FOUNDING MOMENTS IN CONSTITUTIONALISM

Founding moments are landmark events that break ties with the *ancien régime* and lay the foundation for the establishment of a new constitutional order. They are often radically disruptive episodes in the life of a state. They reshape national law, reset political relationships, establish future power structures, and influence happenings in neighbouring countries.

This edited collection brings together leading and emerging scholars to theorise the phenomenon of a founding moment. What is a founding moment? When does the 'founding' process begin and when does it end? Is a founding moment possible without yielding a new constitution? Can a founding moment lead to a partial or incomplete transformation? And should the state be guided by the intentions of those who orchestrated these momentous breaks from the past? Drawing from constitutions around the world, the authors ask these and other fundamental questions about making and remaking constitutions.

Founding Moments in Constitutionalism

Edited by
Richard Albert
Menaka Guruswamy
and
Nishchal Basnyat

•HART•
OXFORD • LONDON • NEW YORK • NEW DELHI • SYDNEY

HART PUBLISHING

Bloomsbury Publishing Plc

Kemp House, Chawley Park, Cumnor Hill, Oxford, OX2 9PH, UK

HART PUBLISHING, the Hart/Stag logo, BLOOMSBURY and the Diana logo are trademarks of Bloomsbury Publishing Plc

First published in Great Britain 2019

A catalogue record for this book is available from the British Library.

Library of Congress Cataloging-in-Publication data

Names: Albert, Richard (Law professor), editor. | Guruswamy, Menaka, 1974-, editor. | Basnyat, Nishchal, editor.

Title: Founding moments in constitutionalism / Edited by Richard Albert, Menaka Guruswamy, Nishchal Basnyat.

Description: Chicago : Hart Publishing, an imprint of Bloomsbury Publishing, 2019. | Includes bibliographical references and index.

Identifiers: LCCN 2019027716 (print) | LCCN 2019027717 (ebook) | ISBN 9781509930975 (hardback) | ISBN 9781509930982 (EPub)

Subjects: LCSH: Constitutional history. | Constitutional law. | Comparative law.

Classification: LCC K3161 .F68 2019 (print) | LCC K3161 (ebook) | DDC 342—dc23

LC record available at https://lccn.loc.gov/2019027716

LC ebook record available at https://lccn.loc.gov/2019027717

ISBN: HB: 978-1-50993-097-5
ePDF: 978-1-50993-099-9
ePub: 978-1-50993-098-2

Typeset by Compuscript Ltd, Shannon

TABLE OF CONTENTS

LIST OF CONTRIBUTORS

Richard Albert is the William Stamps Farish Professor in Law at the University of Texas, Austin.

Mikołaj Barczentewicz is Lecturer in Public Law and Legal Theory at the School of Law, University of Surrey.

Nishchal Basnyat is a graduate of the Yale Law School and currently works in the financial services industry in New York.

Noga Efrat is Senior Lecturer at the Department of History, Philosophy and Judaic Studies, the Open University of Israel.

Simon Gilhooley is Assistant Professor in Political Studies at Bard College.

Menaka Guruswamy is a Senior Advocate at the Supreme Court of India. She was also BR Ambedkar Research Scholar at Columbia Law School from 2017 to 2019.

Swati Jhaveri is Assistant Professor at the Faculty of Law, National University of Singapore.

Maryam S Khan is a Research Fellow at the Institute of Development and Economic Alternatives (IDEAS) in Lahore, Pakistan.

Ming-Sung Kuo is Associate Professor at University of Warwick School of Law.

Chien-Chih Lin is Assistant Research Professor at Institutum Iurisprudentiae, Academia Sinica, Taiwan.

Eugene D Mazo is Visiting Associate Professor of Law at Rutgers University, New Jersey.

Yair Sagy is Senior Lecturer at the University of Haifa Faculty of Law, Israel.

Mel A Topf is Professor in the College of Liberal Arts at Roger Williams University, Rhode Island.

Juliano Zaiden Benvindo is Professor of Constitutional Law at the University of Brasília in Brazil and a Research Fellow at the Brazilian National Council for Scientific and Technological Development.

Introduction

Mapping the Founding

RICHARD ALBERT AND MENAKA GURUSWAMY

Every country lives at least one founding moment. It may be an extraordinary mobilisation of people coming together to create a new state. It may alternatively be an agreement among elites to arrive at a peaceful settlement to start afresh. And it may be the product of externally imposed order after military conquest. Whatever the source, a founding moment is common to peoples the world around, either in fact or in the fictional narratives they tell themselves and pass on to their posterity. Founding moments shape constitutional identities, transform national law, influence surrounding countries, establish power structures and legitimise institutions in the country. But what exactly is a founding moment? When does the 'founding' process begin, when it is ongoing and when does it end? And is a founding moment possible without a new constitution?

Understanding the Founding

It is not always easy to identify and define founding moments. The establishment of a new constitutional identity or the reform of an existing one is almost never encompassed in a single episode, and indeed it may span decades. Some (though not all) founding moments occur at tumultuous times in a country's history, for instance, anti-colonial conflict, civil wars, legitimation crises, power struggles and contests for consolidation. The founding as a unit of analysis should not be studied only as an historical event, but also as a modern reality that influences and often drives our understanding of law. From Iraq to Chile and from Taiwan to Pakistan, many countries around the world are undergoing the birth pangs of founding, constitution and reconstitution. They are waging civil wars, mounting revolutions, writing or rejecting constitutions, or amending constitutions in ways that entirely transform the document and the constitutional order.

It should come as no surprise that founding moments can and do spring from revolutionary uprisings. A totalising revolution seeks to mark a new beginning and set the state on an entirely new course. Even more restrained political revolutions are driven towards a change. In either case, the path from revolution to founding is not linear and raises questions of its own. How does the culmination of a revolution relate to and influence the promulgation of a constitution? How does the promulgation of the constitution trigger crises in the consolidation process? Is there some danger to entrenching the words, symbology and structures of the revolutionary fervour in the codified constitution? We might also consider the phenomenon of an unfinished founding. It may occur when revolutionary groups overthrow a single dictator, but not the entire 'old guard'. To what extent, then, is an event properly called a founding moment if it is a partial or incomplete transformation? How do unfinished foundations influence the identity of the country? What is clear is that founding moments, however they arise, often endow certain elements in civil society, such as revolutionary parties or political leaders, with sociological legitimacy, as distinguished from legal or moral legitimacy.[1] A key line of inquiry therefore concerns the relationship between founding moments and 'founding figures', and the extent to which the future of a nation should be guided by the intentions of those who orchestrated these momentous breaks from the past.

Theorising the Founding

What is a founding moment? Is it the same as a constitutional moment? For the most influential telling of a founding moment, we turn to Bruce Ackerman.[2] He describes it as a moment when 'the People' make a rare collective decision under a special confluence of political and social conditions.[3] This decision is a result of a popular movement that earns the support of a majority of citizens. This special decision must withstand repeated deliberations in fora provided for 'higher lawmaking'. In Ackerman's words, the crescendo of massive and repeated mobilisations of the people are 'acts of citizenship that, when successful, culminate in the proclamation of higher law in the name of We the People'.[4] He recognises four constitutional moments in the US: the Founding, the Reconstruction, the New Deal and the Civil Rights Revolution. The Founding, of course, framed the original US Constitution and the Bill of Rights that followed closely thereafter. The second constitutional moment occurred three generations later, in the struggle that led to the Reconstruction Amendments. The third came in the 1930s with the New Deal revolution confronted by the Old Court, ultimately yielding to the creation of the 'activist welfare state'.[5] The most recent constitutional moment occurred in the

[1] For a discussion of these three forms of legitimacy, see Richard H Fallon, Jr, 'Legitimacy and the Constitution' (2005) 118 *Harvard Law Review* 1787, 1794–1801.

[2] Bruce Ackerman, *Volume I – We the People: Foundations* (Harvard University Press, 1991).

[3] ibid 6.

[4] ibid 7.

[5] ibid 40.

1960s with the enactment of landmark statutes that made good on the promise of equality in the Reconstruction Amendments. Ackerman explains that these four decisive turning points each 'inaugurated' great transformations, ushering in new and distinctive constitutional regimes.[6]

One way to understand a constitutional moment, and perhaps also a founding moment, is as an 'extralegal constitutional change, resorted to because of a failure of the formal rules of constitutional amendment'.[7] This definition would exclude the most critical moment in India's modern history: the creation of the doctrine of basic structure by the Supreme Court of India. The 'basic structure' or 'basic features' doctrine was crafted by the Indian Supreme Court to prevent the national legislature from amending features like secularism, judicial independence and the separation of powers – features the Court identifies as integral to the country's constitutional identity.[8] What makes this moment special is that the Court created this rule out of whole cloth. While it may reflect the contemporary values of Indian political actors and the people, it remains a moment of great significance because it marks a turn in the Court's case law and its conduct in respect of the coordinate branches of government. It is here, then, that we find the country's new beginning.

Another reading of a constitutional moment offers a potentially sharper contrast with a founding moment. A constitutional moment can be understood more narrowly – though no less importantly – as the informal amendment of formal amendment rules.[9] What makes the four episodes Ackerman identifies as constitutional moments similar in kind to the creation of the basic structure doctrine is not that these constitutional changes occurred outside of the formal rules of constitutional amendment;[10] it is instead that Ackerman's four constitutional moments and the rise of the basic structure doctrine in India each on their own altered how their respective constitution is amended and when an amendment is recognised as valid.[11] The four transformations in the US and the creation of the basic structure doctrine in India are therefore all examples of constitutional moments in the Ackermanian sense.[12] Whether these episodes are all properly understood as 'founding moments' is another question altogether.

Emerging insights from around the world suggest that founding moments may not always be a culmination of a people's revolution or a collective movement built upon popular support. Founding moments may also be a culmination of events triggered by civil war, leading to efforts to secure peace and stability. A constitution

[6] ibid 59.

[7] Sujit Choudhry, 'Ackerman's Higher Lawmaking in Comparative Constitutional Perspective: Constitutional Moments as Constitutional Failures?' (2008) 6 *International Journal of Constitutional Law* 193, 214.

[8] See *Golak Nath v State of Punjab*, 1967 AIR 1643, 1967 SCR (2) 762; *Kesavananda Bharati Sripadagalvaru v Kerala*, 1973 SCC (4) 225.

[9] Richard Albert, *Constitutional Amendments: Making, Breaking, Changing Constitutions* (Oxford University Press, 2019), Introduction.

[10] ibid.

[11] ibid.

[12] ibid.

follows, but is soon suspended in a military coup. Soon after the military relinquishes power, the constitution is brought back into force and is subsequently amended time and again to modernise it. This generally tracks the story of Pakistan, as explored in this volume, and all this could amount to a long series of events in a founding moment that continues into the present.

As we suggested above, founding moments may also take the form of a transformative decision by an apex court. It could also follow from the emancipation of a sizeable section of citizens. For instance, in Iraq a sequence of law-making events that resulted from a change of regimes expanded the freedom of women. An entire gender joined the ranks of decision-makers as the legal equals of men. When some challenged this legal transformation and sought to undo it, their efforts met with deep resistance from contemporary society and equality campaigns pushed back very hard to defend the change in the legal status of women, in the end making it virtually impossible to retrench on these newly created rights. This suggests that we might well identify a founding moment retrospectively in light of how difficult it is to undermine or repeal a law, a practice or a socio-political development.

We should also acknowledge that what qualifies as a founding moment may turn on one's philosophy of constitutional interpretation. Originalists, for instance, may see founding moments quite differently from non-originalists. And since originalists have tended for now to be most influential in the US, it may be that the notion of a founding moment is understood differently in that country.

Two important resources help inform our understanding of a founding moment. In *Founding Acts*, Serdar Tekin offers some insight into the idea of a founding moment.[13] Tekin highlights these moments' relation to popular sovereignty and their grounding (or not) in democratic legitimacy. As he states, 'how Constitutions are made (or their pedigree) is morally and politically as significant as what they are made of (or their pedigree)'.[14] He stresses the importance of these moments as experiments of democratic sovereignty in which the people exercise their sovereignty and express their identity-in-formation. For his part, Hans Agne complicates our thinking on founding moments when arguing that in order for a founding to be democratic – that is, to be constituted by the people in a foundational choice of coming-together constitution-making – it must be agreed to by as many persons as possible within and beyond the boundaries of the state.[15] As Agne claims, founding moments and their legitimacy are a key component underpinning the legitimacy of the state itself.[16]

These and other works contribute immensely to our learning about founding moments and their relation to constituent power. Yet there is much more

[13] Serdar Tekin, *Founding Acts: Constitutional Origins in a Democratic Age* (University of Pennsylvania Press, 2016).

[14] ibid 2.

[15] Hans Agne, 'Democratic Founding: We the People and the Others' (2012) 10 *International Journal of Constitutional Law* 866.

[16] ibid 869.

to say about founding moments from theoretical, historical and comparative perspectives, and we offer this volume as a complement to existing works exploring this fundamental reality in the lives of constitutional states. We seek more specifically in this book to explain how founding moments occur, when they occur and what forms they might take.

The Seeds for this Collection

On 16 April 2016, a diverse and expert group of scholars gathered at the Yale Law School for a full-day symposium we hosted on 'Founding Moments in Constitutionalism'. The purpose of the programme was to explore this phenomenon as it has occurred around the world across time and traditions. Our sponsors for this programme were the Oscar M Ruebhausen Fund at Yale Law School and the Gruber Program for Global Justice and Women's Rights. The symposium was structured around five panel discussions in which scholars presented their papers. Each panel was assigned a discussant and was divided into the following subjects: Theorizing Founding Moments; Understanding Founding Moments; Asia's Founding Moments; Founding Moments in the Middle East; and Constitutional Identity and Founding Moments. From the beginning, the purpose of the symposium was to publish the papers in an edited volume. The papers were therefore prepared with this objective in mind and they appear in this volume as thoroughly revised chapters.

In this Volume

This book consists of 11 chapters and a conclusion. The chapters delve deeply in the theory of founding moments, draw from history to identify and contextualise the significance of momentous events in the life of a state, and highlight jurisdictions that do not figure in the conventional list of 'usual suspects' in comparative constitutional studies.

In Chapter 1, 'Between Fact and Norm: Narrative and the Constitutionalisation of Founding Moments', Ming-Sung Kuo seeks to shed light on how the construct of a founding moment is related to the constitution itself, problematising the ambiguities about the relationship between the founding moment and its ensuing constitutional order in constitutional theory. Kuo's chapter takes up these issues at the core of constitutional theory by examining the idea of a founding moment in light of the antimony between fact and norm. He argues that contemporary constitutional theories fail to account for the role of the founding moment in the constitutional order because they are preoccupied by matters of constitutional interpretation and less so by the construction of the constitutional order. He concludes by underlining the implications of the relational approach to the constitutionalisation of the founding moment to constitutional theory in terms of substance, process and structure.

In Chapter 2, 'The Role of Courts in Advancing Constitutional Moments: Constitutionalising the Constitution in Singapore and Hong Kong', Swati Jhaveri explores the role of courts in founding moments. Her chapter draws from Hong Kong and Singapore in particular to highlight that founding moments are necessarily ongoing and cannot be compartmentalised or viewed as fixed periods of time. This analysis is used to further highlight the important work to be done after a 'founding moment' to translate these moments into new and sustainable constitutional orders. Using the Asian experience, her chapter looks beyond political actors and citizens to the role of the courts in legitimising, consolidating and furthering the objectives of founding moments and in their overall translation into the establishment of the new order. National courts, she argues, have played a critical role in transitional situations in one key respect: explicating the 'meta-constitutional identity' of the system.

In Chapter 3, 'Foundation and Revolution: Hannah Arendt and the Problem of Legitimacy and Stability in Constitutional Consolidation', Mel A Topf investigates the relation of revolutionary consolidation to the American constitutional founding. He suggests that the ideas of consolidation and augmentation – and their relation to the question of constitutional legitimacy – have received insufficient attention. He argues that Hannah Arendt's theory of revolution is paradigmatic in this respect, yet adds that she does not give sufficient attention to the pragmatic role of consolidation in acts of constitutional founding. He focuses on Arendt because he believes that within her political thought on what for her was the uniquely successful consolidation of the American Revolution lies an explanation for that success that she herself does not expressly develop.

In Chapter 4, 'I am Not Your (Founding) Father', Mikolaj Barczentewicz distinguishes between an 'agent behind making a constitution as law' and a 'constitution-maker'. In advancing his distinction, he explores three jurisdictions – Australia, Canada and the US – to answer two fundamental questions in constitutionalism: who made the constitution and how do we know? He argues that in order to truly be a maker of the constitution, one must either exercise pre-existing legal authority to make the constitution or have one's intentional act purporting authoritatively to make the constitution as law recognised as the reason for the acceptance of the constitution as law.

Chapter 5, '"And Then They Begin to Look after the History of Their Founders": (Re)configurations of the Founding in the Early Republic' by Simon Gilhooley, turns to an historical assessment of founding moments and offers a reconceptualisation of the American founding itself. Gilhooley suggests that rather than interpreted or narrated anew, the moment of founding itself is reconfigured to be something it previously was not, which is to say that the present relocates the precise temporal moment of the founding in ways that conform to the political necessities of the present. In order to explore this possibility, he turns to three periods during the early American Republic: discussions of the electoral crisis of 1800–01; the debates surrounding *McCulloch v Maryland* in 1819; and the debates around slavery in Washington DC in the early 1830s. He proposes that these accounts show that even in close proximity to the concrete events of a founding, the people who emerge from it can radically reconfigure its history and meaning.

In Chapter 6, 'Under the Shadow of the Constitutional Revolution? Revisiting Israel's Founding Moments', Yair Sagy sets out to analyse and evaluate a new string of recent Israeli literature revisiting the 1950s, Israel's founding decade. In particular, he looks closely at three books, each one published in Hebrew by three distinguished Israeli legal scholars: Nathan Brun, *Law, Passions and Politics: Judges and Lawyers Between the British Mandate and the State of Israel*; Nir Kedar, *Ben-Gurion and the Constitution*; and Daniel Friedmann, *Before the Revolution: Law and Politics in the Age of Innocence*. In critically examining these three books, Yair's chapter highlights common threads and collages them into a distinct appraisal of Israel's founding generation that is represented in them. What results is a novel reconceptualisation of Israel's founding moment and its generation. Sagy states that, however essential, the 1950s were a transitory generation, cut off on both 'ends': that the decade had departed from the pre-state, colonial (British-Mandatory) oppressive constitutional regime, while, at the same time, its constitutional orthodoxy had been arcane and irrelevant to the brave new post-revolutionary constitutional era.

In Chapter 7, 'Path-Dependency in Soviet and Russian Constitution-Making', Eugene D Mazo begins from the proposition that one theory of constitution-making posits that new constitutions result from a path-dependent process. As such, these constitutions tend to reflect those constitutions that were in place before. To understand constitution-making, according to this view, it is necessary to study the period of time between the fall of a one regime and the creation of the new one. This is the period of transitional uncertainty when the 'constitutional moment' takes place. This chapter explains how one constitutional moment was exploited during the Soviet Union's transition from communism. It examines the distinctive features of that transition and why they led many countries in the post-Soviet region to adopt dual-headed executive structures, ones that created a role for a president and a prime minister. There are theories that explain why presidential or parliamentary constitutions are adopted, but few treat dual-headed semi-presidentialism as a distinguishable category. Given that this constitutional model dominates in the post-communist world, the lack of an explanation for why it was chosen seems problematic. This chapter argues that the reason why so many semi-presidential constitutions were adopted in the post-Soviet world is because they already existed there when these states gained their independence. Thus, for Mazo, the theory that goes furthest towards explaining post-communist constitution-making is path-dependency theory.

Chapter 8, '"Founding Moments" in Latin America? The Brazilian and Chilean Constitutional Histories and the Rise of the Forgotten People', features Juliano Zaiden Benvindo's study of Brazil and Chile. He suggests that constitutional scholarship normally connects the concept of 'founding moments' to radical events such as revolutions, but little has been written about the association of this concept to gradual political transitions, and particularly transitions whose constitutional moments differ in the 'timing' of constitution-making. His chapter fills this gap by linking this concept to two relevant experiences in Latin America: Brazil and Chile. By focusing on the distinct 'timing' of their constitution-making – Brazil, where a new constitution was drafted right after the transition to democracy, and Chile, where a new constitution is just now being discussed – this chapter examines whether and how constitution-making may have a significant impact on the founding of a new democratic moment and how it is intertwined with the rise of active and meaningful citizenship.

In Chapter 9, Chien-Chih Lin brings us to Taiwan in 'We the Taiwanese People: A Constitution with Two Antagonistic Constitutional Identities'. He notes that despite the ubiquitous usage of 'We the People' in preambles of national constitutions, the concept of the phrase remains elusive. He observes that the plethora of studies within a 'Eurocentric' context largely ignores ideas of 'constitutional identity' in other corners of the world. His chapter therefore zeroes in on the formation of the constitutional identity embodied in the Constitution of the Republic of China, suggesting that, unlike in many other countries, there are two distinct and antagonistic constitutional identities – the Chinese constitutional identity and the Taiwanese constitutional identity – that have been forged by formal and informal constitutional practice. He concludes that in such a divided society, the development of constitutional identities is deeply embedded in, and reflective of, the dispute over national identities.

Chapter 10 continues our global voyage with Maryam Khan's contribution on 'What is a Founding? Founding Moments and Pakistan's "Permanent Constitution" of 1973'. Khan explores Pakistan's founding, suggesting that rather than the traditional narrative of 'Jinnah's Pakistan' as a founding, the period of constitution-making between 1967 and 1973 was one of greater constitutional trailblazing. Her chapter conceptualises the constitutional bargaining underlying the 1973 Constitution as a founding. She advances the argument that, from the perspective of both the genesis of a democratic constitutional framework and the continuing political identification with that framework, the creation of the 'permanent' Constitution of 1973 is central to Pakistan's constitutional politics and identity. As a legal scholar of Pakistan, Khan makes this claim with a conscious appreciation of Pakistan's troubled constitutional journey, the failure attributed to the 1973 Constitution to forestall military coups, the repeated 'suspension' of the 1973 Constitution and its bill of rights, and the many 'constitutional deviations' introduced into the text by dictators attempting to fundamentally alter the design of the state and its institutions.

In Chapter 11, 'A Founding Moment in Iraq: A Gender Perspective', Noga Efrati focuses on an interim period in Iraq's constitutional past: the period between the introduction of the British-backed Iraqi Constitution in 1925 and the promulgation of the American-backed Transnational Administrative Law in 2004.

In particular, she looks to women's history to argue that a gender perspective undermines the prevailing notion of this period as a constitutional void. She concludes that only when one understands how the 1925 Constitution constructed female citizens of the new Iraqi state can one appreciate the significance of legislation and actions affecting women that were inspired by the constitutional replacement in 1958. She argues that this was a founding moment in Iraqi history.

This volume closes with a concluding chapter by Nishchal Basnyat, in which he continues the discussion that runs through the earlier chapters – asking what is a founding moment and what is its significance to constitutionalism.

An Invitation

The concluding chapter in this book doubles as an invitation for further research and writing on the phenomenon of a founding moment. The phenomenon invites inquiry from a multiplicity of perspectives, including comparative, doctrinal, historical or theoretical. In this volume, the authors collectively survey many jurisdictions ranging from Brazil to the US, Israel to Pakistan, Australia to Hong Kong, Canada to Singapore, and Iraq to Taiwan. There is great breadth in this list, but there remain jurisdictions that could be mined for insights into what a founding moment entails and what follows from it – and these unstudied jurisdictions are worth studying both to examine the rich diversity of experiences in constitutionalism around the world and also to deepen our understanding of founding moments as they occur through popular movements, judicial decisions or political agreement. We stand to learn a great deal from expanding the universe of jurisdictional coverage and from identifying the many different types of founding moments identifiable around the world, both historically and in our modern times. We invite you to join us in analysing the phenomenon of a founding moment and we look forward to reading your findings.

1

Between Fact and Norm

Narrative and the Constitutionalisation of Founding Moments

MING-SUNG KUO

I. Introduction

The character and identity of a constitutional regime (or simply constitutional identity) is not a novel concept in constitutional theory, but has seen a resurgence in recent scholarship.[1] Such anthropomorphic references to the issues resulting from the continuity and change of constitutional orders have proliferated on both sides of the Atlantic and beyond over the past three decades.[2] On this view, a constitution has its genesis. Far from being a unitary construct, the genesis of a constitution has generated a set of topics for further investigation in constitutional theory. The subject who gives birth to a constitution is one; the time when a constitution comes into being is another. Both being part of the multifarious construct of the genesis of a constitution, the constituent power (subject) and

[1] Traditionally, the key question concerning constitutional identity is whether a changing constitutional order should be regarded as the continuation of the original one or as the replacement that is new and distinct from it. Jan-Herman Reestman, 'The Franco-German Constitutional Divide: Reflections on National and Constitutional Identity' (2009) 5 *EuConst* 374, 382–84; Monika Polzin, 'Constitutional Identity, Unconstitutional Amendments and the Idea of Constituent Power: The Development of the Doctrine of Constitutional Identity in German Constitutional Law' (2016) 14 *ICON* 411. Notably, a recent wave of literature on constitutional identity centres on the question of 'identification' and is more or less sociologically oriented (see ibid 412). Under this view, constitutional identity appears to be a special form of national identity. Compare Michel Rosenfeld, *The Identity of the Constitutional Subject: Selfhood, Citizenship, Culture, and Community* (Routledge, 2010) 11–12 with Gary Jeffrey Jacobsohn, *Constitutional Identity* (Harvard University Press, 2010) 9–10. For the present purposes, constitutional identity is understood in its traditional sense.

[2] See, eg, Reestman (n 1); Polzin (n 1); Bruce Ackerman, *We the People, Volume 1: Foundations* (Belknap Press, 1991); Jed Rubenfeld, *Freedom and Time: A Theory of Constitutional Self-Government* (Yale University Press, 2001); Chaihark Hahm and Sung Ho Kim, *Making We the People: Democratic Constitutional Founding in Postwar Japan and South Korea* (Cambridge University Press, 2015).

the founding moment of constitutional orders (time) are intertwined. Bringing the crucial role of momentous constitutional politics in understanding a constitutional order to the fore, Bruce Ackerman's theory of constitutional moment is an exemplar.[3] Yet, as many of his critics have pointed out, how the construct of constitutional moment is related to the constitution itself is unclear. Is it a function of the exiting constitutional order or a manifestation of extra-constitutional power? Is it norm or merely fact? Is it situated within or without the constitutional order?[4]

Although these issues have been at the centre of scholarship on constituent power, they also speak to ambiguities about the relationship between the founding moment and its ensuing constitutional order in constitutional theory. Yet, there is a fundamental difference in character that makes the question of the constitutional status of the founding moment more complex than the idea of constituent power. In contrast to the idea of constituent power, the founding moment is more than a conceptual construct; rather, the founding moment of a constitutional order points to the series of historical events that lead to the adoption of the constitution.[5] This difference suggests that beneath the relationship between the founding moment and its ensuing constitutional order are questions about the identity of constitutional theory itself. Is the historical founding moment relevant to the theorisation of the constitution at all? If so, how is the originary moment being considered in constitutional theories? Is the state of the art satisfactory? Can we rethink the question of the founding moment in constitutionalism beyond current theoretical positions?

This chapter takes up these issues at the core of constitutional theory by examining the question of the founding moment in constitutional scholarship in light of the antinomy between fact and norm. I argue that contemporary constitutional theories fail to account for the role of the founding moment in the constitutional order because they are absorbed in the narrow question of constitutional interpretation at the expense of making sense of the constitutional order. Drawing upon Robert Cover's concept of *nomos*,[6] I contend that with an eye to the understanding of the constitution beyond the interpretation of constitutional norms, the constitutional order needs to be recast as a constitutional *nomos*. As a constitutional *nomos* operates not only on constitutional norms but also on the enriching narratives about the birth and growth of a constitutional

[3] Ackerman (n 2).

[4] See, eg, Andrew Arato, 'Carl Schmitt and the Revival of the Doctrine of the Constituent Power in the United States' (2000) 21 *Cardozo Law Review* 1739.

[5] This distinguishes the Ackermanian constitutional moment from the historical founding moment of a constitutional order. While both point to an extended period of time during which a constitutional order originates or undergoes great transformation, the former turns out to be a theory of constituent power, which is related to but separate from the question of the status of the founding moment in a constitutional order.

[6] Robert M Cover, 'The Supreme Court, 1982 Term – Foreword: *Nomos* and Narrative' (1983) 97 *Harvard Law Review* 4.

order, the founding moment is pivotal to the discovery of constitutional meaning in this broad sense. Through narratives, the founding moment is related to its ensuing constitutional order and thus 'constitutionalised', suggesting a broader understanding of interpretation in constitutional theory than contemporary constitutional theories assume. On this view, the founding moment is neither a mere historical fact nor a placeholder for universal norms, but rather serves as the reference point for constitutional redemption that renders the constitutional order 'jurisgenerative'.[7] Narratives about the founding moment concern more the invigoration of the existing constitutional order than its original foundation. This observation further suggests an alternative attitude towards the unsettling concept of constituent power:[8] the constituent power's appeal does not so much lie in the substitution of a new constitutional order for the existing one as in its rejuvenation of the latter, since it is reincarnated in the narratives-mediated constitutionalised founding moment.

My argument proceeds as follows. In the first place, I shall establish that two opposite views dominate current constitutional scholarship on the question of the founding moment. As I shall explain, under the historicist view, the founding moment is fact only;[9] under the normativist view, it is absorbed into constitutional norms. Neither is satisfactory as the question of the founding moment in constitutionalism is reduced to a methodological debate about constitutional interpretation among specialists (section II). Taking issue with this jurispathic rendering of the founding moment in contemporary constitutional theories, I shall continue to propose a relational approach to the constitutionalisation of the founding moment by drawing upon Cover's ideas in 'Nomos *and Narrative*'.[10] Situated between fact and norm and mediated by narratives, the founding moment conceived of this way will turn the enterprise of constitutional interpretation into one of *nomos*-building that invites revitalising narratives from citizens in the discovery of the meaning of the constitutional project. Thus, the narratives-mediated constitutionalisation of the founding moment also entails an alternative account of the constituent power (section III). To conclude, I shall underline the implications of the relational approach to the constitutionalisation of the founding moment to constitutional theory in terms of substance, process and structure (section IV).

[7] For the distinction between a 'jurisgenerative' and a 'jurispathic' legal order, see ibid 40–44. For a different understanding of whether a legal order is jurisgenerative, see Frank Michelman, 'Law's Republic' (1988) 97 *Yale Law Journal* 1493; Seyla Benhabib, *Another Cosmopolitanism*, Robert Post (ed) (Oxford University Press, 2006) 48–50.

[8] Hahm and Kim (n 1) 35; David Dyzenhaus, 'The Politics of the Question of Constituent Power' in Martin Loughlin and Neil Walker (eds), *The Paradox of Constitutionalism: Constituent Power and Constitutional Form* (Oxford University Press, 2007) 129; Martin Loughlin, 'The Concept of Constituent Power' (2014) 23 *European Journal of Political Theory* 218.

[9] I use the term 'historicist' to denote this particular attitude among historians towards historical events.

[10] Cover (n 6).

II. Fact or Norm? Founding Moments Envisaged in Constitutional Theory

As the question of the founding moment in constitutional theory concerns how to fit historical facts into the conceptualisation of a normative order, I follow in the footsteps of those who have utilised the antinomy between fact and norm as the analytical framework for manifold legal and constitutional issues.[11] Situating theories of the founding moment in constitutionalism in this antinomy, I begin with a discussion of historicist theories in which the founding moment is regarded as fact. Unveiling the interpretive character of constitutional theory, I note that historicist theories oscillate between disregard and fidelity in their attitude towards the founding moment as a matter of fact. Then I turn to the normativist strain. In contrast to the historicist oscillation between disregard and fidelity, normativists effectively equate the founding moment with the original values that underlie constitutional provisions. After disclosing the historicist and normativist views of the founding moment, I discuss why neither is satisfactory as both reflect the gap in constitutional imagination that contemporary constitutional theories of the founding moment help create.

A. When Founding Moments are Historical Facts Only: Disregard, Fidelity and the Identity of Constitutional Theory

A new constitutional order is mostly established in response to the failure of the existing regime. The founding moment of a new constitution is thus a moment of crisis when the old constitutional order breaks down as a result of national liberation movement, civic uprising, military defeat, economic breakdown or other precipitous events.[12] Antipathy towards foreign or colonial regimes,[13] resistance against repressive rulers,[14] anger at failed war plans and strategic blunders,[15] discontent with socio-economic justice,[16] and other socio-psychological responses

[11] Examples include Rosenfeld (n 1) 42; Jürgen Habermas, *Between Facts and Norms: Contributions to a Discourse Theory of Law and Democracy*, William Rehg (trans) (MIT Press, 1996).

[12] See Jon Elster, 'Constitution-Making and Violence' (2012) 4 *Journal of Legal Analysis* 8.

[13] See Ruth Gordon, 'Growing Constitutions' (1999) 1 *University of Pennsylvania Journal of Constitutional Law* 528.

[14] See, eg, Adam Roberts, 'Civil Resistance and the Fate of the Arab Spring' in Adam Roberts et al (eds), *Civil Resistance in the Arab Spring: Triumphs and Disasters* (Oxford University Press, 2016) 270.

[15] See, eg, Yaprak Gürsoy 'Civilian Support and Military Unity in the Outcome of Turkish and Greek Interventions' (2009) 27 *Journal of Political and Military Sociology* 47, 59–60, 65.

[16] See, eg, Rehan Abeyratne, 'Socioeconomic Rights in the Indian Constitution: Toward a Broader Conception of Legitimacy' (2014) 39 *Brooklyn Journal of International Law* 1.

are usually recorded in crises leading up to the founding of a new constitution. To be sure, these reactions to the tumultuous situation in which a new constitutional order originates are not the only occurrences in the founding moment that are recorded. The debates over how to respond to the failure of the old regime, the wrangling over the process and substance of the new constitutional order, and the tabulation of the votes cast in the convention or the referendum on the adoption of the new constitution are also part of the historical record of the founding moment of a constitutional order.[17] All of them are *fact*. Thus, the accuracy of how they are documented and presented underlies the study of the founding moment as a matter of fact.

Driven by the pursuit of historical truth and its accurate representation, scholars of the founding moment dig deeper and deeper into the details of its constitutive episodes. On this view, the founding moment is a historical object to be faithfully represented.[18] Yet, the accurate, specific, comprehensive representation of the founding moment does not tell us much about the relationship between the founding moment and its ensuing constitutional order. Instead, it is a question of how the founding moment as a matter of fact is seen in the eyes of constitutional theory, raising the question of the identity of constitutional theory.

The task of constitutional theory is to provide a language that gives expression to the political life under the constitution.[19] To make sense of the constitutional order as a political project is what constitutional theory is all about. Interpretation (vis-à-vis explanation) underpins the enterprise of making sense of the constitutional order.[20] Noticeably, one defining character of contemporary constitutional theories is the fascination with the question of what norms in the constitutional 'text', which extends beyond the codified constitutional document, mean.[21] This predilection for interpreting norms is not without reason, especially in light of the new frontiers of constitutional scholarship. Studies of constitutional orders have long extended beyond the exegesis of the constitution to issues about how constitutional norms are implemented, what explains the gap between precept and practice, the extent to which the practice has displaced or amended the norms etc.[22] Yet, none of them can be addressed without confronting the question of

[17] See, eg, Max Farrand, *The Framing of the Constitution of the United States* (Yale University Press, 1913).

[18] This corresponds to 'descriptive representation' developed in Hanna Fenichel Pitkin, *The Concept of Representation* (University of California Press, 1967) 60–91.

[19] Sanford Levinson, *Constitutional Faith* (Princeton University Press, 1988) 191–94.

[20] The role of interpretation in making sense of the constitutional order is further discussed in section III.A.

[21] See Jed Rubenfeld, 'The Paradigm-Case Method' (2006) 115 *Yale Law Journal* 1977, 1977; Mark A Graber, *A New Introduction to American Constitutionalism* (Oxford University Press, 2013) 3; Martin Loughlin, 'The Constitutional Imagination' (2015) 78 *MLR* 1, 14. 'Text' here is understood in a broad sense and is not restricted to constitutional provisions or judicial doctrines.

[22] See, eg, Ran Hirschl, *Comparative Matters: The Renaissance of Comparative Constitutional Law* (Oxford University Press, 2014).

what constitutional norms mean. For example, the question of how constitutional norms are implemented is predicated on the cognisance of what to implement. This obtains only when the radius of what constitutional norms stipulate has been determined through interpretation. Interpretation remains indispensable to constitutional studies that centre on the explanation of the gap between the law in books and the law in action too. The reason is simple: if the law in books is unknown, how can we even raise the question of why there is variance between it and the law in action? What the law in books stipulates only becomes clear as a result of interpretation.[23]

I hasten to add that nothing I have said so far suggests that interpretation of constitutional norms is the only legitimate component or the most important characteristic of all theoretical studies of the constitution. Instead, a quick survey of the recent literature on constitutional scholarship will reveal that constitutional theory has extended beyond the matter of interpretation.[24] Nevertheless, the foregoing two examples indicate that interpretation of constitutional norms in the text constitutes the *sine qua non* of constitutional theory.[25] When this interpretive core is revealed, the stance of contemporary constitutional theories towards the founding moment as a matter of fact also transpires.

Considered fact, the founding moment is not necessarily integral to constitutional theory as the constitutional status of the founding moment depends on the theoretical position on the relationship between fact and constitutional interpretation.[26] To put it differently, contemporary constitutional theories oscillate between disregard and fidelity with respect to the historical founding moment. To some, constitutional interpretation amounts to a function of the system of constitutional norms as exemplified in Hans Kelsen's pure theory of law. Under this view, there may be disagreement on whether the focus of emphasis should be on individual constitutional provisions or on the structural relationship between them. Nevertheless, textualists and structuralists share the belief that they confine their determination of the meaning of constitutional norms within the normative system without taking fact into consideration. To be clear, text and structure are not the only constituents of the system of constitutional norms; judicial interpretations of the constitution are also widely considered part of the normative system.[27] However, standing as historical event instead of legal precedent, the founding

[23] See Ming-Sung Kuo, 'A Dubious Montesquieuian Moment in Constitutional Scholarship: Reading the Empirical Turn in Comparative Constitutional Law in Light of William Twining and His Hero' (2013) 4 *Transnational Legal Theory* 487, 496–97.

[24] Hirschl (n 22).

[25] Martin Loughlin even goes further and observes: 'Constitutional scholarship is today driven by a desire to discover an authoritative method of constitutional interpretation.' Loughlin (n 21) 14.

[26] *cf* Grégoire CN Webber, 'Originalism's Constitution' in Grant Huscroft and Bradley W Miller (eds), *The Challenge of Originalism: Theories of Constitutional Interpretation* (Cambridge University Press, 2011) 147, 154.

[27] Akhil Reed Amar, *America's Unwritten Constitution: The Precedents and Principles We Live by* (Basic Books, 2012) ix–xiii.

moment is disregarded by those who adopt an internal view of constitutional interpretation, regardless of whether they take a Kelsenian purist stance or not.[28]

On the opposite end are those who take the view that fact is not only a component of interpretation. Interpretation of constitutional norms cannot be legitimately rendered without receiving guidance from fact. On this view, the founding moment as fact is indispensable to the exercise of constitutional interpretation as well as to the deciphering of the constitutional order in practice. In contemporary constitutional theories, the foremost advocates for reading constitutional norms in light of the founding moment are those dubbed originalists.[29] Among the myriad facts of the founding moment they take into consideration, it is those pertaining to the adoption of constitutional provisions that interest them most. Or, to put it in a slightly exaggerated way, the whole historical record of the founding moment is examined only to determine the content of constitutional norms.[30]

Notably, originalism is not the only way to take account of the historical facts of the founding moment in the interpretation of constitutional norms.[31] Some constitutional scholars cast their eyes beyond constitutional norms in their interpretation of the constitutional order.[32] Even so, what theories in this strain of the historicist stance have in common is the view that the founding moment as historical fact provides the key to the status quo of the constitutional order and the guidance on the way forward.[33] When the founding moment as historical fact is considered in the interpretation of constitutional norms, it is not only one of the many facts to be taken into account. It is given a special status, standing out from other periods of time. This backward-looking attitude results from the special interpretive character of constitutional theory.[34] Framed within a progressive, linear temporality, constitutional interpretation cannot do away with the concept of authorship.[35] However, driven by the anthropomorphic characterisation of the constitutional

[28] See also Frank I Michelman, 'Constitutional Authorship' in Larry Alexander (ed), *Constitutionalism: Philosophical Foundations* (Cambridge University Press, 1998) 64, 68–74.

[29] Rubenfeld (n 2) 63. See also Lael K Weis, 'What Comparativism Tells Us about Originalism' (2013) 11 *ICON* 842.

[30] Ackerman's effort to identify 'constitutional canons' from the practices of constitutional moments is an example. See Suzanna Sherry, 'The Ghost of Liberalism Past' (1992) 105 *Harvard Law Review* 918, 933.

[31] Philip Bobbitt, *Constitutional Fate: Theory of the Constitution* (Oxford University Press, 1982) 9–24.

[32] Ackerman's constitutional theory suggests a broader notion of constitutional interpretation. Nevertheless, it remains focused on the deciphering of the normative imperatives of the existing constitutional order in light of historical occurrences in the preceding constitutional moments. Bruce Ackerman, *We the People, Volume 3: The Civil Rights Revolution* (Belknap Press, 1991) 7, 71.

[33] See also Weis (n 29) 846; Jack M Balkin, *Living Originalism* (Harvard University Press, 2014).

[34] Paul W Kahn, *The Cultural Study of Law: Reconstructing Legal Scholarship* (University of Chicago Press, 1999) 43–49.

[35] Wilfrid J Waluchow, 'Constitutional Interpretation' in Andrei Marmor (ed), *The Routledge Companions to Philosophy of Law* (Routledge, 2012) 417. See also Sotirios A Barber and James E Fleming, *Constitutional Interpretation: The Basic Questions* (Oxford University Press, 2007) 62–63.

order, authorship becomes a conceptual framing of interpretation and is further perceived as the authenticity and primacy of the original intent of the attributed author of constitutional norms.[36] As a result, the founding moment as a matter of fact is not only essential to the interpretation of constitutional norms. The relationship between fact and interpretation becomes one of fidelity. Originalists are just exemplary of those who hold the relationship between the historical founding moment and constitutional norms to be one of fidelity.[37]

B. What if Founding Moments Resolve into Constitutional Norms: A Mere Matter of Interpretation

While the founding moment comprises historical occurrences, it may or may not appear as fact in the eyes of constitutional theory. Just as the Ackermanian constitutional moment is more akin to conceptual construction than historical reality,[38] the founding moment may stand as norm instead of fact to its ensuing constitution. This is what I call the normativist view of the relationship between the founding moment and the constitutional order.

As I have noted above, virtually all constitutional orders have their own historical founding moment. In contrast to historicists, normativists regard the historical events, institutional innovations, prescriptive rules or political actions at the founding moment as the embodiment of normative principles and values.[39] What matters to constitutional theory is not that which actually happens at constitutional founding; instead, it is what lies beneath or behind these historical occurrences that interests constitutional theorists. Through the normativist lens, reading the founding moment is not aimed at digging out some hidden historical fact about constitutional founding that may influence constitutional interpretation. Rather, the founding moment is explored in order to extract the fundamental values and normative principles from the historical episodes that take place at constitutional founding.[40] I emphasise that it is in the values and principles, not the episodes, that normativists are interested. Reading the founding moment in this way is not so much the discovery of historical facts as the interpretation of constitutional

[36] This is the originalist position, which Paul Kahn argues mistakes writership for authorship in constitutional interpretation. See Paul W Kahn, 'Political Time: Sovereignty and the Transtemporal Community' (2006) 28 *Cardozo Law Review* 259; Paul W Kahn, *Making the Case: The Art of the Judicial Opinion* (Yale University Press, 2016) 48–51.

[37] Notably, the requirement of fidelity in constitutional interpretation does not necessarily result in the Scalian style of originalism. See Balkin (n 33).

[38] See Ming-Sung Kuo, 'Reconciling Constitutionalism with Power: Towards a Constitutional Nomos of Political Ordering' (2010) 23 *Ratio Juris* 390, 399.

[39] Ronald Dworkin, *Freedom's Law: The Moral Reading of the American Constitution* (Harvard University Press, 1996) 13.

[40] See generally Alan Gibson, *Interpreting the Founding: Guide to the Enduring Debates over the Origins and Foundations of the American Republic* (University Press of Kansas, 2006).

norms. Thus, studies of the founding moment become part of constitutional interpretation. Both the founding moment and the constitutional order are turned into the objects of an integrated interpretive activity.[41]

Once the fact that both the founding moment and the constitution are incorporated into one comprehensive interpretation of the constitutional order is laid bare, the role of the founding moment in constitutional interpretation naturally transpires. As a norm, the founding moment cannot be taken at face value, but is rather to be viewed as the placeholder of the values and principles that have motivated the rejection of the old regime and further effected the institutional responses as embodied in the new constitution.[42] Yet, with the translation of the principles and normative values at the founding moment into the underlying values and principles of positivised constitutional norms,[43] the relationship between the founding moment and the resulting constitution is also fundamentally transformed under the normativist view. What Jed Rubenfeld calls the 'paradigm case interpretation'[44] illustrates such a transformation.

Under the paradigm case approach to constitutional interpretation, reading a constitutional provision in light of the particular issue its framers intended to tackle at the founding moment, which Rubenfeld calls the paradigm case, is aimed at correctly identifying the purpose that is to guide its application to the case at hand. The founding moment and its paradigm case are thus treated as the primary illustration of the legislative purpose.[45] As reading the founding moment is pivoted to determining the purpose of positivised constitutional norms, the founding moment is absorbed into the post-founding constitutional order itself, in that it resolves into the exercise of constitutional interpretation aimed at discovering the values and principles connoted by the purpose of constitutional norms.

If my observation is correct, the question of the founding moment becomes a matter of the interpretation of constitutional norms through the lens of normativists. As a result, the question of the founding moment seems to become part of the debate over interpretive methodology. Viewed thus, the normativist view of the founding moment comes close to the historicist stance that maintains the founding moment commanding fidelity from the constitution, as both reflect the variations on the method of constitutional interpretation.[46] Taken together, the significance of the founding moment to its ensuing constitutional order appears to be a function of stance-taking or methodological competition in the exercise of constitutional interpretation, regardless of whether it is considered fact or norm.

[41] See Amar (n 27) 51–94.

[42] Rubenfeld (n 2) 183–88.

[43] By positivised constitutional norms, I mean the constitutional provisions in the Big-C Constitution plus judicial doctrines that set out constitutional principles and rules.

[44] Rubenfeld (n 2) 178.

[45] ibid 180–92.

[46] What Jack Balkin calls 'framework originalism' suggests that the distinction is not so rigid between historicist and the normativist stances. See Balkin (n 33) 21–34.

C. Founding Moments Misconceived: A Gap in Constitutional Imagination

My discussion of the historicist and the normativist view of the founding moment shows that their contrasting stances resolve into different methods of interpretation. Yet, this does not mean that the debate surrounding the founding moment is nothing more than a storm in a teacup among constitutional scholars. Rather, an investigation of how the inevitable imaginary of constitutional authorship is reflected in the historicist and the normativist stances towards the founding moment discloses a gap in constitutional imagination and the problem with contemporary constitutional theories.[47]

As I have noted above, the historicists look to the founding moment as the source of fidelity because of its special status in the course of constitutional development. It is regarded as the moment in which the constitutional order is authored, or rather brought into being. On this view, constitutional authorship is reified in the historical founding moment and controlling, demanding fidelity from the future generations.[48] In contrast, the normativist stance towards the character of constitutional authorship is much less straightforward.[49] Through the normativist lens, the founding moment resolves into constitutional norms inasmuch as it is translated into normative purpose. The nature of purpose distinguishes normativists from fidelity-oriented historicists with respect to constitutional authorship. It is noteworthy that normative purpose is different from the 'context' of which interpretation of constitutional norms is supposed to take account: the former is fixed, whereas the latter is changing in nature.[50] I hasten to add that a fixed normative purpose does not necessarily lead to it being inflexible. Quite the contrary: unlike text, purpose is made abstract and general to accommodate changes in context.[51] With respect to the constitution, the purpose of positivised norms is fixed at constitutional founding, but their application and the implications of the purpose to concrete cases can only be determined against the evolving context. Thus, sublimated into purpose, the founding moment in the normativist strain is not as controlling as its rendering in the hands of the fidelity-oriented historicists, suggesting a constitutional authorship that is more abstract and open to the changing context in the future.[52]

[47] See Ming-Sung Kuo, 'Cutting the Gordian Knot of Legitimacy Theory? An Anatomy of Frank Michelman's Presentist Critique of Constitutional Authorship'. (2009) 7 *ICON* 683, 705–13. For a discussion on constitutional imagination that centres on the epistemic (vis-a-vis popular) aspect, see Loughlin (n 21).

[48] See Jack M Balkin, *Constitutional Redemption: Political Faith in an Unjust World* (Harvard University Press, 2011) 2.

[49] See also Alexander Somek, *The Cosmopolitan Constitution* (Oxford University Press, 2014) 128–33.

[50] *cf* Rubenfeld (n 2) 181–83.

[51] ibid 188–91.

[52] ibid 187–88. See also Kahn (2016) (n 36) 51–62.

Yet, the normativist view pays a hefty price to keep the idea of constitutional authorship alive: the abstraction, if not deformation, of the founding moment. As a result, the concreteness of the founding moment as conceived of by the fidelity-oriented historicists appears to be more accessible to the public than the abstract norms into which the founding moment is resolved under the normativist view. More importantly, even though interpretation is never identical to that which is to be represented through interpretation, concreteness is more likely to be associated with the presence of authenticity.[53] In the collective constitutional imagination that extends beyond specialists in constitutional interpretation, the constitutional order and its interpretation are seen as constantly seeking to approach the authenticity or identity of constitutional authorship.[54] Specifically, in the eyes of non-specialists, the historical founding moment is real and the associated representation of constitutional authorship appears to be authentic. All method-guided interpretations are expected to be able to speak to the identity of constitutional authorship at constitutional founding without fail. Yet, to specialists (except those who totally disregard the historical founding moment), neither the historicist nor the normativist view of the founding moment can bring forth the much-longed-for authenticity of authorship. Whether the founding moment plays a controlling or an inspiring role in the constitutional order is a matter of interpretive method. Regardless of being fact or norm, the founding moment as recounted in constitutional interpretation does not concern constitutional authorship. This contrasting attitude towards the semblance of authenticity emanating from historical concreteness explains why originalism is not going away anytime soon.[55]

There is no blaming non-specialists for ignorance in mistaking a particular form of representation of the founding moment (originalism) for its authenticity (the presence of constitutional authorship). Instead, here emerges a gap in constitutional imagination. Not only failing to bridge the gap but widening it, contemporary constitutional theories are flawed in making sense of the founding moment in constitutionalism. Reconceiving the role of the founding moment in the constitutional order will be the first step towards narrowing the gap.

III. Between Fact and Norm: Imagining Founding Moments in the Constitutional *Nomos*

The gap between specialists and the public in constitutional imagination, as noted above, is not so much about the discrepancy between theory and practice as about the role of the founding moment in the constitutional order. Whether through the

[53] See Kahn (2016) (n 36) 126–34.

[54] See Paul W Kahn, *The Reign of Law:* Marbury v. Madison *and the Construction of America* (Yale University Press, 1997) 177–229. See also Larry Alexander, 'Introduction' in Alexander (ed) (n 28) 1, 1.

[55] Balkin (n 33).

historicist or the normativist lens, the founding moment is understood as centring on the articulation of norms and guiding principles implicit in the constitutional order, suggesting a unidirectional relationship between the founding moment and the constitutional order. Regardless of disregard, fidelity or absorption, the founding moment is either left out of the interpretation of the constitutional order (disregard), invoked to hold sway over the interpretation of constitutional norms (fidelity) or integrated into the norms as purpose (absorption). Moreover, such a unidirectional relationship is also 'jurispathic' as the founding moment plays no role in making sense of the ongoing operation of the whole constitutional order apart from settling individual disputes through interpretation, leading to the gap in constitutional imagination. From this perspective, the fidelity-oriented historicist view does not hold out much hope for a less jurspathic relationship between the founding moment and the constitutional order either, since its associated semblance of authenticity only rests on misconception.[56]

Yet, this is not the only way that the founding moment may bear on the constitutional order. Rather, the above unidirectional, jurispathic relationship can be turned genuinely relational and 'jurisgenerative' when the focus of constitutional theory shifts from constitutional interpretation to making sense of the constitutional order as a political project. To disclose what this relational view means to constitutional theory, I first draw upon Cover's discussion of *nomos* and his view on the relationship between interpretation and meaning to lay the foundations for relating the founding moment to the constitutional order through narratives. As this view bears significantly on the genesis of the constitutional order, I then discuss why the founding moment emerging from the relational view can shed new light on the concept of constituent power.

A. Beyond Interpretation: Constitutionalising Founding Moments through Narratives

As I have suggested, constitutional theory is aimed at helping to make sense of the constitutional order as a political project. Interpretation is never an end in itself, but only part of the continuous collective effort to make sense of what it means by organising the political life of a particular political community as a constitutional order. As authenticity can never be exhausted by a particular interpretation,[57] constitutional interpretation cannot be saved from the accusation that it is unauthentic for deviating from the constitution itself.[58] Yet, it is in the never-ending pursuit of authenticity that the meaning of the constitutional order is

[56] See also Paul W Kahn, *Finding Ourselves at the Movies: Philosophy for a New Generation* (Columbia University Press, 2013) 68.

[57] *cf* ibid 41–45, 67–77.

[58] See Balkin (n 48) 103–38. See also Kahn (2016) (n 36) 89–108.

also enriched and revealed through interpretation. In other words, making sense of the meaning of the political life under the constitutional order is embedded in the action taken in the quest for authenticity, namely, interpretation.[59] Thus, persuasion is integral to the political action taken by individual citizens to approach authenticity through interpretation.[60] In sum, the interpretive character of constitutional theory is only the surface manifestation of the unresolved but productive tension between interpretation and authenticity that makes persuasion necessary and keeps the meaning of the constitutional order alive.

Seen in this light, interpretive settlement is provisional at best as it itself is not free from the question that it fails to represent the identity/authenticity of the constitution.[61] And the pathology of contemporary constitutional theories lies in the fascination with a final interpretation through the correct method without keeping the meaning of the constitutional order in sight. Worse still, constitutional interpretation has been commonly understood through the lens of 'modalities', becoming the game among specialists, if you will.[62] Yet, Cover questioned such an attitude towards interpretation in the discovery of the meaning of the law or, rather, the constitutional order. His critique of interpretation as understood in constitutional-legal practice suggests an alternative view of the role of the founding moment in the constitutional order.

According to Cover, the common practice of legal interpretation that focuses on how to apply legal rules and other precepts to individual cases correctly is problematic for the discovery of the meaning in law.[63] Of the practice of constitutional and legal interpretation, Cover observed that the official agent of interpreting the law (the judge in most cases) is tasked with bringing finality and authoritativeness to the legal order of the modern state.[64] To achieve this goal, the agent backs up his interpretation of the legal order with discourse and force when necessary.[65] Obviously, force is disruptive to the pursuit of constitutional meaning when it is invoked to put paid to the debate over the meaning of the constitutional precepts concerned in the public sphere.[66] Besides, Cover further noted that facing the reality of legal pluralism, the judicial discourse gravitates towards objectivity and universalism in the name of neutrality for fear of being seen as taking sides. As a result, ethos and particulars pertaining to individual cases, which give meaning to legal precepts, are obscured in the interpretive gravitation towards objectivity

[59] In other words, the constitutional order is more like performing art to be acted out than like literature text to be interpreted. To be sure, the performer interprets a drama, for example, before and through his performance. Balkin (n 48) 91–94.

[60] ibid 12–13.

[61] This suggests an implicit form of accusing such interpretations of usurping the (constituted) amending power and thus defying the design by the constituent power. William F Harris II, *The Interpretable Constitution* (Johns Hopkins University Press, 1993) 164–208.

[62] Philip Bobbitt, *Constitutional Interpretation* (Blackwell, 1991) 11–22.

[63] Cover (n 6) 6.

[64] ibid 16.

[65] ibid 9–10, 13.

[66] Robert M Cover, 'Violence and the Word' (1986) 95 *Yale Law Journal* 1601.

and universalism.[67] Modalities in theories of constitutional interpretation fail to get to grips with the root cause of this 'jurispathic' character of the common practice of constitutional interpretation.[68] Mistaking authority for persuasion, interpretive modalities do not help very much with the settlement of controversial constitutional issues.[69]

Alternatively, Cover conceived of the law and the constitutional order as not only existing in but also envisaging a whole world, which Cover called a 'nomos'.[70] A *nomos* is the normative universe we inhabit. Specifically: 'The rules and principles of justice, the formal institutions of the law, and the conventions of a social order are … but a small part of [such a] normative universe.'[71] On this view, the meaning of the constitution is more of the understanding of the whole constitutional order than the interpretation of individual constitutional norms, while the enterprise to discover the meaning of the constitution goes beyond the application of the methods of constitutional interpretation.[72] To make sense of the legal institutions or prescriptions, Cover suggested, we need to relate them to 'the narratives that locate [them] and give [them] meaning'.[73] Situated in their discursive context, the legal institutions or prescriptions are no longer the commands of authorities, but have their 'history and destiny, beginning and end'.[74] The purpose and meaning of legal institutions and prescriptions can only be fully grasped along with the underpinning narratives of the constitution order. As Cover further observed, '[legal] prescription [cannot] escape its origin and its end in experience, in the narratives that are the trajectories plotted upon material reality by our imagination'.[75] Given that the 'material reality' on which legal interpretation rests results from our imagination, history, literature and other narratives also find their way into a normative universe.[76] Law as a *nomos* comprises both legal rules and principles and their meaning-embedding narratives.

The role of narratives in building a constitutional *nomos* figures prominently in the relationship between interpretation and the meaning in law as conceived by Cover. Appealing to the idea of commitment, Cover located '[t]he transformation of interpretation into [constitutional] meaning' in the moment 'when someone accepts the demands of interpretation and, *through the personal act of commitment*, affirms the position taken'.[77] This is more than consent to or acceptance of a particular rendering of the constitutional 'text', whether it is written, oral or

[67] See Cover (n 6) 13.
[68] See ibid 40.
[69] See Balkin (n 48) 12–16.
[70] Cover (n 6).
[71] ibid 4.
[72] Compare Harris (n 61) 114–63 with Bobbitt (n 62) 9–30.
[73] Cover (n 6) 4.
[74] ibid 5.
[75] ibid.
[76] ibid. See also Harris (n 61) 103–13, 131–35.
[77] Cover (n 6) 45 (emphasis added).

social.[78] 'Such affirmation entails a [unique] commitment to projecting the understanding of the norm at work in our reality through all possible worlds onto the teleological vision that the interpretation implies.'[79] The creation of constitutional meaning thus requires 'the objectification of that to which one is committed'.[80] In Cover's view, this can only be made possible by telling 'a story of how [the constitution], now object, came to be, and more importantly, how it came to be one's own', namely, a narrative.[81] Narratives operate as the catalyst for persuasion by 'provid[ing] resource for justification, condemnation, and argument by actors within the group, who must struggle to live their [constitution]'.[82] Moreover, by way of telling narratives in the process of persuasion, people of all political persuasions take part in the activity of constitutional (re)interpretation, turning the whole constitutional order into a jurisgenerative project (or simply jurisgenesis).[83] It is also in this way that narratives relate the founding moment to the constitutional order and reshape their relationship.

Through the lens of 'Nomos *and Narrative*', the constitutional order, which is the reification of the political project of citizens living as a community, turns out to be more than the combination of the documental constitution and its supporting institutions. It is a *nomos* in which citizens take part in the constitutional project and jointly give meaning to it. To put it differently, to be a constitutional *nomos*, the constitutional order needs to stand for what citizens aspire to and commit themselves to. Notably, citizens find themselves in the constitutional order not only through their elected representatives or institutions and procedures but also through narratives concerning the birth and growth of the constitutional order.[84] Either by entering into an individual dialogue with existing narratives about the constitutional order or by giving their own account of it, citizens partake of the construction of the constitutional *nomos*. On this view, the meaning of the constitutional order cannot be identified with the interpretation of constitutional norms, but rather materialises in the ongoing jurisgenesis in which 'stories of peoplehood' are told to carry out the constitutional project amid the tension between interpretation and authenticity.[85] The genuine meaning of constitutional norms can only be fully grasped when they are read together with the narratives concerning their creation, contestation and evolution in the life of the whole constitutional order. Thus, neither the normative purpose nor the underlying principles or values suffice to substantiate the meaning of constitutional norms as they are abstracted

[78] See Clifford Geertz, *The Interpretation of Cultures* (Basic Books, 1973) 3–30.
[79] Cover (n 6) 45.
[80] ibid.
[81] See ibid. See also Harris (n 61) 86–96.
[82] See Cover (n 6) 46.
[83] See ibid 15.
[84] See Balkin (n 48) 2–6, 25–32. See also Paul W Kahn and Kiel Brennan-Marquez, 'Statutes and Democratic Self-Authorship' (2014) 56 *William & Mary Law Review* 115, 173–77.
[85] Balkin (n 48) 2; Rogers M Smith, *Stories of Peoplehood: The Politics and Morals of Political Membership* (Cambridge University Press, 2003).

from the context in which the meaning is contained. It is narratives that bring the meaning-rich context to the fore.

Conceived of in this way, the founding moment is related to the constitutional order not just as fact, as the historicists claim, or as norm, as the normativists assert; rather, it is to be narrated in relation to the ongoing constitutional project with an eye to satisfying the longing for identity/authenticity. As noted above, the founding moment exists as historical occurrence in most cases. Recognising this fact does not necessarily result in commanding fidelity from the constitutional order, as some historicists suggest; instead, the relationship between it and the resulting constitutional order is mediated by narratives.[86] Narratives about the founding moment or, rather, the founding episodes are told not to define constitutional norms or settle interpretative disputes. Instead, they are invoked by citizens themselves to invite their fellow citizens living in the same constitutional order to come to terms with its genesis and reflect upon the constitutional project itself. The flawed constitutional order as it is can find redemption by engaging with its own growth trajectory from birth through the flow of fresh narratives.[87] For this reason, relating the founding moment to the ongoing constitutional order does not surrender the present generation's political destiny to the dead hand of the founding fathers and mothers. On the contrary, since the founding moment is related to the constitutional order through narratives, the constitutional *nomos* incorporates and reconstructs the founding moment by generating new narratives about the founding moment. Under the relational view, reciprocity characterises the relationship between the founding moment and its ensuing constitutional order. Giving their own narratives, citizens of the here and now make decisions on the meaning of the life of the constitutional order after the founding moment, but at the same time keep the constitutional project moving by engaging in constant persuasion as they take such decisions in anticipation of disagreement from their fellow citizens.[88] As a result, the relationship between the founding moment and the constitutional order is genuinely relational. It is no longer unidirectional as the stances of disregard, fidelity and absorption connote.

With intermediary narratives, the relational view is also set apart from the normativist stance. Notably, narratives about the founding moment echo the normativist view of the founding moment as they are not aimed at re-enacting or remembering the birth of the constitutional order. Rather, they are employed to bring the foundational values and principles to the fore so that the constitutional *nomos* can thus continue on these normative pillars and evolve alongside the society without being overwhelmed by the vicissitudes of time and fortune. Yet, narratives concern not only normative purpose or foundational values and principles. A successful narrative must be coherent to be persuasive.[89] It is conducted

[86] Kahn (n 56) 27.
[87] Balkin (n 48) 119–23. *cf* Kuo (n 47) 709–11.
[88] Kahn (n 56) 71–77.
[89] ibid 52–58. *cf* Jacco Bomhoff, *Balancing Constitutional Rights: The Origins and Meanings of Postwar Legal Discourse* (Cambridge University Press, 2013) 90–91.

in a structure of unity filled with subjects, events and conflicts.[90] Narratives speak both to the political identity of citizens who find themselves in the constitutional *nomos* and to the identity of the constitutional order itself.[91] Under the relational view, the founding moment is not only an attributed source of values or principles, but also part of the quest for identity in the constitutional project.

Situated in the discovery of the meaning of the constitutional order mediated by narratives, the question of the founding moment in constitutionalism is freed from the grip of specialists in constitutional interpretation. As the founding moment is no longer related to the constitutional order only for the sake of the interpretation of constitutional norms, it cannot be mastered by methodology. Rather, its meaning is intertwined with that of the whole constitutional order, which emerges from and evolves with refreshing narratives from citizens, not the monographs on interpretive methods or modalities from law professors.[92] Instead of leaving the question of the founding moment in constitutionalism in the hands of specialists, citizens relate the founding moment to the constitutional order on their own terms through the medium of narratives.

Under the relational view, the founding moment is brought into contact with the constitutional order through narratives. The founding moment sits between fact and norm instead of being characterised either as fact or as norm, as the historicist and the normativist views suggest. The question of the founding moment in constitutionalism raises fundamental issues concerning the meaning of the constitutional order beyond the interpretation of constitutional norms. The constitutionalisation of the founding moment by virtue of narratives suggests rethinking the constitutional order as a *nomos*, at the core of which is the construction of identity.

B. From Foundation to Invigoration: Founding Moments, Constitutions and the Constituent Power

At the beginning of this chapter, I noted that the constituent power and the founding moment, both of which are the essentials of constitutional genesis, share some characteristics in constitutional theory. One of them is that both stand at the interface of fact and norm.[93] Another concerns their relationship with the constitutional order. As I have argued in the foregoing sections, narratives bring the founding moment into contact with the constitutional order in a way that suggests that it sits between fact and norm instead of being either fact or norm. In terms of the close correspondence between the founding moment and the constituent power, what is

[90] Kahn (2016) (n 36) 62–73, 83–87.

[91] See Balkin (n 48) 2–3.

[92] See Richard S Kay, 'Constituent Authority' (2011) 59 *American Journal of Comparative Law* 715, 756–57.

[93] Carl Schmitt, *Constitutional Theory*, Jeffrey Seitzer (trans) (Duke University Press, 2008) 75–78, 125–35.

the image of the constituent power entailed by the narratives-mediated constitutionalisation of the founding moment? To answer this question, a closer look at the relationship between the constituent power and the constitutional order will help.

The constituent power and the constitutional order are conceptually distinct.[94] The former gives birth to the latter, while the latter only changes within the decisions made by the former. As a corollary, another conceptual distinction is drawn between the constituent power and the constituted power.[95] Viewed thus, the constituent power tends to be associated with action, free will, and freedom; the constituted power is part of the legal order underpinned by rules and other precepts.[96] Acting on the constituted power is not an exercise of free will in full, but is instead a disciplined application of legal provisions concerned aimed at an ordered liberty.[97] That said, the constituent power is not a kind of action to be taken lightly. To the existing constitutional order, the constituent power means disruption, even destruction, in the sense that the latter is invoked to break free of the former's grip. The constituent power can only engender a new beginning by putting the existing constitutional order to death.

Due to its duality of freedom and destruction, the concept of constituent power is unsettling. From the internal perspective of the constitutional order, it can only be remembered, but should not be conceived. It needs to be suppressed to keep the constitutional order going. In contrast, when looked at from the external point of view, the constituent power is the symbol of freedom, the hope for liberation from the incorrigible existing regime, and the agency to bring about a pristine constitutional order.[98] As a result, uneasiness usually looms over how to characterise incidents that disrupt the standing constitutional order.[99] Should an instance of civil disobedience or rioting be seen as the sign of the resurrected constituent power?[100] At what point in time can this characterisation be legitimately determined? Or should disruptive acts of this sort instead be taken as law-breaking behaviours that warrant punishment and even suppression? How about a military coup d'état?[101]

This is not the place for me to dwell on the various positions on the constituent power. Yet, the narratives-mediated constitutionalised founding moment, as suggested above, also points to an alternative reading of the constituent power.[102]

[94] Kuo (n 38) 399–400; Mark Tushnet, 'Peasants with Pitch Forks, and Toilers with Twitter: Constitutional Revolutions and the Constituent Power' (2015) 13 *ICON* 639, 645–46.

[95] Schmitt (n 93) 80, 128; Kuo (n 38) 399.

[96] See also Kahn (n 56) 97–99.

[97] See ibid 84–90.

[98] ibid 97–99.

[99] Kuo (n 38) 395–98.

[100] Andreas Kalyvas, 'Popular Sovereignty, Democracy and the Constituent Power' (2005) 12 *Constellations* 223, 230; Joel I Colón-Ríos, *Weak Constitutionalism: Democratic Legitimacy and the Question of Constituent Power* (Routledge, 2012) 178–83. See also Loughlin (n 8) 233–34.

[101] See Schmitt (n 93) 142; Tayyab Mahmud, 'Jurisprudence of Successful Treason: Coup d'Etat and Common Law' (1994) 27 *Cornell International Law Journal* 49.

[102] *cf* Loughlin (n 8) 228.

I have noted that by way of narratives, the founding moment contributes to the constitutional *nomos* as it is not only associated with the foundational values and principles but also marks the beginning of the growth trajectory of the constitutional order. Moreover, the founding moment that sets out the jurisgenerative constitutional project is also the time when the constituent power asserts itself. Thus, narratives about the founding moment are stories about the invocation of the constituent power too. In this way, when the founding moment interfaces the constitutional order through narratives, the constituent power is also being narrated in relation to the jurisgenesis of the living constitutional *nomos*.

What is important about the duality of narratives on the founding moment and the constituent power is that narratives are not told to remember the past and commemorate landmarks at constitutional genesis; rather, narratives themselves are constitutive of the constitutional *nomos*. They substantiate the rules, norms, institutions and other constitutional precepts with meaning that makes the constitutional order a *nomos* that citizens inhabit. Narratives about the genesis of the constitutional order also help with the reformation of the imperfect constitutional order by bringing the whole constitutional life into focus in the constant reflections on the state of the constitutional order.[103] More importantly, narratives make the democratic pursuit of the meaning of the constitutional project possible. In other words, constitutional genesis is not a mere past of the constitutional order. It continues to work on the present constitutional project by way of narratives about it. Thus, with narratives that bring the founding moment into contact with the ongoing constitutional order, the constituent power morphs from the generative force that brings forth the constitutional order into the rejuvenating energy that breathes new life into the constitutional project. The constituent power not only brings the constitutional order into existence but also sustains the constitutional *nomos* by way of narratives about the founding moment.[104] In a word, the constituent power is reincarnated in the narratives-mediated constitutionalised founding moment.

I hasten to add that the image of the constituent power emerging from the narratives-mediated constitutionalised founding moment does not suggest that the constituent power can or should be domesticated. As a conceptual construct, the constituent power may come in many guises in reality.[105] Nevertheless, the reincarnation of the constituent power in the narratives-mediated constitutionalised founding moment does point out a new temporal orientation of the constituent power. From the internal perspective of the constitutional order, the conventional wisdom has it that the constituent power stays in the past or resurrects in the future only to end the present constitutional order. On this view, the

[103] Balkin (n 48) 2–4.

[104] *cf* Loughlin (n 8) 231–32.

[105] See Andreas Kalyvas, *Democracy and the Politics of the Extraordinary: Max Weber, Carl Schmitt, and Hannah Arendt* (Cambridge University Press, 2008) 294–300.

constituent power has no place in the present jurisgenerative process under the constitutional *nomos*.[106] It is for this reason that scholars who take the external view of the constituent power charge that the constitutional order is aimed at neutralising the constituent power by co-opting it.[107] Unless viewed from the external point of view and regardless of the disruptive effects it may entail, the constituent power is not oriented towards the present.[108]

Yet, the reincarnation of the constituent power in the narratives-mediated constitutionalised founding moment means that the constituent power continuously bears on and reinvigorates the constitutional *nomos* through the narratives about the genesis of the constitutional order. The constituent power as the symbol of freedom is no longer confined to the foundation of the constitutional order; rather, this alternative image of constituent power re-emerges in the invigoration of the constitutional project. Beyond foundation and destruction, the constituent power that is reincarnated in the constitutionalised founding moment works towards the maintenance of the constitutional order. Reincarnated in the narratives about the founding moment, the constituent power is not only remembered as a thing of the past but also relived in the present tense.

IV. Conclusion

Interpretation has dominated contemporary constitutional theories for too long. Studies of the founding moment have either been undertaken as part of the enterprise of constitutional interpretation organised along the divide between fact (fidelity) and norm (absorption) or have simply fallen outside the purview of constitutional theory (disregard). As a result, the formative role of the founding moment in the unfolding of the constitutional project has not yet received the attention it deserves. This not only creates the gap in constitutional imagination between specialists and the public but is also symptomatic of the pathology of contemporary constitutional theories: the more sophisticated constitutional interpretation becomes, the more elusive the meaning of the constitutional order appears to the public.[109]

Alternatively, I have proposed a relational approach to the constitutionalisation of the founding moment, according to which the founding moment sits between fact and norm. The founding moment is related to the constitutional order by virtue of narratives that substantiate the constitutional order with meaning, rendering the constitutional project jurisgenerative. The founding moment

[106] Kuo (n 38) 397–98; Tushnet (n 94) 645–51.

[107] See Antonio Negri, *Insurgencies: Constituent Power and the Modern State*, Maurizia Boscagli (trans) (University of Minnesota Press, 1999).

[108] Notably, in order to alleviate the anxiety over its destructive potential, the constituent power has been recast as civil protest or irritant power. See, eg, Kalyvas (n 105) 230.

[109] *cf* Kahn (2016) (n 36) 117–26.

under the relational view proposed here can be further analysed in three aspects. In terms of substance, constitutional theory will have to extend beyond the debate over interpretive methodology to 'stories of peoplehood'. Surely reframing the historical fact of the founding moment in constitutional terms through narratives is not just another restatement of constitutional theory on the role of history in the interpretation of constitutional norms. Rather, the process of accounting for the founding moment under the relational view recasts the understanding of the constitutional project in democratic terms. The discovery of the meaning of the constitutional order is not constitutional experts' privileged enterprise, but rather requires the democratisation of constitutional (re)interpretation. Narratives epitomise the media via which the meaning of the constitutional project can be democratically discovered. Through the narratives about the founding moment in the democratic pursuit of constitutional meaning, the constituent power can be brought to the fore in the present constitutional order without fearing its unsettling or destructive force.

Apart from substance and process, the structure of narratives about the founding moment is the pivot of the underlying constitutional imagination of the collective constitutional project that involves every member of the political community. Narratives about the founding moment are part of the narratives about the growth trajectory of the constitutional order. They must be told in a structure of unity in order to be coherent and thus persuasive. This is not only an ethics of speaking constitutional language but also makes it possible for citizens to find themselves in the constitutional *nomos*. To make sense of the constitutional order, constitutional theory needs to look beyond interpretation and take the quest for meaning and identity in the constitutional project seriously.

2

The Role of Courts in Advancing Constitutional Moments

Constitutionalising the Constitution in Singapore and Hong Kong

SWATI JHAVERI

I. Introduction

Constitutional lawyers, including the contributors to this volume, have analysed 'constitutional moments' from the perspective of looking at how and when such moments occur, when they are complete, how to identify the product of such moments, the legitimacy (or otherwise) of such moments, the authorship of these moments and/or the question of how to preserve the product of such moments.[1] This chapter, conversely, considers the absence of grand constitutional moments in two post-colonial transitions in Asia: Hong Kong and Singapore. In common with other chapters in this volume, it uses the example of these jurisdictions to problematise how constitutional moments are not always capable of reduction into a single instantiation (however long) or easily identifiable or measurable as being such a moment or even easily to attribute to a particular causal event. This chapter focuses in particular on the fact that in these two jurisdictions, the 'constitutional' nature of the foundational text of the jurisdictions is still unclear. Sections II and III look at the nature of the constitution-making process at the post-colonial founding of the two jurisdictions that contributed to this problem. It highlights how the pragmatic drivers (economic, political and social *stability*) animating the actors involved in the foundings deprioritised discussions relating to more normative questions about the role of the constitutional text in the governance of the jurisdiction.

[1] See, in particular, the chapters in this volume by Ming-Sung Kuo (ch 1), Mel A Topf (ch 3), Yair Sagy (ch 6) and Chien-Chih Lin (ch 9).

The discussion on Hong Kong in Section II highlights how Sino-British negotiations on the transition of Hong Kong from British colonial governance to being a special administrative region of the People's Republic of China prioritised pragmatic concerns of stability, largely financial and economic, over the implementation of a constitutionally led political and democratic governance of Hong Kong.[2] The provisions of the Basic Law of Hong Kong set out only the need for a gradual and incremental transition to self-governance, with much detail left under-defined. These provisions are now being tested with political reform coming to a standstill as civic and political actors on both sides of the border are locked in trenchant disagreement on how the constitutional aspirations behind these provisions should be realised. More importantly, there is a fundamental disagreement about the necessity of realising the constitutional aspirations for the development of democracy in Hong Kong. There are opposing opinions between the local and central actors on the importance of direct elections and democracy and representative government to the task of achieving successful and legitimate governance.[3] As the discussion in Section II highlights, this disagreement stems from mixed understandings of the nature of the Basic Law.

In the context of Singapore, the founding was an unexpected one rather than one subject to protracted negotiation, as was the case in Hong Kong. Singapore's founding occurred on the sudden and unilateral expulsion of Singapore from the Malaysian Federation.[4] Following this event, Singapore parked issues of constitutional design to resolve more immediate and pressing issues relating to the practical needs of its citizens. Most importantly, this included the establishment of 'order' and 'harmony' in a racially charged atmosphere. The latter, in other contexts, would have been an exclusively or predominantly constitutional conversation.[5] However, in the Singapore context, there were only a few constitutional provisions dealing with this major concern.[6] Instead, a lot of this work

[2] Michael Davis, *Constitutional Confrontation in Hong Kong Issues and Implications of the Basic Law* (Palgrave Macmillan, 1990) 1. See also the Sino-British Joint Declaration, which sets out the need to maintain the 'stability and prosperity' of Hong Kong: Jing Cheng, *Hong Kong: In Search of a Future* (Oxford University Press, 1984) 1.

[3] Michael Davis, *Constitutional Confrontation in Hong Kong Issues and Implications of the Basic Law* (Palgrave Macmillan, 1990) ix.

[4] See Kevin Tan, *The Constitution of Singapore: A Contextual Analysis* (Hart Publishing, 2015) for a general discussion of the history of Singapore.

[5] As for example, in the context of South Africa.

[6] Articles 152 (on the responsibility of the government towards minorities and the recognition of the special position of Malays), 153 (a mandate for Parliament to enact legislation for the separate regulation and management of members of the Muslim faith) and 153A (and the recognition of the languages of the four main ethnic groups as official languages) are at the heart of the constitutional provisions on multiculturalism. Interestingly, as a matter of constitutional design, the provisions are not contained in pt IV of the Constitution (which sets out the fundamental rights): art, 15 which sets out the freedom of religion generally, and art 16, which discusses the issue of religion in the context of educational instruction, makes no reference to the Muslim religion, but is neutral in its protection of all religions. The model adopted was to avoid entrenched or institutionalised distinctions based on race and religion and ethnicity, preferring instead aspirational provisions in the Constitution on respecting the special

was done without explicit reference to such constitutional provisions, but through the initiation and management of policy at the executive level. This set the tone of the view taken towards the Constitution: it was not necessary or sufficient to deal with these important transitional issues at the time. As further discussed in Section IV, the endurance and normative importance of the Constitution needs to be assessed against the broader political backdrop in Singapore. The question of the true nature of the Constitution has been a recurring one – most importantly, on questions of constitutionality of legislative and executive action, and on the issue of constitutional amendment and entrenchment.[7]

In both jurisdictions, the founding of the post-colonial jurisdiction was accompanied by a measure of pragmatically driven constitutional agnosticism about the foundational text. The practical motivations behind the constitutional design process (consolidation of political power for economic and social stability over constitutional normativity in the Singapore context, and stability during a major transition in the Hong Kong context) meant that both jurisdictions missed out on the opportunity to have 'grander' conversations about the constitutional core of the systems. Section IV of this chapter therefore looks at how the courts in both jurisdictions will need to play a crucial role in keeping this constitutionalisation exercise alive. It considers key contexts where the national courts may need to or have explicated the 'constitutional' nature of the relevant constitutional text.

II. The Founding of the Hong Kong Special Administrative Region: Collision of Political and Constitutional Ideologies

In order to establish the structure and institutions of government in Hong Kong after the handover, a new constitutional document, the Basic Law, was enacted. The Basic Law Drafting Committee identified five key principles that guided the design of the document: to encapsulate the governing principle of 'One Country Two Systems'; to uphold national unity, while implementing a high degree of autonomy for Hong Kong; to promote economic growth and social stability; to retain the merits of the existing Hong Kong institutions and increase democratic participation; and to begin from the basis of the realities of Hong Kong itself.[8]

position of Malays and the Muslim community, and imposing on the government the job of protecting this (Wee Chong Jin Constitutional Commission, 1965). This was a more gradual approach to dealing with the issue of race and ethnicity in elections. Further changes were made later on to introduce racial representation in Parliament and the office of the Elected President (1988 and 2016, respectively).

[7] See, for example, the most recent amendment exercise relating to the Elected Presidency (Constitutional Commission, *Report of the Constitutional Commission 2016*).

[8] Xiao Weiyun, 'A Study of the Political System of the Hong Kong Special Administrative Region under the Basic Law' (1988) 2 *Journal of Chinese Law* 95.

The relationship between the special administrative region of Hong Kong and Mainland China is encapsulated in the phrase 'one country two systems'. This is a fundamental component of the design of the Basic Law. It is operationalised in Chapter II of the Basic Law, which sets out the division of powers between the local branches of government and the Central Government of China. The latter is responsible for issues relating to foreign and external affairs and defence. The executive, legislature and judiciary in Hong Kong retain their respective powers outside of these contexts. The precise boundaries of the powers have been a highly complex issue. These problems are compounded by uncertainties relating to the nature of the Basic Law and how it is to be interpreted.

Two problems merit particular attention. First, the lack of clarity over the division of governance powers generally between the local and central governments and the precise degree of autonomy that Hong Kong has under the 'one country two systems' principle. Here, the Central Government of China takes the view that Hong Kong only has as much authority as may be determined by China from time to time. For example, in 2007, Wu Bangguo, the head of the Standing Committee of the National People's Congress (NPCSC),[9] stated that Hong Kong only has as much autonomy as Beijing authorises. The scope of the autonomy accorded to Hong Kong under the Basic Law, while referenced in this statement, could therefore be regularly recalibrated by new rulings from the Beijing central government.[10] More recently, President Xi Jinping reiterated China's 'comprehensive jurisdiction' over Hong Kong in his speech at the 19th National Congress of the Communist Party. This could be interpreted to mean that Hong Kong's autonomy would always be subject to the central government's supervision and, presumably, revision.[11]

Second, the lack of clarity over the division of powers of interpretation of the Basic Law has contributed to some of the confusion about the nature of the document. Article 81 of the Basic Law established a Court of Final Appeal within Hong Kong, replacing the Privy Council in London as the final court of appeal for Hong Kong, and Article 82 gave the Court of Final Appeal the power of final adjudication. Furthermore, the Basic Law, in Article 85, explicitly maintains the principle of an independent judiciary. However, these provisions have to be balanced against Article 158, which confers the power of final interpretation of the Basic Law in matters concerning relations between the Hong Kong SAR and China to the NPCSC.[12] This latter provision, especially when it is given a broad

[9] The standing committee of the National People's Congress is convened in between plenary sessions of the legislative body – the National People's Congress. It has the power to interpret laws, including the Constitution.

[10] See 'Wu Bangguo: Hong Kong's Autonomy Laid Down by Beijing' *AsiaNews.it*, www.asianews.it/news-en/Wu-Bangguo:-Hong-Kong%E2%80%99s-autonomy-laid-down-by-Beijing-9487.html.

[11] See http://news.xinhuanet.com/english/special/2017-11/03/c_136725942.htm. This echoes earlier statements made by the State Council in a White Paper on 'The Practice of the "One Country, Two Systems" Policy in the Hong Kong Special Administrative Region' (available at: www.scmp.com/news/hong-kong/article/1529167/full-text-practice-one-country-two-systems-policy-hong-kong-special).

[12] Article 2 states that: 'The National People's Congress authorizes the Hong Kong Special Administrative Region to exercise a high degree of autonomy and enjoy executive, legislative and independent

interpretation, can result in a considerable diminution of the Hong Kong courts' power of final adjudication and at the same time invite the substitution of the political perspective of the NPCSC on the meaning of provisions of the Basic Law for the legal perspective of the Hong Kong judiciary. This limit to the autonomy of the Court of Final Appeal has been the subject of extensive litigation, including immediately after the handover.[13] The difficulties of ascertaining the division of interpretive powers has significant consequences on the way in which the Basic Law is interpreted. Chinese law views it as legislative versus constitutional in nature.[14] It has thus been a big part of the post-handover constitutional project to flesh out the nature of the Basic Law and the approach to constitutional interpretation. This has become an increasingly complex task requiring input from the courts.

III. Founding Moments for the Republic of Singapore: Tension between the de Jure v de Facto Status of the Constitution

One of the most recent texts on constitutional law in Singapore describes it as an unlikely nation with an abrupt beginning.[15] When Singapore separated from Malaysia – its first true post-colonial independent moment – it was left in a

judicial power, including that of final adjudication, in accordance with the provisions of this Law.' Article 5 states that: 'The socialist system and policies shall not be practised in the Hong Kong Special Administrative Region, and the previous capitalist system and way of life shall remain unchanged for 50 years.' Article 8 states that: 'The laws previously in force in Hong Kong, that is, the common law, rules of equity, ordinances, subordinate legislation and customary law shall be maintained, except for any that contravene this Law, and subject to any amendment by the legislature of the Hong Kong Special Administrative Region.' The use of the word 'authorise' in art 2 has recently been read by the PRC government to mean that: 'The high degree of autonomy of the HKSAR [Hong Kong Special Administrative Region] is not full autonomy, nor a decentralised power … It is the power to run local affairs as authorised by the central leadership.' White Paper, State Council of the People's Republic of China, 'The Practice of the "One Country, Two Systems" Policy' (n 11).

[13] *HKSAR v Ma Wai Kwan David* [1997] 1 HKLRD 761, [1997] 2 HKC 315 (CA); and *Ng Ka Ling v Director of Immigration* (1999) 2 HKCFAR 4, [1999] 1 HKLRD 315 (CFA). See also *Ng Ka Ling v Director of Immigration (No 2)* (1999) 2 HKCFAR 141, [1999] 1 HKLRD 577 (CFA). Such confrontations were foreshadowed by commentators during the drafting of the Basic Law of Hong Kong (M Davis, *Constitutional Confrontation in Hong Kong: Issues and Implications of the Basic Law* (Palgrave, 1990)).

[14] Interpretations of the Basic Law by the NPCSC are issued pursuant to art 67(4) of the Chinese Constitution, which gives the NPCSC the power 'to interpret *statutes*'. 'Interpretation' of statutes in the Chinese legal system can include the amendment of text; see Simon Marsden, 'Constitutional Interpretation in Hong Kong: Do Common Law Approaches Apply When the National People's Congress Standing Committee Interprets the Basic Law?' (2006) *LAWASIA Journal* 99.

[15] See Kevin Tan, *The Constitution of Singapore: A Contextual Analysis* (Hart Publishing, 2015) 1. See also Andrew Harding, 'Does the "Basic Structure" Doctrine Apply in Singapore's Constitution? An Inquiry into Some Fundamental Constitutional Premises' in Jaclyn L Neo (ed), *Constitutional Interpretation in Singapore: Theory and Practice* (Routledge, 2016) 32, who argues that the beginning of Singapore was not a 'moment', but 'a process of adjustment which may be regarded as ongoing even after fifty years' (at 36 and 39).

constitutional vacuum. The state-level constitution that applied under the Malaysian Federation Constitution to Singapore no longer extended to Singapore. Therefore, one of the first projects within the nation-building exercise should have been the filling of this gap. The Cabinet were even advised to consult members of governments in the Commonwealth on questions of post-independence constitutional design.

However, soon after, the constitutional project was paused. In the words of Lee Kuan Yew, he felt the need to take a more considered and gradual approach to questions of constitutional design.[16] There could have been a level of uncertainty felt about entrenching a particular constitutional design at such an early stage in the nation's unexpected independence, especially as political power had not been consolidated to a clear majority of one political party at a level that was considered desirable for making important socio-economic decisions to stabilise the nation.[17] The approach was thus a pragmatic one – while having a constitutional document was considered important, it was not yet in itself normatively desirable or paramount at that stage in the nation's history. It was more functionally relevant in empowering the government to maintain economic progress, manage ethnic relations and consolidate political power in order to allow the government to achieve the latter two imperatives.[18] It could be that was achieving the latter imperatives was seen as the source of legitimacy of public power rather than the constitutional framework under which such decisions were made.

Given the relatively pragmatic genesis of the Constitution, there remain fundamental questions to be resolved about its true effect and impact within Singapore: what is its constitutional identity? Article 4 of the Constitution purports to establish a form of constitutional supremacy.[19] Pursuant to Article 5, the Constitution can be amended by a two-thirds majority in Parliament. On the face of it, this appears to 'entrench' the Constitution by imposing this high parliamentary threshold for amendment.[20] However, this needs to be considered against the fact that in

[16] Speech by Mr Lee Kuan Yew in Parliament: http://sprs.parl.gov.sg/search/topic.jsp?currentTopicID=00059192-ZZ&currentPubID=00069470-ZZ&topicKey=00069470-ZZ.00059192-ZZ_1%2Bid002_19840725_S0002_T00021-bill%2B.

[17] Kevin Tan and Li-ann Thio, *Singapore: 50 Constitutional Moments That Defined a Nation* (Marshall-Cavendish, 2015) 46–47.

[18] Kevin Tan, *The Constitution of Singapore: A Contextual Analysis* (Hart Publishing, 2015) 2–3.

[19] Article 4 states that: 'This Constitution is the supreme law of the Republic of Singapore and any law enacted by the Legislature after the commencement of this Constitution which is inconsistent with this Constitution shall, to the extent of the inconsistency, be void.' Harding has previously warned against reading too much into art 4 in light of the fact that it was only introduced in 1979 as a result of the reprinting of the Constitution versus as the result of something that happened at the separation of Singapore from Malaysia that indicated it would be supreme, and, further, it was the product of a legislative process indicating legislative versus constitutional supremacy (Andrew Harding, 'Parliament and the Grundnorm in Singapore' (1983) 25 *Malaya Law Review* 351, 357). However, while this may be historically accurate, the judicial discussion of the supremacy clause has given it impact and meaning. See also Kevin Tan, 'The Evolution of Singapore's Modern Constitution: Developments from 1946 to the Present Day' (1989) 1 *Singapore Academy of Law Journal* 1, 17–23.

[20] Although Singapore is not unique in this respect, with other systems imposing similar, if not higher, thresholds for amendment. See Richard Albert, Xenophon Contiades and Alkmene Fotiadou,

Singapore's Westminster parliamentary system, the People's Action Party (PAP) of Singapore has held such a majority (convincingly) since Singapore's independence. Parliament is unicameral with no convention for a shadow opposition party and voting is done via the whip system.

Various alternative amendment provisions have been introduced from time to time that would shift power to the Elected Presidency and to the citizens via the use of national referenda. However, these options, while introduced into the text of the Constitution, have not been brought into force.[21] Until they are, the power to amend the Constitution remains with the executive – either *qua* executive in the initiation and design of changes or *qua* the majority that passes the amendments in Parliament. It is in this context that commentators have come to the conclusion that Singapore exemplifies a particularly strong form of political constitutionalism.[22] Therefore, while Singapore purports to be a de jure constitutional supremacy, it is in fact a de facto parliamentary supremacy. As a result, the question of the true nature of the Constitutional document has been a recurring one – most importantly, on questions of constitutionality of legislative and executive action and on the issue of constitutional amendment and entrenchment.

The supremacy of the Constitution was tested most prominently in 1989 in a series of cases involving the Internal Security Act.[23] The case involved a group of individuals who had been detained without trial under the Internal Security Act for their involvement in an alleged Marxist conspiracy. They sought to judicially review their detention orders in the case of *Chng Suan Tze v Minister for Home Affairs and Others*.[24] Their challenge was successful on narrow technical grounds

The Foundations and Traditions of Constitutional Amendment (Hart Publishing, 2016) for a comparative overview of amendment provisions. It is the dominance of the PAP in Parliament that makes these provisions unique.

[21] The old art 5(2A) and the new arts 5A, 5B, and 5C introduced in 2016 (but which have yet to be brought into operation). See the 'Entrenchment Framework': Deputy Prime Minister Teo Chee Hean, 'Second Reading, Constitution of the Republic of Singapore (Amendment) Bill' (*Prime Minister's Office Singapore*, 7 November 2016), www.pmo.gov.sg/newsroom/speech-dpm-teo-chee-hean-2nd-reading-constitutional-republic-singapore-amendment-bill.

[22] Kevin YL Tan, *The Constitution of Singapore: A Contextual Analysis* (Hart Publishing, 2015) ch 2; Li-ann Thio, 'In Search of the Singapore Constitution: Retrospect and Prospect' in Li-ann Thio and Kevin YL Tan (eds), *Evolution of a Revolution: Forty Years of the Singapore Constitution* (Routledge, 2008) 355; and Michael Dowdle and Kevin Tan, 'Is Singapore's Constitution Best Considered a Legal or Political Constitution?' in Neo (n 15) 365–72.

[23] Article 149 of the Constitution explicitly permits the possibility of detention without trial. notwithstanding the obvious implications this has for the protection of the rights contained in pt IV of the Constitution (most importantly art 9, which requires that no deprivation of liberty is possible unless it is in accordance with the law).

[24] *Chng Suan Tze v Minister for Home Affairs and Others* [1988] 2 SLR(R) 525, which led to a constitutional amendment to art 149 of the Constitution. The new provision read: 'If, in respect of any proceedings whether instituted before or after 27th January 1989, any question arises in any court as to the validity of any decision made or act done in pursuance of any power conferred upon the President or the Minister by any law referred to in this Article, such question shall be determined in accordance with the provisions of any law as may be enacted by Parliament for this purpose; and nothing in Article 93 shall invalidate any law enacted pursuant to this clause.' The effect of this amendment was to reset the law to the pre-*Chng Suan Tze* position. This amendment was tested (unsuccessfully) in the subsequent case of *Teo Soh Lung v Minister for Home Affairs* [1989] 1 SLR(R) 461, [1990] 1 SLR(R) 347.

(the detention order had been signed and issued by the wrong member of the executive). However, it is the obiter dicta of the judgment that proved to be the trigger for what followed. The Court of Appeal held in *Chng Suan Tze* that it would be prepared to review the legality of detention orders on the normal grounds of judicial review. This led to a swift constitutional amendment to Article 149 of the Constitution, which, in effect, reset the position of the reviewability of detention orders to that which existed prior to *Chng Suan Tze* – namely, very narrow procedural grounds. In doing so, the constitutional amendment furthered the idea of pragmatism over principle (in this case the principle that all power has legal limits and the rule of law) embodied in the *Chng Suan Tze* obiter dicta.[25]

The discussion above has highlighted that depending on the precise shape and contours of the founding event of a jurisdiction, there may be fundamental constitutional questions left for resolution. The next section conceptualises a role for the courts in both jurisdictions in doing just this.

IV. Moving Past the Founding Moment: A Need to Constitutionalise the Constitutional Text

The rest of this chapter will focus on the courts' role in the two jurisdictions. It will look at how the courts can clarify the constitutional nature of the founding documents in light of the problems discussed in Sections II and III above.[26]

A. A Role for the Courts in Hong Kong: Retaining an Interpretive Foothold

How the powers of interpretation are divided between the Hong Kong courts and the NPCSC has significant consequences on the way in which the Basic Law is interpreted. The Basic Law, when viewed from the perspective of Chinese law, is legislative versus constitutional in nature. 'Interpretation' of statutes in the Chinese legal system can include the amendment of text.[27] However, locally, it is

[25] As the Court put it, 'the notion of a subjective or unfettered discretion is contrary to the rule of law. All power has legal limits and the rule of law demands that the courts should be able to examine the exercise of discretionary power'. *Chng Suan Tze* (n 24) 553.

[26] Theories that focus on the role of political actors, more broadly, in the creation and consolidation of constitutional moments are incomplete in excluding this role for the courts. Frank Michelmann, 'Law's Republic' (1988) 97 *Yale Law Journal* 1493 at 1521; and Jean Barnard-Naudé, 'Republican Constitutionalism, Post-Apartheid Jurisgenesis and Kate O'Regan J's Dissent in *Minister of Home Affairs v Fourie*' (2013) 2 *Stellenbosch Law Review* 342, 350 on the court's role in consolidating and advancing constitutionalism in systems.

[27] Interpretations of the Basic Law by the NPCSC are issued pursuant to art 67(4) of the Chinese Constitution, which gives the NPCSC the power 'to interpret *statutes*'. See Marsden (n 14) on the blurred lines between interpretation and amendment of legislation under Chinese law.

viewed as a constitutional document. This imbues the Basic Law with supremacy over local legislation and a meta-structure or value system that is protective of rights and the rule of law.[28] Article 158 provides a conduit for the NPCSC to substitute its political perspective on the Basic Law for the judicial perspective of the Hong Kong judiciary. These different understandings of the nature of the Basic Law are likely to manifest in the interpretation of key provisions.

For example, Article 23 of the Basic Law of Hong Kong mandates the enactment of national security legislation to prohibit, among other things, treason, secession, sedition and subversion against the Central People's Government.[29] The design and prosecution of these offences are likely to bring up issues relating to the freedom of expression, assembly, association and personal liberty. A common law grounded interpretation of Article 23 to resolve issues that come before the courts is likely to be more sensitive to the need to balance rule of law and national security concerns than a political interpretation by the NPCSC.[30]

Aside from Article 23, there are a group of provisions in the Basic Law that are aimed at the realisation of governance by universal suffrage of Hong Kong through locally held elections. The development of a system of direct elections was a significant focus during the Sino-British negotiations prior to Hong Kong's handover to China.[31] The provisions of the Basic Law set out the parameters for reforming the mode of electing the Chief Executive and the members of the Legislative Council (LEGCO) respectively. The process for reform (in terms of the requisite majority in LEGCO, the consent of the Chief Executive and the role of the legislative body of the People's Republic of China (NPCSC)) is also set out in the text. Annexes I and II of the Basic Law state that any changes should 'be reported to the [NPCSC] for the record' (in the case of the election of members of LEGCO) or 'for approval' (in the case of the election of the Chief Executive).[32] While Annexes I and II make clear that the NPCSC has a role to play in political reform, this is only at the end of the reform process once any reform package has been voted on by LEGCO and approved by the Chief Executive. Paragraph 7 of Annex I states that

[28] The constitutional nature of the document and its implications for rights-friendly interpretation was confirmed by the Hong Kong courts early on in the founding of the special administrative region: see *Ng Ka Ling and Others v Director of Immigration* [1999] 1 HKLRD 315 [10], and [73]–[79], per Chief Justice Li, as borne out by arts 4 and 11 of the Basic Law. See Eric Ip, 'The Politics of Constitutional Common Law in Hong Kong under Chinese Sovereignty' (2016) 25(3) *Washington International Law Journal* 565.

[29] The text states that: 'The Hong Kong Special Administrative Region shall enact laws on its own to prohibit any act of treason, secession, sedition, subversion against the Central People's Government, or theft of state secrets, to prohibit foreign political organizations or bodies from conducting political activities in the Region, and to prohibit political organizations or bodies of the Region from establishing ties with foreign political organizations or bodies.'

[30] See Swati Jhaveri, 'Administrative Law as a Modest Guardian of the Rule of Law' in Fiona de Londras and Cora Chan (eds), *China's National Security: Endangering Hong Kong's Rule of Law* (Hart Publishing, forthcoming).

[31] See Michael Davis, *Constitutional Confrontation in Hong Kong Issues and Implications of the Basic Law* (Palgrave Macmillan, 1990) especially 27–29. See also, Swati Jhaveri, 'Reconsitutionalizing Politics in the Hong Kong Special Administrative Region' (2018) 13(1) *Asian Journal of Comparative Law* 27.

[32] Basic Law, Annex II, pt III and Annex I, para 7.

any amendments to the method for selecting the Chief Executive 'shall be reported to the [NPCSC] *for approval*' (emphasis added). Paragraph (III) of Annex II states that any amendments to the method for selecting LEGCO 'shall be reported to the [NPCSC] *for the record*' (emphasis added). The political reform process was therefore envisaged as a process that would be primarily locally initiated, driven and led. However, through various interpretations and decisions relating to the relevant provisions of the Basic Law, the NPCSC have created a new role for themselves at the *inception* of the reform exercise and have then exercised this role in problematic ways. The distinction between a 'decision' and an 'interpretation' by the NPCSC is unclear. The NPCSC has provided no indicators or guidance on when it will issue one over the other on a particular issue, but the purported effect of both instruments appears to be the same from the text of the instruments: they are promulgated as authoritative positions on the particular provision of the Basic Law. These various 'interpretations' and 'decisions' on the meaning and implementation of these provisions of the Basic Law arguably augment and amend the provisions outside the proper constitutional amendment procedures set out in the Basic Law. The gradual increase in input from the NPCSC on the interpretation of the Basic Law could be detrimental from the perspective of furthering interpretations that are sensitive to the rule of law, as practised and understood in Hong Kong.[33]

In this environment, there is a case for a stronger role for the local courts in dealing with these issues and retaining a foothold in the interpretation of the Basic Law. This involves resolving some problematic issues relating to the nature of and approach to interpretation of the Basic Law. Under Article 158(1) of the Basic Law, plenary powers of interpretation are vested in the NPCSC. Under Article 158(2), the NPCSC authorises the Hong Kong courts to interpret 'on their own … the provisions of the Basic Law' in adjudicating cases. However, in respect of certain provisions (described in Article 158(3)), where the courts are unclear about the meaning of those provisions, they must consult the NPCSC for an interpretation before making a decision and then must do so in accordance with the interpretation so provided. Importantly, the role of the Hong Kong courts is in no way *automatically* abridged by the plenary interpretation powers of the NPCSC under Article 158, either as a matter of design or in the way the powers have been utilised to date. Therefore, the lack of clarity in the constitutional set-up should not be utilised to weaken the role of the courts. The Hong Kong courts have discretion on whether or not they should refer something for interpretation to the NPCSC.[34] It is not suggested that the courts challenge the authority of or any legitimate input by the NPCSC or reverse the established jurisprudence

[33] See Albert Chen, 'National Security and the Rule of Law under "One Country, Two Systems"' in de Londras and Chan (n 30).

[34] Cora Chan, 'State Immunity: Reassessing the Boundaries of Judicial Autonomy in Hong Kong' [2012] *Public Law* 601; and Cora Chan, 'Reconceptualising the Relationship between the Mainland Chinese Legal System and the Hong Kong Legal System' (2011) 6 *Asian Journal of Comparative Law* 1.

on the scope of Article 158(3). Instead, it is argued that the courts should not *automatically* assume a deferential and exclusionary role for itself in the area of political reform, but should instead deal with it on a case-by-case basis.

Where the NPCSC issues interpretations outside of any judicial request, the courts can respond to such interpretations in one of four possible ways (in order of decreasing deference). First, the courts are bound by such interpretations and must follow them.[35] Second, the courts could and should apply common law interpretive techniques to any such NPCSC interpretations; they should not accept them at 'face value'. Such common law interpretive techniques include the full remit of constitutional interpretive tools (purposive, originalist, living tree etc).[36] Here the courts could have a role to play in adopting a more Basic Law-consonant and compliant interpretation of an NPCSC interpretation.[37] Third, the courts could evaluate the validity of such 'interpretations' and 'strike them down' should they amount to, for example, 'amendments' via the back door outside the prescribed Article 159 amendment procedure.[38] A fourth possibility, which has not yet been explored in the literature or cases in Hong Kong, is the utilisation of some form of a basic structure or basic features doctrine to evaluate the legitimacy of such interpretations that amount to 'unconstitutional' or 'questionable' 'amendments through interpretation' by the NPCSC. Courts in various common law jurisdictions have sought to identify 'basic features' or the 'basic structure' of the Constitution to varying ends. In India, for example, the Supreme Court of India has stated on multiple occasions that such basic features are beyond amendment by Parliament and the courts will strike down any amendments that seek to limit, constrain or violate such features.[39] This idea of the basic structure or features of a constitution makes particular sense in the Hong Kong context. It could serve as a constitutional hurdle for any decisions or interpretations by the NPCSC that have to comply with certain constitutional fundamentals of the

[35] Po Jen Yap, *Courts and Democracies in Asia* (Cambridge University Press, 2017) ch 12 (relying on *Director of Immigration v Chong Fung Yuen* (2001) 4 HKCFAR 211, 222G–H (Li CJ)).

[36] See Peter W Hogg, 'Canada: From Privy Council to Supreme Court' in Jeffrey Goldsworthy (ed), *Interpreting Constitutions: A Comparative Study* (Oxford University Press, 2006) 82–93 for a summary of the main approaches to constitutional interpretation.

[37] See Cora Chan, 'How Hong Kong's Courts Interpret Beijing's Interpretation of the Basic Law May Yet Surprise' *South China Morning Post* (10 November 2016), www.scmp.com/comment/insight-opinion/article/2044385/how-hong-kongs-courts-interpret-beijings-interpretation.

[38] Following *Ng Ka Ling v Director of Immigration* [1999] 1 HKLRD 315, the Court of Final Appeal asserted such a role for itself. This has not been directly challenged or undermined and some academics argue is still a possible role for the Hong Kong courts; see Cora Chan, 'The Legal Limits on Beijing's Power to Interpret Hong Kong's Basic Law' *HKU Legal Scholarship Blog*, 3 November 2016, http://researchblog.law.hku.hk/2016/11/cora-chan-on-legal-limits-of-beijings.html.

[39] *Kesavananda Bharati v State of Kerala* [1973] AIR SC 1461 (Supreme Court of India); and *Minerva Mills v Union Of India* [1980] AIR SC 1789 (Supreme Court of India). Singapore has a more muted version of the doctrine: *Yong Vui Kong v Public Prosecutor* [2015] 2 SLR 1158; Harding (n 15). See also Swati Jhaveri, 'Recent Judicial Comments on the Basic Structure of the Constitution', *Singapore Public Law Blog*, 20 April 2016, https://singaporepubliclaw.com/2016/04/20/recent-judicial-comments-on-the-basic-structure-of-the-constitution.

Basic Law, including the idea of autonomy and the division of power built into the Basic Law. Article 159(4) states that: 'No amendment to this Law shall contravene the established basic policies of the People's Republic of China regarding Hong Kong.' The interpretive division of powers is a key aspect of these 'basic policies' and one that can be the subject of review by the courts in Hong Kong on the basis of a 'basic features doctrine'-style approach to interpreting NPCSC interpretations and decisions.[40]

As a matter of political reality, the NPCSC and the Central People's Government are unlikely to be invisible in the interpretation of the Basic Law. This is not the direction in which local–central government relations are going, with ever-increasing involvement in the political governance and autonomy of Hong Kong.[41] If the courts took a stronger role in pushing back against or re-interpreting NPCSC interpretations, they might lose their perceived legitimacy and influence once they are viewed as being more active in constitutional adjudication in this area. This could lead to push-back from the NPCSC, which may issue retaliatory interpretations of the Basic Law. Worse still, the NPCSC may issue a 'clarifying' and perhaps contrary interpretation of Article 158 on the conditions for an interpretation by the NPCSC. This could ultimately lead to the diminishment of the judicial role, as the courts would become bound by more interpretations of the Basic Law from the NPCSC in future cases. This could be an irreversible position in the absence of any democratic or constitutional mechanisms to combat any unilateral constitutional usurpation by the NPCSC.[42] However, this section highlights the importance of retaining a role for the courts in Hong Kong and the myriad ways in which this is possible: this is to retain a constitutional identity for the Basic Law. The various postures the courts may adopt range from deferential to activist and can be modulated in response to the political temperature. For the courts to take no role would risk the deconstitutionalisation of the Basic Law.

B. Role of the Courts: Singapore and the Basic Structure of the Constitution

The Constitution of Singapore can be amended by a two-thirds majority (a national referendum is only required where the issue is one of the relinquishment

[40] See Jhaveri (n 31) for an analysis of recent cases that may indicate the court's likely approach.

[41] See n 11.

[42] The concern being that there could be retaliation against strong judicial review. See Po Jen Yap, *Constitutional Dialogue in Common Law Asia* (Oxford University Press, 2015) chs 1 and 12; Samuel Issacharoff, *Fragile Democracies: Contested Power in the Era of Constitutional Courts* (Cambridge University Press, 2017) ch 11; and Stephen Gardbaum, 'Are Strong Constitutional Courts Always a Good Thing for New Democracies?' (2015) 53 *Columbia Journal of Transnational Law* 285, 289.

of sovereignty).[43] Due to the strong majority held by the PAP (since Singapore's independence) in a unicameral parliamentary system, this may not be a significant hurdle, especially as voting is done on the basis of a party whip system. The question of entrenchment in a system committed to constitutional supremacy as part of its text (Article 4) is therefore an important one. This question has been addressed directly by the courts in Singapore in the form of a discussion on the 'basic structure' of the Constitution.

The language of the 'basic structure' or 'basic features doctrine' comes from Indian constitutional law jurisprudence, most notably the case of *Kesavannada Bharati v State of Kerala*,[44] where the Supreme Court of India held that 'every provision of the Constitution can be amended provided in the result the basic foundation and structure of the Constitution remains the same'.[45] The Supreme Court of India has gone on in subsequent cases to identify such fundamental features of the Constitution of India that are beyond the reach of constitutional amendment.[46] The application of this doctrine was first tested in Singapore in the case of *Teo Soh Lung v Minister for Home Affairs*, where the High Court held that 'the *Kesavananda* doctrine is not applicable to our Constitution. Considering the differences in the making of the Indian and our Constitution, it cannot be said that our Parliament's power to amend our Constitution is limited in the same way as the Indian Parliament's power to amend the Indian Constitution'.[47]

This remained the position until the very recent decision of the Singapore Court of Appeal in the case of *Yong Vui Kong v Public Prosecutor*.[48] The applicant in the case had been convicted for trafficking drugs under the Misuse of Drugs Act and received the mandatory sentence of the death penalty under that legislation.[49] The legislation was subsequently amended to permit the imposition of a mandatory life sentence and not less than 15 strokes of the cane. The applicant

[43] While recent changes envisage national referenda for constitutional amendment, these are not yet in force and only envisage referenda in exceptional situations.

[44] *Kesavannada Bharati v State of Kerala* AIR 1973 SC 1461.

[45] ibid [316].

[46] See *Minerva Mills Ltd and Others v Union of India and Others* AIR 1980 SC 1789, where the court held that the limit on absolute power was a fundamental feature of the Constitution; therefore, any constitutional amendment which sought to further enlarge the amendment powers of Parliament and limit judicial power to review this was unconstitutional.

[47] *Teo Soh Lung v Minister for Home Affairs* [1989] 1 SLR(R) 461 [47], per FA Chua J (the Court of Appeal did not consider the issue on appeal). The High Court took a strict originalist interpretation of the origination of the Constitution to reach this conclusion, positing that if 'the framers of the Singapore Constitution had intended limitations on the power of amendment, they would have expressly provided for such limitations'. The applicant had tried to argue that constitutional amendments which sought to immunise national security decisions from judicial review violated the basic structure of the Constitution as being in contravention of the rule of law and the separation of powers and in reliance on the Supreme Court of India's decision in *Minerva Mills* (ibid).

[48] *Yong Vui Kong* (n 39).

[49] The applicant sought to challenge that sentence (and the subsequent refusal to grant him clemency) in numerous unsuccessful constitutional challenges: *Yong Vui Kong v Attorney-General* [2011] 2 SLR 1189, CA; *Yong Vui Kong v PP* [2010] 3 SLR 489; *Yong Vui Kong v Public Prosecutor* [2012] 2 SLR 872, CA.

was re-sentenced under these legislative amendments. He sought to challenge the caning part of his re-sentence on the grounds that it was a form of torture and violated Article 9 (protection of liberty) as being a form of punishment that was contrary to 'law', and that caning was discriminatory in its application to men and therefore violated Article 12, which protected equality of persons before the law. The relevant challenge for the present purposes was the argument that (having failed to convince the court of his arguments under Articles 9 and 12) 'a prohibition against torture and inhuman punishment should be read into the Constitution because such practices violate "first principles of natural law"', all part of the basic structure of the Constitution.[50] The applicant sought to rely on an interim case, *Mohammad Faizal bin Sabtu v Public Prosecutor*,[51] where the High Court had articulated aspects of the basic structure of the Constitution – in that case, the principle of the separation of powers.

The Court of Appeal accepted that this case had introduced the idea that certain aspects of the Constitution are part of its 'basic structure' into the jurisprudence of Singapore. To this the Court of Appeal added that the right to vote may be part of the basic structure of the Constitution,[52] acknowledging its earlier decision in the case of *Vellama d/o Marie Muthu v Attorney-General*,[53] where it held that citizens had a right to a representative in Parliament in the Westminster model of government that is part of the inherent framework of the Constitution. Using these examples, the Court of Appeal concluded in *Yong Vui Kong* that in

[50] *Yong Vui Kong* (n 39) [38].

[51] See *Mohammad Faizal bin Sabtu v Public Prosecutor* [2012] 4 SLR 947, where the High Court held that the principle of separation of powers is part of the 'basic structure' of the Constitution: 'The Singapore Constitution is based on the Westminster model of constitutional government ("the Westminster model"), under which the sovereign power of the State is distributed among three organs of state, viz, the Legislature, the Executive and the Judiciary … the sovereign power of Singapore is shared among the same trinity of constitutional organs, viz, the Legislature (comprising the President of Singapore and the Singapore Parliament), the Executive (the Singapore government) and the Judiciary (the judges of the Supreme Court and the Subordinate Courts). The principle of separation of powers, whether conceived as a sharing or a division of sovereign power between these three organs of state, is therefore part of the basic structure of the Singapore Constitution … All Constitutions based on the Westminster model incorporate the principle of separation of powers as part of their constitutional structure in order to diffuse state power among different organs of state' (at [11] and [12]). The court went on to hold that constitutional supremacy and the exclusiveness of judicial power were part of this idea of the separation of powers. However, it eventually concluded that none of these principles were breached by a legislative provision that sought to structure the sentencing 'discretion' of the judges in the context of certain drug-trafficking offences.

[52] Relying on parliamentary debates where the government acknowledged this to be the case, see Singapore Parliamentary Debates, Official Report (16 May 2001) vol 73 at col 1726 (Wong Kan Seng, Minister for Home Affairs and Leader of the House): 'While the Constitution does not contain an expressed declaration of the right to vote, I have been advised by the Attorney General, even before today, that the right to vote at parliamentary and presidential elections is *implied within the structure of our Constitution*. We have a parliamentary form of government. The Constitution provides for regular general elections to make up Parliament and establishes representative democracy in Singapore. So the right to vote is fundamental to a representative democracy, which we are, and that is why we have the Parliamentary Elections Act to give effect to this right' (emphasis added).

[53] *Vellama d/o Marie Muthu v Attorney-General* [2013] 4 SLR 1.

order for something to be part of the basic structure of the Constitution 'it must be something fundamental and essential to the *political system* that is established thereunder'.[54]

There are therefore two open questions for the court to clarify on the 'basic structure' of the Constitution. The first is what is 'essential to the political system of Singapore'. In *Yong Vui Kong*, the purported prohibition against torture was not considered intrinsically linked to the political system of Singapore and therefore not part of the basic structure of the Constitution.[55] Second, the Court of Appeal did not conclude whether recognising something as part of the 'basic structure' of Singapore had the same impact as the basic features doctrine in India whereby it is beyond the normal amendment process.[56] In India, the basic features doctrine can be used to strike down constitutional amendments (validly passed as a matter of process) as unconstitutional for violating the basic features. In Singapore, the basic structure has a seemingly more subtle impact on legislation and executive action: the validity of both can be assessed using features of the basic structure.[57]

Despite not being a full-blown basic features doctrine, the conversation about the 'basic structure' of the Constitution of Singapore has importance for the purposes of understanding a possible role for the courts in consolidating the advancement of constitutionalism in a system. Given that major architectural issues were not a formative part of the constitutional design deliberations in Singapore, the courts are now able to contribute, however modestly, to a deeper understanding of what constitutes constitutional fundamentals in Singapore.

The court is further able to use the vehicle of the basic structure of the Constitution to advance constitutional dialogue to keep up with changing constitutional conditions. For example, the courts have recently elaborated on the nature of the

[54] *Yong Vui Kong* (n 39) [70], relying on Calvin Liang and Sarah Shi, 'The Constitution of Our Constitution, A Vindication of the Basic Structure Doctrine' *Singapore Law Gazette* (August 2014) 12, at paras 38 and 46: 'The basic structure is intrinsic to, and arises from, the very nature of a constitution and not legislative or even judicial fiat. At its uncontentious minimum, a constitution sets out how political power is organised and divided between the organs of State in a particular society. In other words, the constitution is a power-defining and, therefore, power-limiting tool … the basic structure is a limited doctrine. It is arguable that fundamental rights are not a necessary part of the basic structure of a constitution. This is because fundamental rights relate to rights and liberties of citizens and do not define the limits to the powers of and checks on each organ of the State. What is not fundamental to a constitution cannot form part of its basic structure.'

[55] However, the Court of Appeal was prepared to recognise the presence of a limited prohibition against torture within art 9 of the Constitution: liberty could not be deprived on the basis of evidence obtained through methods that constituted torture. This was reiterated in *Ravi s/o Madasamy v Attorney-General and Other Matters* [2017] 5 SLR 489.

[56] See Harding (n 15) 37, 39, who argues that Singapore should not and does not adopt the Indian basic features doctrine. He notes how the court in cases like *Mohammad Faizal* discuss and accept the idea of the basic structure in the context of interpretation, but cases like *Teo Soh Lung* reject the basic structure doctrine when it is being argued it prevents certain constitutional amendments.

[57] *Mohammad Faizal bin Sabtu* (n 51); *Vellama d/o Marie Muthu* (n 53). See also Harding (n 15); and K Tan, 'Into the Matrix: Interpreting the Westminster Model Constitution' in Neo (n 15); and The Honourable Senior Judge Chan Sek Keong, 'Basic Structure and Supremacy of the Singapore Constitution' (2017) 29 *Singapore Academy of Law Journal* 619.

separation of powers doctrine (part of the basic structure) and its application in Singapore. Previously when the doctrine was elicited, it was used as a tool for judicial restraint. For example, in the case of *Lee Hsien Loong v Review Publishing Co Ltd*,[58] the High Court elaborated on the idea of non-justiciability (as part of its obiter dicta and in rejecting the application of a media privilege against liability for defamation) and in doing so held that:

> In all cases of judicial review, the court should exercise restraint and take cognisance of the fact that our system of government operates within the framework of three co-equal branches; even though all exercise of power must be within constitutional and legal bounds, there are areas of prerogative power that the democratically elected Executive and Legislature are entrusted to take charge of and in this regard it is to the electorate and not the Judiciary that the Executive and Legislature are ultimately accountable.[59]

However, recently the courts have switched the rhetoric of co-equality in favour of judicial review rather than judicial deference. This was in the case of *Tan Seet Eng v Attorney-General*,[60] where the Court of Appeal observed that:

> [T]he specific responsibility for pronouncing on the legality of government actions falls on the Judiciary. It is appropriate at this juncture to parse this. To hold that this is so is not to place the Judiciary in an exalted or superior position relative to the other branches of the government. On the contrary, the Judiciary is one of three co-equal branches of government. But though the branches of government are co-equal this is so only in the sense that none is superior to any other while all are subject to the Constitution. Beyond this, it is a fact that each branch of government has separate and distinct responsibilities. In broad terms, the Legislature has the power to make the laws of our land, and this power extends even to amending the foundation of our entire legal system and indeed, of our nation, the Constitution. The Executive has the power and the responsibility of governing the country within the framework of the laws established by the Legislature. And the Judiciary has the responsibility for the adjudication of controversies which carries with it the power to pronounce authoritatively and conclusively on the meaning of the Constitution and all other laws. It is the nature of this latter responsibility that results in the Judiciary being tasked with the role of pronouncing on the legality of government actions.[61]

What is particularly pertinent is the context in which this happened in the case of *Tan Seet Eng*. This case also involved preventative detention, as did the cases of *Chng* and *Teo Soh Lung*, but this time under the Criminal Law (Temporary Provisions) Act (CLTPA) and, in particular, section 30(a), which states that:

> Whenever the Minister is satisfied with respect to any person … that the person has been associated with activities of a criminal nature, the Minister may, with the consent

[58] *Lee Hsien Loong v Review Publishing Co Ltd* [2007] SGHC 24, [2007] 2 SLR(R) 453 at 490, [98] (which dealt with the question of the proper scope of the law of defamation and its relationship with freedom of expression).

[59] ibid [98(d)].

[60] *Tan Seet Eng v Attorney-General* [2015] SGCA 59.

[61] ibid.

> of the Public Prosecutor – (a) if he is satisfied that it is necessary that the person be detained in the interests of public safety, peace and good order, by order under his hand direct that the person be detained for any period not exceeding 12 months from the date of the order.

The main issue for the Court of Appeal was whether the section 30 ground had been made out and the scope of the court's role in reviewing decisions made under this provision. Despite the constitutional and statutory amendments that sought to scale back the courts' role in reviewing preventative detention decisions under the Internal Security Act, the Court of Appeal in *Tan Seet Eng* can be seen as reviving its position under *Chng Suan Tze* in the context of the CLTPA. One of the issues for the Court of Appeal in *Tan Seet Eng* was whether the approach in *Chng Suan Tze* to reviewing such detention orders continued to be 'good law' outside of the context of the Internal Security Act, given the amendments that followed that case. The Court of Appeal answered this in the affirmative.[62] The foundation for this was the rule of law.[63] Soon after the decision, the Ministry of Home Affairs issued a statement which stated that the '[Ministry] respects and accepts the Court of Appeal's judgment'. It further stated that the Ministry had sought to reissue detention orders with the consent of the Public Prosecutor which would comply with the Court of Appeal's decision in *Tan Seet Eng*. In particular, the Ministry stated that the orders will set out the impact of the applicant's match-fixing activities 'on public safety, peace and good order within Singapore' as per the Court of Appeal's interpretation of section 30 of the CLTPA.[64] The applicant was rearrested less than a week later and the detention order was not challenged.[65] In addition, the Ministry of Home Affairs released a further three detainees under the CLTPA on the basis that it had reviewed the detention orders of those persons following the judgment and had come to the view that they also needed to be revoked. Once released, these detainees were not rearrested under fresh detention orders, but were instead subject to the lesser restraint of a police supervision order.[66] The balanced approach taken to review in *Tan Seet Eng* meant that the 'binary clash'[67]

[62] ibid [67]–[76]. This differs from the courts' position in earlier cases under the Criminal Law (Temporary Provisions) Act (Cap 67, 2000 revised edn): see, most notably, *Re Wong Sin Yee* [2007] 4 SLR(R) 676.

[63] *Tan Seet Eng v Attorney-General* (n 60) [1] and [90], per Sundaresh Menon CJ.

[64] Ministry of Home Affairs, 'MHA Statement on Detention of Dan Tan Seet Eng' (5 December 2015).

[65] 'Alleged Match-Fixer Dan Tan Re-arrested' *The Straits Times* (1 December 2015).

[66] Ministry of Home Affairs, 'MHA Statement on Three Members of Match-Fixing Syndicate Released from Detention and Placed on Police Supervision Orders' (18 January 2016). The government amended the CLTPA to introduce an ouster clause which would restrict judicial review. During parliamentary debates, the Minister clarified that this ousted review on the merits and not review on the basis of the normal grounds of review as were used in *Tan Seet Eng*: s 30(2), which came into effect on 1 January 2019.

[67] See Sundaresh Menon, 'The Rule of Law: The Path to Exceptionalism' (2016) 28 *Singapore Academy of Law Journal* 413 at paras 29 and 35 on the advantages of avoiding such binary clashes between the two branches.

that was apparent post-*Chng Suan Tze* was avoided with the court's input and the government's response to that input being more collaborative versus combative in nature.[68]

The discussion in the cases above places the doctrine of the separation of powers and the idea of limited government squarely within the framework of the Constitution. Earlier discussions undermined the idea of constitutional supremacy. This additional layer of explanation in the recent cases on the separation of powers is an incremental extension of the explanation provided in earlier cases and a move towards consolidating the aspirations behind Article 4.[69] A further clarification by the Court of the Appeal on the nature and function of the basic structure or meta purpose of the Constitution will help to consolidate its identify as just that.

V. Conclusion

The courts in both jurisdictions can have a role to play in clarifying fundamental features of the Constitutional documents, but also, more importantly, the constitutional nature of the foundational texts. They will need to fill a gap that resulted from the more pressing pragmatic and specific concerns of the founding moments in both jurisdictions. This chapter has proposed a role for courts versus the political arms of government in the broader constitutionalism project of a state. It has considered this issue in the context of the particular founding events of the two jurisdictions and in the context of the particular political set-up. It moves beyond idealised visions of the political arms of government to situations with realistic problems that the political arms of government cannot resolve without some input from the courts. The aim has been to cast a spotlight on the voice of the courts as a contributor to the consolidation of founding moments and their role in creating a level of sustainability of a movement.[70] This chapter acknowledges concerns about the judicial role in founding moments: the fact that the judicial branch lacks democratic legitimacy. Thus, this chapter stops short of proposing judicially

[68] Even amendments to the CLTPA made post-*Tan Seet Eng* did not purport to exclude judicial review: Second Reading of the Bill, the Minister for Law, Mr K Shanmugam, Singapore Parliamentary Debates, Official Report (6 February 2018), vol 94.

[69] Here, Harding does express a preference for the resolution of these issues in the future via the process of constitution-making versus leaving it to the courts to explicate via the 'basic structure' concept (Harding (n 15) 44–45). See also Tan (n 57) 50, 71; B Ong, 'The Basic Structure Doctrine in Singapore: A Reply' (2014) *Singapore Law Gazette* (November) 34; and Sudhir Krishnaswamy, *Democracy and Constitutionalism in India: A Study of the Basic Structure Doctrine* (Oxford University Press, 2011) for a detailed discussion of such confrontations.

[70] This will involve reconciling this with more textual approaches to interpretation – a doctrinal issue that is outside of the scope of this chapter. However, see S Jhaveri. 'Reflecting on Constitutional Change in Singapore' in Jaclyn L Neo and Swati Jhaveri (eds), *Constitutional Change in Singapore: Managing the Elected Presidency* (Routledge, 2019, forthcoming).

initiated constitutional moments. In addition, it does not propose a role for the courts in setting out a constitutional theory that will be 'universally or eternally applicable'.[71] Rather, it makes a more modest suggestion of allowing judicial input on these open questions. This discussion engages the usual debate on the balance of constitutional power between the judiciary and political branches. It seeks to set it within a particular political context. Political and constitutional reforms in both of these jurisdictions are top-down exercises, prompted and managed and approved by the executive and legislature. The potential for collective citizen-oriented and initiated reform through referenda is absent in these jurisdictions. This rationalises a stronger role for the courts as a proxy for ventilating issues on the part of the citizens. The discussion is also premised on the existence of constitutional systems that are intended to be of enduring quality versus temporary and transitional in nature.[72]

[71] Harding (n 15) 36.

[72] In the context of Hong Kong, it is still a semi-enduring situation. The Basic Law of Hong Kong establishes the Special Administrative Region of Hong Kong, which will enjoy legal, political and fiscal autonomy for at least the first 50 years post-1997. Thus, even though it is a 50-year-long constitutional arrangement, this is still semi-enduring: first, the 50-year timeframe is optional and, second, this is still a long period of time for a 'transitional or temporary constitution' (see, for example, Varol's definition of temporary constitutions: 'Under the default rule, a constitution lasts in perpetuity … Intended to be durable and long lasting, if not permanent … a constitution or constitutional provision remains in place until its amendment or repeal. The default rule for a temporary constitution is different. A temporary constitution or constitutional provision, as this Essay defines it, limits its own term and lapses at its expiration date unless re-enacted through regular constitutional amendment procedures'; Oran Varol, 'Temporary Constitutions' (2014) 102(2) *California Law Review* 409). See also Iand Zachary Elkins, Tom Ginsburg and James Melton, *The Endurance of National Constitutions* (Cambridge University Press, 2009), who noted that, empirically, a national constitution has a typical life expectancy of 19 years.

3

Foundation and Revolution

Hannah Arendt and the Problem of Legitimacy and Stability in Constitutional Consolidation

MEL A TOPF

This chapter investigates the relations of revolutionary consolidation to the American constitutional founding. The concepts of consolidation and augmentation have received little attention in relation to the central question of constitutional legitimacy. Hannah Arendt's theory of revolution is paradigmatic in this respect. Notwithstanding her influential discussion of foundation, Arendt gives relatively little attention to the pragmatic role of consolidation in acts of constitutional founding. Further, scholarly analyses of Arendt on revolution rarely offer critiques of her concept of foundation in this respect. I focus on Arendt partly owing to her influential theories regarding founding of bodies politic and partly because I believe that within her political thought on what for her was the uniquely successful consolidation of the American Revolution lies an explanation for that success that she herself does not expressly offer. Further, Arendt's thinking may be a useful launchpad in considering the dynamics of founding moments.

The historical barriers to the successful consolidation of revolutionary acts are a function of negotiating the extraordinarily difficult relation of revolution to legitimacy. Arendt's theory of foundation reflects the vexed relation of founding to legitimacy and to the order of stability. 'Arendt is not considered as a thinker of order but as a thinker of … revolutionary beginnings.'[1] I will look at the creation of the early US state constitutions (those developed 1776 to 1780) in order to argue that their purported legitimacy as foundational revolutionary acts was grounded in what Arendt calls the modern identification of fabrication with action, with the consequent reliance on what she calls the 'central position of

[1] Christian Volk, 'The Decline of Order: Hannah Arendt and the Paradoxes of the Nation-State' in Seyla Benhabib (ed), *Politics in Dark Times: Encounters with Hannah Arendt* (Cambridge University Press, 2010) 173.

the concept of process'.[2] I will extend Arendt's view of foundational acts to show that the consolidation phase of the American Revolution was widely perceived as guaranteeing the Revolution's legitimacy by fabricating stable spaces for its augmentation, that is, institutions, which in turn are perceived as made through the force of speech acts – written constitutions. The unprecedented reliance on the *ethos* of fabrication was a crucial ground for the perceived legitimacy of the consolidation of the American Revolution. Everywhere the revolutionaries framed their narrative of events in terms of fabrication, a frame, for that era, of great cognitive power.

This was reinforced by the written and printed nature of the early constitutions, which was crucial to both the making and the consolidation of a constituent and stable post-revolutionary body politic. The emergence of a print culture 'reconceptualized the public sphere' (Gordon Wood) through what was in the 1770s the unprecedented making of constituting documents that had the force and effect of consolidation. The perceived stabilising force of the making of written constituting documents was crucial as 'a foundation never more to be shaken', as one of the framers of the first Pennsylvania Constitution put it. While Arendt, like many writers on revolution and founding, does not explicitly develop this important element at length, I will show that it is crucial to her views on the problem of the relation of revolution and founding on the one hand and to legitimacy, stability and consolidation on the other.

I. Hannah Arendt and the Problem of Revolutionary Consolidation

In her influential book *On Revolution*,[3] Hannah Arendt largely avoids the question of revolutionary consolidation in her treatment of the American Revolution. Somewhat curiously, she seems to adopt that revolution as a kind of norm, against which later revolutions in France, Russia and elsewhere failed, owing mainly to violence. She celebrates, with little attempt at explaining, the relatively non-violent character of the American Revolution. She simply notes, as she put it elsewhere, that the American revolutionaries 'founded a completely new body politic without violence and with the help of a constitution'.[4] She separates the act of foundation from development of a constitution, which, as she says, merely helped.

For Arendt, it is the foundation of a body politic, the *polis*, which is crucial. Central to her thought is that human beings gain their humanity, their very identity as human, only to the extent that they are political. She was inspired by the ancient Greeks, for whom 'outside the body politic man's life was not only and

[2] Hannah Arendt, *The Human Condition*, 2nd edn (University of Chicago Press, 1998) 294–304.
[3] Hannah Arendt, *On Revolution* (Viking Press, 1963; revised edn, 1965).
[4] Hannah Arendt, *Between Past and Future* (Viking Press, 1961) 140.

not even primarily insecure ... it was without meaning and dignity because under no circumstances could it leave any trace behind it'.[5] It is only through action (as opposed to labour and work) that humans can be free, can exercise their unique capacity to initiate, to found, to begin something new. Hence, 'the *raison d'etre* of politics is freedom, and its field of experience is action'.[6] Action is never possible except in the *polis*, in the presence of others in a public space: 'to be isolated is to be deprived of the capacity to act'.[7] Indeed, 'without a space of appearance and without trusting in action and speech as a mode of being together, neither the reality of one's self, of one's own identity, nor the reality of the surrounding world can be established beyond doubt'.[8] This space of appearance, of speech and action, where humans may come together has endurance and stability only because of the human capacity for fabrication. Fabrication is for Arendt a kind of second-order category of the *vita active*, for it is by erecting a concrete world of lasting things that action can be protected and be remembered.[9]

Working against action and fabrication, in danger of destroying them, is the endless cycle of nature, which must, as far as possible, be kept out of the *polis* or at least be marginalised to protect action and fabrication. Humans of course never escape nature. They may act and fabricate, but they also must engage in the third element of the human condition – labour – and they must consume the fruits of labour to survive, since we are always subject to the demands of biological necessity. Labouring and consuming are life processes, the most futile of human endeavours because they leave nothing behind. Labour is opposed to freedom, for labour 'despite its futility is born of great urgency and motivated by a more powerful drive than anything else, because life itself depends upon it'.[10] For Arendt, 'the activity corresponding to the status of poverty was laboring'.[11] Poverty, then, which 'forces free men to act like a slave',[12] can have no place in the *polis* owing to the threat it poses both to freedom and to the very stability of the public realm.

Arendt attributes the relative success of the American Revolution and 'the failure of the men of the French Revolution' to 'the predicament of poverty [that] was absent from the American scene but present everywhere else in the world'.[13] The poor, even with some assurance of self-preservation, are bound by the necessity of labouring and consuming, so that even after 'their self-preservation has been assured ... their lives are without consequence, and ... they remain excluded from the light of the public realm'.[14] For Arendt, the French Revolution failed owing to

[5] ibid 71.
[6] ibid 146.
[7] Arendt (n 2) 167.
[8] ibid 187.
[9] ibid 120.
[10] ibid 76.
[11] ibid 110.
[12] ibid 64.
[13] Arendt (n 3) 62–63.
[14] ibid 63.

the intrusion of poverty – of necessity – into the public realm. There the insidious pressures of compassion demanded not only that the people be liberated from tyranny, as in America, but that the poor 'had to be liberated once more, and compared to this liberation from the yolk of necessity, the original liberation from tyranny must have looked like child's play'.[15]

Arendt's view of the success of the American Revolution has what one writer calls a curious unreality.[16] Arendt does note the role of institutional frameworks and constitutionalism, that is, what might be considered consolidation of the revolution, but, as another writer puts it, she is 'not as concrete as one would like'.[17] In *On Revolution*, 'the American Revolution is rendered in deceptively pure tones … We are presented with a sharp contrast between the violence of the French revolutionaries and the legal fairness of the Americans'.[18] Arendt fails to connect the events of the American Revolution, and especially the concurrent and unprecedented state constitution-making, with its most surprising outcome, compared to the French and subsequent revolutions: the successful founding of stable and enduring constitutional structures. In short, she fails to account for the consolidation of the American Revolution. She never succeeds in explaining the surprising stability, and equally surprising universal perception of the legitimacy, of the revolutionary-era constitutions. The nature of the early constitutions and of the governments they created seems to be of little interest to Arendt. The 'ever-recurring phenomenon of government remained to her a matter of so little urgency, if not indeed one of indifference, despite her relevant discussion of the separation of power principle … the inherent goal of all political action remains oddly obscure. For that goal is decision'.[19]

The problem is twofold. First, Arendt's concept of action foregrounds its unpredictable nature and celebrates the human capacity of beginning, witness and testimony to the human capacity for freedom. 'It is the very nature of a beginning to carry with itself a measure of complete arbitrariness … the beginning has, as it were, nothing whatsoever to hold on to.'[20] A revolution for Arendt occurs only 'when change occurs in a sense of a new beginning, where violence is used to constitute an altogether different form of government, to bring about the formation of a new body politic'.[21] This valorising of new beginnings, of 'initiatory action with all of its inherent spontaneity, uncontrollability, and unpredictability',[22] effectively prevents Arendt from coming to terms with the

[15] ibid 69.

[16] James Miller, 'The Pathos of Novelty: Hannah Arendt's Image of Freedom in the Modern World' in Melvyn A Hill (ed), *Hannah Arendt: The Recovery of the Public World* (St Martin's Press, 1979) 181.

[17] Jeremy Waldron, 'Arendt's Constitutional Politics' in Dana R Villa (ed), *Politics, Philosophy, and Terror: Essays on the Thought of Hannah Arendt* (Princeton University Press, 1999) 210.

[18] Miller (n 16) 181.

[19] Dolf Sternberger, 'The Sunken City: Hannah Arendt's Idea of Politics' (1977) 44 *Social Research* 145.

[20] Arendt (n 3) 207.

[21] ibid 28.

[22] Peter Fuss, 'Hannah Arendt's Concept of Political Community' in Hill (n 16) 159.

mundane goals and the mechanics of their actual operation in the public realm. Hence, Arendt is 'not considered a thinker of order but as a thinker of contingency, of revolutionary beginning'.[23] Another writer observes that Arendt 'was far from being a constitutional engineer; she was far more concerned with the spiritual aspects of politics'.[24] In other words, her interest is in founding and not in consolidation or augmentation. Other than the purported absence of poverty, Arendt never attempts to get to the basis for the American Revolution's success in consolidating the revolution.

Arendt pays little attention to the question – central to explaining the success of the American Revolution – of how this new beginning was consolidated, and how it developed into a stable and legitimate constitutional system and so avoided the chaos, violence and instability of revolutionary governments in France. She notes in passing, and somewhat inconsistently, that America's success can be attributed to 'the relatively nonviolent character of the American Revolution', though she acknowledges only that the stability of the resulting political structures is 'surprising'.[25] The closest she comes, as Jurgen Habermas notes, is to place 'more trust in the venerable figure of the contract than in her own concept of a praxis. She retreats … into the contract theory of natural law'.[26]

Arendt, then, is a thinker of contingency, of revolutionary foundings. Consolidation is simply not a central concern either in her thought on revolution, or for that matter in her thinking about human action and speech and their role in creating a political realm. In one sense, she does not differ from many major writers on revolution. The Marxist analysis of revolution, which Arendt did not accept, has in common with her a lack of interest in consolidation, focusing instead on historical inevitability, so that human action and its capacity for founding play no role. In the Marxist view, consolidation warrants little if any attention because, as Jacques Barzun said, it is almost 'automatic': 'The revolution over, Marx's communist society gets itself established by sheer historic necessity. Communism comes without any special plan.' There is 'an as yet unknown and more cheerful message for the proletariat' on the revolution's other side, but that will come about without human agency.[27]

Marx acknowledges the violence necessary to revolution, speaking of the 'point where war breaks out into open revolution, and where the violent overthrow of the bourgeoisie lays the foundation for the sway of the proletariat'.[28] The next step,

[23] Volk (n 1) 173.

[24] Dick Howard, 'Keeping the Republic: Reading Arendt's *On Revolution* after the Fall of the Berlin Wall' in Benhabib (n 1) 281.

[25] Arendt (n 4) 140.

[26] Jurgen Habermas, 'Hannah Arendt's Communications Concept of Power' (1977) 44 *Social Research* 24.

[27] Jacques Barzun, *Darwin, Marx, and Wagner*, 2nd edn (Doubleday, 1958) 165. See also at 161: the 'Marxian process is almost, but not quite, automatic'.

[28] Karl Marx and Friedrich Engels, *Communist Manifesto* (New York Labour News Co, 1948 [1848]) 31.

the dictatorship of the proletariat, continues the revolutionary violence: the proletariat, now supreme, will 'wrest … all capital from the bourgeoisie, to centralize all instruments of production in the hands of the state'. The coercion and suppression of liberty are 'of course' a requirement: 'Of course, in the beginning, this cannot be effected except by means of despotic inroads into bourgeois rights.'[29] Afterwards, the post-revolutionary state will famously wither away, apparently automatically, leaving what he calls 'free development for all'.[30] Lenin reveals the same pattern. Suppression, he writes, is 'still necessary' during the transition from capitalism to communism, after which the new era will simply arrive. With the state's withering away, the people will somehow '*become accustomed* to the observance of the elementary rules of social life that have been known for centuries', people observing these rules 'without force, without compulsion, without subordination, without the *special apparatus* for compulsion which is called the state'.[31]

II. Consolidation and the Problem of Legitimacy

Arendt, in addressing the American Revolution and its successful consolidation, cannot avoid the vexing question of how a revolution, which by its nature was illegitimate, resulted in a political system that was both stable and legitimate. For her, the 'problem of founding the new body politic was effectively one of legitimacy [deriving] … from the perplexities inherent in every beginning, whose "bewildering spontaneity" means that no cause can be found to prove that the founding act of freedom was necessary and therefore justified. Without such authority, a new legal constitution is at permanent risk of being undone, as was the French constitution, which was replaced fourteen times between 1789 and 1875'.[32]

There can be no consolidation without legitimacy. Arendt, fascinated by the American founders' revolutionary break with the past, never quite accounts for the legitimacy of the extraordinarily successful consolidation of the revolution through constitution-making. For her, Dick Howard writes, the 'need to break with the past in order to found the new means that the new order has itself no proper legitimacy; its only foundation is the violent revolutionary "crime" that destroyed the old order. This was the rock against which the French revolutionary hopes crashed again and again'.[33] The disconnect between revolution and legitimacy 'is precisely the dilemma of revolutionaries: how to establish a legitimate order when the existing order labels that act of establishment as fundamentally illegitimate'.[34]

[29] ibid 44–45.
[30] ibid 47.
[31] VI Lenin, *State and Revolution* (International Publishers, 1932 [1917]) 74.
[32] Finn Bowring, *Hannah Arendt: A Critical Introduction* (Pluto Press, 2011) 73.
[33] Howard (n 24) 278.
[34] John McGowan, 'Must Politics Be Violent? Arendt's Utopian Vision' in Craig Calhoun and John McGowan (eds), *Hannah Arendt and the Meaning of Politics* (University of Minnesota Press, 1997) 277.

To confront this in her study of the American Revolution, Arendt relies not very convincingly on traditional social contract theory and argues for a continuous line of legitimacy from the Mayflower Compact to the US Constitution.[35] For her, the Mayflower Compact is a social contract arising from a group of ship's passengers thrown into a state of nature as their ship arrived at a vast wilderness. Arendt here tips into the view, commonly expressed during the revolutionary era, that independence put the colonies into a state of nature where they would remain until they developed constitutions. Arendt notes neither the then-common confusion between forming a society and framing state governments nor the fact that the framers of the state constitutions never asserted this as a ground for the legitimacy of the new constitutions.[36]

Yet, in revolutionary America, the entirely new and unprecedented constitution-making that began in 1776 was everywhere accepted as the legitimate means of consolidating the revolution. 'By 1776 the idea of a constitution … had almost achieved the status of self-evident truth. That these new constitutions were formulated in writing evoked neither resistance nor amazement at such a novelty.'[37] Arendt appreciates this astonishing constitution-making, but she seems to presume that because the people had a revolutionary (but not yet a legal) right to do so, they had the ability to do so. She does not satisfactorily account, in these terms, for either the success of American constitutions in consolidating the revolution or the failure of the French revolutionary constitutions to do so. The French accepted, as did the Americans, such notions as popular sovereignty, natural law and the social compact, but these failed to give legitimacy to the revolutionary governments in France, constitutional or not, none of which overcame the need for both the rhetoric and the acts of violence.

The unique success of the American Revolution and especially the absence of systemic violence (which so impressed Arendt) 'cannot be fully explained by the theoretical insights' of the founders, who were 'preoccupied by the absence of an absolute authority capable of legitimizing the legal foundations of the new republic'.[38] This is where Arendt relies on her concept of foundation, the establishment of a body politic comprising communities of free people. 'It is this initial step which throughout Hannah Arendt's thinking is so preeminent that political authority can, to her, be flatly traced back to past religious sanction and legitimation, back to the political act of founding and to its enduing presence.'[39]

[35] Bowring (n 32) 77. For Arendt on the Mayflower Compact, see Arendt (n 3) 165–73.

[36] See generally Gordon Wood, *The Creation of the American Republic* (Norton, 1972) 273–74, 282–91. The Mayflower Compact appears to have had little influence on American revolutionary-era writers.

[37] Willi Paul Adams, *The First American Constitutions* (University of North Carolina Press, 1980) 22. At the call of the Continental Congress, all 13 of the new states considered, in legislatures or conventions, the adoption of written constitutions. Eight states adopted constitutions in 1776, two in 1777 and one (Massachusetts) in 1780. Two states, Connecticut and Rhode Island, decided to retain their royal charters with some changes, though not without debate. See ibid 66–68.

[38] Bowring (n 32) 75.

[39] Sternberger (n 19) 139. See Arendt (n 3) 24.

The problem is that Arendt's concepts, at least as applied to the American Revolution, seem, to use James Miller's term, almost 'magical'.[40] True to her theory of action and foundation, but not true to the history of the American Revolution (Arendt's treatment of which Miller somewhat harshly calls 'shoddy'),[41] Arendt marvels at how the American founders came together to found an enduring, stable and legitimate republic; that is, they uniquely consolidated a revolution. She assertively if vaguely attributes the broad acceptance of the new constitutions by the people to the 'organizational impulses of the people themselves'.[42] Here she seems to rely on her concept of spontaneous councils that she believed arise during revolutions. However, she pays little attention to any purported role they may have played in the American Revolution, where much of the activity occurred in duly elected and organised legislatures and conventions on the one hand, and in already-established and constituted town meetings on the other, and not in any spontaneously appearing councils.

The closest the Americans came to any such revolutionary councils were the committees of correspondence that the colonies established in 1773, originally proposed by John Adams for Massachusetts but adopted everywhere. The committees were the colonies' first form of governance that functioned independently of royal authority. The last royal governor of Massachusetts, Thomas Hutchinson, later lamented that independence began with the creation of these committees, calling them 'a most glaring attempt to alter the constitution of the colonies … It was an act which ought to have been considered as an avowal of independency'.[43] It is surprising, then, that Arendt nowhere mentions the committees of correspondence.

Arendt inadequately addresses the difficult question of the consolidation of the revolution in America and does not account for the legitimation that consolidation inevitably required in that, or in any, revolution. We must look at this question of legitimation. Yet, the concept of legitimacy has not been addressed with much success, being neither clearly defined nor related convincingly to political activity, nor much studied empirically. Some 40 years ago, two students of the subject said that 'the nature and underpinnings of legitimacy are among the most neglected aspects of the dynamics of society',[44] and this has changed little since. Whatever the nature of legitimacy, it includes centrally the related elements of consent and perception. An act by those in power must be seen as having arisen from already-established and consented-to communal norms.[45]

[40] Miller (n 16) 183, 181.

[41] ibid 181.

[42] Arendt (n 3) 280.

[43] Thomas Hutchinson, *The History of the Province of Massachusetts Bay from the Year 1750 until June 1774* (first published 1828), quoted in Adams (n 37) 38.

[44] Craig A McEwen and Richard J Maiman, 'In Search of Legitimacy: Toward an Empirical Analysis' (1980) 8 *Law and Policy* 257. But see Mlada Burkovansky, *Legitimacy and Power: The American and French Revolutions in International Political Culture* (Princeton University Press, 2002) 2, 70 (on legitimacy as 'a necessary component of authority and thus of power').

[45] R. Francesconi, 'The Implications of Habermas' Theory of Legitimation for Rhetorical Criticism' (1986) 53 *Communication Monographs* 20; A Hyde, 'The Concept of Legitimation in the Sociology of Law' [1983] *Wisconsin Law Review* 379.

It was the early constitution-making of 1776 to 1780, all observers including Arendt agree, that effectively consolidated the revolution and provided its legitimacy and stability. But what was it about what Arendt calls 'this spontaneous outbreak of constitution-making in all thirteen colonies … so that there existed no gap, no hiatus, hardly a breathing spell between the war of liberation … and the constitution of the new states'[46] that made these early written state constitutions so immediately and broadly perceived as legitimate? While the unprecedented constitution-writing was spontaneous, the documents were framed on the authority of the Continental Congress by formally elected representatives who, with the rejection of the monarchy, saw themselves as sovereign. Popular sovereignty was a necessary but by no means sufficient element of legitimacy, partly, as Gordon Wood and others have shown, because there was widespread disagreement in the revolutionary era as to what this meant in practice, ranging from mob rule to duly elected legislatures and conventions.[47]

For Arendt, 'the legitimacy of rule in general, and the authority of secular law and power in particular had [before the modern era] always been justified by relating them to an absolute source not of this world'. She acknowledges that 'since it was the task of the revolutionaries to establish a new authority, unaided by custom and precedent and the halo of immemorial time, they could not but throw into relief with unparalleled sharpness the old problem … of the source of law which would bestow legality upon positive, posited laws, and the origin of power which would bestow legitimacy upon the powers that be'.[48] But if the 'chief perplexity' of the revolutionaries 'was where to find an absolute from which to derive authority for law and power',[49] Arendt does not succeed, as I have tried to show, in demonstrating what 'absolute' the Americans found that would successfully consolidate their revolution through written constitutions.

While Arendt does not directly offer sufficient explanation, I believe that elsewhere in her thought, she does provide the basis for elucidating the successful consolidation of the American Revolution.

III. Legitimacy and Fabrication

In 1776, the American revolutionaries were amazed by the opportunity independence offered to engage in what Gordon Wood describes as the provocative challenge that was somehow providentially directed at them.[50] They were everywhere 'thrilled at the prospect of forming their own government … Few doubted the extraordinary, almost millennial, character of it all'.[51] Their astonishingly firm

[46] Arendt (n 3) 139–40. Actually, Connecticut and Rhode Island retained their royal charters.
[47] Wood (n 36) 329–30, 362–63, 371–72.
[48] Arendt (n 3) 159.
[49] ibid 160.
[50] Wood (n 36) 127.
[51] Marc W Kruman, *Between Authority and Liberty* (University of North Carolina Press, 1997) 17, 18.

confidence that they could, for the first time, legitimately frame new governments *de novo* – and thereby consolidate the revolution – through written constitutions is itself remarkable. Some observers remarked that the Continental Congress had trouble completing business because so many members went home to participate in framing new state governments. '*Constitutions* employ every pen', wrote Francis Lightfoot Lee in November 1776.[52] That this was the best way, if not the only way, to consolidate the revolution was with equal confidence taken virtually for granted.[53] As soon as the possibility of independence began to be debated, writers seemed to accept with little or no contradiction that Americans could 'erect more eligible systems of government on the ruins of the colonies' monarchial constitutions'.[54] William Gordon of Massachusetts, using the language of fabrication employed everywhere, declared: 'Let Americans mold their governments.'[55] John Adams exulted at 'how few of the human race have ever enjoyed an opportunity of making an election of government, more than of air, soil, or climate for themselves or their children!'[56] James Burgh noted that all previous forms of government were the results of chance or force, but Americans were 'the first people whom heaven has favoured with an opportunity of … choosing the form of government under which they shall live'.[57]

It is these very frequent references to framing, forming, moulding, erecting and such that bring us back to Hannah Arendt. The earlier colonial charters and compacts were not perceived as 'framing' completely new structures of government on, so to speak, their own volition and self-referenced authority. While Arendt is much taken with the Mayflower Compact, her view of it as an instance where 'a group of people could create a valid government for themselves by means of a covenant, compact, or constitution'[58] is not accurate. It sets aside a distinct, in fact unique, characteristic of the revolutionary era's constitution-making: the revolutionaries in America saw themselves as actually, quite literally, fabricating new governments. Their self-awareness in engaging in such a constitutional founding moment was itself unprecedented. In the Mayflower Compact, the group aboard ship vows to 'combine our selues togeather into a ciuill body politick'.[59] But while the Compact states the intention to frame a government, it does not itself do so, and at any rate acknowledges that any such framing derives from the authority of God and the king.

[52] Quoted in Wood (n 36) 128.

[53] ibid 129.

[54] Wood (n 36) 129.

[55] William Gordon, *The Republican* (30 January 1776), quoted in Wood (n 36) 128.

[56] John Adams, *Thoughts on Government* (1775), in *The Revolutionary Writings of John Adams* (Liberty Fund, 2000).

[57] James Burgh, *Political Disquisitions*, quoted in Wood (n 36) 127. On the widespread excitement of the American Revolutionaries, see Kruman (n 51) 17–19; and Wood (n 36) 127–32.

[58] Arendt (n 3) 309.

[59] Mayflower Compact (1620); see the Mayflower webpage, mayflowerhistory.com/mayflower-compact.

Similarly, the colonial charters provided for structures of government, but they invariably and quite emphatically asserted royal authority for doing so. It was the king who did the framing 'by our royal will and pleasure', the charter simply documenting and certifying it, and specifically delegating authority to the colonial leaders to carry it out.[60] Rhode Island's Royal Charter of 1663 is entirely typical in this respect, declaring that King Charles II, who 'by our will and pleasure … and our especial grace, certain knowledge, and mere motion … have ordained, constituted and declared' that the petitioners 'shall be … a body corporate and politic'.[61] The charter creates the offices of governor and others, a judicial system and a legislative body, each with duties specified, but these are created by 'mere motion', by the grace and sheer will of the sovereign.[62] It is a rhetoric of will, not of fabrication.

The early American constitutions in contrast did not designate the frame of government as handed down from a higher authority. How was it that this notion of framing governments simply by the language of a written document was so widely and enthusiastically accepted as an objectively legitimate means of consolidating the revolution? It was in part owing to writing and printing. By the eighteenth century, printing was widely perceived as affirming a document's credibility, to some extent because the text could be relied upon as stable and enduring, and because of the relative ease and cheapness of promulgation.[63] This helped to confirm the central and overriding purpose of constitutions: 'written documents as barriers to encroaching power'.[64] James Cannon of Pennsylvania anxiously asserted that in order to prevent constitutional rights from being 'lost forever', they must be 'written down in immutable documents'.[65] This was a flashpoint in the debates between federalists and anti-federalists over whether the rights and principles of constitutions 'actually have to be specified and written down in order to be in force', reflecting, Gordon Wood notes, 'a basic ambiguity in the American mind about the nature of law that was carried into the Revolution'.[66] But constitutions in their capacity as frames of government were everywhere understood as necessarily written, since they were meant to withstand anticipated challenges to the people's liberties, when the documents would be invoked during inevitable disputes over interpretation and application.

[60] The quote is from Rhode Island's Royal Charter of 1663, in *State of Rhode Island Constitution and Royal Charter* (1986) 30.

[61] ibid 31–32.

[62] The colonial charters are collected in Yale Law School's Avalon Project. See the Avalon website: avalon.law.yale.edu.

[63] See Ian Williams, '"He Credited More the Printed Bookes": Common Lawyers' Receptivity to Print, c. 1550–1640' (2010) 25 *Law and History Review* 39.

[64] Wood (n 36) 268. Closely correlated with this was the unprecedented development of a 'reading public that produced and consumed the numerous pamphlets, newsletter, and books' flooding Europe and America in the eighteenth century. See Carolina Armenteros, 'Epilogue: The Forced Inhabitant of History' in Carolina Armenteros and Richard Lebrun (eds), *The New* Enfant de Siècle: *Joseph de Maistre as a Writer* (University of St Andrews, 2010) 99.

[65] Wood (n 36) 293.

[66] ibid 292–93.

That the early American constitutions were written and printed does not, of course, itself account for the extraordinary confidence the revolutionary era had in the legitimacy of, as it were, constructing governments on paper. That it was extraordinary, that there was nothing inherently automatic about written constitutions as effective consolidators of revolutions, is evidenced by the revolution in France and that country's repeated (and mostly failed) creation of constitutions – some 14 in the 85 years after 1789.

The question remains: why were the early written constitutions so widely and enthusiastically accepted as the legitimate instruments to consolidate the American Revolution? While Hannah Arendt largely failed, as we have seen, to account for the consolidation phase of the American Revolution, I believe she does offer an explanation elsewhere in her work on the human condition, but not addressed in *On Revolution* or her other discussions of revolution. We may find it in Arendt's concept of fabrication and its unique role in the public life of a secular polity.[67] She argues that the powerful, unprecedented forces of secularisation degraded the public realm to the point where we live in a condition of 'worldlessness'. We no longer have or believe in an enduring *polis* that is a place for action and for the talking about and remembering actions.[68] We no longer accept that there are great words and deeds that stand out as singular events and disrupt the endless, futile cycles of daily life, words and deeds that make a world. In this worldless view of modern, mass society, all events are seen as merely parts of processes. 'The modern concept of process … separates the modern age from the past more profoundly than any other single idea. To our modern way of thinking nothing is meaningful in and by itself.'[69]

Because in the modern era nature is the standard by which humans observe themselves, the study of nature – natural science – has become the foundation for all thought. It renders intellectual legitimacy to other systems of thought, and systems that do not pay allegiance to it are on the defensive and at risk of being marginalised. The power of modern science lies in its rejection of anything human. The trouble is, for Arendt, that without a public realm, humans can have no conception of an external reality: 'The reality of the world is guaranteed by the presence of others.'[70] The weird consequence of this is that modern science accounts not for the external world, general opinion notwithstanding, but for a private one whose existence no one can be sure of. Such apparent discoveries as the motion of the earth, the law of inertia, the structure of the atom or the behaviour of matter at velocities approaching the speed of light, the great advances of modern science – none of which can be revealed directly to the senses – all presume a loss of faith in the truth-revealing capacity of the senses. Descartes'

[67] See generally Arendt (n 2) pt V.

[68] Discussion of Arendt's thought on fabrication is based on Arendt (n 2) pts IV and VI; and Arendt (n 4) ch 2. Parts of my discussion are adapted from Mel A Topf, 'Hannah Arendt: Literature and the Public Realm' (1978) 48 *College English* 353, 359–62.

[69] Arendt (n 4) 63.

[70] Arendt (n 2) 178.

doubt-based philosophy so wholly relied on Galileo's work, especially regarding the heliocentric structure of the universe, that he feared that he would have to retract his system of thought if Galileo acknowledged (before the Inquisition) that he was wrong. If 'the movement of the earth is false, all the foundations of my philosophy are also false'.[71]

Sensible reality itself is, Arendt argues, dissolved into the incoherent data of sense perception, so that humans are 'ultimately imprisoned in a non-world of meaningless sensations that no reality and no truth can penetrate'.[72] This worldlessness of the subjective, the darkness of the private, 'the playing of the mind with itself',[73] is for Arendt the primary datum of the modern era. 'Man, whenever he tries to learn about things which neither are himself nor owe their existence to him, will ultimately encounter nothing but himself, his own constructions, and the patterns of his own actions.'[74] Science itself appears to yield certainty where other knowledge seems so contingent only because 'the sheer cognitive concern of consciousness with its own content … must yield certainty, because here nothing is involved except what the mind has produced itself'.[75]

An important consequence is that our own minds can construct whatever world we wish and accept it as reality. 'We can take almost any hypothesis and *act* upon it, with a sequence of results in reality which not only make sense but *work*. This means quite literally that everything is possible not only in the realm of ideas but in the field of reality itself.'[76] Thomas Hobbes (who like Descartes acknowledged his dependence on Galileo and Kepler) knew that understanding *is* knowing how something is made: 'Where is no generation … there no philosophy is perceived.'[77] For Hobbes, Ernst Cassirer writes, we 'understand only what we can cause to develop under our observation … If one wants to "know" something, he must constitute it himself'.[78] Locke's designation of knowing as an action, which he said was an original contribution to philosophy,[79] was grounded in the new conception of understanding as a positive process of 'joining together'.[80]

[71] Descartes' letter to Mersenne, November 1633, quoted in Arendt (n 2) 273. Galileo's trial before the Inquisition, at which he testified to recanting the heliocentric theory, took place in June 1633.

[72] Arendt (n 4) 56.

[73] Arendt (n 2) 258.

[74] Arendt (n 4) 86.

[75] Arendt (n 2) 255.

[76] Arendt (n 4) 87.

[77] Thomas Hobbes, *De Corpore* (1655), quoted in Ernest Cassirer, *Philosophy of the Enlightenment* (Beacon Press, 1955) 254. Hobbes, like Descartes, saw the significance of the new science's rejection of sensible reality. Very early on in his *Leviathan*, setting out the foundations of his political philosophy, he cites Newton's law of inertia, noting that its assertion that 'when a thing is in motion, it will eternally be in motion, unless somewhat els stay it' is something that 'is not so easily assented to'. Thomas Hobbes, *Leviathan* (Dent, 1914 [1651]) 4.

[78] Cassirer (n 77) 254.

[79] In the second letter to Stillingfleet, quoted in AC Fraser's introduction to John Locke, *Essay Concerning Human Understanding* (Dover Publications, 1959 [1690]) liv ('If I have done anything new [in the *Essay*], it has been to describe to others, more particularly than has been done before, what it is their minds do when they perform the action that they call knowing').

[80] Locke (n 79) II, xii, 2.

For Arendt, then, in a world where the decline of the *polis* raises barriers to true action, we are left with fabrication, so that we 'substitute making for action in order to bestow on the realm of human affairs the solidity inherent in work and fabrication'.[81] There is, Arendt notes, a line of thought extending back to Plato expressing uneasiness about the unpredictable and fragile nature of action as the central value of the political realm, so that the Western understanding of political communities has always been menaced by the suspicion of action and by an accompanying desire to substitute fabrication for action.[82] Arendt argues that fabrication rose to become a predominant value in the modern era, evidenced by the crisis of secularisation and the scientific revolution it engendered. Arendt saw that the consequence, that 'everything is possible', engendered the disasters of the twentieth century. These included the totalitarian regimes, the embodiment of the 'abyss of the possible', with the regimes' total domination and limitless capacity for mass crimes, feasible in good part owing to normal people who simply do not believe the monstrosities of totalitarian systems, since they 'don't know that everything is possible'.[83]

However, Arendt does not take into account the prominent place of this new ethos of making in the Enlightenment's striking self-assurance that it could, through sheer "rational reliance on the efficacy of energetic action', remake their world and diminish its many evils through the application of scientific method and its discoveries. This was 'a genuine and far-reaching novelty in human affairs'. Now, 'for the first time in history, confidence was the companion of realism rather than a symptom of the Utopian imagination'.[84] The widely perceived, rarely opposed, legitimacy of the early American constitutions meshed with the equally widespread belief that new governments can be made from scratch, so to speak, without posing any challenge to the legitimacy of these governments. The language of fabrication functioned as a legitimating rhetoric because fabrication was the primary frame, the cognitive model by which founding a new body politic was understood as both possible and legitimate. To paraphrase Hobbes, where there is no generation, there no legitimacy is perceived. For the people of revolutionary America, a written constitution meant 'the active making of a new order, as opposed to its gradual emergence in the course of a continual historical development'. This pointed directly to 'the theoretical foundations of modernity which presume that the structure and values of the political order are neither innate nor revealed by God, but rationally fabricated by men'.[85] To the extent that

[81] Arendt (n 2) 225.

[82] ibid 225–26. See Bowring (n 32) 35–36; and Hill (n 16) 170 (on Arendt's view of Plato as the 'first philosopher … to introduce the categories of fabrication and making into the political realm').

[83] Hannah Arendt, *Origins of Totalitarianism* (Harcourt Brace, 1951) 413, quoting David Rousset, *The Other Kingdom* (1947).

[84] Peter Gay, *The Enlightenment: An Interpretation. Volume II: The Science of Freedom* (Knopf, 1969) 3–4.

[85] Ulrich K Preuss, 'Constitutional Powermaking for the New Polity: Some Deliberation on the Relations between Constituent Power and the Constitution' (1993) 14 *Cardozo Law Review* 639. Preuss comments that 'the relationship between revolution and constitution is extremely ambivalent' (at 640).

violence, through the Revolutionary War, played a role, this is consistent with the nature of fabrication, which begins with acts of violence – cutting down a tree, say, to make a chair – though the violence is a means to that end, a means to consolidate order. For Arendt, the revolution in America was the exception, not showing 'the same combination of the old Roman enthusiasm for the foundation of a new body politic with the glorification of violence as the only means of "making" it'.[86]

The American Revolution's relative absence of violence and the contribution of that absence to the Revolution's consolidation, which so impressed Arendt, have been accounted for by historians pointing to what they believe was the evolutionary nature of events in America. John Phillip Reid, for example, writes that America's constitutional arguments against Britain were consistently based on principles already established and 'familiar' because American constitutional claims were all derived from former and current British constitutions, or the British imperial constitution.[87] Others have similarly seen the early revolutionary constitutions as actually a re-forming, out of already-constituted town governments in already-constituted colonies.[88]

But this sudden 'obsession with constitution making at the inception of the American Revolution'[89] cannot be adequately explained by seeking continuities with the past. Such continuities fail to account for the consolidation of the revolution, that is, for the role of the early constitutions in affirming the newly framed governments' legitimacy and, owing to their legitimacy, their stability. It was the acts of fabricating that were crucial in this respect. Although Arendt does not make the explicit connection, for her, as Jeremy Waldron puts it, 'that politics need *housing*, and that building such housing can be equated with the framing of a *constitution* – this is an image that recurs throughout Arendt's writings'. Whatever images she uses – furniture, fences and boundary walls, bricks and mortar – 'always the emphasis is on artificial structures … which exist as features of a world that men have made for themselves'.[90]

Arendt is not consistent in terms of whether she sees constitution-making as fabricating or as acting.[91] But fabricating is more central to her political thought than observers often note, with their greater interest in her concept of action itself, of her (literally) dramatic 'agonistic conception of politics – politics as a stage for action and distinction', as well as in her yearning for the ancient *polis*.[92] This is owing largely to her neglect, already discussed here, in failing to explain just how the early constitution-making succeeded in consolidating the

[86] Bowring (n 32) 37. On violence as an element of fabrication, see Arendt (n 2) 139–40.

[87] John Phillip Reid, *Constitutional History of the American Revolution: The Authority to Tax* (University of Wisconsin Press, 1987) 17.

[88] eg, Robert Nisbet, 'Hannah Arendt and the American Revolution' (1977) 44 *Social Research* 69.

[89] Kruman (n 51) 168.

[90] Waldron (n 17) 203.

[91] ibid.

[92] ibid.

American Revolution, in framing stable governments with enduring institutions whose legitimacy was not subject to challenge, while many later revolutions – for Arendt all of them – were complete, often disastrous, failures in just this consolidation. One element of the early constitutions to which she pays little attention is that the frames of government in these constitutions all comprised specifically and carefully defined institutions. Habermas makes the connection: 'Owing to its innovative potential, the domain of praxis is highly unstable and in need of protection. In societies organized around a state, this is looked after by political institutions.'[93] Yet, Arendt acknowledges that rights could be protected only by such institutions and also acknowledges that these institutions were designed so that their powers could be checked and balanced, chiefly through the separation of powers.[94]

Institutions are the crucial element in the consolidation of a revolution, and they, not assertions of rights, are what are unprecedented in early American constitution-making. The futility of declaring rights in 'theatrical proclamations' (Waldron's phrase) was the basis of Arendt's criticism of the inefficacy of the French Declaration of the Rights of Man and the Citizen and later such proclamations. But 'the moment human beings … had to fall back on their minimum right, no authority was left to protect them and no institution was willing to guarantee them'.[95] Rights 'need to be built into the civic structures'.[96] Rights themselves were widely understood, and argued, as having always existed, whether or not enumerated in a constitution. Constitutions emphatically were not seen as in and by themselves creating rights *ex nihilo*. Revolutionary-era Americans understood their constitutions framing institutions that protected these rights and, perhaps more important for Arendt, creating an enduring civic realm without which rights would be meaningless abstractions. Indeed, the early constitutions were what Preuss calls institutionalist: 'Institutionalist constitutions … institutionalize the capacity of the people to form and enforce their will in post-revolutionary times.'[97] Once again, Arendt remains above dealing with the nuts and bolts of constitutionally established institutions and their role in revolutionary consolidation, her world of abstractions, as one critic put it, 'largely uncontaminated by mundane things'. Nonetheless, she is engaged, if indirectly, 'with quite familiar issues about institutions, and … how important structure is, even in her most abstract characterizations of human freedom'.[98]

The constitution-making and its institution-building, the acts of foundation that so interested Arendt, could not have contributed so centrally to consolidating

[93] Habermas (n 26) 8.

[94] Arendt (n 3) 149–50, 303–09.

[95] Arendt (n 83) 288; see also at 287–98 (on the relation of rightlessness to the loss of a polity 'willing and able to guarantee' any rights (at 294)).

[96] Waldron (n 17) 207.

[97] Preuss (n 85) 643.

[98] Waldron (n 17) 214.

the American Revolution unless they were perceived as legitimate. Their legitimacy rose from the perception of them as fabricated and so not handed down by some external, higher and transmundane authority, whether divine or royal or tradition. It was in this sense that the revolutionaries so often thought of themselves as being in a state of nature. The people of Massachusetts, for example, during the development of their first constitution, 'imagined themselves creating government for the first time, as if revolution had cast them back into a state of nature wherein they would reestablish government'.[99] Arendt does not explain this in terms of her concept of fabrication since she falls back on 'the venerable figure of the contract' and the contract theory of natural law.[100] Jurgen Habermas, in criticising her for this approach, argues that Arendt is deficient in failing to test her concepts of speech and action (what he insightfully calls her 'anthropology of communicative action').[101] This is, perhaps, because she is not quite willing to proffer a relation between action and fabrication, which, on the one hand, she sees as fundamentally exclusive principles of the human condition and, on the other, argues that making can substitute for action 'in order to bestow upon the realm of human affairs the solidity inherent in work and fabrication'.[102] Mainly, though, Arendt sticks to the sharp distinction between action and fabrication, probably in order to avoid diluting her dramatic, agonistic and character-revealing notion of action by having to acknowledge that action can be a mere means to an end, leading to 'something', and so be conducive to fabrication.

My argument here is that the American revolutionaries, in the face of a potential crisis of legitimacy inherent in any attempt to consolidate a revolution, adopted an unprecedented mode of action that was indeed an act of fabrication. By this act, they could legitimately found a constitutional order, a body politic whose institutions would in turn be perceived, acknowledged and accepted as legitimate, and thereby stable and enduring, and so comprise a consolidation of their revolution. More specifically, the outcomes of the legislatures and conventions that developed the early constitutions were speech acts, and what those speech acts fabricated were constitutional orders. 'What is crucial in their [the founders'] act of founding is linguistic. In J.L. Austin's terms, they used language that might appear denotative … but is actually performative.'[103] What allowed the founders' 'performative language' to succeed? 'How can we explain its being taken up by the populace as constituting an adequate foundation for a new body politic?'[104] Arendt explains only that the American revolutionaries, in what she believed is the only successful attempt at doing so, 'founded a completely new body politic without violence

[99] Kruman (n 51) 31.
[100] Habermas (n 26) 24. On this often-cited social contract view of the early constitutions, see, eg, Kruman (n51) ch 2; and Wood (n 36) 282–91.
[101] Habermas (n 26) 7.
[102] Arendt (n 2) 225.
[103] McGowan (n 34) 276.
[104] ibid.

and with the help of a constitution'.[105] She seems to view a constitution as somewhat marginal, a mere device, which provided 'help'. In fact, constitutions were, and remained, the core of the body politic and of the legitimacy of the American Revolution's consolidation. It is this that needs explanation.

The legitimacy of the constitution-making arose in great part out of the role that fabrication played in modern secular thinking. However, we need to look at how this legitimacy, which is always a function of appearances, was communicated, applying what Habermas calls Arendt's 'communicative praxis'. The problem is that a revolution, which by its nature is illegitimate, is burdened with communicating the legitimacy of any attempted consolidation. Surprisingly little attention has been given to the communication of legitimacy. Studies of legitimacy tend pretty consistently towards exposing social and economic forces that lie behind claims to legitimacy, especially to show that legal and political institutions 'adopt rules which serve the dominant interest groups in society'.[106] This view downgrades legitimacy to window-dressing to cover up the exercise of 'real' power.

Speech acts and fabrication, that is, a message and its context, affect each other dynamically and actually help create each other. The basic principle of linguistic pragmatics, that a sign has meaning only within context, is of course true. But equally true is that context – the world 'out there' – has meaning only in relation to the sign. This rejects the older positivist notion that words and sentences somehow contain meaning, what Gerald Graff calls 'the fallacy of semantic immanence'.[107] The constructivist view of the dynamics of language rightly asserts that 'to speak, to interact with others verbally, is thus to construct the world, to constitute it, not merely to mirror it in words'.

If communication were simply some objective event within an objective world of context, then communication could be observed against a static background of world/context. However, there exists no Newtonian fixed point in an absolute space of context from which a message may be observed and studied as it moves through contextual space. Moreover, the context, the space through which the message takes effect, is relative to the message. There is no communication without perception of the context, but there is no perceiving context without communication. Neither the message alone nor the context alone has reality; only the message-context continuum does. In other words, there exists no objective message or objective context, but there exists an objective relation between the two. This is communication. A message cannot exist outside its context. There is no outside for it to exist in.

This throws some light on the operation of Arendt's communicative praxis and its place in the consolidation of the American Revolution. That we have some

[105] Arendt (n 4) 140.

[106] William Nelson, 'William Nelson Replies to Robert Gordon' (1988) 6 *Law & History Review* 161. Nelson is critical of this view.

[107] Gerald Graff, '"Keep off the Grass", "Drop Dead", and Other Indeterminacies: A Response to Sanford Levinson' (1982) 60 *Texas Law Review* 406.

confidence that our utterances can be communicated is wholly owing to our common presence in a space of shared values and ends. It is the essence of space, as Merleau-Ponty said, to be already constituted,[108] and we communicate with others in terms of our and their place within the already-constituted spaces of institutions. In other words, the spaces in which we share our presence with others are pre-eminently institutional. Conversely, the institutional contexts are reified by speech. Communication supports the 'selective maintenance of relatively stable strictures of images and associations that stem from institutional structures and policies'.[109] 'Our capacity for communication depends on mutual acceptance of a complex of conventions whose visibility and continuity are guaranteed institutionally. Utterances become speech acts only when they are put forth in the presence of others.'[110] We communicate with others in terms of our and their places within the space of institutions.

Action, then, and specifically speech acts (for this is what the constitutional conventions put forth) did fabricate the legitimate institutions that consolidated the American Revolution. The self-assurance with which the Americans of the revolutionary era enthusiastically engaged in constitution-making was grounded in the modern ethos of making not only as a means of understanding reality, but as a means of acting to consciously make a new reality both legitimate and stable by virtue of speech acts – the constitution-making itself – and without the need for reference to divine or royal or traditional authority to secure legitimacy. It never happened before.

[108] WJ Fromm, *Merleau-Ponty Language and the Act of Speech* (Bucknell University Press, 1982) 217.
[109] George Gerbner, 'Communication and Social Environment' (1972) 227 *Scientific American* 159.
[110] J Searle, *Speech Acts* (Cambridge University Press, 1970) 237.

4

I am Not Your (Founding) Father

MIKOŁAJ BARCZENTEWICZ[1]

I. Introduction

In this chapter, my focus is on an aspect of original constitutional founding moments (events that bring about a new constitutional order): the question of who made the constitution as law. Or, in other words, who was the legally authoritative agent (or author) in the making of a constitution? This question, for better or worse, plays a significant role in legal arguments about the legal content of some codified constitutions. I take no position on how significant, if at all, founding moments should be in constitutional law. I only offer a jurisprudential account of who, among the potentially many participants of a founding moment, counts as the legal authority who made the constitution (the constitution-maker).

Lawyers across the globe routinely talk about what the 'founding fathers' or the 'framers' of their constitution (or a founding treaty) meant, expected, intended and so on. The point of this chapter is that some of the founding fathers talk is confused, because it refers to people who did not make the constitution. I dispel the confusion through analysis of what it means to be an agent behind making a constitution as law: what does it mean to be a constitution-maker?

It is not only originalists who are in a habit of invoking the founding fathers. Even anti-originalists do not shy away from supporting their legal positions by reference to what the founding fathers would have wanted. For some reason, the founding fathers feel at home in any legal argument. Perhaps this reason is to be found in the sound intuition that there ought to be a connection between laws and exercises of legitimate authority that bring those laws into being. The problem with the founding fathers talk is that it tends to be at odds with this intuition. In other words, the founding fathers, or the framers, are not the ones who made the

[1] This chapter is partly based on an unpublished manuscript 'Who Made the United States Constitution?', http://ssrn.com/abstract=2323497. My thanks for discussion and feedback to Richard Albert, James Allan, Nicholas Aroney, Nick Barber, Katherine Brabon, Jon Crowe, Richard Ekins, Patrick Emerton, Jeffrey Goldsworthy, Richard Kay, Phil Magness, Alexander Moran, Rob Mullins, Scot Peterson and Charlotte Steinorth.

constitution in question as law. If they were not the constitution-makers, then at least an additional argument is required before one should even think of invoking them in a legal argument concerning the interpretation of a law they did not make. Such additional argument is often missing. In short, lawyers are prone to unreflectively refer to the founding fathers in their legal arguments concerning the interpretation of codified constitutions. In some cases, such references may be unjustifiable, whilst in other cases there is a glaring need for justification – a gaping hole in the legal argument.

This chapter presents a general theory of authoritative agency in constitution-making, with a particular emphasis on group action. On my general account, to be the legally relevant constitution-maker, one has to either: (1) exercise pre-existing legal authority to make the constitution in question; or (2) have one's intentional act purporting authoritatively to make the constitution as law recognised as the reason for the acceptance of the constitution as law. Some, or even many, constitutions may fail to have makers in this sense.

To clarify, I am exclusively concerned here with *original* constitution-makers. I do not investigate the sources of *current* authority of any constitution, merely the sources of authority of historical constitutional changes. Also, for the sake of simplicity, I focus on an important subset of instances of constitutional change: on cases of constitution-*making*, not merely *alteration* of an already-existing constitution (admittedly, Canada is a borderline case). With the analytical toolkit in hand, I consider the cases of Australia, Canada and the US. I identify who was the constitution-maker there and I look at some possible ways of justifying legal uses of historical materials, which constitute legally *unauthoritative* sources. I am using 'unauthoritative' here in a technical sense of being unconnected to the legal authority behind the original making of a constitution (the constitution-maker).

This is not a work on *originalism*. I am not making claims on how any materials associated with the makers of a constitution are supposed to be legally relevant. Strictly speaking, I do not even need to assume that they are of legal relevance. This may very well be a controversial, unsettled issue in a particular constitutional order – with some participants of the legal practice denying them legal relevance and some endorsing it. Also, even those who do not accept that any materials connected with the constitution-makers *constrain* or *determine* the current content of the constitutional law (anti-originalists) are likely to accept some limited, persuasive role of such materials in constitutional interpretation.

My focus is on the structure of legal arguments that are affected by the issue of the identity of constitution-makers. I reflect on one way in which such arguments may be legally invalid: when they invoke people or groups who were not the makers of the constitution in question. It may be that such arguments are legally invalid for other reasons. In particular, they may be invalid because the legal system in question does not make *any* material associated with the constitution-makers relevant for the current legal practice *in any way* (or at least not, for example, as a conclusive factor in the interpretation of a constitutional provision). Also, I do not claim that my theory is *conclusive* as to the content of the positive law in any particular constitutional order. The content of the positive law at any given time is determined by the legal practice at that time.

II. What Does it Mean to be a Constitution-Maker?

Constitutions tend to be drafted, debated, voted on, enacted and so forth. Hence, there may be many people (and arguably groups of people) involved, who are doing the drafting, debating, voting or enacting. Often, once a constitution is made, some of the people involved in its making begin to be referred to as 'the founders', 'the founding fathers' or 'the framers' of the constitution. There are various contexts in which references of this kind are made. I am exclusively interested in one such context: legal reasoning (legal arguments) as to the legal content or legal effect of a codified constitution.

A. Some Clarifications

What counts as a valid legal argument in a given legal system at any given time is always grounded in the practice of that legal system at that time.[2] No philosophical, historical or sociological argument may override even the most outrageous fiction adopted as a matter of legal practice (unless, of course, the practice itself adopts a test of, for example, philosophical propriety).[3] True, legal theory (or jurisprudence) – just like the disciplines of history or sociology – will rarely, if ever, supply a *conclusive* legal argument. However, jurisprudence has a special relationship with particular legal practices. In some cases, jurisprudence provides a good starting point for a strictly legal inquiry into the content of the positive law.

This is so in the case of the legally relevant identity of those who made the particular constitution as law. There are good reasons to presume that this legally relevant maker is the person or the group of people jurisprudence says it is. Such presumption may be rebutted through evidence that the particular legal practice adopts a different understanding, but when such contrary evidence is lacking, a jurisprudential argument has a much better claim to guide legal reasoning than, for example, a historical one. For instance, quite plausibly it does not matter *legally* whether the best historical account of the making of the US Constitution is the one seeing it as a conspiracy of some propertied men.[4] It may be a fascinating and

[2] I adopt here a broadly Hartian jurisprudential framework; see HLA Hart, *The Concept of Law*, 3rd edn (Oxford University Press, 2012).

[3] Stephen E Sachs, 'Originalism as a Theory of Legal Change' (2015) 38 *Harvard Journal of Law and Public Policy* 817, 834.

[4] See, eg, Charles A Beard, 'An Economic Interpretation of the Constitution' in John F Manley and Kenneth M Dolbeare (eds), *The Case against the Constitution* (ME Sharpe, 1987) 49.

important account. Its (historical) truth may perhaps even be a reason to change the law. But the account itself provides no good reason to believe that the conspiracy in question was the legally relevant constitution-maker. On the other hand, the account presented here is of the kind that could plausibly be used in a legal argument about the content of positive law.

My account of identity of constitution-makers relies on the notion of legal, or at least legally recognised, authority to make a constitution as law. This is not necessarily the much-discussed *constituent power*. At least in principle, there is a distinction between the presumptive holder of the ultimate (moral, political) power to effect radical constitutional change (eg, the people) and a person or a group recognised as authority who made some particular constitution as law (eg, a monarch or some representative body). In any historical case, the former may also be the latter, but this is not a necessity. The introduction of the issue of constituent power into the discussion of legally relevant authorship of a constitution as law may obscure that distinction through the sheer immensity of the notion of sovereignty. In particular, the concept of popular sovereignty seems so enticing that some authors are unwilling to look past it and end up committing themselves to very implausible views about agency in constitution-making.[5] Of course, to an extent, this stems from conflating the issue of identifying the historical maker and the issue of identifying the contemporary source of authority of a constitution. As Joseph Raz has shown, it is very likely that in cases of long-lasting constitutions, the answers to the two questions will differ significantly.[6] Here, I am not interested in the latter problem, merely with the search for the historical maker.

Richard Fallon in his helpful discussion of constitutional legitimacy distinguished between 'legal', 'sociological' and 'moral' legitimacy.[7] My argument does not, strictly speaking, concern legitimacy of any constitution. However, issues of legitimacy and of legal authority to make a constitution are closely connected. Fallon's typology helps to clarify the scope of my argument. Legal legitimacy means approximately the same as lawfulness, determined within a legal system (is the action legally permitted? is it a proper exercise of a legal power?).[8] Sociological legitimacy means that individual members of a society accept a constitution (and constitutional institutions).[9] Moral legitimacy means that a constitution is morally justifiable or worthy of respect.[10]

[5] For example, by seeing the people as the maker of a given constitution as law, where the people did not act together to make the constitution as law on the best interpretation of the historical evidence combined with *any* plausible account of group agency (eg, when the members of the alleged 'people' did not see themselves as belonging to one community, where most of them were indifferent to the process of constitution-making etc).

[6] Joseph Raz, 'On the Authority and Interpretation of Constitutions: Some Preliminaries' in *Between Authority and Interpretation: On the Theory of Law and Practical Reason* (Oxford University Press, 2009) 338–52.

[7] Richard Fallon, 'Legitimacy and the Constitution' (2005) 118 *Harvard Law Review* 1787.

[8] ibid 1794–95.

[9] ibid 1795–96.

[10] ibid 1796.

Just like Fallon,[11] I adopt the framework of Hartian legal positivism. This framework entails that for a constitution to exist as law, it means that it is both legally and sociologically legitimate (at least in the social group of legal officials). In fact, legal legitimacy is necessarily grounded in sociological legitimacy among legal officials. I provide more detail of that framework in the next subsection. What is important to note now is that moral legitimacy is not a part of that picture. A constitution has to be sociologically legitimate to exist, but whether it is morally legitimate is a contingent issue. A constitution may be brought into existence, and continue to exist, even if it is morally illegitimate (and when the constitution-makers had no moral mandate to make the constitution or when they were acting immorally in doing so). Hence, my account of agency in bringing about a constitution's existence as law has two legs: one connected to legal legitimacy and one connected to sociological legitimacy. I now turn to that account.

B. The Core Account

On my view, to be a maker of a constitution is to either:

(1) exercise pre-existing legal authority to make the constitution; or
(2) to have one's intentional act purporting authoritatively to make the constitution as law recognised as the reason for acceptance of the constitution as law.

I distinguish between situations where the constitution-maker is designated by the law as it is at the time of the making and where the maker is not so identified. The former may only be the case when the making of a constitution is lawful, that is, when it is either done in accordance with the rules of change – ie, through an exercise of a pre-existing legal power to change the law – or when it is merely validated by the rule of recognition as it is at the time.[12] The rule of recognition is a social rule, which is at the foundation of every legal system and provides the ultimate criteria of what counts as a law of that system (criteria of validity).[13] It could be that the rule of recognition identifies a source of law (and of a new constitution) on which the legal system in question does not already confer a legal power. In particular, the rule of recognition could so identify someone's actions not intended to make law. However, just because it is possible does not mean that it is likely. Practically speaking, we can assume that if making of a constitution is lawful, it is so because of an intentional exercise of a legal power to change the law. This provides us with an easy case of identity of the constitution-maker: it is the person or the body that has exercised its legal power.

The matters are more complicated in the second case: of those constitution-makers who are not designated by the law as it is at the time of the

[11] ibid 1805–06.
[12] On the notion of the rule of recognition, see Hart (n 2) ch 6. See also Mikolaj Barczentewicz, 'The Illuminati Problem and Rules of Recognition' (2018) 38 *OJLS* 500.
[13] ibid.

constitution-making. A person or a group of people may be a constitution-maker if it is for the reason of their (claimed) legal authority that the constitution is accepted as law. What comes into play here is recognition of legal authority to change the law – authority not grounded in the content of the law as it is at the time the authority is purportedly exercised.

An example from Joseph Raz provides a helpful illustration.[14] The Declaration of the Establishment of the State of Israel was proclaimed on 14 May 1948 by the members of the Jewish People's Council. The group of people who had issued the proclamation did not have a legal power to do so conferred on them by any previously existing legal system. And yet, they granted legislative power to themselves as the 'Provisional Council' of the new State of Israel.[15] Raz claims that the group that proclaimed the Declaration had a legal power to make it as law merely because it was later recognised as having such a legal power by the participants of the new Israeli legal system.[16] I do not want to go as far as to say that they in fact had a legal *power*, but I think that the Jewish People's Council was in this case the constitution-maker. This is so because the Declaration was accepted as law *for the reason* that it was made through a purportedly authoritative act of proclamation by the Council.

There are two sides to this coin: (1) one has to act intentionally purporting authoritatively to make a constitution as law; and (2) one's so acting has to be the reason why the constitution is accepted (one has to be a de facto authority). Regarding the first point, I do not claim that all exercises of legal powers are necessarily intentional or that it is impossible to comprehend an unintentional exercise of a legal power. However, exercising an authority to change the law (evenly a merely purported authority to be recognised *ex post*) requires direct intent. Without at least presuming such direct intent, one's actions are not intelligible as actions of an authority.

On the second point, for a constitution to be accepted as law means that it meets the criteria of validity from the rule of recognition.[17] A constitution may be a valid law because the rule of recognition identifies it directly ('eo nomine') or because the rule of recognition identifies the source of the constitution or the way it was made as a source of law.[18] A constitution-making authority figures in this picture as a reason to accept the rule of recognition (or a part of the rule of recognition) that makes it the case that the constitution is law.

HLA Hart famously banished such considerations from jurisprudence, but I think John Finnis is right that some questions about the reasons for acceptance

[14] Joseph Raz, 'Voluntary Obligations and Normative Powers' in Stanley L Paulson (ed), *Normativity and Norms: Critical Perspectives on Kelsenian Themes* (Oxford University Press, 1999) 84–85. For a more detailed background, see Yair Sagy, ch 6 in this volume.

[15] 'Declaration of Establishment of State of Israel 1948', www.mfa.gov.il/mfa/foreignpolicy/peace/guide/pages/declaration%20of%20establishment%20of%20state%20of%20israel.aspx.

[16] Raz (n 14) 84–85.

[17] See above, nn 12–13 and accompanying text.

[18] On the idea of the rule of recognition identifying elements of the law 'eo nomine', see HLA Hart, 'The Morality of the Law' (1965) 78 *Harvard Law Review* 1281, 1295.

of some legal rules as law are valid jurisprudential questions.[19] The issue of legal authority in constitution-making is a good example: it is jurisprudentially interesting that some rules of recognition are accepted for, allegedly, legal reasons. I am not saying that the rule of recognition has to change for a new constitution to become valid law. But it may be that even when the rule of recognition does not change, the reasons for its acceptance change and this is relevant for the issue of identity of the constitution-maker.

Whose acceptance counts? Strictly speaking, acceptance by legal officials is constitutive of legal systems and from a jurisprudential perspective, it does not matter what the position taken by anyone else is.[20] However, in relation to many historical cases of constitution-making, we do not have evidence fine-grained enough to allow us to reliably distinguish between the reasons for acceptance among the general public and those of the officials. Hence, in the applicative part of this chapter, I will not, for the most part, rely on this distinction.

In principle, it could be that on my account there is more than one constitution-maker. On one interpretation, this is what happened in Australia. The Australian Constitution was enacted by the Imperial Parliament, and this is what makes this body the constitution-maker according to my first criterion. However, it may be that the Australian people have accepted the Constitution for the reason that it was adopted in referendums in the colonies, which in turn may suggest, for example, that those who participated in the referendums also have a claim to being the original constitution-maker (on my second criterion). As I will show below, I am sceptical of this interpretation of the events, but it is consistent with my general account.[21]

C. Group Agency

What kinds of entities may be constitution-makers? The simple case of a natural person acting alone as an authority does not fit any of the historical examples discussed here, but it is not unheard of (eg, constitutions enacted by monarchs) and certainly fits my model. Somewhat more controversially, I adopt the view that groups may also satisfy the criteria presented above and thus be constitution-makers. There are two kinds of groups that I will invoke later in the chapter: *institutional* and *ephemeral*. The latter term comes from Christopher Kutz's minimalist account of group agency.[22] Kutz defines ephemeral groups as 'groups whose identity as a group consists just in the fact that a set of persons is acting jointly

[19] John Finnis, 'Revolutions and Continuity of Law' in *Philosophy of Law: Collected Essays Volume IV* (Oxford University Press, 2011) 425, 430–34.

[20] Hart (n 2) 117; Leslie Green, 'The Concept of Law Revisited' (1996) 94 *Michigan Law Review* 1687, 1700–02. See also Barczentewicz (n 12) 507–27.

[21] See below, section IV.B.

[22] Christopher Kutz, 'Acting Together' (2000) 61 *Philosophy and Phenomenological Research* 1, 28.

with overlapping participatory intentions'.[23] This means that an ephemeral group exists and acts only if all the members of the group have overlapping intentions to participate in some common project. Any 'group' of people that does not satisfy this requirement is a mere collection of individuals and has no capacity for group agency. Ephemeral groups may, in principle, be constitution-makers, but as I show below, in practice this is likely to be very rare. Institutional (complex) groups, on the other hand, have rules that specify what individual actions count as actions of the group and in what circumstances (eg, a constitutional convention).[24] If an institutional group is constituted by the law (eg, corporate bodies), then the law defines who counts as members of the group and which actions of those members constitute actions of the group.

One important feature of this account of group agency (both for ephemeral and institutional groups) is that it does not require all the members of a group to intend the achievement of the goal of the project to which they are contributing – it is enough that they 'only know that their actions are likely to contribute to its realization'.[25] Hence, even if a member of a legislative body votes against the enactment of a constitution and the member is outvoted, they still contribute to the group action of making the constitution.[26]

For a group to have the intention required to be a constitution-maker (that this group is acting with authority to make a constitution) means that such an intention is established in a proper way for this kind of group. In the case of an ephemeral group, there needs to be an overlap of individual participatory intentions. Hence, for example, if the people of a country (taken as an ephemeral group) are to act together to make a constitution as an authority, they all need to intend to contribute to that goal or at least a vast majority of them has to have such intentions (even if some of them do not intend that a particular project of a constitution is enacted). Evidence of low popular participation in a process of constitution-making would count heavily against a hypothesis that such an ephemeral group acted. In a sense, matters are simpler with institutional groups. As long as we know what the rules of the group are, then all that needs to be seen is whether the rules are followed.

D. Must there be a Constitution-Maker?

It may well be that some constitutions do not have makers in the sense presented here. To begin with, attributing intentions to groups is controversial and someone might object that if to be a constitution-maker is to act intentionally, then certainly no group could be a constitution-maker. It is not my purpose to defend

[23] ibid.
[24] Christian List and Philip Pettit, *Group Agency* (Oxford University Press, 2011) 76.
[25] Kutz (n 22) 27.
[26] Richard Ekins, *The Nature of Legislative Intent* (Oxford University Press, 2012) 233–34.

the notion of group agency; I will only note that, irrespective of the debates in philosophy of action, acceptance of group agency works well with ordinary legal talk. Among the familiar examples of law-makers, many, if not most, are groups. My argument does not rely on the metaphysical view that groups, strictly speaking, exist. All that is needed is that for legal purposes, we can speak as if they did.

Another argument against the existence of a constitution-maker behind any specific constitution is that the constitution in question was not made law through an exercise of authority. An important example of this is the view that the US Constitution came into being as law *only* through the continuing assent of those it was supposed to govern.[27] In other words, the US Constitution is law because it has been treated as such and not because some authority enacted it (it has been accepted only for content-dependent reasons). In a sense, no one made the Constitution because no one may be considered responsible for it being a part of the legal system. Surely, there were people or groups causally connected with the emergence of the Constitution, but their actions could not bring about the legal validity of the Constitution.

There are two versions of this argument. One I fully endorse. According to this version, there is a special way in which a legislature is responsible for a statute becoming a law (a change in law directly due to an exercise of a normative power to change law). This kind of responsibility for something becoming a law does not take place when a constitution is made by unlawful action. In other words, there can be no normative power to directly change the rule of recognition so that it features a new constitution (unlawfully made).

The other version of the argument also denies the somewhat weaker sense of authority in the process of constitution-making with which I am concerned here. This second approach is more plausible when applied to the problem of accounting for the current legal effect of a long-standing constitution. However, it fails when applied to the period immediately following the making of a constitution. This view does not explain why a particular constitution was accepted as law instead of any alternative or why it was accepted at all. If we ask about the reasons for acceptance, then this inquiry is likely to direct it back towards some constitution-making authority.

For example, plausibly, the American people have accepted the US Constitution because they recognised the authority of those who acted claiming to have authority to make the Constitution as law. Of course, an alternative view is conceivable on which the American people are and always have been philosophical anarchists choosing to accept the Constitution for purely content-dependent reasons. Even so, why would those philosophical anarchists consider acceptance or rejection of *the* Constitution as law if there had been nothing significant about the pronouncement of the document as law (by someone claiming to have authority to make such a pronouncement)?

[27] See, eg, Larry G Simon, 'The Authority of the Framers of the Constitution: Can Originalist Interpretation Be Justified?' (1985) 73 *California Law Review* 1482, 1486.

As Joseph Raz suggests, the special role of the makers of a constitution may be stronger when the constitution is new: the citizens and officials are then more likely to rely on the authority of the makers as a reason to recognise the constitution as binding.[28] This role tends to diminish over time. It could be that, in the early days, the constitution-making power of the authors of the US Constitution provided the document with authority, but with the passage of time, the situation has changed.[29]

It may also be the case that views on who were 'the founders' of the constitutional order in question, and what their significance was, evolve over time. Simon Gilhooley in his chapter in this volume argues this took place in the US Constitution's first decades.[30] I want to stress that such later views are not directly relevant to the identification of an original constitution-maker. However, they may feed into the special significance the law gives to some historical figures, as I will discuss below in section III.C.

One last clarification is in order. I do not wish to suggest that those who initially accept any constitution as law do so *only* for content-independent reasons.[31] Most likely, a mix of content-dependent and content-independent considerations figures in their practical reasoning. Quite plausibly, the US Constitution would not have been accepted if its content had been much less agreeable, even if the same agent had been responsible for making it as something to be accepted (for example, if the ratifying conventions were to ratify a constitution establishing a monarchy). My purpose is to look into the content-independent part of that mix, but this is not to deny the importance of the other part.

III. Proper Legal Uses of the Sources *Unconnected* to Constitution-Makers

Historical materials directly connected to the makers of a constitution as law may appropriately be considered as, prima facie, *authoritative* sources for the purposes of legal reasoning, and for interpretative arguments in particular. Of course, this is so only if the law does not positively deny those materials authoritative status. Also, the law may designate some other historical materials as authoritative. The force of my argument is to provide a starting point for legal reasoning when the law is not otherwise settled. In this section, I look at legal justifications of legal uses of historical materials not created by, or otherwise not testifying to, the actions or thoughts of a constitution-maker.

[28] Raz (n 6) 338–52.
[29] See Simon (n 27) 1491–92.
[30] Simon Gilhooley, ch 5 in this volume.
[31] My thanks to Richard Kay for bringing this point to my attention.

As I do not advance any complete theory of constitutional interpretation, I do not consider systematically the problems with using sources *connected* with constitution-makers. I am also not claiming that it is always prima facie legally proper to rely in legal argumentation on the historical sources connected to constitution-makers. My ambition is much more limited. I only argue that if someone is to use such sources and, explicitly or implicitly, justify that by the legally authoritative role of the associated persons or groups, then it matters whether those persons or groups actually did play such a role. What follows is a discussion of ways to make such references work, even when the persons or groups invoked are not the constitution-maker.

A. Adoption by the Constitution-Maker

Imagine a prince, Alex, who legally holds the exclusive law-making power, but does not himself bother with the hard part of legislating. He does not reflect on the law as it is, and on the reasons for its change, and does not form plans how to change the law. All this is being done by his council. The council submits draft bills to Alex and he invariably signs them into law. It is reasonable to suppose that the legislative intent of the prince is always 'what the council intended'. In other words, his choice is to *adopt* the legislative plan prepared by someone else. Notice that the prince does not form any views on the laws he creates – the legislative plan might just as well be a secret to him.

Now, consider another prince, Roger, who differs from the first prince in that he is very inquisitive as to every plan proposed by his council. He never changes the plan, but he takes pains to understand it fully. He would be very cross if the council had a secret understanding of the plan that was not available for Roger to know (at least potentially). In other words, Alex adopts someone else's plan, whereas Roger legislates his own plan, in which he adopts someone else's proposal to the extent it is epistemically available to him.[32]

The nature of the choice made by a constitution-maker could be like the choices made by Alex or by Roger (naturally, it also may be like neither). If so, this has consequences for the sort of historical material that may be legally relevant, because of the constitution-maker's choice. On the Alex model, even the secret history of drafting by someone who was not the constitution-maker may be made legally relevant by the choice of the constitution-maker. On the Roger model, only the evidence of the intentions or understandings, which were epistemically

[32] The latter option is akin to what in the American literature is sometimes referred to as the reliance-based contract argument: David McGowan, 'Ethos in Law and History: Alexander Hamilton, The Federalist, and the Supreme Court' (2001) 85 *Minnesota Law Review* 755, 756; Vasan Kesavan and Michael Stokes Paulsen, 'Interpretive Force of the Constitution's Secret Drafting History' (2003) 91 *Georgetown Law Journal* 1113, 1152.

available to the constitution-maker, may be legally relevant. Either way, it is the constitution-maker who makes the actions or thoughts of someone else legally relevant to the content of his plan to change the law. Evidence of such actions or thoughts is therefore also, prima facie, *authoritative.*[33]

There are good reasons to think that the particular constitution-maker did not make a choice described by any of the two models. Consider a judge who gives a judgment entirely prepared by his clerk. Uncontroversially, it does not matter if the clerk had some idiosyncratic understanding of the words he used (even if that understanding was epistemically available to the judge – he could have asked); what matters is what the judge intended to convey or at least what he managed to convey by using the words he used (though did not write). Turning back to the case at hand, a careful lawyer would need some positive evidence that the constitution-maker's choice did adopt someone else's plan, even partially. The mere fact that the constitution-maker did not introduce any textual changes (or no significant changes) to a proposal prepared by someone else is far from conclusive.

B. Evidence of Public Meaning

Historical materials associated with the people who were not constitution-makers may also be legally relevant as evidence of *public* meaning of a constitutional text. In this sense, even secret or private documents are potentially relevant – they may even have more probative value as they are likely not to be strategic in the sense that public political speeches are.[34] However, this justification should not be overstated.[35] Drafting a provision is different from speaking in a convention or writing a private letter – the latter are often delivered hastily, without caution.[36] More importantly, if we are looking for the public meaning (the conventional linguistic meaning of a text), then we can only give a very low weight to any particular source (some single other text in that language) – unless, of course, that source itself reports a reliable lexicographic study, but this is unlikely to be the case. It is hard to escape the impression that those who rely on this justification still tend to have a bias favouring the 'illicit' evidence of intentions of non-constitution-makers.[37]

[33] It is beyond the scope of my argument to say with more precision in what sense that evidence is legally relevant or authoritative, as that would require a more robust account of constitutional interpretation.

[34] Kesavan and Paulsen (n 32) 1158, 1164.

[35] John F Manning, 'The Role of the Philadelphia Convention in Constitutional Adjudication' (2012) 80 *George Washington Law Review* 1753, 1770–72, 1792–93.

[36] ibid 1770.

[37] For criticism of such an approach in the American context, see McGowan (n 32) 835; Manning (n 35) 1772 fn 85. See also Jamal Greene, 'On the Origins of Originalism' (2009) 88 *Texas Law Review* 1, 63–64.

C. Special Significance Given by Later Legal Practice

The first two justifications are in an important sense given by the historical event of the making of a constitution as law. However, the law may give legal significance to any sort of material and may do so even against all good reason. It could be that the law makes diaries of a particularly prominent drafter conclusive evidence as to the meaning of the constitutional text. This may be a good or a bad idea, but its goodness or badness only legally matters if the law says so. I will not say much more about this possibility. My aim here is to provide a starting point for thinking about authorities in constitution-making and the relevance of authority-derived materials for constitutional law. However, this starting point is only relevant if the law does not already provide a different answer, which may very well be. Importantly, one needs evidence that *the law* provides such a different answer, as opposed to taking it from some historical or ethical theory that fails to pay sufficient attention to the role of (legal) authority in the law.

IV. Founders, Framers, But Not Makers: Applying the Theory

It is now time to apply the general account to the cases of Australia, Canada and the US. In this section, I identify the most plausible candidates for the makers of these constitutions. I then look at the issue of justifying the legal use of historical materials, which are not connected with the maker of the constitution in question as law.

A. The US

The US Constitution was drafted in 1787 by a special convention (the Philadelphia Convention) of delegates of 12 American states (the thirteenth state, Rhode Island, refused to send delegates). Article VII of the Philadelphia proposal specified that a new US constitution was to be established, to become law, once ratified by state conventions in at least nine states. The ninth state to ratify, New Hampshire, did so in June 1788. The standard view among the sophisticated commentators is that the Constitution was made law by the ratifying conventions.[38] Those conventions,

[38] See, eg, Paul Brest, 'The Misconceived Quest for the Original Understanding' (1980) 60 *Boston University Law Review* 204, 225; Henry P Monaghan, 'Our Perfect Constitution' (1981) 56 *New York University Law Review* 353, 375 fn 130; Akhil Reed Amar, 'Our Forgotten Constitution: A Bicentennial Comment' (1987) 97 *Yale Law Journal* 281, 286–87; Charles A Lofgren, 'The Original Understanding of Original Intent?' (1988) 5 *Constitutional Commentary* 77, 79; McGowan (n 32) 831; Kesavan and Paulsen (n 32) 1137–38; Pauline Maier, *Ratification* (Simon & Schuster, 2010) ix. See also Gilhooley, ch 5 in this volume.

as institutional groups, jointly satisfy the second criterion of being a constitution-maker. They do not satisfy the first condition because, in making the Constitution, they did not exercise pre-existing legal authority.[39]

The conventions saw themselves as having authority to approve the Constitution and thus make it law. Even though some of the delegates to the conventions received purportedly binding instructions, in the end they acted, however reluctantly, as if they were not bound by anyone's will. They considered the proposed Constitution in detail, debated over its clauses, sometimes suggesting amendments, and only after all that, they voted to accept or reject the Constitution.[40] Given the requirement of being a de facto authority, the strongest and the simplest argument for concluding that the Constitution had been accepted for the reason of the authority of the ratifiers is that it was not before and not after their act (ie, ratification) that the Constitution had been accepted as law.[41] Had acceptance happened before ratification, then that would have perhaps meant that the drafters (the members of the Philadelphia Convention) were taken as authority (a view the drafters themselves rejected). Had it happened a long time after ratification, then the view that the content-dependent reasons were decisive in acceptance of the Constitution would have more credence.

This conclusion creates a problem for interpretative arguments relying on the constitution-making authority. As Kesavan and Paulsen note in their helpful discussion of the documentary sources on the ratification:

> It is not the understanding of one, two, or even three ratifying conventions that should constitute sufficient evidence of constitutional meaning, but the understanding of nine state ratifying conventions, or perhaps, all thirteen state ratifying conventions. But such evidence is, as we have seen, simply impossible to extract from the documentary record.[42]

The only plausible evidence of the group intent of the US constitution-maker is the public meaning of the constitutional text adopted. The most popular documentary sources on the constitution-making, *The Records of the Federal Convention* and *The Federalist*, cannot be relied on based on a Roger-type adoption argument (see section III.A above). Both documents were simply unavailable

[39] See, eg, Bruce Ackerman, 'The Storrs Lectures: Discovering the Constitution' (1984) 93 *Yale Law Journal* 1013, 1017; Richard S Kay, 'The Illegality of the Constitution' (1987) 4 *Constitutional Commentary* 57; Bruce A Ackerman and Neal Katyal, 'Our Unconventional Founding' (1995) 62 *University of Chicago Law Review* 475, 489, 506–14. But see Akhil Reed Amar, 'The Consent of the Governed: Constitutional Amendment outside Article V' (1994) 94 *Columbia Law Review* 457, 465; Calvin H Johnson, 'Homage to Clio: The Historical Continuity from the Articles of Confederation into the Constitution' (2003) 20 *Constitutional Commentary* 463.

[40] Eric Parnes, 'They the People: A Third-Party Beneficiary Approach to Constitutional Interpretation' (2003) 43 *Santa Clara Law Review* 495, 527–28.

[41] Gary Lawson and Guy Seidman, 'When Did the Constitution Become Law?' (2001) 77 *Notre Dame Law Review* 1, 1–2.

[42] Kesavan and Paulsen (n 32) 1162 (footnotes ommitted).

for a significant number of the members of the ratifying conventions.[43] As to an Alex-type adoption argument, we know enough about the ratifying conventions to exclude the possibility that their choice was to adopt whatever the Philadelphia Convention (or some its subset) meant, even secretly.[44]

Similarly, one needs to treat with suspicion invocations of materials like the writings of James Madison as evidence for the intent of the ratifiers or for the original public meaning. As to the intent, it is clear that many individual ratifiers were not aware of Madison's views and certainly almost no one was aware of his notes or private correspondence. There is a big justificatory jump from Madison being a 'key framer' to his writings constituting reliable evidence of the group intent of the ratifying conventions.[45] As to the public meaning, the generic objection against relying on a single (arguably biased) data point to establish public meaning suffices (see above, section III.B).

A potentially more fruitful strategy for justifying the legal use of any founding-era materials other than the perfectly ordinary evidence of the public meaning (eg, dictionaries, newspapers, routine legal writing) is to rely not on the legal authority of the constitution-maker, but on the special significance contemporary American law happens to place on the 'founding fathers'.[46] What helps here is the distinction between *interpretation* and *construction* in current originalist theory, where only interpretation is grounded in the original intent or the original public meaning.[47] Some authors, like Balkin or Greene, argue that at the construction stage, it is legitimate to use the kind of 'intent of the founders' arguments that cannot be justified on the grounds discussed above.[48] Greene even considers his view as invoking a theory of 'constitutional authority', yet he does not mean the exercise of authority that was the historical reason for acceptance of the Constitution, but a more nebulous notion of 'national heritage' or 'a set of values that are offered by proponents as uniquely or especially constitutive of American identity'.[49] Balkin made similar claims.[50]

Without attempting to settle the issue, I will merely say that it could be that Greene and Balkin are correct and that the current American legal practice has a technical notion of authority that allows for uses of the founding-era materials unconnected to the constitution-maker.

[43] ibid 1156; Manning (n 35) 1765.

[44] See, eg, Manning (n 35) 1767.

[45] Pace William N Eskridge, Jr, 'Should the Supreme Court Read the Federalist But Not Statutory Legislative History' (1998) 66 *George Washington Law Review* 1301, 1313.

[46] For examples of this strategy, see McGowan (n 32); Kesavan and Paulsen (n 32); Jamal Greene, 'The Case for Original Intent' (2012) 80 *George Washington Law Review* 1683; Jack M Balkin, 'The New Originalism and the Uses of History' (2013) 82 *Fordham Law Review* 641; William Baude, 'Is Originalism Our Law?' (2015) 115 *Columbia Law Review* 2349, 2366.

[47] Lawrence B Solum, 'The Interpretation-Construction Distinction' (2010) 27 *Constitutional Commentary* 95.

[48] Greene (n 46) 1696; Balkin (n 46) 652–53.

[49] Greene (n 46) 1697, 1700.

[50] Balkin (n 46) 653.

B. Australia

Australia is notably different from the US; it does not have the revolutionary past. Australia emerged as a new constitutional order without any unlawfulness.[51] The 'Australian Constitution' is a popular name for the Commonwealth of Australia Constitution Act 1900 (or at least for a part of the Act), a statute enacted by the Imperial Parliament at Westminster. There is broad agreement that the Australian Constitution became law through the enactment of the Imperial Parliament.[52] Hence, the Imperial Parliament is the historical maker of the Australian Constitution. And it is so not only on the first criterion, but arguably also on the second one – the Australian people accepted the Constitution because it had been authoritatively made by the Imperial Parliament, not because of the Australian process by which it had been drafted.[53]

Nevertheless, it may seem that this account fails to give justice to the constitution-making process that involved Australian conventions that drafted the Constitution, as well as constitutional referendums in Australian colonies. Peter Oliver insists that the people of Australia played a legally significant role in the constitution-making.[54] There are several problems with that view. First, it is clear that the Australian drafters acted within the pre-arranged framework that was to end with a request directed to the Queen for an enactment of the Australian Constitution by the Imperial Parliament.[55] Second, those who approved the project of the Constitution in referendums were a minority of those enrolled to vote.[56] This is an issue because it suggests that there was no group action (insufficient overlap of participatory intentions), unless it can be shown that the groups involved were institutional groups that may have acted even without specific participatory intentions on the part of the vast majority of their members. But even if it is possible to overcome this, it is still the case that the explicit role of the referendums was to authorise legislation to ask the Queen for imperial legislation, not to enact a constitution.[57] Also, unlike in the US, there is

[51] Peter C Oliver, *The Constitution of Independence: The Development of Constitutional Theory in Australia, Canada, and New Zealand* (Oxford University Press, 2005); Benjamin Spagnolo, *The Continuity of Legal Systems in Theory and Practice* (Hart Publishing, 2015).

[52] John Daley, 'The Bases for the Authority of the Australian Constitution' (DPhil thesis, University of Oxford, 1999) ch 5; Oliver (n 50) 209, 329; BJ Spagnolo, 'Kelsen and Raz on the Continuity of Legal Systems: Applying the Accounts in an Australian Context' (DPhil thesis, University of Oxford, 2014) 46, 58, 294–95.

[53] I rely here on the account offered by Benjamin Spagnolo, who stresses the significance of the change made by the Imperial Parliament to s 74 compared to the draft Act as well as the general perception of the Imperial Parliament as the ultimate law-making authority for Australia, even after the enactment of the 1900 Act; see Spagnolo (n 52) 298–99.

[54] Oliver (n 51) 207–08, 268, 329–30. See also James Kirk, 'Constitutional Interpretation and a Theory of Evolutionary Originalism' (1999) 27 *Federal Law Review* 323, 342–43.

[55] Daley (n 52) 126.

[56] ibid 109–13.

[57] ibid 126. And so Daley concludes: 'Historically, the will of the Australian people has not been treated as conferring legal validity' (at 127).

no strong personal 'cult' of any of the great men from among those who participated in the Australian constitution-making. Even those who stress the role of other agents (the people, the drafters etc) do not single out any individuals as the constitution-makers.[58]

As a matter of cautious constitutional theory in Australia, a version of original public meaning originalism is especially popular.[59] However, the issue of identity of the constitution-maker may be of relevance even for that position. Given the distance and the already-existing legal differences between Australia and England at the end of the nineteenth century, it is not surprising that the relevant public meaning of the terms used by some constitutional clauses differed between them.[60] Hence, identifying the Imperial Parliament as the constitution-maker could suggest that it is the English understanding that trumps. However, this is too quick a judgement to make. From the fact that the Imperial Parliament was the authority that made the Australian Constitution, it may at most follow that what is relevant to constitutional interpretation is the legislative choice made by the Imperial Parliament. It still could be that the choice had been to change the law for Australia in the way in which the colonies petitioned the imperial authority to do, that is, in accordance with the Australian understanding of the details of the legislative plan. Using the two examples introduced before, this may a case of Alex-type adoption (see above, section III.A).

Jeffrey Goldsworthy suggested that such a 'role' had been thrust upon the Imperial Parliament,[61] whereas I prefer to see this as a proper interpretation of the choice made by that Parliament (which also means that that Parliament could have made a different choice). The crucial consequence of this is that some intentions or understandings of certain other agents may be legally relevant for constitutional interpretation *due to a choice* made by the Imperial Parliament, even if the Parliament was the only constitution-maker that the Australian Constitution had.

C. Canada

The making of the Canadian Constitution shares some similarities with the Australian case. Both the British North America Act, 1867 (now the Constitution Act, 1867) and the Constitution Act, 1982 (which formed a part of the Canada

[58] Jeffrey Goldsworthy, 'Originalism in Constitutional Interpretation' (1997) 25 *Federal Law Review* 1, 25; Oliver (n 51) 268, 329–30.

[59] See, eg, Goldsworthy (n 58); Kirk (n 54); Michael Kirby, 'Constitutional Interpretation and Original Intent: A Form of Ancestor Worship?' (2000) 24 *Melbourne University Law Review* 1; Jeffrey Goldsworthy, 'Interpreting the Constitution in its Second Century' (2000) 24 *Melbourne University Law Review* 677; Lael K Weis, 'What Comparativism Tells Us about Originalism' (2011) 11 *International Journal of Constitutional Law* 842.

[60] An example of this (differing legal meaning of 'excise') was at issue in *Peterswald* (1904) 1 CLR 497.

[61] Goldsworthy (n 58) 25.

Act 1982 (UK) and amended the 1867 Act) were enacted by the Westminster Parliament. By virtue of exercising a legal power to do so, the Westminster Parliament was, in both instances, clearly the maker of the Canadian Constitution as law.[62] However, as the Supreme Court of Canada stated in 1998:

> The proclamation of the Constitution Act, 1982 removed the last vestige of British authority over the Canadian Constitution …
>
> Legal continuity, which requires an orderly transfer of authority, necessitated that the 1982 amendments be made by the Westminster Parliament, but the legitimacy as distinguished from the formal legality of the amendments derived from political decisions taken in Canada within a legal framework which this Court, in the Patriation Reference, had ruled was in accordance with our Constitution.[63]

The constitution-maker has thus removed itself from the picture, so to speak, in the very act of constitution-making. Nevertheless, it does not follow from that alone that the identity of the constitution-maker is not legally relevant. The second interesting point made by the Court is the distinction between 'the legitimacy' and 'the formal legality' of the 1982 constitutional change in Canada. I do not disagree with that point, but I want to stress the specifically legal meaning of authority (see above, section II.B). Even though the ultimate (moral, political) legitimacy of a constitution-making process comes from one body, it may very well be that the maker of the constitution as law is someone else (see above, section II.A). My claim is that the move from X's legal authority (in constitution-making) to X's legal relevance (in constitutional interpretation) is easier to make than the move from X's moral or political legitimacy (in constitution-making) to X's legal relevance.

Even though Canadian constitutional practice is considered to be hostile to originalist arguments, there is at least one respect in which it relies on considerations of historical constitution-making – 'constitutional bargains'.[64] The bargains in question are the political compromises, without which the Constitution would not have had the content that it has. The following question then arises: given the Westminster Parliament's role as the constitution-maker, what is the legal significance of anything that happened *not* in the Parliament and, especially, of the evidence of the political deals struck in Canada? Another example of reliance on the constitution-making in Canadian constitutional law is provided by judicial applications of the Charter of Rights and Freedoms, which forms a part of the Constitution Act, 1982.[65] Some Canadian judges rely expressly on the drafting history of the provisions. The problem is that, as we know, the drafting took place in Canada, by someone else than the constitution-maker.

[62] See also Richard S Kay, 'Canada's Constitutional Cul de Sac' (2005) 35 *American Review of Canadian Studies* 705, 708–10.

[63] *Secession Reference (Reference re Secession of Quebec)* [1998] 2 SCR 217, para 467.

[64] Léonid Sirota and Benjamin Oliphant, 'Originalist Reasoning in Canadian Constitutional Jurisprudence' (2017) 50 *UBC Law Review* 505, 522.

[65] ibid 535.

One plausible way to address this concern is to show (for example, by referencing Hansard) that the Westminster Parliament in fact intended to give effect to the legislative plan prepared in Canada, including the political compromises. However, a more general argument to that effect may be available, at least regarding the 1982 Act. The adoption point made by Goldsworthy in reference to the Australian Constitution is applicable, perhaps even more forcefully, to the Canadian Constitution (see above, sections III.A and IV.B). The Queen's proclamation of the 1982 Act explicitly recognised 'the status of Canada as an independent state' and that the UK Parliament enacted the Canada Act 'at the request and with the consent of Canada'.[66] Hence, there are good reasons to think, even without looking at Hansard, that the constitution-maker adopted the legislative plan prepared in Canada, thus making this Canadian plan legally relevant. Nevertheless, this creates a different problem of deciding who were the authors of the original plan (the drafters).[67] I will not attempt to answer this question, as it requires a different framework from the one modelling authority in constitution-making (see above, section II) that I give. From my perspective, the point is that the drafters (the framers) of the 1982 Act are not the constitution-maker and hence they need another legal reason for their legal relevance.

V. Conclusion

I proposed a general account of legal, or legally recognised, authority in constitution-making, according to which in order to be the legally relevant constitution-maker, one has to either: (1) exercise pre-existing legal authority to make the constitution in question; or (2) have one's intentional act purporting authoritatively to make the constitution as law recognised as the reason for acceptance of the constitution as law. I have also considered the ways in which historical materials unconnected to the constitution-maker of a given constitution may be properly used in a legal argument. I then applied the general account to the cases of Australia, Canada and the US showing some of the justificatory problems stemming from the problem of identity of the constitution-maker.

I did not focus on examples of incautious legal talk, where, for example, inferences are being made from the constitution-making authority of the drafters of a constitution (who clearly are not the maker). Instead, I chose to focus on potential types of justifications for legal relevance of those who participated in the making of a constitution, but were not the authority that made it as law. A general conclusion that stems from the applicative part of my chapter is that there are different bases for legal relevance of such agents in the US on the one hand and in Australia and Canada on the other. In the US, it is exclusively the subsequent legal practice

[66] Oliver (n 51) 182.
[67] Greene (n 37) 65.

that plausibly makes the non-makers relevant in legal reasoning. The practice as it emerged after the making of the US Constitution makes the non-makers legally relevant because of the important, non-legal role played by some of them.[68] It may even be that the US law accepts the ahistorical view, a legal fiction so to speak, that the non-makers were the makers in the sense I am using the term.

In Australia and in Canada, a different argument is available. There, it is arguable that the constitution-maker (in both cases the Parliament at Westminster) *adopted* the legislative plan prepared in Australia and in Canada, thus making that plan (and its authors) legally relevant. The question remains as to which model of adoption is applicable. Did the constitution-maker adopt even the parts of the plan that were not available to it (the 'secret' plan) or did it adopt the plan only to the extent that it had been presented (or at least potentially available) to the maker? Interestingly, in the American context, only the second option is considered (and, for good reasons, dismissed). However, some features of the Australian and Canadian constitution-making (in Canada this is more applicable to the 1982 Act) suggest that the Parliament's choice had been in fact to go with the first option: whatever *your* design is for your constitution, *we* enact it as law.

[68] See n 46 above.

5

'And Then They Begin to Look after the History of Their Founders'

(Re)configurations of the Founding in the Early Republic

SIMON GILHOOLEY

> [A]nd then they begin to look after the history of their founders, and search into their original, when they have outlived the memory of it.[1]

Constitutional theories predicated on a return to the founding are an American motif. From the fairly straightforward appeals of original intent as articulated by Edwin Meese in the 1980s, through the doctrine(s) of original meaning and to the 'Dualist' analysis of Bruce Ackerman, founding moments are seen as the historical points of sovereign action that act as the legitimising basis of the constitutional order.[2] From there, it is a somewhat short step to 'purifying' the corruptions of modern constitutional law by returning to the founding either for constitutional meaning (Meese) or for clarifying authoritative action (Ackerman). To place the singular case of Ackerman for the moment to one side, this logic has operated as a centripetal force on American politics, pulling it ever more tightly to the founding, but also on the founding itself, making it ever simpler and more concrete. Even those scholars such as Jack M Balkin who seek to argue for a more open-ended constitutional order frame their claims in terms of the values of the founding and so reify the role of the founding and de-clutter its myriad ideological commitments.[3] Such simplification lends itself to reducing the founding to a series of manageable characters and so we are quickly reduced to 'fighting over the founders', deploying critiques of the founders and their interpreters

[1] John Locke, *Second Treatise of Government and A Letter Concerning Toleration*, Mark Goldie (ed) (Oxford University Press, 2016) 51.

[2] Edwin Meese, 'The Attorney General's View of the Supreme Court: Toward a Jurisprudence of Original Intention' (1985) 45 *Public Administration Review* 701; Keith Whittington, 'The New Originalism' (2004) 22 *Georgetown Journal of Law & Public Policy* 599; Bruce Ackerman, *We The People: Foundations* (Belknap Press of Harvard University Press, 1991).

[3] Jack M Balkin, *Living Originalism* (Belknap Press of Harvard University Press, 2011).

while simultaneously reaffirming the importance of arguing about the founding.[4] As such, US constitutional history becomes bookended by the events of the founding and the events of the present. Although growing chronologically ever further away from each other, they seem to be ever more tightly linked.

The recurrence to the founding has reified the notion that constitutional legitimacy can be traced to a moment, even if the content of that moment has itself become more contested. But the idea that past and present can be easily bifurcated is not without challenge. In this vein, Anne Norton has written of the founders themselves as both conquering and being conquered by history.[5] In Norton's telling, this return to the founding has worked to make the founders available to future generations in acceptable terms, while at the same time renewing the hold of the founders over the present. Caught in this dialectic, both history and present are intertwined, unable to escape each other, but nonetheless mutually defining. American self-understanding is rooted in an assumption of the founding, but this understanding shifts at different times between accounts and characters in order to make that past legible and digestible. In his chapter in this collection, Ming-Sug Kuo has further suggested that narratives of a founding moment are themselves instances of constituent power active in forging a constitutional *nomos*.[6] For both Norton and Kuo, discussion of constitutional politics is refocused away from interpretation of the founding moment and towards the reconstruction of that moment at different – later – temporal points.

Norton's and Kuo's de-centring of the founding moment in constitutional politics points to a tendency to reconfigure the past in the service of present; to reconstruct a historical moment in terms that expand or contract the political possibilities of the present. For Norton, the founding moment is 'conquered' and so reinterpreted in the present. For Kuo, the founding moment is 'narrated', reanimating the constituent power of the present. I would like to suggest here that another possibility for such de-centring exists in a reconceptualisation of the founding moment itself. Rather than reinterpreted or narrated anew, the moment of founding is itself reconfigured to be something it previously was not, which is to say that the present relocates the precise temporal moment of the founding – redefines that instance of sovereign authority – in ways that conform to the political necessities of the present.

The other chapters within this part of this book highlight the ways in which founding moments are contested and narrated by subsequent political actors.

[4] Jack Jackson, 'Unmapped Politics' [2012] *Harvard Civil Rights-Civil Liberties Review*. I would argue here that in this regard, Ackerman's Dualism is not so different. While demoting the importance of the founding in US constitutional history, he does so only by promoting further singular moments of founding to equal importance. In effect, he does not deny the centrality of founding within the constitutional order so much as systematises its definition in an expansive manner. Each founding moment is still authoritative and legitimises its subsequent constitutional era.

[5] Anne Norton, 'Transubstantiation: The Dialectic of Constitutional Authority' (1988) 55 *University of Chicago Law Review* 458.

[6] Ming-Sug Kuo, ch 1 in this volume.

Yair Sagy's chapter shows that the Israeli founding of the 1950s has undergone a repeated process of historical revisionism as commentators rejected and then re-embraced a Diceyan orthodoxy of parliamentary supremacy.[7] In examining the emergence of the norm of semi-presidentialism in the states of the former USSR, Eugene D Mazo traces the ineluctability of path dependency with projects of constitutional revision, raising the question of precisely when, if at all, a moment of sovereign intervention can be seen to have taken place.[8] In each of these contexts, there are multiple candidates for the historical location of *the* founding moment, opening up opportunities for relocation and redefinition. Taken together, these contributions require scepticism towards the idea of a singular and always-accepted moment of founding. But each account – and in particular Sagy's – also indicates the ways in which contestation over a founding moment is linked to the political pressures and considerations of those engaged in the identification of that founding moment. As a whole, then, they suggest widening our scope of inquiry away from 'the founding moment' alone and instead towards a set of contemporary interpreters engaging with *a founding*.

In order to explore this possibility, I turn to three periods within the early American Republic – discussions of the electoral crisis of 1800–01, the debates surrounding *McCulloch v Maryland* in 1819, and the debates around slavery in Washington DC in the early 1830s. Each represents a moment in which the American founding was reconfigured in order to further contemporary political interests, not just in terms of what the founders advocated, but actually in terms of whom exactly the founders were and what it was that they founded. These accounts show that even in close proximity to the concrete events of a founding, the people that emerge from it can radically reconfigure its history and meaning. The chapter proceeds in three stages. I begin with a discussion of founding moments as theoretical ideas. Next I take up the historical accounts of the three periods noted above. The chapter ends with a reflection on these accounts before exploring the potential significance of them for constitutional theory and design.

I. Past and Present in Founding Moments

John Locke's *Second Treatise* offers the classic account of a founding moment within the social contract tradition. Emerging from the state of nature, individuals come together to pledge commitment to each other and to the project of creating an 'umpire on Earth' to adjudicate disputes between them. In such a way, they create a civil society and erect a government for it. The mechanics of this archetypal moment of founding have been extensively analysed and it does not need to be retraced here. But what I would like to highlight is the hint that Locke offers of

[7] Yair Sagy, ch 6 in this volume.
[8] Eugene D Mazo, ch 7 in this volume.

the relationship between the people and the founders in this account. The people make a relatively late appearance in the process of creating a political society in Chapter 8, 'Of the Beginning of Political Societies'. Locke begins with *independent men* and *individuals*, who make a *community*, then form a *majority* to act for the *whole*. It is as he turns to addressing the ahistorical nature of his argument that the people are invoked:

> Government is every where antecedent to records, and letters seldom come in amongst a people till a long continuation of civil society has, by other necessary arts, provided for their safety, ease, and plenty: then they begin to look after the history of their founders, and search into their *original*, when they have outlived the memory of it.[9]

What I would like to highlight here is the manner in which the concepts of 'the people' and 'the founders' emerge in Locke's account only retrospectively (and simultaneously). Both concepts are weighted with authority, but they come into being only once the founding has been forgotten. In contrast to the timeless individuals and community of Locke's mechanical account of polity-making, the founders and people have a very specific historical location – after a degree of development, after a long continuation of civil society, once the founding is no longer available to memory; in short, once there is a clear 'Past' to compare to – and link to – 'the Present'.

In foregrounding the founding's ambiguity and distance, Locke's account points to the manner in which foundings are created not by the founders, but rather by the people's subsequent recognition of those actors and moments. And, crucially, this means that they can be subject to *re*-cognition by subsequent generations, which is to say that foundings are subject to recognition by different 'the peoples' at different moments in history. Understood this way, rather than being absolutes, foundings are prisms through which contemporary political debates can be exercised.

That the power of recognition lies in the current, not the founding, generation opens up several possibilities for the renewal of constituent power within the present moment. Jason Frank has pointed to the way in which the claim of popular sovereignty gave scope for democratic actors to seek to expand the conception of the people in the early Republic.[10] Creating spaces of 'insurgent citizenship', these actors enacted a politics that pushed the rhetorical commitment embodied in 'We the People' towards greater democracy. In this instance, the members of the democratic-republican societies of the early Republic reached back to the founding not in order to mobilise it for legitimisation of a facet of contemporary politics, but rather to destabilise the claims that were reliant upon it. Through enacting their democratic citizenship, they highlighted the empty rhetoric of those who were claiming authority to act in the name of 'We the People'. Rather than tapping

[9] Locke (n 1) 51.

[10] Jason Frank, *Constituent Moments: Enacting the People in Postrevolutionary America* (Duke University Press, 2010).

the authority of the founding through invocation of its claim to be a moment of 'higher politics', they sought to re-present that moment in a more radically democratic mode.

A similar reflexive dynamic can be seen in Ming-Sung Kuo's chapter to this collection. Kuo argues that rather than seeing constitutional development in terms of a unidirectional 'jurispathic' relationship between founding and present, narration of a founding moment allows us to understand that relationship as genuinely relational and 'jurisgenerative'.[11] Utilising Robert Cover's conception of a constitutional 'nomos' – a 'normative world' in which 'law and narrative are inseparably related'[12] – Kuo suggests that through narrating founding moments, the present generation can constitute the constitutional *nomos*.[13] Breaking the association of constituent power with beginnings, the process of narration can allow a reincarnated constituent power to sustain and shape the constitutional *nomos* in the present. In place of a constitutional order unfolding from the authoritative moment of the founding – or redeeming itself by a return to it – the act of narration ensures a genuinely 'jurisgenerative' order in which 'the creation of legal meaning … takes place always through an essentially cultural medium'.[14]

Both of these instances of constituent power revolve around an interaction between the present and the founding moment. The eruption of contemporary constituent power is predicated on the re-interpretation or renarration of that founding moment in a manner that, hopefully, works to expand democratic horizons. Nevertheless, it is possible to imagine the power of contemporary recognition utilised to reconfigure not the present, but the past. In such a scenario, the recognition of a founding is not adjudication between competing *nomoi* in the present – although it may certainly have that effect – but is rather adjudication between distinct candidates for the title of founding moment in the past. As different contemporary peoples engage the founding, they have the capacity to bestow on different moments (or configurations of the same moment) the authoritative claim to be a founding moment. Perhaps more so than the jurisgenerative order or the tapping of the democratic excesses of founding moments, the act of reconfiguring the founding moment has the potential to narrow the democratic space. In place of the former moves to reinvigorate a constituent power, reconfiguration of the past has the potential to frame the (previous) constituent power in newly constrained ways. Rather than expansive, these acts of recognition-as-reconfiguration could be limiting. It is this possibility that the following discussions of moments in American history explore. In each of these temporal moments, the political actors of the present have sought not merely to revisit a founding moment, but to actually reposition the moment itself in terms of

[11] Kuo, ch 1 in this volume.

[12] Robert M Cover, 'The Supreme Court, 1982 Term – Forward: Nomos and Narrative' 97 *Harvard Law Review* 4, 5.

[13] Kuo, ch 1 in this volume.

[14] Cover (n 12) 11.

temporal location and participants. After laying out the three periods, the chapter will turn to a reflection upon them.

II. Three Moments of Reconfiguration

A. The Electoral Crisis of 1800–01

The 1800 presidential election exposed a weakness in the US Constitution. As the Electoral College ballots were opened, they revealed an equal number of votes for the Republican candidates for president and vice president, Thomas Jefferson and Aaron Burr respectively. A Federalist party-dominated House of Representatives, constitutionally responsible for adjudicating inconclusive presidential elections, sought to exploit the deadlock by refusing to recognise what everyone knew – that Jefferson was the people's choice for president. As the end of President John Adams' term approached, public debate turned to how the impasse could be addressed constitutionally. The ensuing newspaper debates operated within a framework of constitutional understandings that focus on the text and so conceived of constitutional authority in immediate terms.

The newspaper debate over the election was broadly divided along party lines. On the one hand, Mel Laracey has characterised the arguments offered by the Jeffersonian *National Intelligencer* during this period as marked by a constitutional interpretation rooted in ideas of popular will.[15] Writing pseudonymously 'Aristides' argued that the Constitution derived its powers from a popular and express grant of the people themselves. As '[t]he Federal Constitution was the act of *the people* of the United States', the only way to address gaps in the Constitution was through an overt intervention by the people themselves.[16] Without such an intervention or congressional action, 'Aristides' suggested that the office of the president would remain vacant after the expiration of Adams' term. In the same newspaper, 'An American' argued that contemporaneous constitutional practice and understandings ought to be considered in interpreting the Constitution. Central to this argument was the belief that '[t]he spirit of the constitution requires the will of the people to be executed'.[17] This line of argument was picked up and expanded by 'a respectable citizen' who argued: 'No body thought of a remedy for the case quoted, because no body conceived that any other than the force of public opinion was necessary.'[18] For the latter writer, the Constitution was

[15] Mel Laracey, 'The Presidential Newspaper as an Engine of Early American Political Development: The Case of Thomas Jefferson and the Election of 1800' (2008) 11 *Rhetoric & Public Affairs* 7.

[16] 'On the Election of President No 3' *National Intelligencer and Washington Advertiser* (7 January 1801).

[17] 'To the House of Representatives of the United States of America' *National Intelligencer and Washington Advertiser* (22 January 1801).

[18] 'Letter from a Respectable Citizen to a Member of Congress, on the Election of a President' *National Intelligencer and Washington Advertiser* (21 January 1801).

intrinsically tied to popular opinion, such that 'it was necessary to confide in the force of public opinion, for the execution of the constitution'.[19] For all of these writers, the fundamental document of the political order, the Constitution, was a radically present text subject to real-time intervention by its legitimising authority, the people. The founding in this sense was conceptually understood in terms of a popular grant of authority, but was not one that was necessarily located in the past; rather, it was an almost everyday act of witness.

On the other hand, the Federalist presses resisted (in line with the political divide of the period) the authority of the people and instead sought to find a solution to the electoral crisis within the extant constitutional text. While adhering to Blackstonian ideals of intent as defined by the 'reasonable and legal meaning' of the text, Federalist writers argued that a constitutional document could not fail to provide for all eventualities. In marrying the commitments to intent-via-text and the completeness of the constitutional document, writers such as 'Civilis' suggested 'that construction shall be given which is indispensably necessary to preserve the existence of the government'.[20] Such an approach had the desirable consequences of preserving interpretative authority to those trained in legal methods, while simultaneously denying the people an opportunity for contemporary constitutional revision.

One significant example of this came in the form of an essay series published under the pseudonym 'Horatius'.[21] Arguing that a constitution's fundamental commitment must be self-preservation, the author posited that the Constitution must contain a solution to the crisis at hand:

> For such a state of things the constitution ought not to be understood to be unprovided, or it will be understood to be without the means of self preservation.

From this perspective, Horatius identified the clause concerned with the power of removal as the relevant part of the constitution text[22] and reasoned that the order of presidential succession required that an 'officer' of the executive branch act as President after the expiration of Adams' term. The logical choice for such an officer was the most senior executive office holder – the Secretary of State. Bruce Ackerman has suggested that Horatius may well have been John Marshall, then Secretary of State, later the Chief Justice, providing something of a convenient conclusion for Horatius.[23] Nevertheless, the actual solution was perhaps less important than the commitment to the idea, shared by other Federalist writers,

[19] ibid.

[20] 'Who Will Be the Next President Is Uncertain' *Alexandria Advertiser* (22 December 1800).

[21] 'The Presidential Knot' *Washington Federalist* (6 January 1801).

[22] 'In the case of removal of the President from office or of his death, resignation or inability to discharge the power and duties of the said office, the same shall devolve on the Vice President, and Congress may by law provide for the case of removal, death, resignation or inability of both President and Vice-President, declaring what officer shall then act as President, and such officer shall act accordingly until the disability be removed or a President shall be elected.' US Constitution 1787, art II, s 1.

[23] Bruce Ackerman, *The Failure of the Founding Fathers: Jefferson, Marshall, and the Rise of Presidential Democracy* (Belknap Press of Harvard University Press, 2005) 41–45.

that the constitutional text necessarily contained a response to any constitutional crisis when examined by a suitably trained legal mind.

The consequences of this approach for understandings of the founding varied amongst this Federalist grouping. For some Federalists, these textual commitments led to a view of the Constitution as particularly tied to the intentions of the actors of 1787–88. Among this group, 'Eumenes' characterised interpretation as assessing the contemplations of 'the general convention, who framed … [and] the state conventions, who ratified the constitution'.[24] However, other Federalists seemed largely uninterested in how the Constitution came into being or by what authority it operated. Indeed, for 'Horatius', it was crucial to understand intention as derived solely from the document and wholly distinct from the question of the intention of the parties to the document. This latter (and larger) bloc agreed on constitutional premises with their erstwhile Jeffersonian opponents in some significant ways. Both disavowed – openly or through omission – a requirement to return to the actors of 1787–88 in order to garner constitutional insight. Equally and perhaps consequently, they both presented the Constitution as radically immediate. For the Jeffersonians, this was recognised in the people's capacity for contemporary constitutional intervention. For the Federalists, this manifested in the notion of a 'perfect' constitution, able to respond to any and all constitutional questions through recourse only to the text itself.[25] For both groups, then, the 'founding' was not an historical moment, but instead something always being enacted. The relevant actors were the people and the text itself respectively, unanchored in time but nonetheless actualised in the current moment.

B. The People and the States: *McCulloch v Maryland*

The 'Great Bank Case' of 1819, *McCulloch v Maryland*, is often depicted as one of the central decisions of the Marshall Court, placing on record the supremacy of the federal government. Marshall's biographer Albert Beveridge overstated his case when he stated that *McCulloch* 'is considered as only second in importance to the Constitution itself', but the case is certainly a fixture in the pantheon of landmark Supreme Court cases.[26] Concerned with the ability of Maryland to place a tax on the transactions of the Bank of the United States, the case reached the Supreme Court as discontent with the Bank peaked and questions of federal authority became embroiled with the contentious topic of slavery. In such a context, the opinion offered an 'extremely nationalist interpretation of the Constitution'.[27]

[24] 'For the Washington Federalist' *Washington Federalist* (2 February 1801).

[25] Mark Tushnet, '"Our Perfect Constitution" Revisited' in Peter Berkowitz (ed), *Terrorism, the Laws of War, and the Constitution: Debating the Enemy Combatant Cases* (Hoover Institution Press, 2005).

[26] Albert Beveridge, *The Life of John Marshall* (Houghton Mifflin Company, 1919) 168.

[27] Richard E Ellis, *Aggressive Nationalism: McCulloch v Maryland and the Foundation of Federal Authority in the Young Republic* (Oxford University Press, 2007) 105.

As might be expected, such a strident defence of the federal government attracted equally strident criticism. At one level, these critiques engendered a debate about the very nature of constitutional authority within a democratic polity, but intertwined with these debates was a more historically grounded debate about what had actually taken place in 1787–88.

In his opinion, Marshall offered a narrative of the founding which rested firmly on the people's participation in ratification. Referring back to a model of constitution-making advocated during the Ratification by the Federalists, Marshall emphasised that the document was only a proposal until it received popular sanction.[28] While the Philadelphia Convention was indeed elected by the states, 'the instrument, when it came from [the Convention's] hands, was a mere proposal, without obligation, or pretensions to it'.[29] A reflection of the arguments offered by James Wilson in his famous Speech in the State House Yard[30] and by James Madison in *The Federalist Papers*,[31] Marshall suggested that the Philadelphia Convention had acted as scriveners, offering a text for adoption or rejection by the people at large. Within the framework of his *McCulloch* opinion, this was more than a passing note – it was a vitally important assumption of the argument that Marshall developed. Offered in direct contrast to the claim of Maryland's counsel that the Constitution emanated from the 'sovereign and independent States',[32] Marshall's version of the Constitution's creation was the basis for the famed claim 'we must never forget, that it is *a constitution* we are expounding'.[33]

This famous line drew on the arguments offered by William Pinkney in defence of the Bank, but in Marshall's hands, they were made to map onto a popular mode of ratification. Pinkney had argued that the impossibility of including every eventuality in the Constitution text had led the framers to rely upon the implication of powers not specified in the text. Pinkney had suggested that the brevity of the Constitution reflected the impossibility of producing a comprehensive document.[34] Adapting Pinkney's argument, Marshall utilised the brevity of the Constitution in his argument against state regulation of the Bank, but crucially reworked the meaning of it. In the opinion, Marshall wrote:

> A constitution, to contain an accurate detail of all the subdivisions of which its great powers will admit, and of all the means by which they would be carried into execution, would partake of the prolixity of a legal code, and could scarcely be embraced

[28] *cf* Simon J Gilhooley, 'The Framers Themselves: Constitutional Authorship during the Ratification' (2013) 2 *American Political Thought* 62.

[29] *McCulloch v Maryland* (1819) 17 US 316, 402.

[30] Jonathan Elliot (ed), *The Debates in the Several State Conventions on the Adoption of the Federal Constitution as Recommended by the General Convention at Philadelphia in 1787 … in Five Volumes: Volume II* (Burt Franklin, 1968) 434–35.

[31] Gilhooley (n 28).

[32] *McCulloch v Maryland* (n 29).

[33] ibid 407.

[34] It is worth noting here the subtle shift in the presumption of completeness à la the 'perfect constitution' offered by Federalists in 1800–01.

> by the human mind. It would probably never be understood by the public. Its nature, therefore, requires that only its great outlines should be marked.[35]

As with Pinkney, the argument here suggested that the absence of a directly stated power in the constitutional text ought not to be understood as an absence of that power. Leaning on the idea of implied powers, both Marshall and Pinkney sought to show that the federal government held the power to incorporate a national bank free from state interference. However, Marshall reached that point through a claim of popular authority, not, as Pinkney had, through the difficulty of writing a constitutional text. The centrality of this shift to the opinion is reiterated in the series of essays that Marshall penned in its defence. In his 'A Friend of the Constitution' essays, published in the *Alexandria Gazette*,[36] Marshall argued that the Constitution:

> [I]s the act of a people, creating a government, without which they cannot exist as a people. The object of the instrument is not a single one which can be minutely described, with all its circumstances. The attempt to do so, would totally change its nature, and defeat its purpose.[37]

In this telling, the Constitution's brevity – and thus the doctrine of implied powers – is linked to public support for and understanding of the document. Marshall locates the authority of the document in its popular acclamation and sees its nature as a result of this necessity.

As well as establishing the claim to implied powers, the Constitution's basis in popular authority also served to support another pillar of Marshall's opinion. At its heart, *McCulloch v Maryland* was a case about the relative authority of the federal and state governments. Included within this discussion was the question of whether the Supreme Court itself could legitimately adjudicate a dispute between the states and the federal government. Critics of the Court, such as Spencer Roane of the Virginia Supreme Court of Appeals, argued that the Supreme Court of the United States was usurping authority in rendering a decision in *McCulloch*. Pushing back against this argument, Marshall once again used the popular basis of the Constitution to argue that the people had chosen the Supreme Court as the apparatus of federal-state adjudication:

> It is the plain dictate of common sense, and the whole political system is founded on the idea, that the departments of government are the agents of the nation, and will perform within their respective spheres, the duties assigned to them.[38]

The judicial department was assigned the role of rendering decisions in such cases as a consequence of the Constitution – 'this is not now a question open for

[35] *McCulloch v Maryland* (n 29).

[36] Gerald Gunther, *John Marshall's Defense of McCulloch v Maryland* (Stanford University Press, 1969) 15.

[37] ibid 170–71.

[38] ibid 211.

consideration. The constitution has decided it'[39] – and as the Constitution draws its authority directly from the people as an 'act of the people themselves, and not the act of their governments',[40] the state governments have no authority by which to challenge this. As with the doctrine of implied powers, Marshall made recourse to the popular ratification of the Constitution as the basis for the Supreme Court's authority.

The use Marshall made of popular ratification contrasted with the understanding of the Constitution's creation offered by his opponents. In writing 'A Friend of the Constitution' and his earlier essays 'A Friend to the Union', Marshall was seeking to primarily address his Virginian critics.[41] Two series of essays emanating from the Richmond Republican Junto, 'Amphictyon' and 'Hampden', appeared in the *Richmond Enquirer* in the first half of 1819 to attack the *McCulloch* opinion from the position of states' rights advocacy. The authorship of 'Amphictyon' is unsettled, but 'Hampden' was almost certainly Spencer Roane and both shared an understanding of the founding as a process of confederation. While both implicitly agreed with Marshall that the authority of the constitutional order rested on the process of ratification, they understood that process to have played out in a manner supportive of states' rights rather than federal supremacy.

Amphictyon's essays appeared in the spring of 1819 and were framed as a direct response to Marshall's *McCulloch* opinion.[42] Seeking to challenge the idea that the federal government could claim implied powers, the essays quickly turned attention to offering a rival interpretation of the Constitution's creation. Early in the first essay, Amphictyon offered an account of the period 1787–88:

> Who gave birth to the constitution? The history of times, and the instrument itself furnish the ready answer to the question. The federal convention of 1787 was composed of delegates appointed by the respective state legislatures; and who voted by states; the constitution was submitted on their recommendation, to conventions elected by the people of the several states, that is to say, to the states themselves in their highest political, and sovereign authority: by those separate conventions, representing not the whole mass of the population of the United States, but the people only within the limits of the respective sovereign states, the constitution was adopted and brought into existence.[43]

In case the contrast with Marshall was missed, Amphictyon then denied that the Constitution had emerged as a 'grant of the people, without regard to the distinctive features of the states'.[44]

[39] ibid 209.
[40] ibid 203.
[41] ibid 11–17. 'A Friend to the Union' first appeared in the *Philadelphia Union*. The following discussion of the oppositional writings is drawn from Gunther.
[42] The Enquirer's editor, Thomas Ritchie introduced them as an 'exposition of the alarming errors of the Supreme Court … in their late interpretation of the Constitution' and Amphityon himself began with the McCulloch opinion. ibid 52–53.
[43] ibid 55–56.
[44] ibid 56.

For Hampden too, the role of the states in the creation of the Constitution was of profound significance. While initially arguing against implied powers on the basis of the constitutional text and the expectations of the document at the time of its ratification, when arriving at the question of the Supreme Court's authority, Hampden, like Amphictyon, turned to a history of the founding to support his assertions. Beginning with the statement 'The constitution of the United States was not adopted by the people of the United States, as one people', Hampden offered an account of the ratification that had much in common with Amphictyon's:

> [R]atification results not from a majority of the people in the union, nor even from that of a majority of the states; but that it must result from the unanimous assent of all the states that are parties to it, differing no otherwise from their ordinary assent, than its being expressed, not by the legislative authority, but by the *people* themselves.[45]

Citing with approval Madison's Report of 1799, Hampden concluded that 'the powers of the general government result from a *compact*, to which the *states* are parties'.[46] Understanding the creation of the federal government in this manner, Hampden argued the Supreme Court could not be regarded as holding the power to adjudicate between the states and the federal government. Where Marshall claimed the people have devolved this authority to the Supreme Court, Hampden insisted that the 'compact' meant that the parties (the states) alone 'must be the rightful judges … and that, in this respect, there can be no tribunal above their authority'.[47] As with Amphictyon, the ratification of the Constitution by the states worked to deny the authority of the US Supreme Court in this matter.

For both Marshall and his interlocutors, the crucial question for contemporary political authority was the character of the actors during the process of ratification. In Marshall's view, it was the people themselves acting in a sovereign capacity that underpinned the Supreme Court's authority. For the Virginia Republicans, the states had acted in 1787–88 to create a compact, extending the powers of the general 'government' under the Articles of Confederation. As such, the Supreme Court was not recognisable as a tribunal for conflicts between the states and the federal government. However, crucially from the perspective of this chapter, all the parties in this exchange of essays shared an understanding of the pivotal moment of constitutional creation as the process of ratification. Marshall looked to the people, while Amphictyon and Hampden looked to the states, but they all conceived of the founding as a moment of sovereign action. In contrast to the immediacy of 1800–01 and (as we shall see) the centrality of compromise in the 1830s, the founding moment in the debates surrounding *McCulloch* is commonly held as an instance of sovereign delegation enacted through the process of approval of a constitutional text.

[45] ibid 140.
[46] ibid 141.
[47] ibid 148.

C. Abolition, the District of Columbia and the 'Compact'

The early 1830s were marked by the emergence of a strident movement against slavery. The Abolitionist movement coalescing around William Lloyd Garrison in this period made abolition in the District of Columbia a focal point. Arguing that Congress had constitutional authority over this territory, the Abolitionists called for immediate abolition in the nation's capital. In resisting this call, slaveholders and their supporters came to articulate an understanding of the founding that precluded such action. Conceiving of the founding as centred on the Philadelphia Convention and the bargains struck therein, pro-slavery advocates articulated a narrative of the founding that emphasised spirit and consensus, and appealed to a historical 'Compact' as the touchstone of American constitutional identity.

In late 1833, news reached the US of the British Parliament's abolition of slavery in the British colonies. American proponents of abolition digested this information with mixed feelings. On the one hand, this act of abolition marked a significant advance in the Atlantic abolitionist movement, but on the other, it left the US alone in the English-speaking world in sustaining slavery. As *The Abolitionist* noted: 'This glorious act of the British nation, presents a mortifying contrast to the conduct of our own.'[48] In the face of this new reality, Abolitionists would increasingly come to see slavery as a peculiarly American sin, one given form in the continuation of the slave trade through the nation's capital Washington DC To address this, they undertook an aggressive petitioning campaign organised through the emerging network of Abolitionist societies.

Changes in Southern society meant that by the 1830s, slavery was more ferociously defended than it had been during the earlier unsuccessful attempts at abolition in the District of Columbia. The ending of the (legal) foreign slave trade after 1808 and the American cotton boom had the effect of making slaves more expensive.[49] During the same period, ideological support for slavery became more forthright. Arguments grounded in the positive advantages of slavery rather than the difficulties of safely ending it became more common.[50] The *Charleston Courier* argued that slavery was 'neither a sin nor a curse … [but] a practical blessing'.[51] Seeing abolition in the District as the first step towards national emancipation, slaveholders sought not merely to argue against the advisability of abolition in Washington, but to decisively shut down discussion of it.[52]

To shut down such discussion, advocates of slavery (and those opposed to the Abolitionists) advanced a vision of the founding denoted by the idea of

[48] 'Slavery and the Slave Trade in the District of Columbia' (1833) 1 *The Abolitionist* 145.

[49] Robert Evans Jr, 'The Economics of American Negro Slavery, 1830–1860', *Aspects of Labor Economics* (Princeton University Press, 1962) 199.

[50] Matthew Mason, *Slavery and Politics in the Early American Republic* (University of North Carolina Press, 2006).

[51] 'The Crisis' *Charleston Courier* (14 November 1835).

[52] Which they achieved in Congress through the 'gag rule'.

the 'Compact'. The American tradition of constitutional settlements as compacts has a lineage stretching back to the Mayflower Compact, but the 1830s Compact placed special emphasis on the mode of compacting rather than the binding consequences of the compact. The citizens of Albany explained the commitment involved in the Compact in the following way:

> [T]he constitution of the United States carries with it an adjustment of all questions involved in the deliberations which led to its adoption, and that the compromise of interests in which it was founded, is binding in honor and good faith, *independently of the force of agreement*, on all who live under its protection and participate in the benefits of which it is the source.[53]

The Compact of the 1830s articulated not merely fidelity to the Constitution, but also to the spirit of compromise and to the assumptions and understandings that enabled that compromise to take place. In other words, the Compact encompassed the attitude of Federalists in 1787–88 in addition to the text that they produced.

Developed systematically by Henry Laurens Pinckney in his *Report … Upon the Subject of Slavery in the District of Columbia* for the House of Representatives in 1836, the Compact sought to draw equivalency between federal regulation of slavery in the District of Columbia and in the states.[54] Recognising that there was no textual basis for arguing against abolition in the District, Pinckney argued that there was something more fundamental than the constitutional text – a spirit that enabled the agreement it represented. Seeing the cession of the territory of the District of Columbia as a central part of the constitutional agreement, Pinckney saw attempts to address slavery there as a violation of public faith. To the extent that the Constitution was itself predicated on such faith, abolition in DC was a direct attack on the constitutional settlement:

> Why are all compacts or promises made by Governments held to be irrevocably binding? Why, but because they cannot break them without committing perfidy, and destroying all confidence in their justice and integrity?[55]

In light of this, Pinckney concluded that 'the obligations of Congress not to act on [slavery in DC] are as fully binding and insuperable as a positive constitutional interdict, or an open acknowledgement of want of power'.[56] The argument here – that a spirit of agreement and the intentions infused with it trump the actual content of the agreement – formed the basic commitments of the 'Compact'.

[53] *Opinions of Martin Van Buren Vice President of the United States, Upon the Powers and Duties of Congress, in Reference to the Abolition of Slavery Either in the Slaveholding States or in the District of Columbia* (Blair & Rives, 1836).

[54] *Report of the Select Committee Upon the Subject of Slavery in the District of Columbia, Made by Hon H L Pinckney, to the House of Representatives, May 18, 1836* (Blair & Rives, 1836).

[55] ibid 11.

[56] ibid 14.

While the Compact provided a useful response to Abolitionist pressure, it also contained within it a particular understanding of what the founding actually was. At the core of the Compact was a commitment to the idea that the founding was a deeply historicised compromise. As the idea of the Compact spread and gained purchase in different parts of the US, it was couched in a commitment to this idea that was not evident in 1819 or 1800. Where the debates of 1819 had emphasised the process of ratification and its democratic basis, and those of 1800 had sought to comprehend constitutional action in contemporary moments, the 1830s were marked by a desire not to betray the negotiation of interests achieved in the constitutional settlement.

In 1836, the governments of the various states issued a series of communications condemning abolition and articulating the basis for their condemnation. These communications shared a commitment to the Compact. In Maine, the Legislature located the origin of the compact in 'the spirit of deference, conciliation and mutual forbearance, which pervaded the then independent States'.[57] The General Assembly in Kentucky resolved that the creation of Abolitionist societies was 'a violation of the original basis of the federal compact', and Michigan followed suit, finding them to be 'in direct violation of the obligations of the compact of our Union'.[58] Martin Van Buren would suggest during his 1836 presidential campaign that abolition in DC would 'destroy at once that compromise of interests *which lies at the basis of our social compact*'[59] and in his inaugural address that blocking such attempts would be 'in accordance with the spirit that actuated the venerated fathers of the Republic'.[60]

Once made rhetorically available, these appeals to the negotiations of 1787 were hard to resist, and even the Abolitionists succumbed. To an increasing extent, debates over constitutional meaning became centred on what the intentions of the framers had been and, as they did, they privileged the actors and exchanges engaged with forming the constitutional document rather than ratifying it. In place of the robust exchanges in 1819 over who had authorised the Constitution, Abolitionists and their opponents came to understand constitutional debate as, in the words of Rhode Island Abolitionists, an 'effort … to *regain the ground which liberty occupied in 1787*'.[61] Within this founding imaginary, the debates of the Philadelphia Convention were the historical moment of founding which could be tapped for a greater understanding of legitimate framework of contemporary political action.

[57] *Communication from the Governor, transmitting a report and resolutions adopted by the Legislature of the state of Maine, relative to the subject of slavery* (5 April 1836), 3.

[58] *Communication from the Governor, transmitting resolutions from the Legislature of Kentucky on the subject of abolition societies* (21 March 1836), 5; *Communication from the Governor, transmitting a preamble and resolutions of the Legislature of Michigan, in relation to slavery* (19 March 1836), 4.

[59] *Opinions of Martin Van Buren* (n 53).

[60] Martin Van Buren, 'Inaugural Address' (4 March 1837).

[61] *Proceedings of the Rhode-Island Anti-Slavery Convention, Held in Providence, on the 2d, 3d, and 4th of February, 1836* (HH Brown, 1836).

D. Reconfiguring the Founding

The idea of subsequent generations revisiting a moment of founding in the service of their own political ends is not an alien one. As noted at the outset, a motif of contemporary American constitutionalism is the urge – verging on a civic religious need[62] – to return to the founding for legitimisation. While the originalist project has made a return to the founding its overt aim since Edwin Meese's promise 'to press for a Jurisprudence of Original Intention',[63] countervailing attempts to render the Constitution more open-ended have been equally drawn to the founding, even if only to problematise or attempt to recast it. Nonetheless, I would like to suggest that the three moments traced here reflect a somewhat different interaction with the founding than we are used to seeing today or has been theorised above.

The debates of 1800–01, 1819 and the 1830s did not follow the democratic-republican societies documented by Jason Frank in advancing a radically democratic vision of the founding.[64] Indeed, each debate was marked by the presence of actors seeking to limit the voice of proponents of a larger democratic space. Moreover, the debates did not rely or centre upon the same founding moment as a touchstone of authority. Instead, they invoke wholly distinct configurations of the founding moment that reflect the ideational imperatives of their time. The debates equally provide scant evidence of the conquest of the present by the past sketched out by Anne Norton. Instead, even over the relatively short period from 1800 to 1836, ideas about the nature of the American founding varied significantly in relation to the politics of the day. As the terrain of political conflict moved between partisan, governmental and material-ideological rivalries, so too did the reigning understandings of what the founding was within political debate.

This radical 'availability' of the founding moment to the contemporary generation suggests that too great a focus on founding moments as authoritative points may be misleading. In a variety of ways, the contributors to this collection have highlighted the instability of the category of 'founding moments'. Maryam S Khan has highlighted Pakistan's 'Permanent Constitution' of 1973 as a founding moment not in the form of a stabilised constitutional settlement, but rather as a 'site of struggle',[65] while Juliano Zaiden Benvido has pointed to the potential for incrementalism to characterise founding 'moments'.[66] Mel A Topf's discussion of the American founding similarly moves away from seeing significance in a moment of rupture, but instead in the practices of consolidation enabled by that moment.[67]

[62] *cf* Paul W Kahn, 'Sacrificial Nation' [2010] *The Utopian*.
[63] Meese (n 2) 704. Of course, originalism is now largely associated with original meaning rather than intent.
[64] Frank (n 10).
[65] Maryam S Khan, ch 10 in this volume.
[66] Juliano Zaiden Benvido, ch 8 in this volume.
[67] Mel A Topf, ch 3 in this volume.

Shorn of clarity and stability, and thus predictability, it is perhaps the case that founding moments should be treated as less constitutionally authoritative than current practice suggests. This unsettling of founding moments suggests that founders themselves should perhaps be more cognisant of the limits of their power to constrain the future.

Indeed, one conclusion that we might draw from the historical accounts offered here is that it is not foundings that present us with a paradox, but endings. The instability of founding moments as points for the initiation of a constitutional order begs the question of what must occur for an order to come to an end; if the present is substantially free to reconfigure the founding, then why not always reconfigure rather than found anew? Here a return to Cover might be of use. Cover's suggestion that the state plays a 'jurispathic' role in killing rival *nomoi* through the courts reinforces the claim that the focus of inquiries into constitutional founding ought to be the present rather than the recapturing of a past.[68] But it also highlights the manner in which the continuation of a constitutional order relies upon the state's capacity to 'prune' the various potentialities arising from a jurisgenerative founding. Positing the problem of 'too much law' as the challenge emerging from the ability of narration to generate new *nomoi*, Cover characterises the role of the courts as identifying a legal tradition from the emergent multitude and 'assert[ing] that *this one* is law and destroy[ing] or try[ing] to destroy the rest' (emphasis in original).[69]

However, such action raises the prospect of rival constitutional *nomoi* claiming sufficient strength and institutional support that the courts are unable to decisively adjudicate between them. A present dominated by two (or more) constitutional *nomoi* that defy any jurispathic mechanism would represent a moment in which the jurisgenerative potential of a constitutional order comes to threaten 'the founding' itself. Arguably, the collapsing of the first constitutional order of the US in the run-up to the Civil War reflects such a tendency. One can see the weak power of the Supreme Court in adjudicating *nomoi* in the response of critics of slavery to the *Dred Scott* decision. While not defying the Court in its proximate decision, Abraham Lincoln's speech at Springfield on 26 June 1857 indicates no recognition of its authority to settle the legal tradition of the US in favour of slavery. Indeed, the speech makes explicit Lincoln's belief that absent a compelling claim to be part of a shared and established legal *nomos*, critics of the decision are under no obligation to give up opposition to it:

> If this important decision had been made by the unanimous concurrence of the judges, and without any apparent partisan bias, and in accordance with legal public expectation, and with the steady practice of the departments throughout our history, and had been in no part, based on assumed historical facts which are not really true; or, if wanting in some of these, it had been before the court more than once, and had there been

[68] Cover (n 12) 40.
[69] ibid 53.

> affirmed and re-affirmed through a course of years, it then might be, perhaps would be, factious, nay, even revolutionary, to not acquiesce in it as a precedent.
>
> But when, as it is true we find it wanting in all these claims to the public confidence, it is not resistance, it is not factious, it is not even disrespectful, to treat it as not having yet quite established a settled doctrine for the country[70]

Absent the Court's ability to kill one of the rival conceptions of the constitutional order – pro-slavery or anti-slavery – resolution of the crisis was reached through overt violence and an enforced renewal of the constitutional order on the basis of a rewritten text and the legitimacy of the Union's victory.

It is worth noting that this possibility brings us full circle to a new moment of founding. But it is a moment of founding that is obscured by the Civil War and continuity from the previous constitutional order. From when in the mid-nineteenth century should we date the new constitutional order? The final defeat of the South? The ratification of the Fourteenth Amendment? The re-entry of the seceded states into the Union? Or the collapse of the old order? In the midst of modern records and a highly bureaucratised state, we meet with imprecision on a foundational moment. Here we can see the origin of that obscurity not in the nature of the founding, but in the difficulty of identifying the ending of the older order. Recognition of a precise moment of death eludes us, given the extent to which a regime does not instantaneously expire, but rather gradually deflates. This difficulty is perhaps the very reason most Americans continue to date their constitution from 1787–88, despite its abject failure to hold the Union together between 1861 and 1865. The difficulty of locating an end of the previous order tempts us to obscure the extent to which a founding took place. Once again, we see the present reconfiguring the founding in order that it might make sense to the politics of today. Here we are returned to that state sketched out by Locke above – heirs to a founding only to the extent that we have difficulty in readily identifying it.[71]

III. Conclusion

The case studies detailed above show that from a debate in 1800 that posited the founding as radically present, through the states versus people debates of 1819, and finally in the 'Compact' of the early 1830s, the founding and the founders were regularly reconfigured within the lifetimes of the founders. Moving beyond our contemporary genuflections to the founding and the founding fathers, political actors in the early Republic undertook this reconfiguration in ways that both enhanced democratic agency (1800) and ultimately significantly constrained it (the 1830s). Given this fact, we should not be overly sanguine about the results of

[70] Abraham Lincoln, 'Speech at Springfield, Illinois' in Roy P Basler (ed), *Collected Works of Abraham Lincoln, Volume 2* (Rutgers University Press, 1953) 401.

[71] Or maybe only descendants of those heirs if we accept the 1930s or 1960s as subsequent foundings.

such reconfigurations. But perhaps these examples suggest we should be willing to engage the American founding in more demanding and reflexive ways than contemporary constitutional debates allow for. They direct us to move away from founding moments as definitive authorities and instead consider constitutional orders in their entirety as requiring explanation and analysis. Rather than beginning with foundings as an explanation for the present or seeking to locate authority for the present in the founding moment, the ability to reconfigure foundings urges an engagement with constitutional orders as ongoing projects. Moreover, it suggests that we look to the moments in which those projects break down and are subject to renewal as worthy of as much reflection and consideration as those of founding. Indeed, it might be that endings are as significant as foundings.

6

Under the Shadow of the Constitutional Revolution?

Revisiting Israel's Founding Moments

YAIR SAGY

I. Introduction

The dramatic events surrounding the establishment of the State of Israel in May 1948 had the unmistakable trappings of founding moments, as expounded by Ming-Sung Kuo's chapter in this volume. Israel emerged as an independent state in the midst of multinational, terrible armed conflict. Moreover, it was established following a contested colonial (Mandatory) rule. True, the exact timeframe of Israel's founding moment may be disputed. Still, it seems defendable to include within its ambit events stretching from the decision to adopt a formal constitution upon the state's foundation until it became known – already in 1950, if not sooner – that a different route would be pursued.

But the Israeli case has its complexities, certainly when considering Kou's observation that 'the founding moment of a constitutional order points to the series of historical events *that lead to the adoption of the constitution*' (emphasis added). Israel's constitutional history presents an anomaly in this respect, even compared to the two exceptions of Britain and Taiwan cited by Kuo. For, contrary to Britain, Israel *did* eventually (albeit belatedly) produce a codified constitution of sorts. Likewise, as discussed later in this book by Chien-Chi Lin, it may be said that Taiwan had had a formal constitution before it emerged as a distinct political entity. Contrarily, although it obviously took further time for it to more fully materialise, a distinct Israeli constitutional order – but no comprehensive, formal constitution – emerged only *following* the tumultuous events accompanying its establishment. Israel, it appears, had a clear founding moment, yet it did not produce a formal constitution.

To make things even more complicated, about four decades after the foundation, the Israeli 'Constitutional Revolution'[1] took place, following the adoption of two basic laws in 1992 enumerating a short list of human rights.[2] In the epoch-defining 1995 *United Mizrachi Bank* case,[3] the Supreme Court pronounced the latter two – as well as all other – basic laws the supreme law of the land. Israel, Chief Justice Barak declared, relinquished in 1992 the British constitutional tradition and finally embraced the US-style constitutional framework. To many, a circle was thus closed, however imperfectly. The founding generation's failure to draft a formal constitution (including a bill of rights) upon the state's foundation moment – even though it had promised to do so in the Declaration of the Establishment of the State of Israel[4] – was at long last rectified.

The time lag between Israel's founding moment and the emergence of its formal constitution in the 1990s raises deep questions: could a persuasive link – more than 40 years long – be drawn between the two? Had the constitutional model entrenched at the founding moment indeed been fundamentally defective? Was it still flawed in the 1990s, so that a constitutional revolution – the Revolution – was called for? The first question occupied central stage in the *United Mizrachi Bank* case. The latter two questions are a potent gravitational point in a new string of legal history of Israel. This new literature is the subject of this chapter.

The chapter examines three books in particular, all published recently in Israel (in Hebrew) and authored by three distinguished Israeli legal scholars: Nathan Brun, *Law, Passions and Politics: Judges and Lawyers Between the British Mandate and the State of Israel*;[5] Nir Kedar, *Ben-Gurion and the Constitution*;[6] and Daniel Friedmann, *Before the Revolution: Law and Politics in the Age of Innocence*.[7] Ron Harris' *The Israeli Law – The Formative Years: 1948–1977*[8] will also repeatedly figure in the chapter, although it is only a 'stepbrother' to the other three manuscripts. While its theses do not necessarily comply with the key *normative* propositions advanced in the three other books, on a *descriptive* level, it is their fellow-traveller for its analyses have clear traces of, and contribute greatly to, this literature's re-engagement with Israel's founding moment.

[1] eg, R Hirschl, *Towards Juristocracy: The Origins and Consequences of the New Constitutionalism* (Harvard University Press, 2004) 21–24; G Sapir, *Constitutional Revolution in Israel: Past Present Future* (Bar-Ilan University Press, 2010) (Hebrew); B Medina and A Rubinstein, *The Constitutional Law of The State of Israel*, 6th edn (Schocken Publishing House, 2005) 221, 225–26 (Hebrew).

[2] Basic Law: Freedom of Occupation 1994, LSI 1454 p 90 (Isr); Basic Law: Human Dignity and Liberty 1992, LSI 1391 p 150 (Isr).

[3] CA 6821/93 *United Mizrachi Bank* v *Migdal* 49 (4) PD 221 [1995] (Isr).

[4] The State of Israel Declaration of Independence 14 May 1948 (Hebrew).

[5] N Brun, *Law, Passions and Politics: Judges and Lawyers between the British Mandate and the State of Israel* (Steimatzkty, 2014) (Hebrew).

[6] N Kedar, *Ben-Gurion and the Constitution* (Kinneret, Zmora-Bitan, Dvir 2015) (Hebrew).

[7] D Friedmann, *Before the Revolution: Law and Politics in the Age of Innocence* (Miskal, 2015) (Hebrew).

[8] R Harris, *The Israeli Law – The Formative Years: 1948–1977* (Hakkibbutz Hameuchad, 2014) (Hebrew).

In critically surveying the three books, this chapter highlights common threads running through them and collages them into a distinct appraisal of Israel's founding generation that is embedded in them. The resultant collage is surprising and important. In fact, the chapter suggests that it signifies the emergence of a novel generational reassessment of Israel's founding moment and its time. On this reading, the fact that Big-C, formal constitution, was not delivered upon foundation should not be regarded as a deplorable failure, but rather as a boon and the constitutional framework of those days as a cause for admiration. The chapter will not only identify the rise of this new original historiography, but will also trace its origins. It will argue that this new appraisal of Israel's founding moment cannot be understood detachedly from the Constitutional Revolution. In fact, it is suggested that it is best understood as an unfavourable reaction to the 1990s Revolution.

One does not have to share this literature's judgement of the 1950s (or of the 1990s) to appreciate its great contributions to extant scholarship. As illustrated below, the three books – here, with Harris' forceful assistance – deepen our understanding of the 1950s in three major respects: first, they insightfully straddle the legal and political history of early statehood; second, their (re)reading of early Israeli law is particularly detailed and colourful largely because they line up an extraordinarily long list of legal and political figures as a vital part of their discussions; and, third, this new literature employs an impressive array of methodologies, ranging from personal history to empirical legal studies.

The chapter's historiographical explorations add a vital layer to this collection's analysis. Notably, it joins the insightful dialogue between Kuo and Simon Gilhooley, where they highlight the potential of founding moments to reinvigorate, but also narrow, later generations' 'democratic horizons', depending on the manners in which those generations (re)construct their past. The chapter goes in the same direction, emphasising that founding moments – or, more accurately, present reconstructions thereof – may certainly become battlegrounds where the very definition of a state's democratic nature – at present – is fought over. For, in order to say whether a particular invocation of a founding moment limits or expands democratic horizons, it should be made clear what 'democracy' means for the specific polity in question (eg, are judicial review of legislation and codified constitution vital components thereof?). This chapter illustrates that the founding moment may be relied upon for that exact purpose.

The chapter proceeds as follows. Section II will outline a standard rendition of the history of constitution-making and the constitutional tradition in Israel. Next, section III will introduce the main theses of the three books. Section IV will examine how the new literature relates to previous legal historiographies of the jurisprudence of the 1950s Supreme Court. Section V will examine the new corpus' understanding of the interface between the Mandatory era and early statehood, a topic of great relevance to our discussion, as Israel's foundation was decidedly cast, inter alia, in the shadow of the Mandatory regime. In section VI, I will offer several critical observations regarding this literature's historiography, as well as highlighting its presentist orientation and its nostalgic and revisionist approach. I will also assess its treatment of the interplay between law and politics. Section VII concludes.

II. A Brief History of Israel's Quest for a Bill of Rights

We begin with a shorthand, standard explanation of why, to this day, Israel does not have a unitary, formal, comprehensive, human rights-upholding, US-like constitution.[9]

The State of Israel was founded following three decades of British Mandatory rule over Palestine. As the Mandate drew to a close, the establishment of an independent Jewish state (alongside an Arab state) was envisaged in the United Nations General Assembly Resolution 181 of 29 November 1947.[10] Resolution 181 specifically ordained the writing of the constitutions of the two states to be composed by their respective constituent assemblies, whose elections had been also contemplated in the Resolution. The political leadership of the *Yishuv*, the organised Jewish population in Palestine, embraced the Resolution.[11] It seemed at first to follow it to the letter, at least as far as the writing of a constitution for the Jewish state was concerned. The *Yishuv*'s adherence to the roadmap drawn up in Resolution 181 for constitution-drafting was writ large in the Declaration on the Establishment of the State of Israel. The latter outlined a tight schedule for the election of a constituent assembly and the writing of a constitution. Taking another step in the same direction, the Constituent Assembly was indeed elected, albeit later than prescribed in the Declaration.[12]

It did not take long to realise that the Israeli Constituent Assembly baulked at the task of writing a constitution for the State of Israel. Soon after its inaugural convention, the Assembly made known its refusal to write a unified document comprising the constitution of the newborn state by proclaiming itself a 'regular' parliament of Israel (a 'regular' Knesset), rather than the constitutive, idiosyncratic Constituent Assembly of the State.[13] Further, in 1950, it went for a new course of action with respect to the drafting of the state's constitution. In the famous Harari Resolution of that year, it reformulated its constitutional mission.[14] Rather

[9] eg, I Zamir and A Zysblat, *Public Law in Israel* (Oxford University Press, 1996); D Barak-Erez, 'Form an Unwritten Constitution to a Written Constitution: The Israeli Challenge in American Perspective' (1995) 26 *Columbia Human Rights Law Review* 309.

[10] United Nation, General Assembly Resolution 181 (Partition Plan of Palestine) 1947.

[11] Anita Shapira, *Israel: A History* (Brandeis University Press, 2012) 155; Suzie Navot, *The Constitution of Israel: A Contextual Analysis* (Hart Publishing, 2014) 4–5.

[12] Medina and Rubinstein (n 1) 34–36.

[13] See Navot (n 11) 8–9; The Transition to the Second Knesset Act, 5713-1951, LSI 73 104 (Isr).

[14] 5th Knesset Protocol 1717, 1743; Amos Shapira, 'Judicial Review without a Constitution: The Israeli Paradox' (1983) 56 *Temple Law Quarterly* 405, 408–10.

than drawing up a unitary, comprehensive constitution, as had been initially contemplated, it chose to pursue a piecemeal process, whereby a series of 'basic laws' would be gradually enacted. Probably chastened by its failure to compose a constitution, the Resolution did not even set a timetable for the constitutional enterprise.

The First Knesset – again, originally known as the Constituent Assembly – essentially sufficed itself with adopting the Harari Resolution, failing to enact any basic law. It took the Knesset an additional eight years to actually embark on the road charted in the Harari Resolution. Only in 1958 did the Knesset adopt the first basic law – Basic Law: The Knesset. Subsequently, in a protracted progression, a total of nine basic laws were put on the books from 1958 up until 1988.[15] What united this first string of constitutional legislation was its distinctly institutional character. The nine basic laws focused on the three major branches of government and were mostly confined to these and other state institutions, such as the President of the State, and the State's General Comptroller.

How were basic law treated by the courts? Before the Revolution, Israeli constitutional jurisprudence had a clear dominant orientation: the British-Diceyan framework (or the Westminster model).[16] The fulcrum of the Diceyan orthodoxy rested on the supremacy of parliament. As parliament reigned supreme, there was no place for a formal constitution restricting its powers. Nor was there room for judicial meddling in the business of parliament. Therefore, while British courts could develop human rights (and gained great fame for so doing), they were allowed to do so only between the cracks of parliamentary legislation.[17] Likewise in Israel, where as a rule (although with a limited exception), pre-Revolution courts did certainly not pass judgment on legislative acts of the Knesset.[18] Just as important was the role taken by Israeli courts, under the dominance of the Supreme Court, in constituting a judicial bill of rights in a common law fashion.[19] Still, as part of the orthodox doctrine, there was a clear limit to the Court's frolicking with the development of an Israeli common law of human rights: legislative edicts. Faced with the acts of the Knesset, the courts had to bow and comply.[20]

[15] Basic Law: The Knesset 1958, LSI 244 69 (Isr); Basic law: The Government 1968, LSI 540 226 (Isr); Basic Law: The President of The State 1969, LSI 428 116 (Isr); Basic Law: Israel Lands 1960, LSI 312 56 (Isr); Basic Law: The State Economy 1975, LSI 777 206 (Isr); Basic Law: The Military 1976, LSI 806 154 (Isr); Basic Law: Jerusalem, The Capital of Israel 1980, LSI 980 186 (Isr); Basic Law: The Judiciary 1984, LSI 1110 78 (Isr).

[16] S Aharonson, 'Constitution to Israel: David Ben Gurion British Model' (1998) 2 *Politics* 9 (Hebrew); Z Segal, 'A Constitution without a Constitution: The Israeli Experience and the American Impact' (1992) 21 *Capital University Law Review* 1.

[17] M Bevir, 'The Westminster Model, Governance and Judicial Reform' (2008) 61 *Parliamentary Affairs* 559; D Lino, 'Albert Venn Dicey and the Constitutional Theory of Empire' (2016) 36 *OJLS* 751.

[18] JM Albert, 'Constitutional Adjudication without a Constitution: The Case of Israel' (1969) 82 *Harvard Law Review* 1245; E Likhovski, 'The Courts and the Legislative Supremacy of the Knesset' (1968) 3 *Israel Law Review* 345.

[19] MB Nimmer, 'The Uses of Judicial Review in Israel's Quest for a Constitution' (1970) 70 *Columbia Law Review* 1217.

[20] eg, HCJ 188/63 *Bezul v The Minister of Home Affairs* 19(1) PD 337 [1965] (Isr).

Yet, also in this context, Israel had its complexities, for Israeli parliaments occasionally challenged Dicey. First, as noted, several Knessets adopted a series of 'basic laws', thus seemingly introducing a pyramidal structure of legal norms in which some laws were normatively superior to other, ordinary forms of legislation. However, it must be noted at once that, prior to the Constitutional Revolution, the Court was adamant that as a rule, basic laws were just like any other laws.[21] There was an exception to that rule, which concerned the next, second Knesset's contra-Dicey step. Occasionally, the Knesset included entrenched provisions in basic laws, whose contravention required the support of a special majority of Knesset Members.[22] In so doing, the Knesset appeared to disrupt the Diceyan model's article of faith that the plenary power of the current parliament could not be checked – surely, not by courts, and not even by pervious parliaments. However, in the 1969 landmark case of *Bergman v Minister of Finance*, the Supreme Court ruled that formally entrenched provisions *would* be biding upon later Knessets, as long as the Knesset decided to leave them in place.[23]

The resultant constitutional framework, going both with and against the grain of Dicey, was convoluted. More troubling to many, before and after *Bergman*, was the lingering conviction that the Israeli constitutional framework, which to a large extent stayed in the rut of its founding moment, was fundamentally deficient. Indeed, laments for Israel's lack of a comprehensive (formal) constitution also persisted as the list of ('institutional') basic laws grew longer. Notably, the absence of two items from the unfolding list was steadfastly and increasingly noted along the way: one dealing with fundamental human rights, and the other laying out the procedure for the adoption and amendment of basic laws, which were – and are – enacted just like any other legislation, as well as setting the terms for judicial review of legislation based on them.[24] However, this perception of the founding moment's legacy and its constitutional offspring was never accepted across the board. Over the years, a duo of opposing camps locked horns, disputing the founding generation's constitutional legacy and correspondingly the preferable constitutional model to be pursued by Israelis.

According to the first camp, the 1950s certainly left a mark of Cain on Israeli constitutionalism.[25] And, to many, Israel's exceptionalism in the field of constitutional law, throughout the bulk of its history, served as a painful reminder of that mark.[26] Hence, according to members of the Israeli pro-Constitution

[21] eg, HCJ 148/73 *Kniel v The Minister of Justice* 27(1) PD 794 [1973] (Isr).

[22] See especially Basic Law: The Knesset (n 15) §§ 4, 45, 46.

[23] HCJ 98/69 *Bergman v The Minister of Treasury* 23(1) PD 693 [1969] (Isr).

[24] M Shamgar, 'On the Written Constitution' (1974) 9 *Israel Law Review* 467.

[25] eg, M Ben-Porat, 'Symposium: An Israeli Constitutions Whether and When' (1986) 11 *Tel-Aviv University Law Review* 19 (Hebrew); A Shapira, 'Why Israel Has No Constitution, But Should and Likely Will, Have One' (1992–93) 37 *St Louis Law Review* 283.

[26] M Tushnet, 'Constitution' in Michel Rosenfeld and Andras Sajo (eds), *Comparative Constitutional Law* (Oxford University Press, 2012) 221.

camp, even *if* the founding generation of Israelis had good reasons to disown its constitutional undertaking, due to security and economic considerations, they had still condemned Israelis to live in a profoundly flawed legal system.[27] Members of the latter camp were obviously emboldened by the fact that over time, Dicey was increasingly challenged not only in Israel, of course. Most tellingly, even its motherland cast aside its shibboleth and introduced its version of judicial review of legislation with the closing of the twentieth century, thus finally succumbing to the global, post-Second World War trend of adopting US-style constitutionalism.[28]

Still, not all Israelis were willing to embrace the US constitutional tradition, not even in the wake of Britain's about-face. Notably, Chief Justice Moshe Landau remained a stanch supporter of the British model throughout.[29] Landau persisted in his opposition even as additional ('institutional') basic laws were enacted and as the terms of the debate narrowed down, centring on the desirability of providing the state with a formal bill of rights to be judicially guarded.[30] Landau (who retired from the bench in 1982) kept his running quarrel with the Americanised version of constitutionalism before and after the Israeli Constitutional Revolution. He and others raised the spectre of a politicised judiciary should it be drawn into polemics concerning controversial matters of principle and personal faith.[31] According to this approach, human rights legislation is fraught with such divisive, toxic issues. Therefore, judicial review of a piece of legislation arguably infringing on human rights would readily implicate courts in political strife. The costs of importing such a practice to Israel – above all, in terms of the judiciary's popular standing and its constitutional independence – might be devastating. In any event, it was also argued, the protection offered by Israeli courts to human rights, under the orthodox legal framework, was commendable.[32]

United Mizrachi Bank evidently stands for a contrary approach. It made it abundantly clear that, by the 1990s, the Court unabashedly joined those calling for placing constitutional checks on the Knesset and a departure from the British orthodoxy.[33] It seems that with the Court's new credo came a greater willingness

[27] eg, Y Dinstein, 'Human Rights in Israel' (1973) *Tel-Aviv University Law Review* 619 (Hebrew); Amnon Rubinstein, 'Israel's Partial Constitution: The Basic Laws' in Mitchell G Bard and David Nachmias (eds), *Israel Studies: An Anthology* (American-Israeli Cooperative Enterprise, 2012).

[28] Tushnet (n 26) 221; P Leyland, *The Constitution of the United Kingdom: A Contextual Analysis* (Hart Publishing, 2012) 192–96.

[29] M Landau, 'The Constitution as the Supreme Law of the State?' (1971) 28 *Israel Bar Law Review* 30 (Hebrew).

[30] A Shapira and B Bracha, 'The Constitutional Status of Individual Freedoms' (1972) 2 *Tel-Aviv University Law Review* 20 (Hebrew).

[31] M Landau, 'The Supreme Court as a Constitution Maker for Israel' (1996) 3 *Haifa University Law Review* 697 (Hebrew).

[32] M Elon, 'Basic Laws: Methods of Enactment and Interpretation Form Where to and Where' (1995) 12 *Bar-Ilan University Law Review* 253, 256–57 (Hebrew).

[33] But see R Weil, '*United Mizrahi Bank*'s Twentieth Anniversary: On the Piquant Story of the Hybrid Israeli Constitution' (2016) 38 *Tel-Aviv University Law Review* 510 (Hebrew).

on its part to publicly depict the pre-revolutionary age as flawed.[34] To the justices and scholars subscribing to this vision of the 1950s, the dramatic events of 1992–95 were long overdue. Only once the Revolution took place were key fundamentals of a true liberal-democratic constitutional order finally installed on Israeli soil. Significantly, under such a progressive rendition of the history of Israel constitutional law, the old Court's efforts to put in place the essentials of a liberal-democratic human rights regime – commendable as they were – could not have been anything other than a stepping stone – essential as it was – towards a more complete constitutional arrangement.[35] Finally, on this understanding, only with the Revolution could the Court, unencumbered by Dicey's orthodoxy, finally lend a hand where the old Court could not.[36]

III. Overview of the New Literature

This section introduces the three books and indicates their contribution to our understanding of the processes and debates outlined in the previous section. The following sketches surely do not do justice to the books. They will not encompass their richness, but merely point to their relevance to the chapter's overall theses. Following a review of the books, I will introduce themes running through them and the overall perception of the 1950s – essentially, Israel's founding decade – that emerges from bringing them together.

A. The Books

Law, Passions and Politics was published in 2014 following Nathan Brun's earlier tome (of 2008) dedicated to the history of the judiciary in the territory known as 'Palestine'.[37] The first book canvassed the Ottoman judiciary in the land and related the transition from Ottoman-run to British-run legal system at the end of the First World War. Brun's latest manuscript, which occupies us here, explores a chain of episodes, some (in)famous, others thus-far unknown, concerning courts and judges in the late Mandate and early statehood eras. For the most part, judges are the focal points of the book. It presents a gallery of Mandatory and Israeli judges. The different chapters describe various judges' personal background and ideological predilections before and after nomination, difficulties they encountered as

[34] Y Sagy, 'A Case That Made History: A Historiographical Inquiry into *The United Mizrahi* Case' (2018) 19 *Haifa University Law Review* 325 (Hebrew).

[35] ibid.

[36] Medina and Rubinstein (n 1) 54–57, 255–59; Aharon Barak, 'The Rule of Law and the Supremacy of the Constitution' (2000) 5 *Haifa University Law Review* 375, 377–78, 382–83 (Hebrew).

[37] N Brun, *Judges and Jurists in Erez-Israel: Between Constantinople and Jerusalem 1900–1930* (Hebrew University Magness Press, 2008) (Hebrew).

their appointment to judicial positions (as judges, justices or chiefs of courts) was at issue, and noteworthy cases they handled. It is clearly to Brun's credit that he showcases myriad legal players; not only Justices but also other judges, as well as attorneys and their clients, occupy central stage in the book's chapters.

Nir Kedar's aspiration in writing *Ben-Gurion and the Constitution*, which revolves around the founding father and the first Prime Minister of Israel, is quite straightforward. Kedar writes against the pervasive conception that Ben-Gurion shunned – thus effectively nipping in the bud – the campaign to write a formal constitution for Israel for ephemeral, even small-time political considerations. There are two interlocking prongs to Kedar's effort to rationalise the Ben-Gurion position. First, Ben-Gurion's campaign against the vogue of constitution-making was based on solid, principled and justifiable arguments. Second, Ben-Gurion did indeed rebuke the drive toward a Big-C Constitution, but he was just as relentless in putting in place a lasting Small-C Israeli (Jewish) liberal-democratic constitution. Kedar sympathetically portrays Ben-Gurion as well as several questionable actions taken by him as the reverberations of a deep commitment to liberal democracy.

Taken together, the two prongs assert that Ben-Gurion was driven by an overarching, coherent vision: Israel must be founded on established liberal-democratic principles (such as the rule of law and general free elections), yet these principles would not gain traction among the public by codifying them in a written constitution. Rather, they would have to be won, by each generation anew, through the dynamic, on-the-ground practice of state organs and the citizenry pursuing such principles. Kedar makes the case that Ben-Gurion got it right in the constitutional debate of early statehood. According to Kedar, it simply did not make sense to dedicate the required time and energy and face the political turmoil involved in drafting a constitution for the embattled state.[38]

In an impressive feat, Daniel Friedmann – a former Minister of Justice and an eminent legal scholar – has recently published two tomes covering the past five centuries(!) in the history of the territory stretching to the west of the Jordan River: first came *The Purse and the Sword: The Trials of the Israeli Legal Revolution* (2013),[39] which spans the period from the late 1970s to the near present, and then *Before the Revolution*, which is dedicated to the lengthy period from the fifteenth century to the mid-twentieth century. The two relate momentous events that took place during Ottoman, Mandatory and Israeli rule over that piece of land, although Friedmann's two-volume enterprise devotes much more attention to post-Israeli independence events than to pre-independence affairs.

As indicated in the title of the second book, which is more pertinent to the present discussion, there are two focal points to Friedmann's discussions: the legal

[38] See also O Rozin, 'Forming a Collective Identity: The Debate over the Proposed Constitution, 1948–1950' (2007) 26 *Journal of Israeli History* 251.

[39] D Friedmann, *The Purse and the Sword: The Trials of the Israeli Legal Revolution* (Miskal, 2013) (Hebrew). An English translation of a revised version of this book was published by Oxford University Press in 2016.

sphere and the political sphere. Around the first focal point, Friedmann canvasses major developments in the law of the land during the relevant eras, whether they took the form of legislation, the constitution of novel legal institutions or epoch-defining litigation and courts' rulings. The second focal point revolves in the main around policies and ideologies advanced by dominant (mostly Jewish) political organisations, the Knesset and, even more so, Israeli governments. Friedmann's scathing rebuke of the new, post-1970s Court cuts across the analyses in both books. His theses will resurface time and again in the ensuing discussion.

B. Connecting the Dots

Taking a bird's-eye view over the historiography encapsulated in the three manuscripts, an overarching theme emerges: a reassessment of the Israeli-Diceyan constitutional model. Specifically, in revisiting the 1950s, the books buttress both sides of the Diceyan model as applied in the Israeli context: they applaud both the absence of a formal constitution and the 'old' Court's protection of human rights in the young state. Intertwined in these two counter-arguments is the proposition that constitution-making is hardly a cost-free endeavour. It is far from clear that the benefits that might have resulted from the adoption of a constitution in fledgling Israel would have outweighed the costs incurred in the process by Israeli society and the courts of that time.[40]

Further, it appears that, according to the account provided in this literature, Israeli constitutional law of the 1950s was in quite good shape. An impressive line of judges and justices, the political elite of the day, and a dedicated state apparatus made sure that nascent Israel would have a decent, well-functioning legal system; moreover, they made sure that human rights would be protected in Israel. Miraculously, all this was done in the face of enormous security, economic and social challenges that beset the young state.

As part of this reassessment of the pre- and post-Constitutional Revolution eras, the books revisit the 1950s judiciary and especially the Supreme Court – their composition, jurisprudence and interplay with the other branches of government. In so doing, they implicitly and even explicitly draw comparisons with the latter-day Court. All in all, the authors describe the courts of the 1950s as highly competent, entirely respected, reasonably efficient, dutifully modest and appropriately deferential to the other branches of government. In fact, several sections in their analyses suggest that the courts of the 1950s better served their callings – the protection of human rights included – than do contemporary courts.[41]

Friedmann in particular suggests that the old Court fared better than the new Court because the former did its best to distance itself from ideologically charged

[40] Kedar (n 6) 225–27.

[41] Friedmann (n 7) 486–87, 506; Friedmann (n 39) 595.

issues and plain politics, and even more so from any engagement with the divisive business of legislation.[42] Friedmann harkens back to the Landau-Dicey approach and embraces Landau in more than one way. First, on a personal level, according to Friedmann, 'in many respects Landau was an ideal judge'.[43] Friedmann commends in particular the fact that Landau's judgmanship was 'totally objective, as it was founded on legal principles and detached from personal and political views'.[44] Also laudable, to Friedmann, was Landau's unwavering – allegedly, as opposed to the new Court's faltering – commitment to the preservation of the State of Israel and a robust Zionist vision thereof.[45] Likewise, Landau's deference to the government's security considerations, and his general conservatism and penchant for judicial restraint are explicitly and favourably contrasted by Friedmann with the activism of the new Court.[46] Finally, not only does Landau's judicial ideology fare better in Friedmann's account, but so too does his style of judging, especially Landau's (and his brethren's) clear tendency of writing short opinions.[47] Clearly, Friedmann wholeheartedly sides with Landau in the debate surrounding the Constitutional Revolution. Echoing familiar arguments put against the practice of judicial review of legislation, Friedmann too holds that it is democratically undefendable, as it subverts the will of the people and is injurious to the courts, which are thereby drawn into the political arena.[48]

Now, taking a panoramic view over the three books, I wish to argue that, taken together, they construct the following argument regarding 1950s Israeli constitutionalism:

(a) *since* – as demonstrated mainly by Friedmann and Brun – *even without a formal constitution, human rights were generally preserved in Israel during early statehood thanks to the robust, yet balanced, efforts of the courts*; and
(b) *since* – as forcefully argued by Friedmann – *courts should not be implicated in political processes typifying legislation*;[49] and
(c) *since* – as illustrated by Kedar – *the writing of a constitution would have been a costly, maybe even a dangerous, enterprise*;

therefore, the founding generation set in place the right constitutional framework for that time and age – and maybe even for our age.

[42] Friedmann (n 7) 319, 347, 455–58, 523. See also Brun (n 5) 531.
[43] Friedmann (n 7) 457.
[44] ibid. See also Brun (n 5) 420–40.
[45] ibid 333–34; M Landau, 'On Zionism in Our Days' in Aharon Barak (ed), *The Shamgar Book: A Life Story* (Israel Bar Press, 2003) (Hebrew).
[46] Friedmann (n 7) 424–25, 459, 495.
[47] ibid 250, 473.
[48] Friedmann (n 7) 209, 470–74, 495–502, 525–26, 595; Friedmann (n 39) 559–69, 582–84; D Friedmann, 'Does Israel Have a Constitution and Who Wrote it?' (2012) 14 *IDC Law Review* 117 (Hebrew). It goes beyond the purvey of this article to assess these arguments.
[49] Friedmann (n 7) 470–74, 495–502, 525–26; Friedmann (n 39) 114–15, 559–69.

No doubt, especially in light of the discussion in the previous section, this argument is plainly critical of the Constitutional Revolution and thus of the revolutionary Court that made it a reality.

IV. The Old and New Courts: Three Generations of Scholarship

As we have just seen, according to Friedmann, the old Court – Landau's Court – was a better court than the new Court, pure and simple, and the former also proceeded on a sounder constitutional theory. This section positions this estimation within the general sweep of the Court's historiography. It argues that the new literature signals the dawn of a new, third approach in the historiography of the 1950s Court, which follows a first generation's hagiography of the Court as well as a second generation's more critical approach that emerged around the late 1980s. In short, this third generation regards with favour the Court's performance during the 1950s, thus rekindling the hagiographical tradition. The following discussion will chart the course of this triad of generations.

Over the years, several characterisations of the Court's jurisprudence during the formative 1950s were put forward. As insightfully suggested by Harris, the various characterisations could be organised along three axes: ideological (potentially relevant options include the socialist, collectivist-nationalist and individualist categorisations); institutional (namely, how deferential was the Court to the other branches of government? Was it conservative or activist in this respect?); and its style of decision-making (in Menachem Mautner's influential description, was it 'formalistic' or 'value-laden'?).[50] The resultant matrix is complex. Consequently – and this is one of Harris' fine emphases – the general tenor of that jurisprudence escapes bright-line characterisations. There are simply sufficient major cases, in which the three axes point to contrary orientations, to ruffle the now-familiar collectivist, conservative and formalistic portrayal of the 1950s.

The new literature reminds us that beneath the various attempts to neatly depict the 1950s Court lies a seemingly simple question – namely, to what extent was the Court in fact the bastion of human rights in Israel of the 1950s? For years, justices – on and off the bench – prided themselves in championing the cause of human rights. Numerous scholars followed suit, highlighting the Court's achievements against a backdrop of the immense challenges faced by the fledgling state, the lingering legacy of Mandatory legislation, which predominated post-independence Israeli law, the absence of a formal constitution, as well as the harsh ideological

[50] Harris (n 8) 73–75; M Mauntner, *The Decline of Formalism and the Rise of Values in Israeli Law* (Ma'agalay Da'at Publishing House, 1993) (Hebrew).

environment surrounding the Court of early statehood.[51] This environment was, or so the story went, collectivist and thus averse to human rights that smacked of liberal individualism.

As a general matter, as far as the Court's history was concerned, for decades the literature treated it with much favour. The important 1980 book of (future Justice) Elyakim Rubinstein on the history of the Court[52] was a significant high point of that generous approach, which subsequently almost petered out. Pnina Lahav, Yoram Shachar, Menachem Mautner and others played a decisive role in ushering in a new generation of scholarship, stirring the Court's historiography to more balanced and critical grounds.[53] Thus, for example, Lahav opines that the 1950s Court's record 'was far from uniform'. She writes that: 'In a number of cases, [it] allowed the suppression of the rights … because of national security considerations applied by the executive branch.'[54] Several scholars followed suit, thus supplementing the extant hagiography with novel and rich historiography.[55] Especially following Mautner, it became commonplace to generally regard the 1950s Court as formalistic and its days as the days of judicial restraint.[56]

It is therefore only to be expected that, in revisiting the 1950s jurisprudence, the new literature critically explores the breadth of public law issues the Court handled throughout its history. 'Standing' and 'justiciability' are two particularly relevant legal categories here, and it is commonly accepted that the more expansive the Court's interpretations thereof is, the wider the range of public law disputes engaged with by the Court is. Also undisputed is the fact that the Shamgar and Barak Courts (of 1983–95 and 1995–2006, respectively) adopted a sprawling approach on both counts.[57]

The transformation of standing and justiciability doctrine in Israeli law during the 1980s met with some opposition among justices and scholars,[58] yet this opposition did not derail it. Consequently, an increasing number of cases, which had

[51] A Maoz, 'Defending Civil Liberties without a Constitution: The Israeli Experience' (1988) 16 *Melbourne University Law Review* 815.

[52] E Rubinstein, *Judges of the Land* (Schocken, 1981) (Hebrew).

[53] eg, Pnina Lahav, *Judgment in Jerusalem: Chief Justice Simon Agranat and the Zionist Century* (University of California Press, 1997); Y Shachar, 'The History of the Supreme Court' (2003) 19 *Bar-Ilan University Law Review* 397 (Hebrew).

[54] P Lahav, 'Rights and Democracy: The Court's Performance' in E Spirnzak and L Diamond (eds), *Israeli Democracy Under Stress* (Lynn Reinner, 1993) 125, 138.

[55] eg, G Forman and A Kedar, 'From Arab Land to Israel Lands: The Legal Dispossession of the Palestinians Displaced by Israel in the Wake of 1948' (2004) 22 *Environment and Planning D: Society and Space* 809; I Saban, 'Theorising and Tracing the Legal Dimensions of a Control Framework: Law and the Arab-Palestinian Minority in Israel's First Three Decades (1948–1978)' (2011) *Emory International Law Review* 29.

[56] M Mauntner, *Law and Culture in Israel* (Oxford University Press, 2011). *cf* D Friedmann, 'Formalism and Values: Legal Certainty and Judicial Activism' (2007) 11 *College of Management Law Review* 9 (Hebrew).

[57] HCJ 910/86 *Ressler v Minister of Defense* 42(2) PD 441 [1988] (Isr).

[58] R Gavison, M Kremnitzer and Y Dotan, *Judicial Activism in the Israeli High Court of Justice* (Hebrew University Magness Press, 2000) (Hebrew).

been traditionally barred from the Court due to their 'political' nature, were now regularly dealt with by the Court. While Friedmann's rhetoric is particularly sharp in this case, he is certainly not alone in observing that during the past generation, most, if not all, political controversies – controversies concerning political parties, intra-coalition rifts, appointments of high-ranking governmental officials etc – found their way to, and subsequently were reviewed by, the Court.[59]

Friedmann maintains in this context that, contrary to the new Court, the founding Court kept to its own. It was much more careful not to overstep its 'proper' authority, circumspectly shunning away from political, grand public-policy issues. When it was forced into a political affair, the former Court only reluctantly entered the fray – in stark contrast to the Court of the later generation, which revelled in dealing with such issues.[60]

This line of attack censures the latter Court for patronising over the old-fashioned, 'simple' adjudication – adjudication done between the cracks of legislation – and for thinking it is capable of resolving complicated public policy issues. It is actually argued that the Court invests in policy-making *at the expense* of good old adjudication, since policy-making detracts from the Court's limited resources.[61] These accusations amount to faulting the new Court with damaging the old Court's Herculean undertaking of putting in place and entrenching human rights in the young and vulnerable State of Israel.

Furthermore, according to its detractors, the new Court's appetite for what they regard as essentially political controversies is damaging to the Court's institutional legitimacy among Israelis. An equation is drawn between the degree to which the Court has minded its own business and its 'approval rating', so to speak.[62] Under this approach, the old Court, although immersed in rights-averse environment, was widely respected *because* it kept to itself. In a mirror image, the new Court faces frontal opposition from large segments of the Israeli population *because* it routinely meddles in daily politics. Thus viewed, as Landau had foreseen, in the final analysis, the new Court's activist stance has made it less effective in performing its duties – the duties it has taken upon itself to tend to under the banner of activism (above all, political disputes), but also and more damagingly, its traditional judicial duties.

In light of all of the above, it may come as no surprise that one current in the new literature goes so far as to claim that the old Court was more effective than the new Court in actually promoting human rights in Israel.[63] Although no empirical findings are provided in support of such claims, they are certainly not insignificant. They evidence how sceptical the new literature is of the new Court's

[59] Friedmann (n 7) 236, 346–47, 396, 408, 443, 495–502, 526; Friedmann (n 39) 445–59. See also Harris (n 8) ch 6.

[60] Friedmann (n 7) 455–58, 473–74; Friedmann (n 39) 343–47.

[61] Friedmann (n 7) 526; Friedmann (n 39) 343, 347.

[62] Friedmann (n 39) 344–48. See also Brun (n 5) 531.

[63] See also, eg, J Segev, 'Rights Talk after the Constitutional Revolution: Did the Constitutional Revolution Improve the Protection of Rights in Israel?' (2013) 17 *IDC Law Review* 235 (Hebrew).

overall performance. This scepticism is particularly poignant when it comes to the Court's foremost project of advancing a constitutional revolution in the cause of safeguarding human rights in Israel.

To conclude, the recent wave of denouncing the new Court carries with it a revived adulation of the older Court, in the vein of the literature of the Elyakim Rubenstein generation. Thus, the Court of the 1950s become today a benchmark against which the new Court may be attacked for various reasons: for its activism, alleged arrogance, style of reasoning, missing the mark on human rights protection, and even justices' persona and professional mien. However observers attack the new, and from whatever angle, they universally give the impression that the old Court was a superb – nay, a superior – court of law.

V. The Mandate's Legacy

The Jewish population in the young State of Israel was generally highly hostile to the British Mandatory regime. Simply put, the British colonial rulers were seen as oppressors.[64] This unfavourable impression of the Mandate epoch found its way into Israeli case law, as justices had the occasion to reflect on the age preceding the establishment of the sovereign State of Israel or, indeed, on the auspicious event of its very foundation.[65]

With all their repugnance for the Mandatory rulers, Israeli (Jewish) jurists could not have denied the fact that upon independence – and for an extended period thereafter – the Israeli legal system was in many respects a direct extension of the Mandatory legal system. Almost all sources of law that had been valid on the eve of the British parting of Palestine remained in place in the sovereign state.[66]

At the same time, while the contribution of the Mandate to the Israeli legal system could not be denied, the degree to which the latter lived, for decades following independence, in the shadow of the former could be toned down. As a general matter, it seems that for a long while, Israeli judges and legal scholars were inclined to downplay the continuities between pre- and post-independence periods, arguing for a chasm lying between the colonial and the sovereign entities.[67]

The new literature pushes in the other direction. It is not the first to highlight continuities stretching from the Mandatory to the Israeli legal system, even in the area of human rights, which had traditionally been regarded as antithetical to the colonial-Mandatory legal framework.[68] Still, the new literature's espousal of

[64] C Shenhav, *The British Mandate A Shattered Dream* (Am Oved Publishers, 2007) 48–59 (Hebrew).

[65] D Barak-Erez, 'And Thou Shalt Tell Thy Son: History and Memory in the Court' (2002) 26 *Tel-Aviv University Law Review* 773 (Hebrew).

[66] eg, Navot (n 11) 57.

[67] A Barak, 'Fifty Years of Justice in Israel' (2001) 1 *Eli-Mishpat* 9 (Hebrew).

[68] A Likhovski, 'Between Mandate and State: Re-thinking the Periodization of Israeli Legal History' (1998) 19 *Journal of Israeli History* 39.

the Mandate-Israel continuity thesis is surprising. After all, this thesis is mainly identified with critical legal historiography. The orthodoxy in this case too adulates the founding Israeli Court. Revealing how indebted embryonic Israeli law was to the Mandate seemed to detract, as it were, from the achievements of the Israeli founders.

It is thus interesting that a few chapters in the new literature argue for quite a strong version of the continuity thesis. The root of the argument is that both Mandatory and Israeli courts share the most fundamental, most basic feature: they were both run by human beings who, as all human beings – British or Israelis – were naturally driven by similar human sentiments and desires. To Brun, who epitomises this approach, the life of law is cast in the shape of the particular life of the particular law officer. On his approach, both in Palestine and Israel, judges ruled in accordance with their personal conviction. Before we proceed, it should be noted that one implication of this approach is self-evident: the new Court's jurisprudence and the Constitutional Revolution must be of its very own doing.

VI. Critical Assessment

Before concluding, I wish to make a few general observations on this literature's historiography and the exchange between law and politics.

The new literature as a whole challenges a progressive narrative of Israeli law that, as noted, was advanced by the Court and others as part of an effort to legitimise the Constitutional Revolution. This narrative charted the trajectory of Israeli constitutionalism as moving from the rights-denying Mandate to the rights-upholding Court cases of the early statehood era, culminating with the rights constitutionalisation of the 1990s. Contrarily, the novel literature signals an emerging revisionist historiography of Israel's founding moment. It is revisionist as it questions the concept that the 1950s was a *lost* constitutional moment. After all, it is now maintained, the 1950s laid the foundations for a working democracy, sustained by a state apparatus respectful of the rule of law and supported by a competent and effective judiciary. Viewed through the prism of this scholarship, it appears that the 1950s encapsulated a *realised* constitutional moment, even though – or perhaps because – they had not produced a formal constitutional document.

But isn't the latter perception overly nostalgic and exaggeratedly tainted by present concerns? After all, the books reconsider the country's founding moment of the 1950s in the wake of the 1990s Constitutional Revolution. It may come as no surprise, then, that this literature has a clear presentist orientation.[69]

[69] This is especially conspicuous in the case of the Friedmann project, as indicated even by the sequence in which the two works were published: the second volume, focusing on the Supreme Court's jurisprudence from the 1970s to the present, was published prior to the second volume (ie, *Before the Revolution*), which covers earlier epochs.

As we have seen, its analyses attest to a discomfort with the role assigned to the courts – by the Court – in the post-revolutionary constitutional configuration and/or with the heated – and to the authors, unnecessary and unconstructive – debate within Israeli polity which was unleashed by the Revolution.[70] Consequently, whether it openly acknowledged this or not, it may be characterised as post-Revolution afterthoughts – maybe even second thoughts – on the post- and pre-Revolution times in Israel.

While a certain amount of presentism is unavoidable in the writing of history,[71] it may still be questioned whether the books' assessment of the 1950s is not overly skewed by their unfavourable assessment of the Constitutional Revolution. Specifically, it seems that part of their portrayal of Israeli law of the 1950s is excessively charitable. Notably, this scholarship appears to downplay patent instances of human rights violations in the nascent Israel, especially with respect to the Arab minority, which was placed under martial law well into the 1960s.[72] Moreover, with respect to Friedmann's manuscript in particular, I wonder whether its nostalgic tenor allows for a truly balanced appraisal of the 1950s in general, and the 1950s Court's jurisprudence and disposition in particular, especially considering the all-powerful executive branch of the time.[73]

At the same time, this literature should be commended for advancing our grasp of Israeli law. It broadens our perception of it in more than one way. First, as I have noted especially apropos Brun's manuscript, it persuasively makes the case that a longer-than-usual list of players – justices and Ministers of Justice but also lower-court judges, law clerks, politicians, court administrators, Ministry of Justice officials, parties to litigation[74] and so on – should be incorporated into a portrayal of the (1950s) Israeli law in action. This emphasis surely adds important layers to the existing literature. In addition, this literature, with the vital companion of Harris, makes great strides in deploying an exciting selection of historical methodologies.[75]

Another contribution of this literature lies in its engagement with politics.[76] To begin with, a running theme throughout the books is the conception that law has come to occupy exceedingly more volume in Israeli polity throughout the decades, and the contrast between the 1950s and the 1980s and 1990s is said to be striking.[77] More generally, this group of books openly entertains the

[70] Kedar (n 6) 225–27.

[71] DH Fisher, *Historian Fallacies: Toward a Logic of Historical Thought* (Harper Perennial, 1970) 135–37; *cf* L Fendler, 'The Upside of Presentism' (2008) 44 *Pedagogica Historica* 677.

[72] Shapira (n 11) 196–98. See, eg, Saban (n 55); Forman and Kedar (n 55).

[73] eg, B Kimerling, 'Legislation and Jurisdiction in an Immigrant-Settler Society' (2000) 16 *Bar Ilan University Law Review* 18 (Hebrew).

[74] See also Harris (n 8) ch 4.

[75] See Orit Rozin, 'Israeli Legal History: A Methodological Analysis' (2018) 168 *Cathedra* 155 (Hebrew).

[76] Indeed, particularly to Friedmann, the category of the 'political' consists mainly, if not solely, of those issues that occupy parliamentary parties. This view, however, relies on a very narrow concept of 'politics'. *cf*, eg, MJ Horwitz, 'The Conservative Tradition in the Writing of American Legal History' (1973) 17 *American Journal of Legal History* 275.

[77] See also Harris (n 8) ch 6.

conception that ideological rifts, personal convictions and plain politics shape the law to a considerable extent. Their analyses demonstrate how such 'non-legal' forces bore on law-making in the young State of Israel and even on courts' decisions. This in itself is not new in the existing Israeli legal history.[78] Rather, the novelty lies in the degree to which this literature makes politics and *political figures* an integral part of Israeli *legal* history, thus further bridging the gap between the legal and political histories of Israel.

It seems fair to say that thus far, the Israeli legal history gave the impression that it was first and foremost a series of jurists who gave shape, before and after independence, to Israeli law. Traditionally, the first Israeli Justices and high-ranking legal officials in the Ministry of Justice were quite exclusively designated as the founding fathers of Israel's legal system, and their decisions and policies direct that historiography. The new literature supplements the extant legal history by bringing to the fore several legal and political protagonists, whose role as law-makers – as personas that had a role in the design of Israel law – was hardly noted in that historiography. First among them is Ben-Gurion, whose influence on Israeli law is slowly becoming more fully acknowledged in the literature. The advent of a Ben-Gurion revival in the legal-history literature is important for it thickens, and more fully integrates between, the Ben-Gurion and the general sweep of political-social-cultural Israeli historiographies, on the one hand, and the legal history of early statehood, on the other.

Furthermore, the literature under review not only incorporates politics into law but also law into politics. For it could certainly also be read as revealing how intertwined law-making, broadly defined, was with politics-making, just as broadly defined. Thus, notably, Kedar's is a narrative about Ben-Gurion, the founding father of Israel, who must also be credited as a founding brother of the Israeli legal system. Namely, in assessing Ben-Gurion's overall achievements, failures and vision, his actions and views with respect to legal issues must be made part of the analysis and must be evaluated together with closely related reforms he sought to advance. Kedar's study does exactly that, as he examines Ben-Gurion's standing on the constitution dilemma and the re-establishment of the Israeli judiciary alongside other reforms he advanced.

However, there are problematic sides to the literature's bridging the politics-law divide. At times, it seems that its treatment of politics is somewhat idealistic, as if only lofty principles – as opposed to tit-for-tat or even 'petty' personal motives – drive it. For example, Kedar leaves little room to such motives in accounting for Ben-Gurion's actions. On the other hand, Brun seems to go to the other extreme, giving the impression that politics and public policy is solely about personal and ideological issues, and has also certainly been so during Mandatory times

[78] See, eg, A Shapira, 'The Supreme Court Self-Restraint and Ensuring Civil Rights' (1973) 3 *Tel-Aviv University Law Review* 640 (Hebrew); P Lahav, 'The Supreme Court of Israel: Formative Years' (1989) 14 *Tel-Aviv University Law Review* 479 (Hebrew).

and the 1950s. Yet, this latter perception does not account for the structural dimensions in politics (and law): procedures, practices and constitutional conventions (which had been so dear to Dicey). As new institutionalism taught us, such structures may constrain and enable, channel and obstruct political – and legal – actions. Indeed, new institutionalism appears to offer a middle ground between Kedar's vision of politics on the one hand and Brun's on the other. I therefore believe that the 1950s legal historiography may substantially benefit from consulting new institutionalist historiography.[79]

VII. Conclusion

It is only natural that an event of the magnitude of the Constitutional Revolution will have an effect on the future of Israeli law. Even more remarkably, as this chapter demonstrates, the Revolution may even have an effect on its *history*. Having reviewed a recent body of literature studying law and politics in 1950s Israel, this chapter has argued that it heralds a new approach to the legal historiography of that foundational era. It has illustrated that this literature is bi-focal, having one eye on the Israel's founding moment and the other on its Constitutional Revolution and the controversy surrounding it. Bluntly put, the literature takes the 1950s' side *against* that of the 1990s. It favours the constitutional framework and the Court's jurisprudence of the former over those of the latter. The new literature's grasp of the 1950s legal legacy is undoubtedly rich and perceptive. Nevertheless, as illustrated in this chapter, one may wonder whether its depiction of that eventful era is not overly generous and forgiving.

[79] *cf* ED Mazo, ch 7 in this volume; and see also Y Sagy, 'The Missing Link: Legal Historical Institutionalism & the Israeli High Court of Justice' (2015) 31 *Arizona Journal of International & Comparative Law* 1.

7

Path-Dependency in Soviet and Russian Constitution-Making

EUGENE D MAZO*

I. Introduction

The world witnessed an enormous new wave of constitution-making take place during the 1990s. Just as Samuel Huntington famously hypothesised that democratic transitions come in waves,[1] with many countries experiencing their move away from authoritarianism close together in time, so too has constitution-making come in waves. In fact, the waves of constitution-making have historically followed the waves of democratic transitions. As with Huntington's waves of transitions, there has been a contagion effect witnessed in the waves of constitution-making. Jon Elster was perhaps the first scholar to identify these waves. He wrote about how 'new constitutions almost always are written in the wake of a crisis or exceptional circumstances of some sort' and he found 'the link between crisis and constitution-making [to be] quite robust'.[2] He observed that the reason that constitution-making comes in waves is because the creation of new constitutions is often 'triggered by the same event'.[3]

By Elster's estimation, the world has witnessed seven waves of constitution-making. The first began in the late eighteenth century when, between 1780 and 1791, constitutions were written for the American colonies and for the US, Poland and France. From here:

> The [second] wave occurred in the wake of the 1848 revolutions in Europe … A third wave broke out after the First World War. The newly created or recreated states of

* Thanks to my friend Bob Condlin of the University of Maryland for reading and providing comments on an earlier draft, Sue McCarty and Jenny Rensler of Maryland's Thurgood Marshall Law Library for helping to track down hard-to-find sources, and Valeriya Zavyalova-Antonsen for assisting with the Russian transliteration.

[1] SP Huntington, *The Third Wave: Democratization in the Twentieth Century* (University of Oklahoma Press, 1991) 13–16.

[2] J Elster, 'Forces and Mechanisms in the Constitution-Making Process' (2005) 45 *Duke Law Journal* 364, 370.

[3] ibid 372.

> Poland and Czechoslovakia wrote their constitutions. The defeated German state adopted the Weimar Constitution. Next, the fourth wave occurred after the Second World War. The defeated nations – Japan, Germany and Italy – adopted new constitutions under the more or less strict tutelage of the Allied Powers. A fifth wave was connected with the breakup of the French and British colonial empires. It began in India and Pakistan in the 1940s, but the process did not really gain momentum until the 1960s. In many cases, the new constitutions were modeled closely on those of the former colonial powers … A [sixth] wave is linked to the fall of the dictatorships in Southern Europe in the mid-1970s. Finally, a number of former Communist countries in Eastern and Central Europe adopted new constitutions [in the seventh wave] after the fall of communism in 1989.[4]

The vast majority of the world's constitutions were adopted in the last three of Elster's waves. In fact, only 15 of the world's existing states promulgated their current constitution prior to the Second World War, while 14 more adopted their constitution prior to 1960.[5] Between 1960 and 1974, approximately 50 additional states adopted new constitutions. This means that all the rest of the world's remaining states possess constitutions that were adopted after the fall of communism occurred and Huntington's famous 'third wave' of democratisation began in 1989.

Constitution-making episodes that come in waves provide social scientists with unique data to test their theories. Generalisations about the constitution-making process are easier to make when a group of countries with similar histories or similar paths towards democratisation exhibit a similar set of constitution-making characteristics. In seeking to advance a better understanding of the constitution-making process, scholars have often focused on the period of uncertainty during a democratic transition. This is the period of time when political actors have the opportunity to create a new constitution[6] and when a nation's 'constitutional moment' most often takes place.[7] But does a founding moment always have to represent a clean break from the past? Or can the past also influence it? Recently, the literature in comparative constitutionalism has emphasised that founding moments may be influenced by historical legacy.[8] Moreover, scholars have discovered that most constitutions, when examined closely, actually exhibit a high degree of similarity over time. Ozan Varol refers to this phenomenon as 'constitutional stickiness',[9] explaining how the path of constitutional history can constrain future constitutional paths: 'Even in transitions from one regime type to another or in constitution-making processes following exogenous shocks such as revolution

[4] ibid 368–69.

[5] AP Blaustein, *The Influence of the United States Constitution Abroad* (Washington Institute for Values in Public Policy, 1986) 33 fn 25.

[6] G O'Donnell and PC Schmitter, *Transitions from Authoritarian Rule: Tentative Conclusions about Uncertain Democracies* (Johns Hopkins University Press, 1986) 6–7.

[7] B Ackerman, *The Future of Liberal Revolution* (Yale University Press, 1992) 46–50.

[8] ED Mazo, 'The Upstream Problem in Constitutionalism' (2015) 50 *Wake Forest Law Review* 795.

[9] O Varol, 'Constitutional Stickiness' (2016) 49 *UC Davis Law Review* 899; see also Z Elkins, T Ginsburg and J Melton, *The Endurance of National Constitutions* (Cambridge University Press, 2009).

or war – when one might expect tectonic constitutional shifts – the resulting constitutional changes are relatively minor.'[10]

The theory of constitutional stickiness essentially posits that new constitutions result from a path-dependent process. Path-dependency is a broad term and can be used to convey many different ideas. But the main idea it conveys is that one's range of future options is constrained by what was in place before. Path-dependency tells us that political institutions may be circumscribed by their predecessors. When new constitutions are written during regime transitions, they are often based on the constitutions that previously existed. Indeed, this makes sense, as constitutional framers rarely work in a vacuum. During a regime transition, a temporary void is created during which a new state more likely than not inherits its old institutions, under which it must function for a short period of time until its constitutional framers decide how to amend these old institutions or else scrap them in order to put something else in their place. These old institutions often wind up heavily influencing their successors.

One particularly powerful path-dependency theory is 'sequencing path-dependency'. Sequencing path-dependency stands for the broad idea that an outcome or decision is shaped by the historical path that specifically or systematically leads to it. This theory signifies the existence of a causal relationship between stages in a temporal sequence, where each stage strongly influences the direction of the stage that follows.[11] As William Sewell observes, 'what happened at an earlier point in time will affect the possible outcomes of a sequence of events occurring at a later point in time'.[12] Sequencing path-dependency finds that the order in which choices are presented can significantly affect later outcomes and even predict them.

When we say that a path-dependent historical or temporal process is one characterised by a self-reinforcing sequence of events, we mean that *when* a particular event occurs in a sequence is important, because small events early on can have disproportionately large effects later.[13] During the early stages of a sequence – during the moment often referred to as the 'critical juncture' – things are relatively permissive. However, they get more restrictive as one moves down the path. The further one goes down the path, the more change becomes 'bounded'.[14] Sequencing path-dependency involves three phases. The first is the 'critical juncture'. This is the phase at which an event triggers a move down a particular path. The second is the 'period of reproduction', when positive feedback mechanisms reinforce movement along that path. The third happens when the new path comes

[10] ibid 903.

[11] K Arrow, *Social Choice and Individual Values* (Wiley, 1963).

[12] WH Sewell Jr, 'Three Temporalities: Toward an Eventful Sociology' in TJ MacDonald (ed), *The Historic Turn in the Human Sciences* (University of Michigan Press, 1996) 262–63.

[13] P Pierson, 'Not Just What, But *When*: Timing and Sequence in Political Processes' (2000) 14 *Studies in American Political Development* 72, 74–77.

[14] ibid 76.

to an end. At that point in time, new events work to dislodge the old, long-lasting equilibrium. Every path begins and ends with a 'critical juncture', which is essentially a kind of punctuated equilibrium. As James Mahoney observes:

> [P]ath dependence characterizes specifically those historical sequences in which contingent events set into motion institutional patterns or event chains that have deterministic properties. The identification of path dependence therefore involves both tracing a given outcome back to a particular set of historical events, and showing how these events are themselves contingent occurrences that cannot be explained on the basis of prior historical conditions.[15]

This chapter focuses on the wave of constitution-making that took place in the countries of the former Soviet Union after the fall of communism and explains how it was influenced by path-dependency and the constitutional changes that occurred in the Soviet Union before that country ceased to exist. There are numerous distinctions that characterise the founding constitutional moments in the post-Soviet space. First, many of these countries rejected popular constitutionalism and drafted new constitutions through the ordinary political process.[16] As William Partlett explains, 'parliaments became the locus for both ordinary legislation and constitutional lawmaking' in these countries.[17] As such, second, constitution-making in the post-Soviet space often lacked a sense of citizen engagement.[18] Indeed, founding constitutional moments in these countries did not always turn out to be specific moments or events. Finally, many of the countries in this region adopted semi-presidential systems of government, even though the literature strongly cautioned against this[19] – and even though the Soviet constitutional system had experienced no such thing itself for most of its long existence.

This chapter explains how path-dependency worked to influence the post-Soviet region's constitutional choices. Specifically, it examines the distinctive features of the transition from communism in the former Soviet Union and how this transition led many countries in the post-Soviet space to adopt semi-presidential executive organs and structures, ones that created a role for a president to function alongside a prime minister. Today, this constitutional separation of powers model dominates in the post-communist world, but there has been little scholarly explanation for why it has been chosen.[20] This chapter argues that the

[15] J Mahoney, 'Path Dependence in Historical Sociology' (2000) 29 *Theory and Society* 507, 507–08.

[16] W Partlett, 'The Dangers of Popular Constitution-Making' (2012) 38 *Brooklyn Journal of International Law* 193, 196; R Teitel, 'Transnational Jurisprudence: The Role of Law in Political Transformation' (1997) 106 *Yale Law Journal* 2009, 2069.

[17] Partlett (n 16) 205.

[18] A Sajó, 'Constitution without the Constitution Moment: A View from the New Member States' (2005) 3 *International Journal of Constitutional Law* 243.

[19] J Linz, 'Presidential or Parliamentary Democracy: Does it Make a Difference?' in J Linz and A Valenzuela (eds), *The Failure of Presidential Democracy* (Johns Hopkins University Press, 1994) 3–89.

[20] See R Elgie, *Semi-Presidentialism: Subtypes and Democratic Performance* (Oxford University Press, 2011); R Elgie and S Moestrup (eds), *Semi-Presidentialism in Central and Eastern Europe* (Manchester University Press, 2008).

reason this separation of powers model was adopted in these countries is because it already existed there shortly before the post-Soviet states gained their independence. Thus, the theory that goes furthest towards explaining post-communist constitutional choice is path-dependency.

Like all path-dependent processes, the origin of the constitutional moments that occurred in the post-Soviet world can be traced back to an early event. In this case, that event was Mikhail Gorbachev's decision in 1990 to superimpose a presidency over the existing constitutional architecture of the Soviet Union. Gorbachev created his presidency in a deliberate attempt to make the Soviet Union a semi-presidential republic. In a matter of months, his decision would lead to presidencies being created in most of the union republics of the Soviet Union. When the time came for these union republics to write new constitutions as independent states, they happened to adopt similar constitutional systems. Thus, the original reforms to the Soviet Union's constitution enacted by Gorbachev influenced the constitutional reforms in the Soviet republics at all subsequent points in time. This chapter explains how this process unfolded.

II. The Soviet Union's Constitutional Structure

Mikhail Gorbachev's election to become the Soviet Union's first President on 14 March 1990 was the 'critical juncture' in the path leading to the creation of all subsequent presidential regimes throughout the post-Soviet world. Before long, new constitutional systems based largely on the model that Gorbachev created would be reproduced at lower levels of the Soviet political hierarchy, so that by the end of 1991, when the union republics gained their independence, almost all of them would possess the same type of constitutional system. These republics' presidencies were established, in sequencing terms, *before* each republic gained its formal independence. This meant that when the time came for these republics to write new constitutions as independent states, an additional institutional actor was present who had a stake in the final outcome. As such, a presidential constitutional regime was bound to result. To understand in more depth how this process unfolded, it is first necessary to examine how the Soviet Union's political institutions functioned before Gorbachev's presidency was created.

A. The Formal Constitutional Structure

The Soviet Constitution of 1977 formally divided political power between two state institutions, the Supreme Soviet and the Council of Ministers.[21] In form

[21] For a history of the 1977 Constitution, see R Sharlet, *The New Soviet Constitution of 1977: Analysis and Texts* (King's Court Communications, 1978); WE Butler, *Basic Documents on the Soviet Legal System* (Oceana Publications, 1983) 3–32.

though not function, the system resembled a parliamentary republic. The Supreme Soviet was the Soviet Union's parliament. Its duties were outlined in Chapter 15 of the 1977 Constitution, where it was described as being 'the supreme body of state power' in the USSR.[22] A large body, the Supreme Soviet was split into two chambers which met twice a year. These were called the Council of the Union and the Council of Nationalities.[23] The Presidium of the Supreme Soviet, a smaller body that possessed greater formal powers, including the power to issue laws, ratify treaties, and form and abolish ministries, met every two months and fulfilled some of the functions of a working parliament. The Chairman of the Presidium of the Supreme Soviet carried out the tasks of signing legislation into law and receiving foreign ambassadors. He was considered by Westerners to be the head of state and was referred to as 'the Soviet president'.[24] In practice, however, he was not the major figure such a term would imply and his role was rather ceremonial.[25] Indeed, his power derived more from his membership in the Politburo.

The duties of the executive branch were outlined in Chapter 16 of the 1977 Constitution, which referred to the Council of Ministers as the 'highest executive and administrative body' in the USSR.[26] The Council of Ministers had 106 members. Though this proved to be too large to allow it to function as a working cabinet, it too contained a smaller body within it, called the Presidium of the Council of Ministers, which carried out most of its duties. The Presidium of the Council of Ministers was directed by a Chairman, often referred to by Westerners as 'the Soviet prime minister'.[27] The Council of Ministers could issue decrees within its areas of expertise, but it did not possess the power to adopt statutes, which was reserved for the Supreme Soviet. Formally, the Presidium of the Supreme Soviet was responsible for appointing and removing members of the Council of Ministers.[28] Just as the legislature has the power to select and remove governments in parliamentary systems, the legislature formally had this power in the Soviet system. When a new Supreme Soviet was elected every five years, the Council of Ministers would be appointed by the Supreme Soviet anew.

Although the Soviet Union's political system may have followed the parliamentary model formally, functionally Soviet governments were made and unmade not by the Supreme Soviet, but by the Communist Party of the Soviet Union (CPSU). Article 6 of the 1977 Constitution pronounced the CPSU to be the 'leading and guiding force of Soviet society, the nucleus of its political system, and of all state and public organizations'.[29] Even this description was an understatement

[22] 1977 USSR Constitution, art 108.

[23] ibid arts 110, 112.

[24] J Hough and M Fainsod, *How the Soviet Union is Governed* (Harvard University Press, 1979) 371.

[25] This only changed in 1977, when Leonid Brezhnev became the Chairman of the Presidium of the Supreme Soviet, thus uniting the roles of leader of the Communist Party and that of head of state in the same person.

[26] 1977 USSR Constitution, art. 128.

[27] ibid art 132.

[28] ibid art 129.

[29] ibid art 6.

regarding the power that the CPSU held. Most serious analysts of the Soviet political system found that the highest echelons of the Communist Party enjoyed a higher authority and wielded greater power than any state institutions.[30] Writing about the Soviet political system in 1979, Jerry Hough and Merle Fainsod explained how:

> The Communist Party is clearly the dominant institution in the Soviet Union. The active participants in the political process are … almost all party members, and the ultimate policymaking organs both in the center and in the lower territorial units are the respective collective party bodies. In functional terms the real cabinet of the Soviet political system is the party Politburo, the real parliament is the party Central Committee, and the real prime minister is the party General Secretary.[31]

Still, while the Communist Party was the country's dominant institution, other institutions nonetheless also made policy, including the Council of Ministers and the ministries. Within the Soviet system, the Communist Party was clearly the dominant of the two institutions, but the Council of Ministers nonetheless played an important role in the governance of the country.

B. The Literature on the Soviet Executive

Although the Communist Party was the dominant institution in Soviet politics, it is important to understand the state institutions that co-existed with it. The Council of Ministers, which served as the Soviet Union's 'government', was the most significant of these. Moreover, its existence was not unique to the Soviet system. Similar 'governments' could be found in other communist countries. However, these formal executive institutions were traditionally accorded little attention by Western scholars of communist politics.[32] In their 576-page book *How the Soviet Union is Governed*, Jerry Hough and Merle Fainsod devoted only five pages to the Soviet Council of Ministers, even then admitting how '[n]othing is known about the work of the Presidium of the Council of Ministers, not even the frequency of its meetings. On the surface there should be great overlap in function between the Presidium and the Central Committee Secretariat, but the division of labor between the two committees is obscure'.[33]

Such obscurity existed when it came to understanding the government functions of the Soviet Union's union republics as well, although it was known that these republics traditionally replicated the structure of government at the federal level.

[30] See L Schapiro, *The Communist Party of the Soviet Union* (Random House, 1971); DP Hammer, *USSR: The Politics of Oligarchy* (Westview Press, 1986) 77–100, 110–18.

[31] Hough and Fainsod (n 24) 362.

[32] For a similar conclusion, see W White, J Gardner and G Schöpflin, *Communist Political Systems: An Introduction* (St Martin's Press, 1982) 75. A noteworthy exception is the study of the Soviet industrial ministries by S Whitefield, *Industrial Power and the Soviet State* (Oxford University Press, 1993).

[33] Hough and Fainsod (n 24) 382.

As such, each of the 15 union republics likewise possessed a formal legislature, also called a Supreme Soviet, which contained a smaller Presidium to carry out its business between sessions. Each of the union republics also possessed a formal executive branch, composed of a republican Council of Ministers, which oversaw the work of these republics' administrative agencies or ministries.[34] Despite the fact that the scholarly literature on the Soviet political system had neglected analysis of the Soviet Union's executive branch – and had almost nothing to say about the executive branches of the individual republics – its very *existence* would become important when Gorbachev began dismantling communism and shifting power from the Communist Party to the Soviet state.[35]

III. Gorbachev's Constitutional Reforms

A. Original Reform Plans

When Gorbachev became General Secretary of the CPSU in March 1985, his agenda did not include amending the Soviet Constitution or creating a presidency. On the contrary, Gorbachev initially aspired to make the Communist Party the instrument for carrying out his reforms.[36] At first, he began consolidating his power by making cautious personnel changes within the top ranks of the CPSU. Then, in order to revive the Soviet Union's stagnating economy, he turned to curbing the power of the ministries that were responsible for economic output.[37] He attempted to do this by decreasing the influence of the Communist Party over these ministries and by reducing their number.[38] The Council of Ministers vigorously resisted Gorbachev's reform efforts. Eventually, conservatives within the party would also begin to retaliate, and there would even be attempts to depose Gorbachev.[39]

When the party and the ministries proved resistant, Gorbachev concluded that the only way to achieve his economic reforms would be to breathe new life into the political system.[40] He wanted to accomplish this by democratising state institutions and reducing the influence of the party over them. He envisioned creating several new political institutions. He intended to put them in place by amending the

[34] ibid 485.

[35] For a similar conclusion, see E Huskey, 'Introduction' in E Huskey (ed), *Executive Power and Soviet Politics: The Rise and Decline of the Soviet State* (ME Sharpe, 1992) xi–xiii.

[36] AS Cherniaev, *Shest' let s Gorbachevym* (Progress, 1993) 90.

[37] Gorbachev's initial preoccupation was with economic reform, or what he called *uskorenie*. He later turned his efforts to a rebuilding programme that became known by the term *perestroika*.

[38] C Ross, 'Party-State Relations' in Huskey (ed) (n 35) 61.

[39] ibid.

[40] M Gorbachev, *Zhizn' i reformy* (Novosti, 1995) 227–30. For an English translation, see M Gorbachev, *Memoirs* (Doubleday, 1996).

Soviet Union's existing Constitution. In 1987, on the date of its tenth anniversary, the Soviet Constitution had been amended only once. By late 1988, nearly one-third of its articles would be rewritten.[41] Though numerous changes took place, here I wish to focus only on the constitutional changes of the late Soviet period that affected the country's separation of powers. Three such changes were particularly important. These included Gorbachev's efforts to democratise the Soviet legislature, to downgrade the 'leading role' of the Communist Party and to create the new institution of a presidency.[42]

B. Democratising the Soviet Legislature

The first step towards reshaping the Soviet political system began with a wave of constitutional amendments proposed by Gorbachev at the end of 1988. With the five-year mandate of the Supreme Soviet coming to an end in 1989, Gorbachev publicly announced in June 1988, at the Nineteenth Party Conference, that the old Supreme Soviet would be restructured and a new, democratically elected parliament would be created.[43] In late 1988, the Presidium of the Supreme Soviet formed a working group, headed by Anatolii Lukianov, to draft the constitutional amendments that would create this new two-tier parliament. Fearing a backlash from the Communist Party's leadership, whose own influence would be threatened by a democratic parliament, Gorbachev relied on a small group of advisors to draft the detailed rules for his new legislature.[44] The Supreme Soviet then amended the existing Constitution on 1 December 1988, changing Chapter 15, which dealt with the functions of the old USSR Supreme Soviet, to create a new parliament in its place.[45]

The lower tier of this new parliament, the Congress of People's Deputies, was to consist of 2,250 deputies. Of these, 750 would be elected from single-member constituencies that were apportioned strictly based on population; 750 would be elected from national-territorial districts that were meant to represent the union's

[41] R Sharlet, *Soviet Constitutional Crisis: From De-Stalinization to Disintegration* (ME Sharpe, 1992) 86; GB Smith, *Reforming the Russian Legal System* (Cambridge University Press, 1996) 84. According to Richard Sakwa, a total of 55 of the Constitution's 174 articles were changed. R Sakwa, *Gorbachev and His Reforms, 1985–1990* (Prentice Hall, 1990) 129.

[42] An excellent synopsis of all of the constitutional reforms can be found in A Yakovlev with D Gibson, *The Bear that Wouldn't Dance: Failed Attempts to Reform the Constitution of the Former Soviet Union* (Legal Research Institute of the University of Manitoba, 1992).

[43] For the remarks at the Nineteenth Party Conference, see M Gorbachev, *Izrbrannye rechi i stat'i*, vol 6 (Politicheskaia Literatura, 1989) 358–67. Holding open elections to a democratic parliament had been proposed even earlier to Gorbachev, in 1985. See A Iakovlev, *Gor'kaia chasha: bol'shevizm i reformatsiia Rossii* (Verkhne-Volozhskoe Knizhnoe izdatel'stvo, 1994) 205–12.

[44] These advisors included Anatolii Cherniaev, Anatolii Lukianov, Valerii Boldin, Ivan Frolov and Georgii Shakhnazarov. See Cherniaev (n 36) 214.

[45] For the constitutional changes, see *Vedomosti verkhovnogo soveta SSSR*, No 49, Items 727–731 (1988) 813–60. For an analysis of the constitutional changes from 1988, see LV Lazarev and A Sliva, 'Konstitutsionnaia Reforma: Pervyi Etap' (1989) 3 *Sovetskoe gosudarstvo i pravo* 3–14.

various ethnic groups and territories; and 750 would be selected by societal organisations and unions, including the Communist Party, which was guaranteed 100 deputy seats of its own. During its first meeting, the Congress of People's Deputies itself was to elect, from among its members, the upper tier of parliament, to be called the Supreme Soviet, which would be responsible for legislating on a more full-time basis. This new Supreme Soviet was to be composed of 542 deputies, who would be divided evenly between its two chambers, the Council of the Union and the Council of Nationalities. Elections for the new Congress of People's Deputies were held in March of 1989.[46] The new Congress of People's Deputies was soon given sweeping legislative powers, including the power to amend the existing Constitution and the power to adopt a new constitution. It was also given the power to appoint the new Chairman of the new Supreme Soviet. At its first meeting in the spring of 1989, Gorbachev was duly elected to this post by the members of the Congress.

The new separation of powers system put in place also allowed the Congress to unilaterally appoint the Council of Ministers – not just formally, but also functionally now. Before long, the Congress of People's Deputies and the Supreme Soviet began asserting greater control over the Council of Ministers. For example, in the summer of 1989, the Congress appointed a new Council of Ministers by considering, for the first time, the nomination of each minister to the government individually rather than the government's slate as a whole.[47] Although Nikolai Ryzhkov, the Chairman of the Presidium of the Council on Ministers, was returned to his old position, the Supreme Soviet rejected nine other nominees and even appointed one minister who was not a member of the Communist Party.[48] Given that the Soviet Union's parliament now effectively had the sole power of appointing and recalling the government, Gorbachev had created more or less what looked like a parliamentary system.[49] However, getting used to the new separation of powers system was not easy. Ryzhkov, for his part, admitted that 'a situation of uncertainty' had been created between the Council of Ministers, the Communist Party and the Congress of People's Deputies, as the ministers, who were used to taking orders from the highest ranks of the party, now had to obey a different master.[50]

C. Downgrading the Leading Role of the Communist Party

By the beginning of 1990, it had also become clear to Gorbachev that the Council of Ministers could no longer be effectively overseen by two large, cumbersome

[46] Just how 'democratic' these elections were for the Soviet Union's first democratic parliament has been debated. See S White, R Rose and I McAllister, *How Russia Votes* (Chatham House, 1997) 22–29.

[47] E Huskey, 'Executive-Legislative Relations' in E Huskey (ed) (n 35) 85–89.

[48] Ross (n 38) 64; Sakwa (n 41) 150–51.

[49] B Horrigan and T Karasik, 'The Rise of Presidential Power under Gorbachev' in Huskey (ed) (n 35) 107.

[50] N Ryzhkov, *Perestroika: istoriia predatel'stv* (Novosti 1992) 291.

legislative bodies. If Gorbachev originally envisioned a government that would be responsible to the legislative branch, what he created instead was a parliamentary system in which a parliament with no legislative experience or history of multiparty politics suddenly had to take control of a government that had long ago become accustomed to taking orders from someone else. Gorbachev's creation of a functioning parliament in place of a non-functioning one ensured that another serious institution would now play a role in Soviet politics, in addition to the Communist Party and the Council of Ministers. As the balance of power within the system shifted, a fierce battle began being waged among these three institutions to influence policy. Meanwhile, just as the government was brought under parliament's control, the party's influence over the state began to erode. Soon, there were calls for Gorbachev to scrap Article 6 of the Soviet Constitution, which for years had enshrined the 'leading role' of the party in Soviet life.[51]

The shifting balance of power within the Soviet political system did not exactly prove to be ideal for Gorbachev, who soon found that he possessed no formal institutional base from which to govern effectively. He could no longer rely on his role as General Secretary of the Communist Party, since its authority was waning. His position as Chairman of the Supreme Soviet did not provide him with enough power to oversee the Council of Ministers either. To fill the need for authority, he decided to create an executive presidency.[52] In March 1990, Article 127 on the role of the presidency was added to the existing Soviet Constitution. At the same time, Article 6 was amended so that the Communist Party no longer played the leading role in political life.[53] These tit-for-tat institutional reforms proved to be a 'critical juncture' in the history of Soviet constitutionalism. As Gorbachev himself would later explain: 'The amendment of article 6 and the addition of article 127 to the basic law were organically related. The first meant that our state would cease to be a single-party … state and that one of the main principles of democracy – ideological and political pluralism – would be introduced. The second meant the reorganization of a no less important principle of this democracy, namely the separation of powers.'[54] In effect, the position in the political system previously occupied by the Communist Party was now superseded by a new presidency. This was an important moment in the history of Soviet constitutionalism and it is also where Soviet semi-presidentialism originated.

[51] For the evolution of Gorbachev's thinking about Article 6, see A Brown, *Seven Years that Changed the World: Perestroika in Perspective* (Oxford University Press, 2007) 306–09. The idea to alter Article 6 was proposed as early as 1985, when Aleksandr Iakovlev, one of Gorbachev's advisors, argued that the Communist Party should be split into smaller entities that could compete with one another. See Iakovlev (n 43) 205–12.

[52] See V Medvedev, *V komande Gorbacheva* (Bylina, 1994) 107–09.

[53] Article 6 was not deleted. Rather, its language was changed to say that the 'Communist Party of the Soviet Union, other political parties, as well as trade unions, youth, and other social organizations and mass movements … shall participate in working out the policy of the Soviet State and in the administration of State and social affairs'. *Vedomosti s"ezda narodnykh deputatov SSSR i verkhovnogo soveta SSSR*, No 12, Item 109 (1990).

[54] Gorbachev, *Memoirs* (n 40) 317.

D. Creating the Soviet Presidency

Creating a presidency had been considered at several earlier points in Soviet history. A plan for a Soviet presidency was debated when the 1936 Constitution was adopted, although Stalin ultimately rejected the idea.[55] In 1964, the idea of a presidency was considered again, this time by Nikita Khrushchev, who recommended that a presidency be created to the constitutional commission that was then preparing his new constitution. A chapter on a new presidency had in fact been drafted for that document, but when Khrushchev was forced out of power later that year, discussion of creating a Soviet presidency ceased. The constitutional commission was dissolved after Khrushchev's ouster, and by the time another constitutional commission was reinstated in the 1970s to begin drafting a new constitution for Leonid Brezhnev, its members no longer saw the need to create a national presidency.[56]

Gorbachev also initially resisted the idea of creating a national presidency. In 1985, after he rose to the position of General Secretary, two of his closest advisors, Georgii Shakhnazarov and Vadim Medvedev, put forward the idea of creating a presidency for the Soviet Union.[57] But Gorbachev reacted coolly to it. He believed that a strong President would overwhelm the power of the parliament and that this institution would only serve to re-establish a 'cult of personality' in Soviet politics.[58] In his memoirs, he would later write: 'I have to admit that it took me some time to realize that it was necessary to crown our new institutional structure with the office of President. I rejected the arguments of some of my associates and specialists who advanced similar proposals.'[59] However, even without Gorbachev's backing, the idea for creating a presidency was debated in Soviet newspapers and in parliament. As Shakhnazarov recalls, people were 'speaking about the president of the United States, the president of France, and in this connection it came to mind that having a president would be a good thing'.[60]

During the summer of 1988, when the idea for a presidency was discussed seriously by Gorbachev and his advisors for the second time, few of them had any solid understanding of what form this institution would take. Some of Gorbachev's advisors urged him to unite the roles of General Secretary of the Communist Party and Chairman of the Council of Ministers into one. Others argued that the government and the party needed to remain separate. Still others insisted that an office

[55] Stalin argued that a popularly elected presidency would do a disservice by opposing the Supreme Soviet, thus taking popular legitimacy away from it, and that, in any case, the Supreme Soviet was like a 'collective presidency'. I Stalin, *Sochineniia*, vol I (XIV) (Hoover Institution Press, 1967) 177.

[56] BM Lazarev, 'Prezident SSSR' (1990) 7 *Sovetskoe gosudarstvo i pravo* 3–4.

[57] G Shakhnazarov, 'We've Got a Special Way of Thinking: On the Establishment of the Soviet Presidency' (1994) 2 *Demokratizatsiya* 228; Medvedev (n 52) 109.

[58] Horrigan and Karasik (n 49) 107.

[59] Gorbachev, *Memoirs* (n 40) 317–18.

[60] Shakhnazarov (n 57) 228.

of an elected presidency should be superimposed over these other institutions or made to exist alongside them.[61] Gorbachev continued to resist the idea of a presidency because he believed the institution would 'concentrate too much power in the hands of a single person'.[62] As a compromise, he agreed to create the position of the Chairman of the Supreme Soviet.[63]

Nonetheless, the idea of creating a presidency continued to surface within society. Fedor Burlatskii, a noted scholar and former member of the working group that tried to draft the never-completed constitution for Khrushchev in the 1960s, published an article outlining the benefits of the presidential model in the summer of 1988, after the Nineteenth Party Conference.[64] In 1989, when Andrei Sakharov circulated a new draft constitution for the Soviet Union in the Congress of People's Deputies, that document contained a role for a popularly elected President who was to serve for a five-year term.[65] However, what finally convinced Gorbachev of the need to create a presidency was not this discussion going on in the public sphere, but rather the discussion that took place among his close-knit group of advisors. Reforms had been progressing slower than expected and Gorbachev came to realise that in order to proceed with his economic agenda, the Soviet government could not continue to be overseen by the Congress of People's Deputies and Supreme Soviet. Once he had come to accept this, in late 1989 he again began discussing with Shakhnazarov and Medvedev the idea of creating a Soviet presidency.

At this point, a debate among Gorbachev's closest advisors proceeded to take place over what form of presidentialism should be adopted. The two main models debated were that of the French Fifth Republic and the US.[66] Gorbachev initially favoured the American model. His argument in favour of pure presidentialism was based on his belief that the authority of an American-style President would give him better leverage in implementing difficult reforms. He also believed a president would be better suited to running a federation.[67] Shakhnazarov and Medvedev lobbied Gorbachev to adopt a French-style presidency.[68] Shakhnazarov argued that having a separate premier run the government would lessen the administrative

[61] S White, *Russia's New Politics: The Management of a Post-Communist Society* (Cambridge University Press, 2000) 72. For a detailed account of the suggestions proposed, see EL Kuznetsov, 'Iz istorii sozdaniia instituta Prezidenta SSSR' (1996) 5 *Gosudarstvo i pravo* 95.

[62] *XIX Vsesoiuznaia konferentsiia Kommunisticheskoi partii Sovetskogo Soiuza 28 iiunia-1 iiulia 1988*, Stenograficheskii otchet, vol I (Politizdat, 1988) 59 and vol II, 129.

[63] ibid vol II, 138.

[64] F Burlatskii, 'O Sovetskom Parlamentarizme' *Literaturnaia gazeta*, No 24 (15 June 1988) 2. For more on Burlatskii's role and his ideas about presidential institutions, see F Burlatskii, *Vozhdi i sovetniki: O Khrushcheve, Andropove, i ne tol'ko o nikh* (Politizdat, 1990) 177.

[65] A Sakharov, 'Draft Constitution of the Union of Soviet Republics of Europe and Asia' (1989) 52 *Novoe vremia* 26–28. See also A Sakharov, *Trevoga i nadezhda* (Inter-verso, 1990) 258–59, 272–74.

[66] A Brown, *The Gorbachev Factor* (Oxford University Press, 1996) 198.

[67] ibid.

[68] G Shakhnazarov, *Tsena svobody: reformatsiia Gorbacheva glazami ego pomoshchnika* (Rossika, 1993) 136–39.

burden placed on the president. As he explained in his memoirs: 'I stood for the French model, most of all, because it allowed the president to keep his role as an arbiter, rather than to become a whipping boy after every setback the government might have. While the American model might not be bad, it better suits a country with a stable political system and with a high level of economic attainment.'[69] Shakhnazarov probably got the idea for adopting the French system from his friend Fedor Burlatskii.[70] However, it was Shakhnazarov who first described the proposal to Gorbachev in a memorandum that he co-authored with Medvedev in the autumn of 1989 and that he thereafter circulated to Gorbachev on 29 November 1989.[71]

Although Gorbachev's advisors believed they were adopting French-style semi-presidentialism in principle, it is obvious from their negotiations that they did not know how it would work in practice. Many details concerning the internal dynamics of their new semi-presidential system were left to be ironed out. For example, should the Soviet President have the power to dissolve the Congress of People's Deputies and Supreme Soviet as the French President had to dissolve the National Assembly?[72] Such questions seem to have been hotly debated by the members of the constitutional commission's working group responsible for drafting changes to the existing Constitution's text. Yet these debates, unlike those of the Congress of People's Deputies and the Supreme Soviet, were never published.[73] One thing we do know is that this working group, which was chaired by Gorbachev himself, decided not to give the President the right to dissolve parliament.[74] Gorbachev believed that this power would only increase potential elements of authoritarianism in the office of the presidency.

The records of the negotiations between Gorbachev and his advisors make clear that several of the powers that were given to the new presidency came about in an effort to settle internal disputes among the members of the working group. For example, Anatolii Lukianov believed that the president should have the right to chair the meetings of the Council of Ministers, the Supreme Soviet *and* Congress, while others disagreed, arguing that this would entirely defeat the logic behind the separation of powers. Only the issue of giving the President the power to dismiss the Council of Ministers received universal support.[75] No doubt, the details concerning the internal workings of this system were not understood by the deputies

[69] ibid 138.

[70] Burlatskii has also been recognised as the author of the Soviet law on the presidency by several others. See BP Kurashvili, *Strana na rasputʹe* (Iuridicheskaia Literatura, 1990) 104–07; D Doder and L Branson, *Gorbachev: Heretic in the Kremlin* (Viking, 1990) 279–80.

[71] For a copy of this memorandum, see 'The Structure of the Highest Bodies of Authority' (1994) 2(2) *Demokratizatsiya* 317–22; Shakhnazarov (n 68), 441–43.

[72] E Teague, 'The Powers of the Soviet Presidency' (1990) 2(12) *Radio Liberty Report on the USSR* 4–7.

[73] Y Kuznetsov, 'The Making of a President: A Glimpse into the History of the Top Executive Post in the USSR' (1994) 2 *Demokratizatsiya* 222, 224.

[74] ibid.

[75] ibid 225.

when the constitutional changes were presented to parliament for approval. At a meeting of several deputies that took place in February 1990, at which the future presidency was discussed, Egor Kuznetsov recalled that many deputies did not actually see much difference between the post of a President and that of Chairman of the Supreme Soviet. As long as one of these posts promised to protect Gorbachev from the Communist Party, they were willing to give their support to whatever institution was created and whatever constitutional amendments were sought.[76]

At the time that these discussions took place, Gorbachev's advisors also began debating a much more salient issue – how the new President would be elected. While everyone realised that the President would have more authority if he were popularly elected, most of Gorbachev's advisors conservatively leaned towards having the Congress of People's Deputies elect the Soviet President the first time around. The time needed to organise an election and its unpredictable results, especially given the rising popularity of Boris Yeltsin, were two of the reasons given against holding a popular election, which Shakhnazarov, in particular, opposed. Yet there were other matters of substance that also persuaded Gorbachev's advisors against holding a popular election. For example, to secure the popular election of a new Soviet President would have raised delicate procedural issues. Gorbachev's advisors thought that the new President would need to garner the support not just of a majority of citizens but also of a majority of the republics, given that the Soviet Union was a federation.[77] After a lengthy debate, his advisors decided to write the law on the presidency in a way that would allow the Soviet Union's first President to be selected by its parliament – the Congress of People's Deputies.[78]

The Supreme Soviet approved Gorbachev's proposal to establish the Office of the President of the USSR on 27 February 1990. Two weeks later, the Congress of People's Deputies officially amended the country's Constitution to create this office. This was accomplished by inserting a Chapter 15-1 (on the powers of the presidency) into the Constitution of 1977, wedging it between Chapter 15 (on the Congress and Supreme Soviet) and Chapter 16 (on the Council of Ministers). On 14 March 1990, the Congress then elected Gorbachev as the Soviet Union's first President. Although Gorbachev ran unopposed, he was surprised to find that only 59 per cent of the deputies voted for him.[79] Just as this presidency was created, the language referring to the leading role of the Communist Party was removed from the Constitution. This allowed the presidency to take the place of the party within the country's new political hierarchy, completing the re-alignment of power that

[76] ibid 224.

[77] Lazarev (n 56) 9; Kuznetsov (n 61) 96–97.

[78] For Gorbachev's discussion of this in his memoirs, see Gorbachev, *Zhizn' i reformy* (n 40) vol 1, 483–90. See also Horrigan and Karasik (n 49) 107.

[79] Gorbachev received only 1,329 of the 2,245 votes cast. See White, Rose and McAllister (n 46) 35; Horrigan and Karasik (n 49) 107.

had been happening all year.[80] At the same time, the Soviet legislature found it had to cede much of its influence and stature to this new presidency. One scholar referred to the new Soviet presidency as a 'hastily-conceived institutional reform'.[81]

E. Gorbachev's Evolving Powers: March to September 1990

The Soviet presidency provided Gorbachev with many new powers, including the power to veto legislation, appoint government officials and sign international treaties. He was given the power of calling national referenda, declaring martial law and overruling government decisions that he believed violated the Constitution.[82] While the new Soviet President also had the power to propose candidates for the premiership, it seemed from the text of the Constitution that the Council of Ministers would still be controlled by parliament. For instance, rather than being given the power to 'nominate' the Chairman of the Council of Ministers, the new Article 127-3(6) stated that the President shall 'submit to the USSR Supreme Soviet candidacies for the post of Chairman'. Meanwhile, Article 127-3(7) did not grant the President the power to 'dismiss' this Chairman outright, but, rather more delicately, only gave him the power to 'raise the question before the USSR Supreme Soviet of the resignation or of accepting the resignation of the USSR Council of Ministers'. If the President wanted to remove individual ministers, he could do so only 'in agreement with' the Chairman of the Council of Ministers. Meanwhile, Article 129 tied the Council of Ministers' term to that of the Supreme Soviet, not to that of the new President. Gorbachev could not appoint ministers without the Supreme Soviet, but the Supreme Soviet had the power to force the resignation of the government on its own.[83]

In order to get the presidency through Congress, Gorbachev was forced to agree that several important changes would be made to the amendments creating the presidency. One of these was that the President not be given the sole right to declare a state of emergency in the USSR; instead, he had to wait for the Supreme Soviet to agree to such a measure. Another, as mentioned, was that the President also lost the power to dismiss the Chairman of the Supreme Soviet. A third was that the President's power to veto the Supreme Soviet's laws was taken away.[84] Nonetheless, according to Article 127-3(9), the President was given the power to suspend the decrees of the Council of Ministers. And while he did not have the right to issue decrees himself, Article 127-7 allowed him to promulgate 'edicts' that had binding force.

[80] Huskey (n 47) 90.

[81] ibid 89.

[82] *Vedomosti s"ezda narodnykh deputatov SSSR i verkhovnogo soveta SSSR*, No 12, Item 189 (1990). For an enumeration of the new presidency's powers, see 'Novye polnomochiia prezidenta' (1990) 39 *Argumenty i fakty* 1–2.

[83] For a text of the law on the presidency, see *Vedomosti s"ezda narodnykh deputatov SSSR i verkhovnogo soveta SSSR*, No 12, Item 189 (1990).

[84] D Mann, '*Ukaz* and Effect: Gorbachev is Granted Additional Powers' (1991) 2(40) *Radio Liberty Report on the USSR* 2–3. Elizabeth Teague also notes that depriving Gorbachev of the power to dismiss the Chairman of the Supreme Soviet was one of the major concessions he had to make, in addition to relinquishing the power to nominate the members of the Constitutional Review Committee. See Teague (n 72) 6.

Before long, a 'war of laws' ensued as Congress' laws, the Council of Ministers' decrees and the President's edicts began to compete for dominance in an unintelligible chaos of legislation, with no enforcement mechanism in existence to ensure that the proper hierarchy was being respected.[85] Since Gorbachev was not given the power to dissolve parliament, no simple resolution to the conflict could be found.

To deal with the situation, Gorbachev returned to the Supreme Soviet in September of 1990, when the Soviet presidency was barely six months old, to seek additional powers. He argued that emergencies in the country were growing 'while the system of executive power is not functioning'.[86] His immediate concern was his inability to get the Council of Ministers and the central ministries to respond to his edicts, which often went ignored.[87] On 24 September 1990, the Supreme Soviet granted the Soviet presidency temporary additional powers for a six-month period, until 31 March 1991.[88] These new temporary powers included the right to issue unrestricted decrees concerning the economy, law and order, and government personnel, the right to inject direct presidential rule in troubled regions, and the right to create any new bodies or structures necessary to 'accelerate the formation of an all-Union market and ensure cooperation between Union and autonomous regions'.[89] However, the new constitutional changes said nothing about how the Soviet President would be able to *enforce* his new decree powers, particularly over the Council of Ministers. Speaking to the Supreme Soviet on 26 September 1990, the jurist Anatolii Sobchak lamented the absence of a vertical power structure in the Soviet Union. The result was a situation where 'there is a president who cannot put anything into effect, and a Council of Ministers that cannot do anything'.[90]

F. The Move Towards Pure Presidentialism: November 1990

With neither his edicts nor his new decrees being obeyed, Gorbachev decided in November 1990 that he would try to reorganise the separation of powers along the lines of a pure presidential system.[91] 'Having opted in early 1990 for a French-style executive, with a president governing through a prime minister and council of ministers', explain Brenda Horrigan and Theodore Karasik, 'Gorbachev now sought to establish presidential government based on the American model, which

[85] Huskey (n 47) 91. A so-called Constitutional Review Committee (Komitet konstitutsionnogo nadzora) was created to settle disputes regarding conflicting legislation, but there is evidence to suggest that resistance to parliamentary laws continued and that this was encouraged by the Prime Minister, individual cabinet ministers and the President himself. ibid 94.

[86] Mann (n 84) 1–2.

[87] Horrigan and Karasik (n 49) 109.

[88] Mann (n 84) 1–3.

[89] See *Vedomosti s"ezda narodnykh deputatov SSSR i verkhovnogo soveta SSSR*, No 40, Item 802 (1990).

[90] Mann (n 84) 4.

[91] See 'President Proposes His Program' *Izvestiia* (17 November 1990), reprinted in (1990) 46 *Current Digest of the Soviet Press* 10–11; S Chugaev, 'The USSR's President's Proposals are Supported' *Izvestiia* (5 December 1990), in (1990) 49 *Current Digest of the Soviet Press* 13.

he hoped would arrest the country's deepening economic and social crises.'[92] The new changes granted Gorbachev more direct control of the government ministries, which before had always been overseen by a Prime Minister. As part of the new reforms, the Council of Ministers was transformed into a new 'Cabinet of Ministers'.

The overarching goal of moving from a Council of Ministers to a Cabinet of Ministers was to subordinate all executive power under a single institutional hierarchy. The new Cabinet's leadership was still to be in the hands of a Prime Minister. However, whereas the previous Council of Ministers had been subordinate to the Soviet legislature, the Cabinet of Ministers reported to the President directly.[93] In creating this new Cabinet, Gorbachev managed to amend the Constitution in three subtle but important ways. First, he made it so that the Supreme Soviet no longer confirmed (in Russian 'utverzhdaet') the Cabinet of Ministers, but merely gave its agreement ('daet svoe soglasie') to the President's nominees.[94] Second, he made it so that the President alone now had the power to hire and fire leading members of the government as well as the heads of ministries. Finally, whereas previously the president proposed ministerial candidates to parliament 'in agreement with the Chairman of the Council of Ministers', Gorbachev made it so that now the President formally appointed them ('naznachaet') by decree.[95] Parliament still retained the power to overturn a presidential appointment, but the presumption was that this would rarely, if ever, happen. In instituting these reforms, Gorbachev tried to change the order of command, so that the Soviet government would answer to the president first and to the legislature second. As Eugene Huskey elaborates: 'Parliament was increasingly forced into "take or leave it" decisions on executive proposals, a traditional mark of executive dominance of the legislature.'[96] Perhaps the strongest symbol of this shift was the constitutional change regarding the tenure of the Cabinet of Ministers. Whereas the term of the Council of Ministers had always been tied to the election of the Supreme Soviet, it was now linked directly to the term of Office of the President.[97] Thus, when the election of a new President occurred, the Cabinet of Ministers would submit its resignation and allow the new President to pick a new team.[98]

The creation of the Cabinet of Ministers was also accompanied by a proliferation of new presidential institutions. In addition to the Security Council and Federation Council, which had been added in March 1990, the Office of a Vice Presidency was now added to the presidential administration. Gorbachev had fought for this office in the past, but without success.[99] Now, it was meant

[92] Horrigan and Karasik (n 49) 110.
[93] ibid 111.
[94] See *Vedomosti s"ezda narodnykh deputatov SSSR i verkhovnogo soveta SSSR*, No 1, Item 3 (1991).
[95] Mann (n 84) 1–4.
[96] Huskey (n 47) 95.
[97] Horrigan and Karasik (n 49) 111.
[98] The powers of the Cabinet of Ministers are documented in ibid 110–16. The original changes can be found in Russian in the new law on the Cabinet of Ministers. See 'Zakon Soiuza Sovetskikh Sotsialisticheskikh Respublik: O kabinete ministrov SSSR' *Izvestiia* (28 March 1991) 2–4.
[99] Kuznetsov (n 73) 225–26.

to provide a way for a presidential loyalist to take the place of the President if he should become incapacitated and not be able to carry out his duties. The amended Constitution specified that if the President died, the Vice President would assume the post of President for 60 days, until a new election could be held.[100] Gorbachev nominated Gennadii Ianaev to be the Soviet Union's first Vice President, and the Congress confirmed him on 27 December 1990.[101] An Office of Prime Minister was also created. Whereas in Soviet times the Chairman of the Presidium of the Council of Ministers had carried the unofficial title of 'Prime Minister', now there would be an official Prime Minister who would direct the work of the Cabinet of Ministers. Once again, the Soviet President gained the right to nominate this individual before his candidacy was submitted to parliament for approval. In January 1991, the Congress of People's Deputies approved Gorbachev's nominee, Valentin Pavlov, to replace Nikolai Ryzhkov, and thus to become the first official Prime Minister of the Soviet Union.

G. The August 1991 Coup and its Aftermath

Gorbachev claimed his new constitutional changes were engineered to place the Cabinet of Ministers more strictly under the presidential hierarchy to reflect the 'American model'. But even after a third round of changes, the constitutional system remained semi-presidential. In fact, it could be argued that Gorbachev's late 1990 constitutional reforms helped preserve semi-presidentialism much more than they undermined it. This was because the Soviet Union's new Prime Minister and Vice President worked in tandem to strengthen the powers of their *own* offices, not Gorbachev's, and eventually they conspired to depose him altogether. Gorbachev had repeatedly tried to draw a more direct line of authority down from the Soviet presidency in an effort to streamline the Soviet Union's executive branch. Yet when Pavlov became Prime Minister, he moved things in the opposite direction. Pavlov pushed for the Cabinet of Ministers to free itself from presidential control and for the Prime Minister's powers to be increased. Shortly after taking office, he also decided to move the physical offices of the Cabinet of Ministers to a new location outside the Kremlin. In June 1991, he even went to parliament to seek additional powers for his new office, arguing that the President's working day was too long and that there were many tasks he could not accomplish alone.

Gorbachev was trying to strengthen the new presidency and Pavlov's attempt to expand prime ministerial power flew in the face of what Gorbachev's November 1990 reforms sought to accomplish. Rather than support Gorbachev, Ianaev backed Pavlov, assuring the press 'that Pavlov's search for greater power was not

[100] GB Smith, *Soviet Politics: Struggling with Change* (St Martin's Press, 1992) 137.
[101] Horrigan and Karasik (n 49) 123.

politically motivated'.[102] Gorbachev soon convinced the Congress to deny his Prime Minister expanded authority. Ultimately, Gorbachev's efforts to strengthen the presidency – and to take power, in turn, away from the Cabinet of Ministers – led to his own undoing. The Cabinet of Ministers included many conservatives who were desperate to preserve the Soviet Union. Joining forces, they staged a coup against Gorbachev in August 1991. This coup was launched on the eve of the signing of a new Union Treaty, a document that, if passed, would have stripped the Cabinet of Ministers of considerable power. Many ministers supported the coup. As Horrigan and Karasik observe, 'those who supported the president's ouster were figures who had a long history within the Government apparatus'.[103]

After the coup, the Soviet 'government' lost most of its powers. Leaders from the republics insisted that Gorbachev's Federation Council, which had been created in March, now be replaced by a State Council, a new institution composed of the leaders of the 15 union republics. Gorbachev had but one vote out of 16 in this new institution, meaning that his own power became diluted. Soon thereafter, Yeltsin and his allies launched an assault on the Soviet ministries, expropriating their property and assets for the Russian republic. During the final days of the Soviet Union, the institution that had once been known as the Council of Ministers was controlled by neither the President nor parliament. In a sense, perhaps it no longer mattered, given that on 25 December 1991, the Soviet Union itself ceased to exist.

IV. Constitutional Path-Dependency in the Republics

A. Copying All-Union Institutions at the Republican Level

Knowing how the Soviet presidency evolved during the twilight years of Gorbachev's rule is essential to understanding the separation of powers systems that emerged in the republics. In the same way that Gorbachev tried to centralise power by creating a new presidency, republican leaders tried to strengthen their own power vis-a-vis Moscow by copying the federal presidency at the republican level. As Shakhnazarov would later reflect: 'When the law on the presidency was being prepared, I advised having only one president in the Union.'[104] Gorbachev also had not originally envisioned creating multiple presidencies at the republican level. 'To be frank', he admits in his memoirs, 'the creation of the office of President in the union republics was not part of my plans.'[105] However, he never openly spoke out against the idea either, for otherwise he risked losing the support of

[102] ibid 114.
[103] ibid 120.
[104] Shakhnazarov (n 57) 232.
[105] Gorbachev, *Memoirs* (n 40) 319–20.

these republics' leaders for his own institutional reforms. When he was asked in February 1990 about how the relationship among multiple future presidents at the republican level might be regulated, Shakhnazarov urged him to say that the Soviet Union should have just one President. But Gorbachev answered by saying that he was 'not opposed to thirty-four presidents', an answer no doubt given to placate any potential criticism within the republics.[106]

Although creating republican presidencies may not have been part of Gorbachev's plans, once the all-union presidency was established, he found there was little he could do to stop leaders in the republics from following suit. After agreeing to give Gorbachev additional powers and prerogatives, the leaders of the republics demanded to have the same institutions as existed in Moscow. Gorbachev firmly believed his hands were tied. In describing the meeting of the Congress of People's Deputies at which the Union's new presidential institutions were debated, he noted that, while the leader of the Kazakh republic, Nursultan Nazarbaev:

> [S]upported the establishment of the office of President and my candidacy, at the same time he spoke strongly in favor of using the same model in the republics, in order, as he put it, 'to eliminate contradictions between the notion of the presidency and the desire of the republics to broaden their authority'. In other words, the republics immediately realized that the central power was being strengthened and, not wishing to yield the independence they had gained, decided to seize the opportunity to secure themselves. Nazarbayev, an experienced and clever politician, was playing a no-lose game.[107]

Yet the desire to create presidencies on the part of the republics should not have surprised Gorbachev either, given that each of the 15 union republics had already reorganised its other institutions to copy those at the federal level. Less than a year after competitive elections were held for the USSR's Congress of People's Deputies in March of 1989, the republics held popular elections for their own new legislatures. These elections extended over a period of nine months in 1990. Twelve of the republics elected new legislatures between January and March, another did so in May, and two more held their elections in September and October 1990. The close timing of these republican parliamentary elections in 1990, as Table 7.1 shows below, is evidence that they were all influenced by events happening at the time in Moscow and at the all-union level.[108]

[106] This incident is recounted in Kuznetsov (n 61) 98–99. The number 'thirty-four' refers to the number of all-union and autonomous republics that might have had their own presidential institutions.

[107] Gorbachev, *Memoirs* (n 40) 319.

[108] On the republican elections, see White, Rose and McAllister (n 46) 29–34. Only the Russian Soviet Federative Socialist Republic (RSFSR) decided to keep the complicated two-tier parliamentary system and continue to have a smaller Supreme Soviet elected from within the larger Congress of People's Deputies; all of the other republics opted to elect their Supreme Soviets by popular vote. ibid 30; see also D Slider, 'The Soviet Union' (1990) 9 *Electoral Studies* 295; R Taagepera, 'Baltic Elections, February–April 1990' (1990) 9 *Electoral Studies* 303–11.

Table 7.1 The path to the presidency in the Soviet republics

Name of republic	Name of leader	Election of democratic parliament	Number of seats in parliament	Number of candidates in election	Compete index	Turnout (%)	Election of chairman of parliament	Popular election as president	Existence of president at independence?
Armenia	Ter-Petrosian	20 May 1990	259	1,390	5.4	60.4	Aug 1990	16 Oct 1991	Yes
Azerbaijan	Mutalibov	30 Sept 1990	250	N/A	N/A	81.0	May 1990	8 Sept 1991	Yes
Belarus	Shushkevich	4 Mar 1990	310	1,473	4.8	86.5	Sept 1991	None	No
Estonia	Rüütel	18 Mar 1990	105	392	3.7	78.2	March 1990	None	No
Georgia	Gamsakhurdia	28 Oct 1990	250	N/A	N/A	69.9	Oct 1990	26 May 1991	Yes
Kazakhstan	Nazarbaev	25 Mar 1990	270	1,031	3.8	83.9	April 1990	1 Dec 1991	Yes
Kyrgyzstan	Akaev	25 Feb 1990	350	878	2.5	92.0	Oct 1990	12 Oct 1991	Yes
Latvia	Gorbunovs	18 Mar 1990	201	395	2.0	81.2	Oct 1990	None	No
Lithuania	Landsbergis	24 Feb 1990	141	471	3.3	75.0	Mar 1990	None	No
Moldova	Snegur	25 Feb 1990	380	1,892	5.0	83.4	Sept 1991	8 Dec 1991	Yes
Russia	Yeltsin	4 Mar 1990	1,068	6,705	6.3	77.0	May 1990	12 June 1991	Yes
Tajikistan	Nabiev	25 Feb 1990	230	1,035	4.5	91.2	Sept 1991	25 Nov 1991	Yes
Turkmenistan	Niiazov	27 Oct 1990	175	526	3.0	93.6	Jan 1990	21 June 1991	Yes
Ukraine	Kravchuk	4 Mar 1990	450	3,901	8.7	84.7	July 1990	1 Dec 1991	Yes
Uzbekistan	Karimov	18 Jan 1990	500	1,094	2.2	93.5	May 1990	29 Dec 1991	Yes

Source: Based on information provided in S White, R Rose and I McAllister, *How Russia Votes* (Chatham House, 1997) 31; and DC Booker, 'Founding Presidents of Soviet Successor States: A Comparative Study' (2004) 12(1) *Demokratizatsiya* 133–45, later amended by the author. The 'index' is the ratio of the total number of candidates divided by the number of seats. The three Baltic leaders and the leaders of Belarus were not technically 'presidents'. Uzbekistan held its popular election on 29 December 1991, by which time the Soviet Union no longer existed, but the election had been scheduled beforehand.

Likewise, soon after Gorbachev was elected to the Soviet presidency in March 1990, the new republican legislatures began drafting legislation to create republican presidencies – and, on their heels, official premierships – to match what was happening in Moscow. Gordon Hahn calls what followed 'the parade of presidencies'.[109] As evidence that the ideas were taken from above, we might note how the majority of the new presidential terms were to be exactly five years in length, just like Gorbachev's. Following Gorbachev's example, most of the republican leaders also came to occupy their new presidential offices through a two-step process. First, these leaders were elected chairmen of their republican parliaments. As Table 7.1 shows, all of the republican leaders were elected chairmen of their respective parliaments between April and October 1990. The only exceptions to this general rule were the leaders of Belarus and Tajikistan – Stanislau Shushkevich and Rakhmon Nibayev, respectively – who were chosen to lead their respective parliaments more than a year later, in September 1991, after their predecessors had been deposed for their involvement in the August 1991 coup.[110]

The second step was taken when these republics then created presidential institutions so that their parliamentary leaders could be elected presidents. The sequencing of these elections again replicated the example set by the centre. However, unlike Gorbachev's election to his presidency, a crucially important difference in this second step was undertaken in the republics – namely, rather than be elected to the presidency by their republican parliaments, the republics' leaders overwhelmingly chose to stand for popular election.[111] This was done deliberately to strengthen their authority vis-a-vis Moscow and to send a message of rivalry to Gorbachev, who had not been popularly elected. The only republican leaders who did not take this route were Stanislau Shushkevich of Belarus and the three Baltic leaders – Anatolijs Gorbunovs of Latvia, Vytautas Landsbergis of Lithuania and Arnold Rüütel of Estonia – but there were legitimate reasons for these exceptions.[112] Most of the direct presidential elections were scheduled very quickly after August 1991, with nine of the 11 republican presidential elections being held between September and December. Prior to the August coup, only two republics had held a popular presidential election: Georgia's citizens chose Zviad Gamakhurdia as their President in April 1991 and the citizens of Russia elected Boris Yeltsin in June.[113] By contrast,

[109] GM Hahn, *Russia's Revolution from Above, 1986–2000: Reform, Transition, and Revolution in the Fall of the Soviet Communist Regime* (Transaction Publishers, 2002) 275.

[110] The leader of Belarus in 1990 was Nikolai Dimentei, who was later removed for his participation in the August coup attempt of 1991. Shushkevich then came to power to fill the void as a compromise figure who was mutually agreeable to the Belarussian Parliament and to Moscow.

[111] For a pattern of how these presidencies were created, see PH O'Neil, 'Hungary: Political Transition and Executive Conflict: The Balance or Fragmentation of Power?' in R Taras (ed), *Postcommunist Presidencies* (Cambridge University Press, 1997) 197–201.

[112] See DC Booker, 'Founding Presidents of Soviet Successor States: A Comparative Study' (2004) 12(1) *Demokratizatsiya* 133–34.

[113] T Karasik, *USSR: Facts and Figures Annual* (Academic International Press, 1992).

by 25 December 1991 – the last day of the Soviet Union – only one republic had *not* yet elected its President by popular vote, although even this task was taken care of by 29 December, when Islam Karimov coasted to a resounding presidential victory in Uzbekistan.

When the Soviet Union ceased to exist, these republics' Presidents became the founding fathers of new countries – indeed, sometimes unexpectedly so – when a previously republican institution, the presidency, suddenly became a new *national* institution. The sequencing of events is important here, for all of these presidential institutions were created, and most of these Presidents elected, *before* these countries gained their independence. As a result, when the time came for these states to write new constitutions as independent countries, a 'President' already played a role in running them. This meant that each of these states now possessed an additional stakeholder who would seek to participate in the constitution-making process and would have an interest in its outcome. Although the rush to form presidencies in the republics has been documented elsewhere, it is the timing that I wish to emphasise here. For had these parliaments tried to create presidencies after independence, had independence come sooner or had independence never come at all, the outcome might very well have been different.

Figure 7.1 Sequencing path-dependency during the Soviet transitions

B. The Independence of the Council of Ministers

In his memoirs, Gorbachev recalls being frustrated in his unsuccessful efforts to gain control of the federal Council of Ministers. His admits that: 'After making the proper decision to introduce the office of the president, we failed to think the issues though to the end [on the Council of Ministers].'[114] What he failed to think

[114] Gorbachev, *Memoirs* (n 40) 324.

through was how, specifically, the Soviet separation of powers should work and what mechanisms had to be put in place in order for the government to be effectively controlled by the presidency. As Gorbachev writes:

> The concern of our government for its powers was the major factor that worked against the consistent introduction of a presidential republic. Ryzhkov and his associates feared that the Council of Ministers would be downgraded, shoved into the background, transformed … They strongly objected, while at the same time I did not have sufficient grounds or any intention to quarrel with Nikolai Ivanovich [Ryzhkov]. I was hearing convincing arguments from my advisors that the President should not be saddled directly with the burden of managing the economy. Problems were accumulating and he would have to answer for every trifling detail. In short, it was decided at the time that the functions of the Council of Ministers would not be re-examined. I subsequently realized that this was a major contradiction.[115]

However, even if Gorbachev's advisors *had* steered him elsewhere, adopting an American-style system would have been difficult. It would have meant subordinating an institution with a very long history – a history which could be traced from pre-revolutionary times to its evolution into the Sovnarkom in 1918, its transformation into the Council of Ministers in 1946, its official recognition in the Constitution of 1977 and its reincarnation as the Cabinet of Ministers in 1990 – under a presidency that was barely a year old. Whether this could have been accomplished is a matter of conjecture. Yet, the fact remains that it was not accomplished in the Soviet Union. In retrospect, Gorbachev reasoned that he would have needed to adopt a new constitution, rather than merely 'patching up' and amending the existing one, to achieve this goal.[116]

Yet the Soviet republics *did* adopt new constitutions and the outcome proved to be not very different; a dual-headed, semi-presidential separation of powers system still emerged as the model of choice. Indeed, equally important to what was happening in Moscow was the story of how each republic mirrored the centre in establishing its new governmental institutions. By mid-1991, many of the republics had turned their republican Councils of Ministers into Cabinets of Ministers and renamed the post of Chairman of the Council of Ministers to become 'Prime Minister'. Soon, constitution-making in these republics would also evolve into a battle over whether the President or parliament would have ultimate control of the Cabinet of Ministers. The historic and partly autonomous role of this unique executive institution was contested at the republican level just as it was at the all-union level during the constitution-making process in each republic. Indeed, when the time came for these republics to adopt new constitutions after independence, their framers found that their politics forced them to copy the Soviet constitutional

[115] ibid.
[116] ibid 325.

model. When it came to creating new political institutions, Gorbachev would later say: 'Theory is theory, but practice – real politics – always has the last word.'[117] This chapter has tried to show that while that may be true, 'real politics' also does not happen in a vacuum. Rather, the real politics of constitution-making are often the result of a historical sequence, one in which one temporal stage influences the direction of the next. This is what happened in Russia and its neighbouring former Soviet republics when they gained independence from the Soviet Union and it came time for them to design the separations of powers models for their new constitutions.

[117] ibid 324.

8

'Founding Moments' in Latin America?

The Brazilian and Chilean Constitutional Histories and the Rise of the Forgotten People

JULIANO ZAIDEN BENVINDO

I. Introduction

'A Foundation is a promise', said Jacques Derrida in his fascinating article 'Force of Law: The Mystical Foundation of Authority'.[1] No founding moment is pure, for there is always 'a call for self-conserving repetition'.[2] It is in this paradoxical conflation of the promise and the past that the legal literature usually interprets the founding of a new constitutional moment. A new beginning, with its inherent crises and breakthroughs, is normally associated with the idea that the origins of democracy and constitutionalism, while both interacting with – and being mediated by – each other, will lead to a vicious circle and infinite regress.[3] However, whereas the famous 'chicken-and-egg paradox of politics'[4] appears in philosophical debates over the origins and the limits of constitutional democracy, connecting it to events like revolutions or structural political transitions, little has been done to associate the concept of 'founding moment' with not so radical events like these ones.[5] After all, if this concept is marked by controversies over how and to what extent the past and the promise connect to each other, what exactly makes a moment a 'founding moment'? And how radical should it be in order to be deemed a 'founding moment'?

[1] Jacques Derrida, 'Force of Law: The Mystical Foundation of Authority' (1990) 11 *Cardozo Law Review* 919.

[2] ibid.

[3] See Lasse Thomassen, 'A Bizarre, Even Opaque Practice: Habermas on Constitutionalism and Democracy' in Lasse Thomassen (ed), *The Derrida-Habermas Reader* (University of Chicago Press, 2006) 176; Bonnie Honig, *Emergency Politics: Paradox, Law, Democracy* (Princeton University Press, 2009) 12.

[4] Honig (n 3) 15.

[5] See Maryam S Kham, ch 10 in this volume, who argues that the founding moment 'need not have revolutionary origins, nor break completely with the old legal order'.

This chapter will challenge the concept of 'founding moment', usually related to those radical events by examining two interesting democratic transitions in Latin America: Brazil and Chile. This region has historically experienced unique challenges in constitutionalism, particularly involving its strong presidential and centralist tradition and the aim to provide an egalitarian constitution where inequality is still a very disturbing reality.[6] It is no wonder that this region has endured varied forms of constitutional and political transitions and practices. Some of them have led to what the legal literature calls 'abusive constitutionalism',[7] 'competitive authoritarianism'[8] and the like; others have led to rather promising democracies, where the mechanisms of democracy[9] have somehow gained momentum. While the first group has received great attention, normally associating it with radical events in the region like the 'Bolivarian Revolution' in Venezuela or the 'National Democratic Revolution' in Bolivia, the second has been relatively set aside.

Derived from the so-called 'post-liberal constitutionalism',[10] whose focus consists in granting new rights to historically oppressed social groups through a new process of constitutionalisation[11] challenging some of the liberal constitutional standards, the first group has been in the spotlight of Latin American studies. Yet, Latin American, with its rich history of distinct forms of constitutionalisation and transitions from dictatorships to democracies, has plenty of other experiences that provide valuable insights about how their different moments founded new constitutional realities. Particularly interesting is how these transitions led to different moments of constitutionalisation. On the one hand, as happened in Brazil, the immediate outcome of this new moment was the drafting of a new constitutional text with a very extensive bill of individual and social rights, in clear opposition to the dark years of military rule. On the other hand, as was the case in Chile, despite the violent and authoritarian years of dictatorship, the aftermath of the transition to democracy did not spur a movement towards drafting a new text, but a distinct development of simply amending the 1980 Constitution, drafted during Augusto Pinochet's military dictatorship.

Brazil and Chile are two relevant democracies in Latin America, and both endured years of military dictatorship that deeply affected their institutions and social life. They have since achieved a fairly stable process of democratisation, although some inflection points of instability have surfaced.[12] Still, even though

[6] See Roberto Gargarella, *Latin American Constitutionalism, 1810–2010* (Oxford University Press, 2013).

[7] David Landau, 'Abusive Constitutionalism' (2013) 47 *UC Davies Law Review* 189.

[8] See Steven Levitsky and Lucan A. Way. *Competitive Authoritarianism: Hybrid Regimes after the Cold War* (Cambridge University Press, 2010).

[9] See Adrian Vermeule, *Mechanisms of Democracy* (Oxford University Press, 2007).

[10] Cristiano Paixão, 'Autonomia, Democracia e Poder Constituinte: Disputas Conceituais na Experiência Constitucional Brasileira (1964–2014)' (2014) 43 *Quaderni Fiorentini* 415, 422.

[11] ibid.

[12] This is, for instance, the situation for the former Brazilian President Dilma Roussef, who was impeached after a controversial move in Congress on 31 August 2016, which paved the way for the election of the far-right President Jair Bolsonaro on 27 October 2018.

these moments of instability follow a common trajectory in Latin America and despite the current rise in social and political polarisation (especially in Brazil), both countries seem to have spurred a more pragmatic process of accommodation of the structural tensions among the different sectors of society. Moreover, the elites, albeit their long-standing untouchable privileges, have had to negotiate some of their positions in order to face the new challenges of the very process of democratisation. If these circumstances may have led to a sort of 'democracy by undemocratic means',[13] with many ambiguous and questionable policies and bargains in order to achieve this new democratic order, it may also have created some of the structural conditions that could maintain relative stability over time.

Frances Hagopian, when examining the Brazilian transition to democracy, clearly pointed out that if those negotiated agreements could by some means bring about stability,[14] many political obstacles remained strong after the transition, then leading to the conclusion that those 'pacts did not broaden and deepen democracy, nor did the politicians who forged them create strong democratic institutions and resolve to adhere to democratic political practice'.[15] However, despite the most recent events leading to a presidential impeachment and the rise of a President who reflects much of a still-strong authoritarian mindset in Brazilian society, Brazil has, since the transition to democracy, 'made significant strides toward nascent pluralism',[16] which has played an important role in enhancing the mechanisms of democracy.[17] Chile, by the same token, can be portrayed as one of the Latin American countries whose political institutions are 'the least conducive to effective democracy'.[18] Yet, paradoxically, it can also be recognised 'as among the most successful in Latin America, and in regional perspective the country has one of the best records of democratic governability'.[19]

In this regard, whereas both countries can be categorised in a distinct classification from those 'post-liberal constitutionalisms'[20] and have many aspects in common, their transitions to democracy were nonetheless marked by distinct forms of 'founding moments'. In Brazil, the transition to democracy immediately meant a new constitutional moment and a new constitution, with an opening to civil society[21] during the deliberative proceedings. In Chile, the transition to

[13] Frances Hagopian, '"Democracy by Undemocratic Means"?: Elites, Political Pacts, and Regime Transition in Brazil' (1987) 23 *Comparative Political Studies* 147.

[14] ibid 149.

[15] ibid 166.

[16] Daron Acemoglu and James A Robinson *Why Nations Fail: The Origins of Power, Prosperity and Poverty*, (Crown Business, 2012) 436.

[17] See Vermeule (n 9).

[18] Peter Siavelis, 'Accomodating Informal Institutions and Chilean Democracy' in Steven Levitsky and Gretchen Helmke (eds), *Informal Institutions and Democracy: Lessons from Latin America* (John Hopkins University Press, 2006) 33.

[19] ibid.

[20] Paixão (n 12) 422.

[21] See LAA Barbosa, *História Constitucional Brasileira: Mudança Constitucional, Autoritarismo e Democracia no Brasil Pós-1964* (Biblioteca Digital da Câmara dos Deputados, 2012) 230.

democracy was characterised by the accommodation of informal institutions,[22] with an 'awkward institutional framework'[23] that did not engender a constitutional moment with a new constitution, but rather the maintenance of a constitution drafted during Pinochet's dictatorship, despite some reforms taking place after the return to democracy. The 1980 Chilean Constitution would thus represent a paramount example of what Tom Ginsburg calls 'transformational authoritarian constitutions', which are drafted with the purpose of laying the groundwork for a future democracy, though keeping untouched authoritarian enclaves impeding a stronger democratisation process.[24] Therefore, while in Brazil the impetus for change led to a democratic founding moment with a new constitutional text through political bargaining and the direct participation of civil society, in Chile, the impetus for change was instead accommodated by formal and informal institutions that kept alive a constitutional text originally from the dictatorship era, even though it was paradoxically characterised by many republican principles and individual rights. Only in 2015 could Chile initiate the expected discussion of launching a constituent assembly to draft a new constitution,[25] though the outcome was unsuccessful in the end.[26]

The underlying question of the constitutional movements of both countries is how the drafting of a new constitution after the transition to democracy impacts the founding of a democratic moment. A new constitution or the simple accommodation of the old constitution to the new era may play distinct roles during that very moment. Evidently, constitutional transitions are complex phenomena, and constitutional text does not mean constitutionalism. Still, it is intriguing to observe that countries with some similar patterns followed such contrasting avenues. This chapter will therefore explore these two constitutional realities and transitions in order to discuss whether and how the timing of drafting a new constitution may affect the very concept of 'founding moments'.

For this purpose, the chapter begins by discussing some aspects of Brazilian (section II) and Chilean (section III) constitutional realities and stressing how different the aftermaths of their transitions to democracy were, at least in relation

[22] See Siavelis (n 18) 34.

[23] ibid 35.

[24] Tom Ginsburg, '¿Fruto de la Parra Envenenada? Algunas Observaciones Comparadas sobre la Constitución Chilena' (2014) 133 *Estudios Públicos* 1, who argues that 'transformational authoritarian constitutions … (1) are explicitly framed as helping to structure a return to electoral democracy after a period of time; (2) reflects certain policy goals designed to be permanent and (3) contain an enforcement mechanism to ensure that both these goals are met').

[25] See Claudia Heiss and Oya Yegen, 'The Constitution-Making Process in Chile: A Cautionary Tale from Turkey', *ICON Blog*, 19 June 2015, www.iconnectblog.com/2015/06/the-constitution-making-process-in-chile-a-cautionary-tale-from-turkey; Alberto Coddou Mc Manus, 'The Chilean Constituent Process: A Long and Winding Road', *ICON Blog*, 4 May 2016, www.iconnectblog.com/2016/05/the-chilean-constituent-process-a-long-and-winding-road.

[26] See Sergio Verdugo and Jorge Contesse, 'The Rise and Fall of a Constitutional Moment: Lessons from the Chilean Experiment and the Failure of Bachelet's Project', *ICON Blog*, 13 March 2018, www.iconnectblog.com/2018/03/the-rise-and-fall-of-a-constitutional-moment-lessons-from-the-chilean-experiment-and-the-failure-of-bachelets-project.

to their constitutions. The chapter concludes (section IV) by connecting both constitutional realities to the concept of founding moments, arguing that for such a complex phenomenon of democratic transitions, a new constitution may indeed be relevant for a new beginning, at least at a symbolic level. However, this conclusion does not mean that a new constitutional text alone is able to enhance democracy, but simply that the founding moment, 'the act as archive as well as the act as performance',[27] must maintain the link with the legitimacy of the new moment or, as Derrida calls it, 'must maintain within itself the signature'.[28] In other words, although the constitutional text is only the tip of the iceberg of constitutionalism, the constitutional text may matter as a legitimating sign of a new founding moment.

II. Constitutional Change Through a New Constitutional Text: The Brazilian Transition to Democracy

Among the Latin American countries marked by years of military dictatorship, Brazil stands out as a prominent example of a transition to democracy wherein the timing for change also meant the timing for a new constitution. After the end of the military dictatorship in 1985, already in 1987 a constituent assembly was established to draft a new constitution to replace the authoritarian Constitution of 1967, with its amendment no 1 of 1969. As a constitutional moment also characterised by the founding of a new democratic moment, the reminiscences of that past still played a significant role in determining how constitutionalism should be interpreted and practised from that moment onwards. The Constituent Assembly of 1987/1988 was thereby the result of a bumpy road towards democracy. Until 1987, the military regime, although having left office in 1985, was relatively successful in controlling how the transition should take place.[29] The motto was 'safe, slow, and gradual opening'. Democracy, according to this motto, was then a simple achievement after 21 years of military rule, which was responsible for laying the groundwork for this new future.

Everything seemed to be heading towards an appeasing transition controlled by the regime and the elites. Frances Hagopian, for example, argued that all the transition took place as a 'negotiated settlement on the part of the political elites'.[30] It was not an effective process of liberalisation and rupture, but rather a 'series of political pacts'[31] that could best cope with a civil society eager for change and

[27] Jacques Derrida, 'Declarations of Independence' in Jacques Derrida (ed), *Negotiations: Inteventions and Interviews, 1971–2001* (Stanford University Press, 2002) 48.
[28] ibid.
[29] See Paixão (n 12) 439.
[30] Hagopian (n 13) 149.
[31] ibid.

which was increasingly promoting mass protests all over the country, while the military and the elites could not lose privileges and positions. Political bargains[32] characterised this transition, with serious impacts on how Brazilian democracy would evolve thereafter. According to Hagopian, Brazil would not experience a 'vibrant democracy, but a perverted one skewed toward the representation of elite interests',[33] especially in a country that had thus far experienced a frail democratic framework.[34]

Still, history might have proven that Hagopian's thesis only gave one side of the story, at least if we look at those events from today's perspective.[35] Naturally, many forms of bargains and political accommodations brought about serious consequences for Brazilian democracy. Nonetheless, the Constituent Assembly of 1987/1988 also did something unprecedented in Brazilian history: it was not framed from above by a group of experts who were representatives of those elites.[36] Instead, it resulted from the work of some democratically elected congressmen (most of them without legal skills),[37] the strong participation of civil society,[38] institutional mechanisms of popular participation and the decentralised dynamics of numerous committees and subcommittees on distinct matters working simultaneously without any preliminary draft of a constitutional text.[39]

Pluralism was visible during these preparatory works, despite the encroachment of some privileged sectors of civil society and the military upon the constituent assembly. It was, to quote Leonardo Barbosa, 'an authentic polyphony'.[40] While it signalled that the military's hegemony was in crisis, no longer being able to control the transition, no other leadership or alternative political bloc emerged that could unilaterally control how the game would then be played.[41] President José Sarney, a civilian with strong ties to the military,[42] was visibly weak and was not able to

[32] ibid.

[33] ibid 160. See also Frances Hagopian and Scott Mainwaring, 'Democracy in Brazil: Problems and Prospects' (1987) 4 *World Policy Journal* 485, 486.

[34] Hagopian (n 13) 148.

[35] Hagopian's papers on Brazil were mostly written during the transition to democracy and the 1990s. Brazil has since significantly changed at the institutional and social levels.

[36] See Cristiano Paixão, 'Direito, Política, Autoritarismo e Democracia no Brasil: Da Revolução de 30 à Promulgação da Constituição da República de 1988' (2011) 26 *Araucária* 146, 164.

[37] However, these congressmen were not elected for the specific purpose of the constituent assembly, but rather for an ordinary legislature elected in November 1986, which was granted constituent powers. See Barbosa (n 21) 193; Cristiano Paixão, 'Past and Future of Authoritarian Regimes: Constitution, Transition to Democracy and Amnesty in Brazil and Chile' (2015) 30 *Giornale di Storia Costituzionale* 89, 93.

[38] From 1977 to 1985, there was increasing pressure from distinct social groups to make the Constituent Assembly a reality. See Bernardo Kucinsky, *O Fim da Ditadura Militar: O Colapso do 'Milagre Econômico', a Volta aos Quartéis, a Luta pela Democracia* (Contexto, 2001) 165.

[39] See Barbosa (n 21) 147.

[40] ibid.

[41] See Marcos Nobre, 'Indeterminação e Estabilidade: Os 20 Anos da Constituição Federal e as Tarefas da Pesquisa em Direito' (2008) 82 *Novos Estudos CEBRAP* 97, 98; Cícero Araújo, 'O Processo Constituinte Brasileiro, a Transição e o Poder Constituinte' (2013) *Lua Nova* 327, 378; Barbosa (n 21) 211.

[42] President José Sarney took office after the death Tancredo Neves, the first civilian indirectly elected to the presidency.

prevent society from becoming more actively involved in the constitution-making process. Moreover, despite their intention to control the transition, the military, which left office in 1985, had not previously drafted a document that could bind how the constituent assembly would operate.[43] The 'intense and influential participation of organized civil society',[44] the 'contradictory plurality of actors'[45] was then a feature of the constituent assembly, setting up a scenario of deep indeterminacy towards the future.[46] Both movements – the political bargains and the direct participation of civil society – co-existed in an environment in which the idea of continuity or rupture with the past struggled with each other in building this new democratic founding moment.

The Brazilian democratic founding moment after years of military dictatorship was thereby marked by conflicting interpretations of how the promise and the past should be intertwined with each other from that moment onwards. The idea of pacific transition and not of a rupture with the past gained momentum, especially in the early stages of its procedures.[47] However, such a transition was marked by the growing pluralism of the Constituent Assembly. While the Constituent Assembly opened its proceedings with the Brazilian Supreme Court Justice Moreira Alves saying that 'by installing this National Constituent Assembly, the final term of the period of transition is reached, whereby, without constitutional rupture and via conciliation, the revolutionary cycle comes to an end',[48] its following proceedings were nonetheless characterised by 'a decentralized dynamics in more than two dozen theme subcommittees without the guidance of any preliminary draft of a Constitution'.[49] Its discussions and procedural rules were marked by an effort to extend the dialogue to society,[50] while creating some institutional constraints on Congress in order to lessen the risks of a hegemonic bloc controlling its results.[51]

There are some social reasons for this phenomenon. After years of mass protests and public mobilisation, especially from the late 1970s onwards, Brazil was living a special moment of increasing democratic learning and practice. There was a 'creative and participatory potential that was dammed',[52] only expecting the moment to be released.[53] This participatory potential took place both in the

[43] See Paixão (n 36) 89.
[44] Nobre (n 41) 98.
[45] Araújo (n 41) 378.
[46] ibid.
[47] This argument was quite recently employed by the Brazilian Supreme Court to confirm the constitutionality of the amnesty law (Law 6.683/1979). See ADPF 153 (STF, DJU 4 May 2012).
[48] Diário da Assembleia Nacional Constituinte (2 February 1987).
[49] See Barbosa (n 21) 164.
[50] ibid 218.
[51] See Jefferson Goulart, 'Processo Constituinte e Arranjo Federativo' (2013) 88 *Lua Nova* 185; Júlio Aurélio Vianna, *A Carta da Democracia: O Processo Constituinte da Ordem Pública de 1988* (Topbooks, 2008); Nobre (n 41) 97. See also Hagopian and Mainwaring (n 33) 485, who instead emphasise the clear negotiation among elite groups during the Constitutional Assembly.
[52] Paixão (n 36) 164.
[53] Before the Constitutional Assembly of 1987/1988, massive popular movements accelerated these characteristics, such as: (a) the strikes and demonstrations in distinct regions of Brazil; (b) the campaign for a wide, general and unrestricted amnesty in 1979, which, after some comings and goings,

form of popular lobbies and institutional mechanisms at the heart of the Constituent Assembly. Examples as such could be found in the possibility of submitting suggestions, holding public hearings, proposing popular amendments to the Constitution.[54] Moreover, the procedures and deliberations of the Constituent Assembly were broadcast nationwide.[55] In the end, this paradox of the old regime and those political bargains along with this experience of popular groups dialoguing with the Constituent Assembly drafted the Constitution that cannot be exactly called harmonious or coherent, but is certainly the most dynamic and democratic in Brazilian history.

The ongoing disagreement over continuity and rupture of this constitutional moment was reflected in a constitutional text characterised by many norms that seem unfinished – thereby needing subsequent regulation – or in clearly opposing sides.[56] This is naturally a side-effect of a process that aimed at being controlled, but that became quite uncontrolled in the end, where the deep paradoxical nature of the interests involved co-existed with a high degree of indeterminacy. The 'authentic polyphony'[57] of this moment paved the way for drafting a constitutional text marked by its comprehensiveness, with a vast bill of individual and social rights, followed by distinct institutional mechanisms to protect them, whereas many other provisions related to the political system and entrenched benefits were kept virtually untouched.[58] Some will argue that, despite this increment of citizenship, Brazil endured, in the end, a 'long and highly negotiated democratic transition, marked by a very limited reformism'.[59] Others, in turn, will point out that this living citizenship would push the framers to sign the constitutional text through a 'renewed idea of legitimacy and representation, which gives rise to a reflection on the very meaning of the principle of popular sovereignty'.[60]

Despite this insurmountable paradoxical nature of this moment, the simple fact that it gave rise to a new constitution is nevertheless a milestone of a 'new beginning', which certainly holds a symbolic power over Brazilian society, as a

resulted in Law No 6.683/1979; (c) the movement Diretas Já (*Direct Elections Now*) in 1983/1984, which gathered more than one and a half million people all over the country, but whose results were frustrated by Congress. See Paixão (n 36) 165; Domingos Leonelli and Dante de Oliveira, *Diretas Já: 15 Meses que Abalaram a Ditadura* (Record, 2004); Alberto Tosi Rodrigues, *Diretas Já: O Grito Preso na Garganta* (Fundação Perseo Abramo, 2003); Flamarion Maués and Zilah Wendel Abramo, *Pela Democracia, contra o Arbítrio: A Oposição Democrática, do Golpe de 1964 à Campanha das Diretas Já* (Fundação Perseu Abramo, 2006).

[54] See Barbosa (n 21) 230; Carlos Michiles et al, *Cidadão Constituinte: A Saga das Emendas Populares* (Paz e Terra, 1989).

[55] Paixão (n 36) 164.

[56] See Nobre (n 41) 98.

[57] Barbosa (n 21) 147.

[58] For instance, the judiciary in general, and the Brazilian Supreme Court in particular, strongly lobbied to keep many of its privileges untouched. See Andrei Koerner and Lígia Barros de Freitas, 'O Supremo na Constituinte e a Constituinte no Supremo' (2013) 88 *Lua Nova* 141. For a broader discussion of other cases, see Edson Teles and Vladimir Pinheiro Safatle, *O que Resta da Ditadura* (Boitempo Editorial, 2015).

[59] Nobre (n 41) 98.

[60] Barbosa (n 21) 245.

democratic achievement that reminds us of how we should enshrine its values in our daily lives. Still, all the processes of framing the constitutional text and the experience of that moment, when the controlled past was challenged by the uncontrolled future, yielded a much greater impact upon the very significance of Brazilian constitutionalism. It is a severe undermining of that moment to interpret it overlooking those clashes, dilemmas and, above all, this emerging citizenship. A constitution, after all, is not simply text, although it inscribes much of this temporality in its own words. There is always, especially in paradoxical moments as such, a performative utterance that exceeds the reality or, as Derrida says, there is always 'this obscurity, this undecidability between, let us say, a performative structure and a constative structure'.[61] When the Brazilian framers viewed themselves in face of this living citizenship, the Constitution had already been substantially transformed. Their signature was thereby deeply affected.[62] A 'new beginning', although still marked by many permanencies in the text and practices, was born. A new constitution for launching this new moment was therefore not only meaningful because of a text enshrining democratic values, but, above all, because it catalysed the effective practice of these democratic values in the very process of constitution-making.

The paradoxical emergence of Brazilian democratic constitutionalism makes it clear that transitions as such, while not revolutionary, are strong enough to lay the groundwork for a gradual evolutionary process[63] wherein political[64] and economic[65] inclusive institutions become more real. Despite the backlash driven by many actors who feel that their privileges and benefits are in serious jeopardy during this new moment and who will do whatever it takes to keep them untouched, even by unsettling the constitutional system, pluralism – as Brazilian transition proves – helps dissolve and distribute much of their strength, thereby weakening their capacity to twist the institutional framework to serve their exclusive interests.[66] This feature leads to new negotiations and agreements that, little by little, may engender inclusive institutions.[67] By institutionalising mechanisms that foster pluralism, the consequence may also be a progressive gain of stability.[68]

[61] Derrida (n 27) 49.

[62] ibid.

[63] See Jürgen Habermas, 'Towards a Reconstruction of Historical Materialism' (2007) 2 *Theory and Society* 297: 'the first step in the social evolutionary learning process is the establishment of a new form of social integration which permits an increase in the productive forces and an expansion of the system's complexity'.

[64] See Daron Acemoglu and James A Robinson, *Why Nations Fail: The Origins of Power, Prosperity, and Poverty* (Crown Business, 2012) 460: 'the empowerment at the grass-roots level in Brazil ensured that the transition to democracy corresponded to a move toward inclusive political institutions'.

[65] See Douglass C North, *Understanding the Process of Economic Change* (Princeton University Press, 2005) 158: 'the ideal economic model comprises a set of economic institutions that provide incentives for individuals and organizations to engage in productive activity'.

[66] See Daron Acemoglu, 'Why Not a Political Coase Theorem? Social Conflict, Commitment, and Politics' (2003) 31 *Journal of Comparative Economics* 620.

[67] See Acemoglu and Robinson (n 16) 79.

[68] See Mel A Topf, ch 3 in this volume.

Therefore, rather than a radical confrontation, sometimes a strategic move is to narrow the scope and slow down the pace of change, gaining ground to bolster, in the medium to long run, even more pluralism and thereby more stability.

The Brazilian transition to democracy has followed the path of attempting to settle its disputes without confronting its past. This aspect does not mean that Brazilians have not resented their past; yet, by not confronting it, they have laid the groundwork for some serious threats to Brazil's democratic achievements, such as the recent rise of President Jair Bolsonaro, a far-right politician who praises the civil–military dictatorship.[69] Although the new constitution and its founding moment may impose a new posture towards this past, history has proven that whenever a more radical avenue gains momentum, Brazilian institutions manage to place it into a course of action that is less offensive to the status quo. This can bring greater stability and the need to continuously reach compromises, but evidently at the cost of slowing down the pace of some necessary transformations.

Examples of the process of how Brazilian democracy has managed to settle its disputes appear in distinct forms of constitutional change. Tom Ginsburg and James Melton argue that Brazil, along with India and Mexico, has its Constitution amended practically every year, and this may signal 'the virtue of being frequently changed through internal mechanisms, avoiding the more costly route of a total replacement'.[70] Their thesis is based on cultural grounds, as though in Brazil there is little cultural resistance to amend the Constitution.[71] Still, if cultural reasons play a relevant role in such a phenomenon, the very paradoxical characteristic of Brazilian constitutionalism may explain it even further. The Constitution of 1988 is, after all, the upshot of this complex of interests that flourished through a procedure that moved from a controlled to a relatively uncontrolled transition, where the 'past' had to negotiate with the 'new beginning' and where the inherent vulnerability of some of these compromises would demand an ongoing negotiation process in the following years.

Therefore, the Brazilian Constitution of 1988 is a paramount example of a learning process that took place before 1988 and went way beyond that moment.[72] Many of its promises were either not kept or failed to face the challenges of a society that was structurally unequal and still marked by an authoritarian mindset. It is no wonder that the Constitution has been continuously challenged by several

[69] Brazil, for example, has not directly confronted the amnesty law and many of the atrocities happened under the military dictatorship. This oblivion of the past may have contributed to the rise of President Jair Bolsonaro, who clearly defends a revisionist interpretation of the civil-military dictatorship (1964–85).

[70] Tom Ginsburg and James Melton, 'Does the Constitutional Amendment Rule Matter at All? Amendments Cultures and the Challenges of Measuring Amendment Difficulty' (2015) 13 *ICON* 689.

[71] ibid.

[72] See Marcelo Andrade Cattoni de Oliveira and Rafael Dilly Patrus, 'Constituição e Poder Constituinte no Brasil Pós-1964: O Processo de Constitucionalização Brasileiro entre 'Transição e Ruptura'' (2016) 45 *Quaderni Fiorentini* 187.

attempts to regain control over its meaning and re-signify its comprehensiveness.[73] The natural avenue has been to amend the Constitution, although an empirical examination has proven that most amendments have had little effect on engendering structural changes to the constitutional text.[74] Other avenues, such as attempts to launch fast-track procedures of constitutional change circumventing the formal requirements of constitutional amendment, although repeatedly proposed, have all failed.[75]

Mechanisms of informal amendment to the Constitution[76] have also gained momentum in Brazil,[77] showing how the Constitution has become a gravitational centre of Brazilian social life. No one can deny the significant role the Brazilian Supreme Court plays in the definition of relevant national matters, clearly pointing to a broader interpretation of its authority to areas now seen as part of constitutionalism at large. However, this turning point in the Supreme Court's behaviour is also marked by a contrasting feature of Brazilian constitutionalism.[78] On the one hand, it has actively provided decisions that have fostered equality rights, such as those relating to same-sex unions[79] and quotas for black students in public universities,[80] or that have affected the political system, like the prohibition of corporate campaign contributions.[81] On the other hand, it has steadily acted to maintain the entrenched benefits of some social groups and corporations,[82] which in many respects evidences 'a form of self-interested *hegemonic preservation*'.[83]

The concurrence of an increasing pluralistic and democratic impetus fostered by this founding moment and a 'past' stubbornly reacting to more radical reforms is thereby the main feature of Brazilian constitutionalism, which, also because of

[73] See Barbosa (n 21) 251; Juliano Zaiden Benvindo, 'The Brazilian Constitutional Amendment Rate: A Culture of Change?', *ICON Blog*, 10 August 2016, www.iconnectblog.com/2016/08/the-brazilian-constitutional-amendment-rate-a-culture-of-change.

[74] ibid.

[75] Barbosa (n 21) 251.

[76] See Bruce Ackerman, *We The People: Foundations* (Harvard University Press, 1991), who also presents the theory of 'constitutional moments' for informal constitutional change in the US; and Rosalind Dixon, 'Constitutional Drafting and Distrust' (2016) 13 *ICON* 819, who shows the merits of formal and informal mechanisms of constitutional drafting.

[77] See Juliano Zaiden Benvindo, *On the Limits of Constitutional Adjudication: Deconstructing Balancing and Judicial Activism* (Springer, 2010) 83.

[78] See Swati Jhaveri, ch 2 in this volume, who shows, based on the experiences of Singapore and Hong Kong, how the judiciary matters for keeping the founding moment, and thereby the role of citizenry, in transitional contexts.

[79] STF, ADI 4277 (DJe 5 May 2011).

[80] STF, ADPF 132 (DJe 3 November 2014).

[81] See STF, ADI 4650 (DJe 24 February 2015). See also Juliano Zaiden Benvindo, 'Corporate Campaign Contributions in Brazil: Of Courts, Congresses, and the Agendas of Individual Justices', *ICON Blog*, 3 July 2015, www.iconnectblog.com/2015/07/corporate-campaign-contributions-in-brazil-of-courts-congresses-and-the-agendas-of-individual-justices.

[82] See Alexandre Araújo Costa and Juliano Zaiden Benvindo, 'A Quem Interessa o Controle Concentrado De Constitucionalidade? O Descompasso entre Teoria e Prática na Defesa dos Direitos Fundamentais' (2014), http://ssrn.com/abstract=2509541.

[83] Ran Hirschl, *Towards Juristocracy: The Origins and Consequences of the New Constitutionalism* (Harvard University Press, 2004) 11.

such a feature, moves backwards in some circumstances as is currently the case with the political scenario in the country. In any case, Brazil has built mechanisms that are somewhat able to direct some of the inevitable tensions and backlashes through institutional channels, and this may explain why the Constitution is frequently formally and informally amended. More structural and radical solutions to the long-standing misfortunes of Brazilian society have normally been transformed into pragmatic actions aimed at fostering some change without, however, affecting entrenched privileges. Yet, the simple fact of having drafted a democratic constitution through legitimate forms of civil participation has brought about a symbolic power which has gradually fostered pluralism. Despite the inevitable resistance of the status quo, such a pluralism has been a relevant driving force behind the gradual rise of inclusive political institutions.[84] Obviously, backlashes, such as the recent impeachment of President Dilma Roussef or the Supreme Court's preservationist role, still occur as the outcome of the conflicting positions of a country marked by long-standing inequalities. Nevertheless, they do not deny the power of that founding moment: a constitutional transition that inscribed in Brazilian history the strength of its pluralism.

III. Constitutional Change without a Constitutional Text: The Chilean Transition to Democracy

Like Brazil, Chile also endured years of military dictatorship and its transition to democracy was characterised by strategies to control it until the very end. Yet, unlike Brazil, Chile is a paramount example of a country whose transition to democracy did not correspond to drafting a new constitution. Instead, Chile, up to the present day, still adopts the Constitution of 1980, which was drafted during the military dictatorship (1973–89) to replace the previous Constitution of 1925. As a product of a thoughtful strategy to preserve the status quo and hamper structural changes to its text, the 1980 Constitution was the result of a deep disbelief in the capacity of Chilean society to solve, through democratic means, most of its challenges.[85] Created by the so-called 'Ortúzar Committee' as the symbol of a necessary founding moment[86] for Chilean society that, unlike the previous constitutional text, could best face the dangers of 'the forces of the Marxist left',[87]

[84] See Acemoglu and Robinson (n 78) 460.

[85] See Peter Siavelis, *President and Congress in Postauthoritarian Chile: Institutional Constraints to Democratic Consolidation* (Pennsylvania State University Press, 2000) 1.

[86] See Paixão (n 36) 95: 'the dictatorship always asserted its foundational project'. According to him, unlike in Brazil, where the military called their rise to power a 'revolution', in Chile, the idea of a revolution never gained momentum. As he says, 'the Chilean regime had a foundational proposal, but that foundation was not a revolutionary one'.

[87] J Samuel Valenzuela, 'La Constitución de 1980 y el Inicio de la Redemocratización' (2007) Kellogg Institute, Working Paper fn 242 4, https://kellogg.nd.edu/sites/default/files/old_files/documents/242_0.pdf.

the 1980 Constitution is in reality an outcome of a strategic decision to control the future.[88] Indeed, Jaime Guzmán, the most influential member of that Committee, saw in democracy, albeit inevitable and even necessary, a very dangerous regime that could be used for populist goals.[89]

This committee, which was appointed in the immediate aftermath of the coup[90] and gained momentum in 1977,[91] would be responsible for designing a constitutional system which would be sustained even after Chile's transition to democracy. A constitutional text strategically drafted during a dictatorship that would lay the groundwork for a controlled democracy is in some ways profoundly paradoxical, but Chile reveals how founding moments, such as its transition to democracy in 1989, are also very much still the 'past'.

Many authoritarian legacies would be inscribed in its text, with disruptive effects on the new democracy, such as an exclusionary electoral system through proportional representation, in which minorities would have little say, life-tenured senators, the judicial system, a National Security Council responsible for overseeing matters of national security and a very rigid mechanism of constitutional change, especially for those provisions that would affect some entrenched interests. Following a common path of Latin American constitutions,[92] the 1980 Constitution would also concentrate excessive powers on the President,[93] bestow many privileges on the military and its role of overseeing the state,[94] undermine much of the role of Parliament and the possibility of reaching majorities,[95] and limit mechanisms of civilian participation as a way to 'prevent the reemergence of the dynamics of polarization and instability of the early 1970s'[96] and also safeguard the positive economic legacy of the authoritarian period.[97] Rather than a fragmented and divided society and party system[98] that could lead to the emergence

[88] See Paixão (n 36) 95.

[89] See Javier Couso, 'Models of Democracy and Models of Constitutionalism: The Case of Chile's Constitutional Court, 1970–2010' (2011) 89 *Texas Law Review* 1531, who states that Guzmán 'was heavily conditioned by a conception of democracy as an inevitable, but rather dangerous, regime – one that any modern society should have but that was susceptible to manipulation by demagogues to the detriment of private property rights'.

[90] As a sign that the dictatorship's project was foundational since its inception, this Committee's work started just 13 days after the coup d'état.

[91] The coup against Salvador Allende took place on 11 September 1973, and the Ortúzar Commission was created on 25 October 1973. In 1977, General Augusto Pinochet, after presumably accepting the argument that a new constitution was needed, asked this Committee to draft the constitutional text, obviously incorporating many of his ideas. See Valenzuela (n 87) 8.

[92] See Gargarella (n 6).

[93] See 1980 Constitution of the Republic of Chile, arts 62, 70, 71.

[94] See Valenzuela (n 87) 9.

[95] See Paixão (n 36) 97, who argues that 'the electoral rules virtually prevent the formation of a consistent majority in Parliament'.

[96] Siavelis (n 85) 1.

[97] ibid 2.

[98] According to Siavelis, 'military leaders sought to design a system that would limit party-system fragmentation and in the process lead to a formation of a two-party system, which they viewed as the most stable, moderate, and desirable option for Chile'. Siavelis (n 85) 32.

of populist leaders, the constitutional framework would transform any reform into compromised and moderate solutions, and thus foster what scholars call a 'protected democracy',[99] as did Guzmán,[100] or 'defensive constitutionalism'.[101] The constitutional architecture was thereby designed to prevent the reach of qualified majorities that could unleash its potential to change the core structure of the constitution, even after the return of democracy.[102]

Still, beneath all this strategic design, General Augusto Pinochet, as the President and Commander-in-Chief during most of the authoritarian years, played a significant role, as his steps were aimed at concentrating more power and curbing any opposition to his actions.[103] When Pinochet was convinced that a new constitution and a transition to democracy was necessary, even though this would be a controlled, 'protected, and even 'authoritarian' one,[104] many of his ideas prevailed.[105] Some of them were negotiated in less extreme ways,[106] but he could, after a series of comings and goings, establish 29 temporary constitutional provisions, many with clear authoritarian content,[107] which suspended the application of many permanent provisions.[108] Among them, the thirteenth transitory provision provided that the 'presidential term which will commence to govern from the entry into force of this Constitution will last [for] the time which Article 25 establishes', while the following one explicitly indicated that 'during the term indicated in the preceding provision, the current President, General of the Army, Augusto Pinochet Ugarte, will continue as President of the Republic, [and] will remain in the position until the end of said term'. In other words, this meant that Pinochet would remain in power for the next eight years with effect from 11 March 1981. He could even stay in power for a further eight years, but, in order to do so, he needed to be 'legitimised' by a national plebiscite.[109]

Because of his popularity, Pinochet really believed that he could win this plebiscite.[110] In fact, the 1980 Constitution, with its permanent and transitory provisions, was itself the subject of a plebiscite on 11 September 1980, thereby indicating that Pinochet had some popular support and presumably providing some legitimacy to its text, although the credibility of the results was highly contested.[111] From this moment on, the 1980 Constitution became a strategic argument for Pinochet's authoritarian actions. In a sort of paradoxical symbiosis,

[99] ibid 2.
[100] See Couso (n 89) 1531.
[101] Paixão (n 36) 97.
[102] See Couso (n 89) 1532.
[103] See Valenzuela (n 87) 6.
[104] ibid 8.
[105] ibid 9.
[106] See Siavelis (n 85) 13: 'the process of negotiation ultimately served to water down Pinochet's extreme proposals, though his plan for a "protected" democracy is still evident in the constitution'.
[107] See, among others, the 15th and 24th Transitory Provisions of the 1980 Chilean Constitution.
[108] See ibid, 21st Transitory Provision.
[109] See ibid, 28th Transitory Provision.
[110] See Siavelis (n 85) 13; Valenzuela (n 87) 12.
[111] See Kamel Cazor Aliste, 'Democracya y Constitucion en Chile' (2000) XI *Revista de Derecho* 27, 27.

both authoritarianism and 'protected' democracy would be combined into the constitutional text. Pinochet was defeated in the national plebiscite on 5 October 1988 and, unlike the previous plebiscite the 1980, the Constitutional Court played a relevant role in overseeing the regularity of the electoral procedures and defending it against attempts by the government to apply the previous electoral framework and other tactics that would jeopardise the participation of the opposition and other safeguards.[112] A strong popular mobilisation took place and the 'no' campaign gained momentum, demonstrating that there would be no better opportunity to topple Pinochet's authoritarian regime.

However, the process that would culminate in the transition to democracy was quite distinct from what happened in Brazil. Instead of the impetus for transforming the democratic transition into a constitutional transition, the 1980 Chilean Constitution became a key element of an achieved consensus for the new democratic model, although it required some structural changes.[113] Since the 1980 Constitution was an instrument of the military rule but already provided some democratic achievements, the negotiation led to the conclusion that in order to prevent Pinochet from any attempt to regain power, there was no better alternative than maintaining it and bringing about some reforms. These reforms, especially now that the opposition was getting stronger and would obtain some electoral victories, would also mean a way to institutionally restrain any further radical moves.

However, according to the twenty-first transitory provision then in force, any amendment to the constitutional text needed to be made by the Government Junta, which exerted legislative and constituent powers, and be approved by a plebiscite.[114] Such a procedure would nonetheless possibly strengthen even further the opposition and maybe encourage a constitutional replacement, which was unacceptable to the right-wing parties and the military.[115] On the other hand, the very procedure for constitutional amendment, when combined with the electoral rules, provided an excessively rigid framework[116] and gave substantial powers to the President,[117] which made negotiations during the transition period

[112] See Couso (n 89) 1531; Valenzuela (n 87) 14.

[113] ibid 24.

[114] See Constitution of Chile, 21st Transitory Provision.

[115] See Valenzuela (n 87) 38

[116] According to Siavelis, 'while these quorums may not seem particularly high in comparative perspective, one should again bear in mind the complete constellation of institutional variables inherited from the previous regime'. Siavelis (n 18) 41.

[117] According to art 116, 'the bill of reform will require for its approval, in each Chamber, the confirming vote of three-fifths of the Deputies and Senators in office'. Moreover, according to art 117, 'if the President of the Republic partially objects to a bill of reform approved by the Congress, the objections will be understood to have been approved with the confirming vote of the absolute majority of the members in office of each Chamber, and it will be returned to the President for its promulgation'. Some other provisions required an even more rigid system. Article 118 provided that: 'The constitutional reforms which have for their object to modify the norms on plebiscites prescribed in the preceding article, to diminish the faculties of the President of the Republic [and] to grant greater attributions to the Congress or new prerogatives to the parliamentarians, will require, in every case, the concurrence of both the wills of both the President of the Republic and of two-thirds of the members in office of each Chamber, and a plebiscite will not proceed in [this] respect.'

more complex. While the left-wing parties were growing in strength but needed to control their more radical impulses, the right-wing parties needed to participate in some changes or they would be accused of still being at Pinochet's behest.

As a 'protected democracy', the constitutional designers made every effort to avoid changes in such circumstances, and their framework proved to be very successful. Yet, there was no formal obstacle to change the very system of constitutional amendment, which could lead to a revamp of the Constitution by circumventing the original rules. This scenario of multiple possibilities over the constitutional text prompted a series of negotiations and bargains in which both the left-wing and right-wing parties – above all, Concertación and Renovación Nacional – attempted to find solutions that would not lead to an uncontrolled reform procedure, but could bring some democratic elements into the constitutional text, such as a four-year term for presidents and a substantial overhaul of Chapter XIV, which addresses the rules for constitutional amendment.[118] However, the military still received a good amount of benefits and retained much of their tutelary role[119] of the state, some senators could still be appointed by the President, and the electoral system, although slightly changed, remained largely exclusionary. In some respects, although ousted from government, the military was successful in setting up mechanisms to steadily control the civilian government, in a form of constitutional design that would prevent the new government from making many of the expected changes. No wonder, as Fredrik Uggla posits it, 'more than any other democracy, Chile would remain characterized by the institutions inherited from the previous regime'.[120]

The new government of Patricio Aylwin was initiated in this environment where the military, still under Pinochet's command, exerted a strong influence on national affairs, while Parliament was regulated by electoral rules that were strong enough to hinder the achievement of majorities for change. In other words, while 'Augusto Pinochet simply packed his desk at La Moneda (the presidential palace) and moved across Santiago's main street to the Ministry of Defense',[121] the government could not promote more structural reforms because of its incapacity, according to the electoral rules, to achieve a qualified majority in Congress. In a more structural view, the transition to democracy was so linked to the purpose of assuring a peaceful future, perpetuating the rules of the game already crafted, and maintaining the same economic model[122] that a new democratic model needed

[118] See Valenzuela (n 87) 25.

[119] See Siavelis (n 18) 36.

[120] Fredrik Uggla, '"For a Few Senators More"? Negotiating Constitutional Changes during Chile's Transition to Democracy' (2008) 47 *Latin American Politics and Society* 55.

[121] See Siavelis (n 18) 36.

[122] See Laura Tedesco and Jonathan R Barton, *The State of Democracy in Latin America: Post-transitional Conflicts in Argentina and Chile* (Routledge, 2004) 147: 'the struggle for a peaceful transition and the perpetuation of the economic model put in place during the mid-1970s took precedence over questions of the form of democratic social relations, the values that would shape them, and the nature of the institutions that would give the ensuing social contract its structure'.

much greater involvement of the citizenship to effectively overcome the authoritarian enclaves[123] of the Pinochet era.

Yet, Chile has endured this reality with relative stability[124] and has raised interesting discussions on how to re-signify that 'past', progressively reforming some norms of that authoritarian period. Moreover, some provisions drafted during Pinochet's regime, despite their original authoritarian intent, proved to be a major factor in Chile's stability, especially in terms of how the political coalitions are formed.[125] Informal institutions[126] have also exerted a relevant role in relation to how the political system manages its differences,[127] transforming the cumbersome institutional framework into an example of success in Latin America despite its strong presidentialism and multiparty system.[128] As Siavelis points out, 'these institutions, in turn, have facilitated the functioning of other formal and informal institutions, underwritten the stability of Chile's coalitional configuration, mitigated the most negative characteristics of exaggerated presidentialism, and contributed to the success of Chilean democracy'.[129]

Based on these practices sustained both by formal and informal institutions, the following governments have pushed some progressive agendas aimed at further democratising the institutions and practices, although some more structural changes could not take place, either because of political compromises[130] or obstructions created by the right-wing parties.[131] By the same token, the judiciary has progressively evaluated that past with less complacent eyes. The Chilean Constitutional Court has followed this path towards democratisation to a certain extent. While, during Pinochet's era, it was designed to ensure the awkward constitutional

[123] See Manuel Antonio Garretón, *Incomplete Democracy* (University of North Carolina Press, 2003) 150.

[124] ibid 103: 'From the 1939s on, there were not recurrent cycles of democracy and authoritarianism in Chile, as there were in other countries.'

[125] See John M. Carey and Peter Siavelis, 'Election Insurance and Coalition Survival: Formal and Informal Institutions in Chile' in Steven Levitsky and Gretchen Helmke (eds), *Informal Institutions and Democracy: Lessons from Latin America* (John Hopkins University Press, 2006): 'Chile's coalition ought to be immune from the ills frequently attributed to loose presidential.' See also Garretón (n 123) 148, who contends that one of the success of Chile's transition 'is the government-led constitution of a majoritarian coalition'.

[126] See Siavelis (n 18) 34: 'informal institutions are most likely to be found where political actors face difficulty operating within formal institutions, or where there is a lack of congruence between political reality and formal institutional arrangements'.

[127] ibid: 'a complex network of informal institutions helped attenuate the problems that might otherwise have developed as a result of Chile's awkward institutional arrangements, and also helped moderate the actions of presidents who have the formal powers to be quite authoritarian'.

[128] See ibid 36. See also Tedesco and Barton (n 122) 145: 'over the last three decades, Chile has been widely regarded as the most successful Latin American', although 'it remains one of the most inequitable societies in Latin America'; Couso (n 89) 1522, who argues that Chile 'has long been considered one where legality and constitutionalism have reached relatively high degrees of consolidation'; Simon Collier and William F Sater, *A History of Chile, 1808–2002* (Cambridge University Press, 2004).

[129] Siavelis (n 18) 36.

[130] See Garretón (n 123) 151.

[131] See Collier and Sater (n 128) 393, who show how the right in Congress blocked many proposals made by Concertación's Presidents.

design of an expected 'protected democracy', as the 'Ortúzar Committee' designed it,[132] in practice it has gradually become a more conventional constitutional court aimed at defending basic rights,[133] whilst sometimes playing a more activist role.[134]

Chile, like Brazil, faces this ongoing struggle between the 'past' and the aim to consolidate itself as a new future. This 'protected democracy' or 'defensive constitutionalism', although bringing about stability both by formal and informal institutions, still represents a stain upon a history that seems somehow incomplete.[135] True, a 'transformational authoritarian constitution'[136] like the Chilean Constitution does not necessarily mean that democracy under such a document is doomed to fail – indeed, as Tom Ginsburg mentions, 56 per cent of all current constitutions were drafted under dictatorial regimes,[137] and Chile, as we have seen, is regarded as one of the most successful cases of democratisation in Latin America[138] – but, at least symbolically, there is a call for change. As Alberto Coddou Mc Manus puts it, 'it seems that Chileans have to discuss, design and implement every policy under the shadow of Pinochet's constitution'.[139]

These words show the symbolic power of those authoritarian vestiges and how they affect the very perception of the role of constitutionalism, still marked by an undemocratic founding moment. Even if relative progress has come about from some aspects of this awkward constitutional design that created a hyper-presidential system with few checks and a weak Parliament, the act of founding – and when and how it is founded – transcends the idea that a simple learning democratic process could over time legitimise a constitution. The connection of the concept of the founding moment with that of citizenship, a feature that has gained strength in Chile[140] (like what happened in Brazil during the Constituent Assembly of 1987/1988), is at the root of also transforming Chile's democratic transition into a constitutional transition.

However, the remaining question is how strong the ability of the citizenship is to craft a constitution in times of relative normality,[141] even if Pinochet's ghost

[132] See Couso (n 89) 1532, who argues that the Constitutional Court 'was just one of an array of institutions designed to prevent the dismantling of the system under democratic rule'.

[133] ibid 1528, arguing that, during Pinochet's government, the Constitutional Court acted 'as an insurance mechanism aimed at protecting the constitutional design introduced by the authoritarian regime against the perceived danger posed by what was seen as the inevitable return to democratic rule', while nowadays it has become 'a more conventional constitutional court in that it actively promotes and defends the fundamental rights of individuals and groups'.

[134] ibid, contending that, after some reforms, the Chilean Constitutional Court has applied 'an ever expanding set of constitutional rights – not only civil and political, but also social, cultural, and economic'.

[135] See Garretón (n 123) 149: 'the resulting opportunity to address the political aspects per se and complete the transition by overcoming the authoritarian enclaves, regrettably, was not taken'.

[136] Ginsburg (n 24) 7.

[137] ibid.

[138] The *Democracy Index 2018*, from *The Economist* Intelligence Unit, places Chile as the third most democratic country in the region. *Democracy Index 2018: Me Too? Political Participation, Protest and Demcoracy* (*The Economist* Intelligence Unit, 2019), www.eiu.com/Handlers/WhitepaperHandler.ashx?fi=Democracy_Index_2018.pdf&mode=wp&campaignid=Democracy2018.

[139] Manus (n 25).

[140] ibid.

[141] ibid, contending that 'Chile could show to the world the possibility of debating a new constitutional arrangement under more or less normal times'.

might paradoxically be one of the reasons for such an outcome. It is a normality that still reproduces the 'past' and uses many tools of this 'past', but it is at the same time ashamed of this 'past'. It is also one that, while strongly believing in its institutional arrangements, still places the citizenship in an inferior position, thereby forgetting its own people.[142]

In this regard, the constitutional moment which, during Michelle Bachelet's presidency, seemed to lead to a constitutional replacement was visibly aimed at placing the citizenship at the forefront through distinct mechanisms of popular participation.[143] However, this 'past' is still very much entrenched in Chilean constitutionalism and it is no wonder that it would adopt all possible tactics to unsettle a more participatory constitution-making process that would affect some of its privileges and benefits. Sergio Verdugo and Jorge Contesse were, in this regard, very precise when they called this process 'the rise and fall of a constitution moment',[144] arguing that a more pragmatic approach to constitution-making is needed to emerge from that shadow. As they said, 'so far, political consensus without public participation had been the norm for constitutional change in Chile. Bachelet aimed to change it, but the pendulum swung too far. The challenge for successful constitution-making while keeping the legitimating elements of public participation remains'.[145] Chile is indeed a paradox: it has become one of the most democratic countries in the region based on a constitution that fears more democracy. It is a shadow that may have worked quite well so far, but the legitimacy gap is increasingly challenging the ghost that has stubbornly managed to control Chile's future.

IV. Conclusion

Derrida, in his fascinating text *Declarations of Independence*,[146] right after writing that 'the founding act of an institution – the act as archive as well as the act as performance – *must maintain within itself the signature*',[147] stressed the value and strength of constituent words since they transcend the reality and defy the temporality. Still, the *signature* itself – these constituent words – is as such understood as long as it poses the following question: 'But just whose signature exactly?'[148] There is no *signature* that detaches itself from the 'ultimate signers',[149] those people who 'do *not* exist as an entity, the entity does *not* exist *before* this declaration, not *as such*'.[150] Founding moments, the acts of constituting a new beginning and a new

[142] According to Garretón, this seems an old feature of Chilean democracy. As he says, 'it was a country with a strong political system but a weak civil society'. Garretón (n 123) 104.

[143] See Manus (n 25).

[144] Verdugo and Contesse (n 26).

[145] ibid.

[146] See Derrida (n 27) 46.

[147] ibid 48.

[148] ibid.

[149] ibid 47.

[150] ibid 48.

future, are thereby always involved in this ongoing quest for legitimacy for the people who are made sovereign by the very constituent process.

Brazil and Chile are two countries whose histories challenge this *signature*, the constituent words that transformed their realities and moulded their democracies. Brazil's democratic transition cannot be separated from its constitutional transition, and particularly from the dichotomy control/loss of control of the constituent process, but which continues to deal with a 'past' that stubbornly attempts to regain the reins of power. Chile's democratic transition, on the other hand, also means a constitutional permanence that steadily delays the expected but unreachable future. Brazil's dictatorship, although having laid the groundwork for a transition that should be 'conciliatory' to and a 'continuity' of the 'revolutionary' period, as the military argued, became in the end a relatively uncontrolled transition marked by the surge of citizenship. Nonetheless, it has since been challenged by the strategic moves of elite groups to regain control over it. Chile's dictatorship, in turn, not only was successful in negotiating a 'peaceful' transition, but also limited much of the expected future and the exercise of citizenship through constitutional means. While in Brazil, the *signature* points to the 'ultimate signer' who does not exist as an entity but who is there threatening the conquered citizenship, in Chile, the *signature* is itself the very entity in a current battle with the rising citizenship.

Therefore, the *timing* of the constitutional moment certainly matters as a foundational moment that identifies itself with the rising of citizenship and pluralism. However, the ghost of 'reconciliation', 'compromises' and 'bargains' is always threatening a history whose contingencies engendered a foundational moment that is held by the Brazilian people with pride. The reality has proven how that moment – and the 'conciliatory' interpretation of it – has also been used as a tool to twist the constitutional text by recalling that 'past'. The recent episodes such as the impeachment of President Dilma Roussef and the election of President Jair Bolsonaro are serious reminders of how this 'past' is always there waiting for the ideal moment to attack the very foundations of a constitutional moment whose strength of citizenship is its prime feature. On the other hand, although the 'conciliatory' discourse still strongly resonates in Chile and the formal and informal institutions act to hamper more structural changes to the Constitution, Chile has made important strides towards the encounter of the *signature* with the *forgotten people*, even in spite of the recent failure of Bachelet's project for a new constitution.

Founding moments need an active citizenship, and Brazil and Chile, through different means and timings, are learning how to deal with the insurmountable dilemmas of their transitional histories and democratic experiences. They are also learning how to challenge their ghosts. If a founding moment is a central concept for constitutionalism, it is because it defies its own dilemmas by making constitutionalism not an enemy of the citizenship, but the citizenship the very reason for constitutionalism.

9

We the Taiwanese People

A Constitution with Two Antagonistic Constitutional Identities

CHIEN-CHIH LIN*

I. Introduction

The identity of 'We the People' has always been an intriguing issue that puzzles every student of constitutional law. Founding fathers worldwide have penned similar words to celebrate the promulgation of a new constitution. Hence, phrases such as 'We the Japanese people' and 'We the People of South Africa' have become prevalent in the preambles of national constitutions. Despite the ubiquity of this usage, the concept of 'We the People' remains elusive and slippery. Indeed, the confusion results partly from the lack of a clear founding moment. The founding moment is a period that signifies the political break with the *ancien régime*, a period in which a series of landmark events ultimately lead to the adoption of a constitution. What happens during this period is not simply episodes of constitutional memories, but also embodies certain normative values and principles.[1] It follows that the founding moment not only influences constitutional interpretation, but also shapes the contour of constitutional identity as an imagined community. Recently, the issue of national and constitutional identities has once again become a hotly debated topic in Europe.[2] Nonetheless, these

* I would like to thank Richard Albert, Nishchal Basnyat, Cristina Blanco Sio-Lopez and all other participants of the Symposium on Founding Moments in Constitutionalism in Yale. Also, I am grateful to Wen-Chen Chang, Tom Ginsburg, Cheng-Yi Huang, Jau-Yuan Hwang, Jimmy Chia-Shin Hsu, Ming-Sung Kuo, Shao-Man Lee and Yen-Tu Su for their comments and suggestions on the draft of this chapter. All mistakes are mine.

[1] See Ming-Sung Kuo, ch 1 in this volume.

[2] B Davies, 'Resistance to European Law and Constitutional Identity in Germany' (2015) 21 *European Law Journal* 434; JW Müller, 'Constitutional Patriotism Beyond the Nation-State' (2012) 33 *Cardozo Law Review* 1923, 1929–33; JH Reestman, 'The Franco-German Constitutional Divide: Reflections on National and Constitutional Identity' (2009) 5 *European Constitutional Law Review* 374; A Śledzińska-Simon, 'Constitutional Identity in 3D' (2015) 13 *International Journal of Constitutional Law* 124, 129; JHH Weiler, 'On the Power of the World: Europe's Constitutional Iconography' (2005)

arguments are 'strongly Eurocentric.'[3] How these ideas have developed in other corners of the world has not received adequate scholarly attention.

To address this academic lacuna, this chapter focuses on the formation of the constitutional identity embodied in the Constitution of the Republic of China (hereinafter the ROC Constitution), suggesting that, unlike many other countries, there are two distinct and antagonistic constitutional identities – the Chinese constitutional identity and the Taiwanese constitutional identity – that have been forged by formal and informal constitutional practice. The Chinese constitutional identity emerged from a relatively clear constitutional moment in 1947, when the ROC Constitution was promulgated in China. By contrast, there is no dramatic and radical founding moment in terms of the Taiwanese constitutional identity. In this sense, it is roughly similar to the situation in Brazil, Chile,[4] Hong Kong[5] or Pakistan,[6] where political transitions and constitutional replacements have followed a more incremental path.

Constitutional identity often evolves over time through a process of negation, metaphor and metonymy.[7] Nevertheless, a sharp break exists between the Chinese constitutional identity and the Taiwanese constitutional identity: the latter did not evolve from the former, and the former did not cease to exist after the emergence of the latter. Rather, they are two distinct constitutional identities that cohabit in the ROC Constitution, at least after political liberation in Taiwan. This peculiarity results from the entanglements between large-C Constitution and small-c constitution, as well as between constitutional and socio-political developments. Research into the constitutional identities of the ROC Constitution may be fruitful partly because of the ambiguous international status of the ROC (Taiwan). Many people believe they are Taiwanese rather than Chinese, while some spare no effort to maintain the original Chinese identity embodied in the original Constitution of the Republic of China, which is completely different from the current People's Republic of China (PRC), politically and constitutionally speaking. In such a divided society,[8] the development of constitutional identities is deeply embedded in, and reflective of, the dispute over national identities.

The rest of this chapter proceeds as follows. Section II briefly introduces the concept of constitutional identity by reviewing current literature. Section III elaborates upon the formation of the Chinese and the Taiwanese constitutional identities, arguing that the ROC Constitution has embodied two diametric

3 *International Journal of Constitutional Law* 173; GJ Jacobsohn, *Constitutional Identity* (Harvard University Press, 2010) 348–55; M Rosenfeld, *The Identity of the Constitutional Subject* (Routledge, 2009) 17–36.

[3] M Tushnet, 'How Do Constitutions Constitute Constitutional Identity?' (2010) 8 *International Journal of Constitutional Law* 671, 676.

[4] See Juliano Zaiden Benvindo, ch 8 in this volume.

[5] See Swati Jhaveri, ch 2 in this volume.

[6] See Maryam S Khan, ch 10 in this volume.

[7] M Rosenfeld, *The Identity of the Constitutional Subject* (Routledge, 2009) 37–69.

[8] J-R Yeh, 'Presidential Politics and the Judicial Facilitation of Dialogue between Political Actors in New Asian Democracies' (2010) 8 *International Journal of Constitutional Law* 911, 919–20.

identities over time with the social and political progress in Taiwan. Section IV addresses several topics in Taiwan through the prism of constitutional identity. Section V concludes.

II. National Identity and Constitutional Identity

Before discussing the idea of constitutional identity, the concept of national identity must be introduced. In its simplest definition, national identity refers to one's identity of belonging to one sovereign nation. It is forged both by objective elements and subjective factors.[9] Constitutional identity, like national identity, is also an imagined community.[10] It refers to the identity of a constitutional subject, which in turn means 'the collectivity of strangers that become encompassed within the same constitutional order'.[11] Moreover, constitutional identity is versatile[12] and will adapt to the ever-changing socio-political environment.[13] Despite its fluidity, it can be apprehended more concretely and easily, because it is 'the self-identity of the … polity framed by the Constitution'.[14] Namely, one can better appreciate the concept of constitutional identity through constitutional texts, constitutional amendments, judicial decisions and political implementation.

Specifically, the original constitutional text is a starting point[15] because it is the documentary record of a constitutional moment.[16] Few events are more cardinal than constitution-making in shaping the constitutional identity of a country. Even though the original text can be revised or rewritten later, its spirit may persist and be incorporated into new constitutions. This does not mean that the original constitutional text is the only authority in studying constitutional identity. Most constitutions experience constitutional change, and both formal[17] and informal constitutional changes[18] remodel constitutional identity. In theory, constitution-making creates a new constitutional identity, whereas constitutional amendments do not. The difference is usually a matter of degree: the more antique a constitution is, the more possible constitutional identity has been changed by constitutional amendments.

[9] L Williams, 'National Identity and the Nation State' in K Cameron (ed), *National Identity* (Intellect, 1999).

[10] B Anderson, *Imagined Communities* (Verso, 2006) 6–7.

[11] Rosenfeld (n 7) 18.

[12] GJ Jacobson, *Constitutional Identity* (Harvard University Press, 2010) 13; N Walker, 'Rosenfeld's Plural Constitutionalism' (2010) 8 *International Journal of Constitutional Law* 677, 679.

[13] M Rosenfeld, 'Modern Constitutionalism as Interplay between Identity and Diversity' (1993) 14 *Cardozo Law Review* 497, 508.

[14] Rosenfeld (n 7) 40.

[15] B Breslin, *From Words to Worlds: Exploring Constitutional Functionality* (Johns Hopkins University Press, 2009) 4–5; Jacobson (n 12) 348–49.

[16] B Ackerman, *We the People: Foundations*, vol 1 (Harvard University Press, 1993) 272–77.

[17] See R Dixon, 'Amending Constitutional Identity' (2012) 33 *Cardozo Law Review* 1847, 1857–58.

[18] Rosenfeld (n 7) 127.

In addition, 'a nation's constitutional identity extends beyond the text itself'.[19] Constitutional provisions that prescribe how to amend the constitution should not be the only mechanism of constitutional revision.[20] Instead, judicial interpretations and landmark statutes are sometimes 'the primary vehicle for the legal expression of popular sovereignty'.[21] Like it or not, the judiciary often plays a critical role in shaping constitutional identity when interpreting the constitution.[22] Some crucial decisions become the crux of constitutional identity by filling the gap between constitutional norms and practices. Finally, charismatic political figures also have the capability to shape constitutional identity without constitutional revision.[23] Politicians may appeal to popular sovereignty more easily because they are directly elected by the public. In the US, for instance, some laws, such as the Civil Rights Act, are called 'super statutes' in the sense that they have reshaped the whole country's constitutional understanding.[24] This suggests that politicians can alter constitutional identity without revising or rewriting the constitution.

In terms of the relationship and interaction of the two identities, people with the same national identity usually share the same constitutional identity, although constitutional identity is by no means equivalent to national identity.[25] Given that a constitution is one of the most important symbols of a nation, the two concepts overlap to a considerable extent. Citing pre-Second World War Germany as an example, Rosenfeld points out that Hitler's Third Reich abolished the Weimar constitutional identity, but not the German national identity.[26] Conversely, Taiwan is not yet an independent country recognised by global society, but this political reality does not hamper the growth of Taiwanese constitutional identity as an imagined constitutional community. In other words, a group of people can possibly change their constitutional identity without altering national identity and vice versa. As a corollary, constitutional identity 'does not need a nation for its existence'.[27] In this regard, the rise of Taiwanese constitutional identity may be a good example. Furthermore, the scope of constitutional identity may be broader than national identity. The debate surrounding constitutional patriotism[28] clearly indicates that some constitutional ideals can travel beyond national borders.

[19] GJ Jacobson, 'Rights and American Constitutional Identity' (2011) 43 *Polity* 420.

[20] B Ackerman, *We the People: Transformations*, vol 2 (Harvard University Press, 2000) 15–17; B Ackerman, *We the People: The Civil Rights Revolution*, vol 3 (Harvard University Press, 2014) 11; AR Amar, 'The Consent of the Governed: Constitutional Amendment outside Article V' (1994) 94 *Columbia Law Review* 457, 458–61.

[21] Ackerman, *We the People: The Civil Rights Revolution* (n 20) 8–9; AR Amar, *America's Unwritten Constitution* (Basic Books, 2012) 267.

[22] A Norton, 'Transubstantiation: The Dialectic of Constitutional Authority' (1988) 55 *University of Chicago Law Review* 458, 469–71.

[23] KE Whittington, *Political Foundations of Judicial Supremacy* (Princeton University Press, 2007) 291.

[24] JM Balkin, *Living Originalism* (Harvard University Press, 2011) 5; WN Eskridge, Jr and J Ferejohn, 'Super-Statutes' (2001) 50 *Duke Law Journal* 1215, 1216–17.

[25] S Rigger, 'Competing Conceptions of Taiwan's Identity' (1997) 6 *Journal of Contemporary China* 307, 307.

[26] Rosenfeld (n 7) 23.

[27] Śledzińska-Simon (n 2) 127.

[28] Symposium, 'Constitutional Patriotism' (2008) 6 *International Journal of Constitutional Law* 67.

Despite the conceptual distinction, the two identities usually grow symbiotically, because a stable political environment breeds an endurable constitution.[29] In return, constitutional identity may also undergird national identity when the latter faces pressure from regional integration. In the context of the EU, for example, 'the concept of constitutional identity is typically used to defend national identity (sovereignty) against the supremacy of EU law'.[30] In addition, constitutional identity may provide an alternative imagination of national identity. Therefore, how constitutional identity and national identity interact with each other in the context of the ROC Constitution in Taiwan is particularly intriguing, given the cataclysm in 1949 when the Kuomintang (KMT) lost the Chinese mainland to the Chinese Communist Party (CCP) and then brought the just-promulgated Constitution to Taiwan.

III. Constitutional Identities in the ROC Constitution

Constitutional identity is an amorphous concept that changes over time; indeed, no constitutional identity has remained fixed once forged. Theoretically, three major models of constitutional evolution exist. In the first model, one constitution embodies one evolving constitutional identity. During evolution, an old constitutional identity is either replaced or re-incorporated into a new one, but it is still the same constitutional identity. The development of most constitutional identities follows this path. Second, multiple constitutional frameworks and constitutional identities exist, and one constitutional identity continues to grow and eventually overlaps with another. This phenomenon is best illustrated by the interaction between European countries and the EU. A person may regard herself both as a citizen of a European country and a European,[31] and strive to strike a balance between domestic and transnational constitutional attachment.[32]

Much has been written on the first two models. This chapter instead focuses on the third one, in which two mutually antagonistic identities are forged by the same constitution, and neither includes the other.[33] The ROC Constitution is such a case. At one time, it embodied the Chinese constitutional identity that was carved out in China seven decades ago. After democratisation in 1987, the Taiwanese constitutional identity gradually surfaced through a series of constitutional amendments and judicial interpretations. Stimulated in part by the Taiwan

[29] Z Elkins, T Ginsburg and J Melton, *The Endurance of National Constitutions* (Cambridge University Press, 2009) 137.

[30] Śledzińska-Simon (n 2) 129.

[31] J Habermas, 'Citizenship and National Identity' in B van Steenbergen (ed), *The Condition of Citizenship* (Sage, 1994).

[32] JW Müller, *Constitutional Patriotism* (Princeton University Press, 2007) 93–139.

[33] H Lerner, *Making Constitutions in Deeply Divided Societies* (Cambridge University Press, 2011) 43–44.

independence movement, it is distinct from the Chinese constitutional identity that derives from, and still embraces, the one-China paradigm. Note that the old Chinese identity does not perish, but persists up to the present day. The following paragraphs articulate how the two constitutional identities are forged and how they interact with each other at three different stages: the founding moment; the authoritarian era; and political liberation.

A. The Founding Moment

In 1912, the KMT terminated the era of imperial China and established the Republic of China. Because of armed conflicts between the central government and local warlords, the constitution-building project was seriously postponed. After winning the first civil war, the KMT government promulgated the draft of the ROC Constitution.[34] It was again tabled because of the second Sino-Japanese war,[35] which heralded the beginning of the Second World War. After the end of warfare, unfortunately, another civil war between the KMT and the CCP ensued, and the former decided to unilaterally convene the constituent assembly, which was boycotted by the CCP. The constituent assembly enacted the ROC Constitution,[36] which took effect in 1947 and became the supreme law of mainland China for two years. During the constitution-making process, 17 representatives from then Taiwan Province, along with representatives from other provinces, participated in the constituent convention.[37] Although these token Taiwanese representatives did not participate in the constitution-building project substantively,[38] their appearance in Nanjing, China reinforces the argument that the constitutional subject of the ROC Constitution included all Chinese people, including people in Taiwan at that time.

i. The Chinese Constitutional Identity

The promulgation of the ROC Constitution marked the constitutional moment and the watershed of constitution-building in China, fitting neatly in the revolution-based model,[39] and became the first modern constitution in Chinese history.

[34] J Fa, 'Constitutional Developments in Taiwan: The Role of the Council of Grand Justices' (1991) 40 *International and Comparative Law Quarterly* 198, 199.

[35] C-C Lin, 'Constitutions and Courts in Chinese Authoritarian Regimes' (2016) 14 *International Journal of Constitutional Law* 351, 355.

[36] ROC Constitution 1947 (Taiwan).

[37] J-R Yeh and W-C Chang, 'The Emergence of East Asian Constitutionalism: Features in Comparison' (2011) 59 *American Journal of Comparative Law* 805, 819.

[38] C-J Chen, 'A Feminist Critique of History and Traditions in Judicial Review' (2007) 7 *Academia Sinica Law Journal* 81, 94–95 (Chinese).

[39] Rosenfeld (n 7) 188–91.

Given that the ROC Constitution was enacted in China by the Chinese people, the original constitutional text naturally embodies the Chinese constitutional identity, which is evident from both its preamble and its text. Specifically, the preamble clearly states that the Constitution was enacted in accordance with the legacy of Sun Yet-san, the founding father of the ROC. In the main text, Article I prescribes that the ROC is founded on the Three Principles of the People, which is also part of Sun's political theory. Furthermore, the institution of National Assembly was also a legacy of Sun's design, which imitated the Soviet Union's Supreme Council. Certain congressional seats were reserved for overseas Chinese and representatives from both Tibet and Mongolia,[40] who also had the power of self-government to a certain degree.[41] In summary, the original constitutional design demonstrated the Chinese constitutional identity: it was enacted in accordance with the founding father's political theory, it was passed by representatives from all provinces in China, its congress comprised representatives of both domestic and overseas Chinese, and both its bill of rights and government structure reflected politicians' concerns at that time.

ii. The Taiwanese Constitutional Identity

From 1895 to 1945, Taiwan was part of the Empire of Japan as a result of the first Sino-Japanese war. During the period of colonisation, the Meiji Constitution was implemented, albeit only ostensibly, in Taiwan.[42] Meanwhile, Taiwan consciousness had emerged, notwithstanding some disagreements as to the exact timing. Some say it first appeared in 1895 before the annexation by the Japanese Empire;[43] others suggest that it did not surface until the 1920s, when the Taiwan Cultural Association was founded.[44] Regardless of the date, the birth of Taiwan consciousness did not translate into an identifiable Taiwanese constitutional identity in the Meiji Constitution. After the end of the Second World War, the ROC controlled Taiwan and allowed some Taiwanese representatives to participate in the constituent assembly. Nonetheless, the February 28 incident in 1947, in which the KMT regime slaughtered thousands of Taiwanese, fuelled the formation of the Taiwanese national identity[45] and planted the seed of the Taiwanese constitutional identity.

[40] ROC Constitution, art 64.

[41] ibid arts 119 and 120.

[42] T-S Wang and I-H Chou, 'The Emergence of Modern Constitutional Culture in Taiwan' (2010) 5 *NTU Law Review* 1, 5–13.

[43] C Hsu, *In Search of New Coordinate for Taiwan* (Independence Evening Post Publishing, 1993) 41.

[44] M-K Chang, 'On the Origins and Transformation of Taiwanese National Identity' in Paul R Katz and Murray A Rubinstein (eds), *Religion and the Formation of Taiwanese Identities* (Palgrave Macmillan, 2003); LTS Ching, *Becoming 'Japanese'* (University of California Press, 2001) 57–88; Y-H Chu and J-W Lin, 'Political Development in 20th-Century Taiwan' (2001) 165 *China Quarterly* 102, 108; S-B Su, 'Typography and Taiwan Consciousness' (2011) 109 *Mass Communication Research* 1, 6.

[45] L-C Chen and WM Reisman, 'Who Owns Taiwan' (1972) 81 *Yale LJ* 599, 613; R Edmondson, 'The February 28 Incident and National Identity' in Stépnane Corcuff (ed), *Memories of the Future* (ME Sharpe, 2002).

B. The Authoritarian Period

Unlike most constitutions that symbolise the end of warfare, the promulgation of the ROC Constitution intensified the armed conflict between the KMT and the CCP. Eventually, the KMT lost the civil war and mainland China to the CCP, fleeing to Taiwan with the nascent ROC Constitution in tow in 1949.[46] From then on, the jurisdiction of the Constitution has been limited to Taiwan and several neighbouring isles. However, the jurisdictional change did not result in the immediate transformation of constitutional identity.

i. The Chinese Constitutional Identity

After the political catastrophe in 1949, the ROC Constitution lost almost all of its subjects and territory. Nevertheless, the Chinese constitutional identity did not disappear after the defeat of the KMT, thanks to political efforts and judicial decisions. The KMT refused to rewrite a new constitution even after realising that the ROC Constitution was impractical in Taiwan. One of the reasons for this is because the KMT wanted to bring the original constitution back to where it was born.[47] Another reason is that any repeal of the Constitution would be conceptually unconstitutional as it lacked the consent of all Chinese people, including people in mainland China under the PRC regime. Namely, the KMT strived to fortify the Chinese constitutional identity by freezing the Constitution. Admittedly, although the KMT did not rewrite a new constitution, it did enact the Temporary Provisions Effective during the Period of Communist Rebellion, which were essentially constitutional amendments.[48] Nevertheless, the fact that the Temporary Provisions were not officially named constitutional amendments reveals the KMT's reluctance to alter the nascent Constitution that was enacted in the name of all Chinese people. Even in the Temporary Provisions, the KMT emphasised that congressmen should be elected and convened 'nationally' to secure the symbolic legitimacy of the Constitution and the government over mainland China.

Furthermore, judicial decisions helped consolidate the Chinese constitutional identity as well. The most paradigmatic one is Interpretation No 31, in which the Constitutional Court justified the suspension of national elections by arguing that 'our state has been undergoing a severe calamity, which makes re-election … de facto impossible … all of the first-term Members of both the Legislative and Control Yuans shall continue to exercise their respective powers'.[49] In fact, the real reason was that these old representatives could not be replaced because they

[46] Wang and Chou (n 42).

[47] J-R Yeh, 'Changing Forces of Constitutional and Regulatory Reform in Taiwan' (1990) 4 *Journal of Chinese Law* 83, 88.

[48] Office of the President, Republic of China (Taiwan), Temporary Provisions, http://english.president.gov.tw/Default.aspx?tabid=434#02.

[49] Shih Tzu (Interpretation of Council of Grand Justices) No 31 (1954).

were elected from mainland China and represented the sovereignty of all Chinese people. The existence of these people represented 'the legally authentic succession within a regime',[50] a concept that might justify the KMT's claim of being the sole legitimate Chinese government in the world. Although local Taiwanese people were disproportionately under-represented in congress, it was constitutionally acceptable because 'We the People' in the ROC Constitution referred to the whole Chinese people, not merely Taiwanese people.

Ideally, the personnel of a government, which should generally mirror the composition of the population, can be a proxy of a constitutional subject. However, during the authoritarian period, all important positions prescribed in the Constitution were staffed by people in proportion to the population in each province before the civil war to maintain the façade that the government represented all Chinese people (but not simply Taiwanese people).[51] By contrast, local Taiwanese occupied only two per cent of seats,[52] despite the fact that about 85 per cent of the population was native Taiwanese. This scenario was no exception with the composition of the Court. In the first term, only one justice (out of 17) was born in Taiwan, and the concern of provincial origin was not removed until the sixth term.

ii. The Taiwanese Constitutional Identity

Although Taiwanese consciousness was suppressed vehemently during the authoritarian period, it did not disappear completely. The 1979 Kaohsiung Incident, also known as Formosa Incident, further fuelled the Taiwanese national identity. In 1986, the Democratic Progressive Party (DPP) was established before the KMT lifted the party ban. Many pro-independence activists had returned from abroad in the 1980s. All these events involving alternative imagination of national identity heralded the emergence of the Taiwanese constitutional identity, which blossomed during the Lee Teng-hui administration.[53] Lee was the first ROC President who was popularly elected; more importantly, he was the first president born in Taiwan. During his rule, Taiwan launched the project of constitutional amendments.

C. Political Liberation

The lifting of martial law in 1987 marked the turning point of constitutional identity in the ROC Constitution. The Chinese constitutional identity faded, but did

[50] J Yeh, 'The Cult of *Fatung*: Representational Manipulation and Reconstruction in Taiwan' in G Hassall and C Saunders (eds), *The People's Representatives: Electoral Systems in the Asia-Pacific Region* (Allen & Unwin, 1997).

[51] F-C Wang, 'A Prolonged Exile: National Imagination of the KMT Regime in Postwar Taiwan' (2013) 52 *Oriens Extremus* 137, 149 and 153.

[52] ibid.

[53] S Corcuff, 'The Symbolic Dimension of Democratization and the Transition of National Identity under Lee Teng-hui' in Stépnane Corcuff (ed), *Memories of the Future* (ME Sharpe, 2002).

not dissipate completely. Meanwhile, the Taiwanese constitutional identity was officially recognised in the constitutional amendments, judicial decisions and political practice.

i. *The Chinese Constitutional Identity*

After political liberation, seven rounds of constitutional amendments ensued. The preamble of the constitutional amendments unmistakably stated that the purpose of enacting constitutional amendments is to prepare for unification with mainland China. Moreover, the amendments sustained the policy stipulated in the original constitution that certain parliamentary seats should be reserved for 'citizens residing abroad', who were, according to Sun Yet-san, 'mothers of revolution'. To acknowledge their contribution and consolidate the claim that the constitutional subject of the ROC Constitution includes both domestic and overseas Chinese, this policy was enshrined in the Constitution from the very beginning. From this perspective, the continuance of this policy is to maintain the composition of the constitutional subject as it was in Nanjing in 1947. Moreover, the Control Yuan, which is modelled on the Censorate, a high-level supervisory agency in ancient China,[54] remains untouched, despite the call to repeal it. Besides, the Mongolian and Tibetan Affairs Commission remained untouched until 2017. This implies that Mongolians and Tibetans were still regarded as part of the constitutional subject of the ROC Constitution, and the Chinese constitutional identity persists even after democratisation. Finally, the Court is granted the power to dissolve a political party if its goals or activities endanger the existence of the Republic of China. Initially, this power was mainly to check the DPP, which attempts to declare the independence of Taiwan and enact a brand new constitution.[55]

In addition to constitutional text, judicial decisions continue to undergird the Chinese constitutional identity by invoking original intent and Chinese history. For example, in a drug case that involved the death penalty, the Court opined that: 'From the end of the [Q]ing Dynasty to the founding of the Republic of China, a period of nearly a hundred years, narcotics had a profound and negative impact on our nation.'[56] Evidently, the constitutional identity perceived by the justices refers to the Chinese constitutional identity that inherited imperial China. This notion further supported the argument that 'pre-revolutionary traditions are not completely eradicated but transformed and selectively incorporated into the new order'.[57] In addition to majority opinions, individual justices sometimes invoke the original intent to support their contentions in separate opinions. In Interpretation

[54] H-D Chiu, 'Constitutional Development and Reform in the Republic of China on Taiwan' in B-J Lin and JT Meyers (eds), *Contemporary China and the Changing International Community* (University of South Carolina Press, 1994).

[55] T Ginsburg, 'Constitutional Courts in East Asia: Understanding Variation' in A Harding and P Leyland (eds), *Constitutional Courts: A Comparative Study* (Simmonds and Hill Publishing, 2009).

[56] Shih Tzu (Interpretation of Council of Grand Justices) No 476 (1999).

[57] Rosenfeld (n 7) 39.

No 392, for instance, Justice Sun appealed to the May Fifth Constitutional Draft to refute the majority opinion in his dissenting opinion, as did Justice Wu in Interpretation No 404. Finally, the Court maintained that agreements between Taiwan and China are not international agreements.[58] In this connection, the Court also insisted on one-China ideology in which the PRC is not recognised as a foreign country.

Although no super statute fundamentally transforms the constitutional understanding in Taiwan, some statutes do play an important role in shaping the constitutional identity. Required by Article 11 of the constitutional amendments, the legislature enacts the Act Governing Relations between the People of the Taiwan Area and the Mainland Area, in which it also clearly identifies national unification as one of the ultimate goals. Both the constitutional mandate and the Act become the straitjacket of the Taiwan independence movement by repeatedly stressing the Chinese constitutional identity. Finally, the role of the so-called 1992 Consensus, which endorses the one-China policy, cannot be ignored. Notwithstanding the controversy over its existence and content, the 1992 Consensus has been espoused by both the CCP and the KMT. In accordance with the ROC Constitution, former President Ma Ying-jeou has emphasised that both mainland China and Taiwan are parts of China, although there is disagreement as to which China it is.

In a nutshell, the constitutional subject in the ROC Constitution includes not only local Taiwanese and mainlanders but also overseas Chinese and Mongolians. It follows that the identity of such constitutional subject will inevitably be Chinese. Behind the Chinese constitutional identity is a constitutional framework that generally embodies the one-China paradigm and the constitutional theory of Sun Yet-san.

ii. The Taiwanese Constitutional Identity

Not until the late 1980s did the Taiwanese constitutional identity gradually emerge. Nevertheless, the Taiwanese constitutional identity is growing steadily, and the pace is becoming increasingly rapid. Interpretation No 261 is the most pivotal decision in terms of democratisation and the inception of the Taiwanese constitutional identity. In this decision, the Court has realised that interpreting the Constitution in light of the Chinese constitutional identity is onerous and anachronistic. In this decision, the Court encountered the same issue it had already ruled in the aforementioned Interpretation No 31: whether national elections can be suspended indefinitely as a result of national cataclysm. In the prior decision, justices endorsed the suspension; this time, they mandated a new national election and designated a date before which all old representatives should step down. The Court essentially nullified the Temporary Provisions, and the nullification indicates the weakening of the Chinese constitutional identity for three reasons.

[58] Shih Tzu (Interpretation of Council of Grand Justices) No 329 (1993).

First, the constitutional subject must 'forge its identity through the medium of a constitutional discourse' that ultimately predicates on open-ended contexts and subjects to transformations,[59] and Interpretation No 261 serves as the critical constitutional discourse that officially recognises this transformation. Decades after the Chinese civil war, the Taiwanese speak in the name of 'We the People' in Taiwan now. The Court correctly recognised that the constitutional subject of the Constitution has changed dramatically, and the term 'national elections' from then on refers to elections held in Taiwan, but not in China. Second, the Temporary Provisions were written by representatives elected from mainland China. The passage of this quasi-constitutional amendment had little to do with the Taiwanese people; instead, it was used to oppress their will. Third, the Temporary Provisions abolished the term limit of presidents to prolong Chiang Kai-shek's dictatorship, which was built on the fantasy of the one-China policy. Its nullification implied the end of such a myth and the possibility for Taiwan to become a normal state. In short, the most important result this decision brought about is that it re-interprets the one-China paradigm and 'brings the system in line with the [Taiwanese] people's will'[60] in addition to precipitating democracy in Taiwan.

Echoing this decision, politicians have passed constitutional amendments seven times in which many revisions further confirm the rise of the Taiwanese constitutional identity. First, it distinguishes Taiwanese people from Chinese people, and all political powers are reserved for the former. In addition, the original Constitution adopted a parliamentary system, according to which the President has only ceremonial powers and is elected indirectly. Currently, the President is popularly elected by all Taiwanese and wields immense powers, a crucial change that has resulted in the 'Taiwanisation' or 'localisation'[61] of the ROC Constitution. This reinforced the legitimacy of both the KMT and the Constitution domestically. Furthermore, the constitutional amendment essentially repealed Taiwan Province, which was a legacy of the one-China paradigm. Finally, parliamentary seats that were reserved for racial groups in frontier regions are now reserved for indigenous people in Taiwan. Theoretically, the allocation of parliamentary seats should reflect the composition of 'We the People' to ensure democratic accountability. Therefore, the constitutional revision in this part suggests that the Constitution has recognised the change of constitutional subject. In sum, about one-quarter of original constitutional provisions have been replaced by constitutional amendments after seven rounds of constitutional revision. The scale and content of constitutional revision further facilitate establishing the Taiwanese constitutional identity.

In a *Deutsche Welle* interview, former President Lee commented the symbolic meaning of constitutional amendments, maintaining that: 'The 1991 constitutional amendments have designated cross-strait relations as a state-to-state relationship

[59] Rosenfeld (n 7) 41.
[60] T Ginsburg, *Judicial Review in New Democracies* (Cambridge University Press, 2003) 146.
[61] J-R Yeh, *The Constitution of Taiwan: A Contextual Analysis* (Hart Publishing, 2016) 4.

or at least a special state-to-state relationship, rather than an internal relationship between a legitimate government and a renegade group, or between a central government and a local government.' Being President of the ROC at that time, his speech was not only a personal opinion, but also one kind of authoritative interpretation made by a constitutional organ.

In addition to Interpretation No 261, other judicial decisions also helped cultivate the Taiwanese constitutional identity. In 1993, the Court faced the issue of demarcating the territorial boundaries of the ROC. Given the political reality and the impossibility of recapturing mainland China, whether the territory of the ROC includes mainland China and Mongolia became a sensitive issue during the early stages of democratic transition. Although the Court strategically avoided answering this question by invoking the doctrine of political question,[62] the reluctance itself is telling. As a corollary, this issue must eventually be settled by the Taiwanese people themselves because the judiciary has decided not to decide. Moreover, the Court mandated that the current ROC government in Taiwan did not need to pay the debts owed by the ROC government in mainland China before the retreat.[63] The reasoning implicitly indicated that the ROC in Taiwan was no longer the ROC founded in Nanjing. Finally, the Court ruled that the term 'Republic of China' was no longer required to be included in the name of nationwide organisations. Although the Court based its reasoning on procedural grounds, this decision further proved that the Chinese constitutional identity had gradually faded away.

In addition to government structure, the definition of citizens also reflects the change in constitutional identity because citizens are the core element of the constitutional subject.[64] In this regard, the Court had justified the distinction of citizens based on national origin, a suspect classification that usually demands strict scrutiny.[65] To illustrate this, Chinese people who have converted and become Taiwanese citizens are treated differently from citizens born in Taiwan, even in the domain of fundamental rights. In 2006, the Court ruled that Taiwanese citizens who were born in China cannot serve public roles unless they have had a household registration in Taiwan for 10 years because of concerns over their loyalty. Even though this rule is discrimination based on national origin, the Court upheld the law, arguing that people with Chinese national origin 'may not be as familiar with the constitutional structure of a free democracy as the Taiwanese people'.[66] The Court averred that some of the most suspicious forms of discrimination can be justified because Chinese people per se are not regarded as Taiwanese people, constitutionally speaking. The constitutional subject embodied in the current ROC Constitution clearly excludes certain Taiwanese citizens of Chinese

[62] Shih Tzu (Interpretation of Council of Grand Justices) No 328 (1993).
[63] Shih Tzu (Interpretation of Council of Grand Justices) No 475 (1999).
[64] Rosenfeld (n 7) 211.
[65] MP Burgdorf and R Burgdorf, Jr, 'A History of Unequal Treatment' (1975) 15 *Santa Clara Law Review* 855, 902 fn 302.
[66] JY Interpretation No 618 (2006).

national origin unless some conditions are met, let alone people with the nationality of the PRC. In this decision, the Court applied what Professor Rosenfeld called 'negation' to carve out a constitutional identity.[67] Other decisions dealing with similar issues include Interpretation Nos 497, 558, 710 and 712. None of these decisions articulates the relationship between China and Taiwan, but all implicitly recognise that these two jurisdictions are separate and controlled by different sovereign governments.

The enactment of the Indigenous Peoples Basic Law and the signature of the Convention on the Elimination of all Forms of Discrimination Against Women (CEDAW), the International Covenant on Civil and Political Rights (ICCPR) and the International Covenant on Economic, Social and Cultural Rights (ICESCR) also shape the constitutional subject in Taiwan. For one thing, the Basic Law entrenches the equal status and autonomy of indigenous people. Combined with the reserved seats in congress, indigenous people have been recognised as part of the constitutional subject. Furthermore, the signature of international conventions and the passage of the Act to Implement the ICCPR and the ICESCR also suggest that transnational constitutionalism has taken place in Taiwan.[68] The Court and individual justices have referenced international treaties both in the majority and separate opinions. The convergence of international human rights law and the Constitution, either through statutory incorporation or judicial interpretation, has crafted a new constitutional identity for the Taiwanese people.

Finally, the role of popular constitutionalism[69] must not be ignored. Many scholars have pointed out that the power of constitutional interpretation should not be monopolised by either politicians or judges.[70] In Taiwan, social movements have played a substantial role in the process of constitutional construction. Starting from the Wild Lily movement, which ultimately resulted in the first direct national election, cause lawyers and non-governmental organisations (NGOs) have successfully used litigation as a strategy to bring about social change.[71] Civic constitutionalism reached its zenith in the 2014 Sunflower Movement, which 'demonstrated a continuous civil engagement in the process of democratic constitutional reform'.[72] Despite their different appeals, most of these social movements aim to consolidate the Taiwanese identity.

[67] Rosenfeld (n 7) 46–51.

[68] W-C Chang, 'An Isolated Nation with Global-minded Citizens' (2009) 4 *NTU Law Review* 203.

[69] LD Kramer, 'The Supreme Court 2000 Term – Foreword: We the Court' (2001–02) 115 *Harvard Law Review* 5, 16–74; Larry D. Kramer, *The People Themselves* (Oxford University Press, 2004); R Post and R Siegel, '*Roe* Rage: Democratic Constitutionalism and Backlash' (2007) 42 *Harvard Civil Rights–Civil Liberties Law Review* 373.

[70] M Tushnet, *Taking the Constitution Away from the Courts* (Princeton University Press, 1999) 154–76.

[71] W-C Chang, 'Public-Interest Litigation in Taiwan' in PJ Yap and H Lau (eds), *Public Interest Litigation in Asia* (Routledge, 2011).

[72] J-R Yeh, 'Marching towards Civic Constitutionalism with Sunflowers' (2015) 45 *Honk Kong Law Journal* 315, 316. For more discussion on this event, see Symposium, 'Taiwan's Sunflower Movement' (2015) 45 *Hong Kong Law Journal* 189.

In sum, the constitutional subject now includes not only native Taiwanese but also mainlanders and indigenous people. In contrast to the one-China paradigm implied by the Chinese constitutional identity, the Taiwanese constitutional identity originates from the rise of Taiwan consciousness. It prefers the traditional presidential system to the grotesque five-branch model plus a national assembly and a nominal president. Instead of sticking to the framers' intent, it embraces and incorporates multiculturalism and international human rights conventions into the constitutional order.

D. Interaction between Constitutional Identities and National Identities

Some may still doubt whether the Taiwanese constitutional identity is indeed a constitutional identity distinct from the Chinese constitutional identity. The answer ultimately hinges on the role of the Constitution in people's lives, because a constitutional identity is 'a constitutive narrative through which people imagines themselves as a people, with shared memories, goals, aspirations, values, duties, and ambitions'.[73] In this light, people who embrace the Taiwanese constitutional identity obviously share completely different 'memories, goals, aspirations, values, duties, and ambitions' from people who still possess nostalgia for China.

Regarding the interaction between constitutional identity and national identity, the rise of the Taiwanese national identity is undoubtedly much earlier than the formation of the Taiwanese constitutional identity. During the authoritarian period when the Constitution was suspended and the Court was deferential, the Taiwanese constitutional identity was unlikely to sprout. At that time, constitutional identity was exclusively Chinese, which obstructed the awakening of Taiwan consciousness. However, after Interpretation No 261, the two developed symbiotically: the rise of Taiwan consciousness provides alternative imagination of constitutional identity, whereas the growth of the Taiwanese constitutional identity provides legal ammunition for the discourse of Taiwan independence movement.

Specifically, the most pivotal reason that contributes to the formation of the Taiwanese constitutional identity is the surge of Taiwanese consciousness. In addition to the aforementioned political events, the Taiwanese media[74] and local literature[75] also play an influential role in crafting Taiwanese identity. Public

[73] Balkin (n 24) 61.
[74] CJ Hsu, *The Construction of National Identity in Taiwan's Media, 1896–2012* (Brill, 2014) 156–224.
[75] A-C Hsiau, *Contemporary Taiwanese Cultural Nationalism* (Routledge, 2000) 79–116; D Tsai, 'Shifting National Identities in Public Spheres' in PR Katz and MA Rubinstein (eds), *Religion and the Formation of Taiwanese Identities* (Palgrave Macmillan, 2003).

opinion surveys show that an increasing number of people see themselves as Taiwanese rather than Chinese.[76] Of course, the percentages fluctuate, depending in part on ethnicity,[77] but the trend is undisputable: 'The popular aspiration for an independent Taiwan became increasingly crystallized and cohesive at the close of the 20th century.'[78] The Taiwanese constitutional identity contributes to, and simultaneously results from, the transformation of national identity from the one-China paradigm to an independent Taiwan Republic. However, this relationship is unsatisfying to some radicals, who have suggested that any constitutional identity under the regime of the ROC Constitution will ultimately be Chinese. In fact, the DPP government did endeavour to enact a new Taiwan constitution, but the project was eventually aborted because it did not garner sufficient popular support at that time. Admittedly, the final goal may be the perfect combination of national identity and constitutional identity. However, before that, this one-step-at-a-time strategy may be more practical under the shadow of military invasion from the PRC.[79]

Notably, the Taiwanese constitutional identity is not simply a byproduct of Taiwanese independence movement. Constitutional identity is distinct from national identity because 'the "We" who gives itself a constitution must project beyond itself'.[80] The Taiwanese constitutional identity originated from Taiwan consciousness that opposes the one-China paradigm. Nevertheless, the constitutional subject in Taiwan includes not only native Taiwanese but also indigenous people and mainlanders who come to Taiwan. Moreover, the incorporation of international human rights has become an important dimension of the Taiwanese constitutional identity, but some pro-independence activists may still reject it. Same-sex marriage and the abolition of death penalty are two paradigmatic examples. In a word, constitutional identity refers to the attachment to constitutional norms, values and principles. Conceptually, it is not identical to national identity.[81]

The development of the Taiwanese constitutional identity cannot neatly fit into the prototypes of the major constitutional and constitutional-making modes. Unlike former colonies in Africa and Asia, Taiwan did not enact a brand new constitution after the Second World War or after democratisation. The Taiwanese constitutional identity is not created *ex nihilo*, but emerges gradually through constitutional change. It is also different from the American model[82] in the sense

[76] Y Li, 'The Consolidation of Taiwanese Constitutional Identity and its Impact on Cross-Strait Relations', http://blogs.nottingham.ac.uk/chinapolicyinstitute/2016/01/08/the-consolidating-new-taiwanese-identity-and-its-impact-on-cross-strait-relations; Election Study Center of the National Chengchi University, 'Taiwan National Security Surveys', http://sites.duke.edu/pass/data.

[77] S Corcuff, 'Taiwan's Mainlanders: New Taiwanese?' and R Marsh, 'National Identity and Ethnicity in Taiwan', both in S Corcuff (ed), *Memories of the Future* (ME Sharpe, 2002).

[78] Chu and Lin (n 44) 103.

[79] R-R Wu, 'Toward a Pragmatic Nationalism' in Corcuff (ed) (n 77).

[80] Rosenfeld (n 7) 10–11.

[81] Müller (n 32) 1.

[82] Rosenfeld (n 7) 158–63.

that constitutional promulgation did not result in the establishment of a new country. Furthermore, unlike France or Germany, Taiwan has never been a state that was based either on demos or ethnos[83] before revolution.

In essence, the Taiwanese constitutional identity is *sui generis* precisely because neither a Taiwan Constitution nor a Taiwan Republic exists. Both are unlikely to happen in the near future. Internationally, the PRC still insists that Taiwan is part of China, and the Preamble of the PRC Constitution plainly claims as much. Domestically, neither can garner enough popular support, partly because of China's military intimidation. Taiwan is still a very divided society in which consensuses regarding both issues are insufficient. The attitude of many Taiwanese remains ambiguous and practical: they prefer the status quo to immediate independence, and unification with China is the least of their priorities. Given that enacting a Taiwan constitution and founding a Taiwan republic are difficult to achieve, building the Taiwanese constitutional identity in the ROC Constitution becomes the best available choice, at least in the short term. In this sense, the Taiwanese constitutional identity in the ROC Constitution is not only a compromise between people with heterogeneous imaginations towards national identity, but is also an interim goal of the Taiwan independence movement. Taiwanese people's attitudes toward the national flag vividly portray this point. At one time, the national flag was regarded as an emblem of the Chinese constitutional identity because it was derived from the party flag of the KMT. Nevertheless, an increasing number of people, including the DPP supporters, accept it as a symbol of the Taiwanese constitutional identity when facing international communities, particularly the PRC. This transformation epitomises the complexity of constitutional identities in Taiwan.

From this perspective, the ROC Constitution and the Taiwanese constitutional identity are mutually dependent: the endurance of the ROC Constitution should be partly attributed to the effort of Taiwanisation; and the Taiwanese constitutional identity is recognised through the constitutional amendments and judicial decisions. By contrast, today only a few people still espouse the Chinese national identity and think of themselves as Chinese rather than Taiwanese. In a series of surveys, the overall proportion of people who identify themselves as Taiwanese has increased substantially over the course of the past two decades, and this pattern takes place across ethnic lines and party affiliations.[84]

Still, some remnants of the Chinese constitutional identity are deeply rooted in the Constitution, even though they have been marginalised from mainstream society. The two constitutional identities are ideologically antagonistic, but neither can effectively eliminate the other.

[83] UK Preuss, 'Constitutional Powermaking' in M Rosenfeld (ed), *Constitutionalism, Identity, Difference, and Legitimacy* (Duke University Press, 1994).

[84] TY Wang, 'Changing Boundaries: The Development of the Taiwan Voters' Identity' in CH Achen and TY Wang (eds), *The Taiwan Voter* (University of Michigan Press, 2017).

IV. Normative Implications of Parallel Constitutional Identities

As one Taiwanese justice has pointed out, a divided country will naturally breed divided constitutional personality.[85] Although many may disagree as to whether Taiwan is a divided country, Justice Su is correct that two distinct and diametric constitutional identities have emerged from the Constitution. The juxtaposition of both Chinese and Taiwanese identities has shed new light on several constitutional issues, such as constitutional endurance, judicial dialogue and originalism.

A. Constitutional Endurance

Similar to the Constitution of Japan, it is sometimes argued that the ROC Constitution was imposed upon Taiwanese notwithstanding the fact that some Taiwanese representatives did participate in the constituent convention.[86] The argument has some merit, but it fails to answer why the Constitution has endured up to the present day. Intimidation from the PRC may explain why Taiwan has not yet enacted a new constitution, but this explanation alone is hardly satisfying. To what extent the Constitution should be labelled as an imposed one is unclear because there are different levels of imposition.[87]

In fact, the endurance of the Constitution can be better appreciated through the prism of constitutional identity. A symbiotic relationship exists between the stability of the ROC Constitution and constitutional identity, particularly the Taiwanese constitutional identity. The Constitution provides fertile ground for the development of constitutional identity, and constitutional identity that has been repeatedly confirmed in constitutional amendments and judicial decisions in turn renders the Constitution more entrenched in Taiwanese society. Specifically, the first three rounds of constitutional amendments not only supported the legitimacy of the Constitution and prolonged its longevity, but also simultaneously cultivated Taiwanese constitutional identity by reinforcing domestic representation.[88] Subsequently, the DPP, the long-time opposition party, also participated in amending rather than rewriting the Constitution. Its cooperation with the KMT in the last four rounds of constitutional amendments has further domesticated the Constitution. In this light, the Taiwanese constitutional identity has been firmly entwined with the ROC Constitution. The emergence of the Taiwanese constitutional identity as another constitutional identity embodied in the Constitution saves the latter from being repealed.

[85] Y-C Su, *Constitutionalism at the Dawn of New Century* (Angel, 2002) 162 (Chinese).

[86] Chen (n 38). W-C Chang, 'East Asian Foundations for Constitutionalism: Three Models Reconstructed' (2008) 3 *NTU Law Review* 111, 129; Yeh (n 61) 24–25.

[87] F Schauer, 'On the Migration of Constitutional Ideas' 37 (2005) *Connecticut Law Review* 907, 907–09.

[88] J-R Yeh, *Democratic Transition and Constitution Development* (Angel, 2003) 30–35 (Chinese).

The development of the ROC Constitution in Taiwan suggests that an inclusive drafting process may be less influential than inclusive constitutional provisions in determining the durability and self-enforcement of a constitution.[89] From this perspective, the issue of inclusion in the context of constitution-making is a matter of constitutional identity. Moreover, the relationship between constitutional identity and constitutional stability may be reciprocal: an enduring constitution makes it easier to foster constitutional identity, whereas constitutional identity raises people's loyalty to and respect for the Constitution.

B. Judicial Dialogue and Originalism

With the wide spread of judicial review and constitutional courts after the third wave of democratisation, recent decades have witnessed the rise of transnational constitutionalism and the rampant growth of judicial dialogue among apex courts.[90] In Taiwan, the Court does not expressly engage in judicial dialogue very frequently. Quantitatively, only about one per cent of the majority opinions explicitly cited foreign decisions.[91] This number increases considerably to 16 per cent as far as separate opinions are concerned.[92] Among all these opinions, the major reference jurisdictions are Germany, the US, Japan, the European Court of Justice (ECJ) and the European Court of Human Rights (ECtHR).[93] Furthermore, 'constitutional ideas may be migrating in the absence of explicit judicial borrowing'.[94] In addition to explicit citations, the Court is quite receptive to foreign legal doctrines, particularly in the domains of free speech and equal protection.[95]

How do we explain judges' choice of their reference jurisdictions? All of the traditional arguments are plausible, but the role of constitutional identity is often neglected. To specify: 'A court's position and how it views its role with respect to sociopolitical struggles over the polity's collective identity is at least as significant a factor in explaining judicial choices of foreign reference as any structural, linguistic, or legal factor.'[96] In this view, the Supreme Court of Israel selectively looks to Western courts, regardless of the differences in language, legal tradition

[89] Elkins, Ginsburg and Melton (n 29) 79–81.

[90] V Jackson, *Constitutional Engagement in a Transnational Era* (Oxford University Press, 2010) 71–102; C Saunders, 'Judicial Engagement with Comparative Law' in T Ginsburg and R Dixon (eds), *Comparative Constitutional Law* (Cambridge University Press, 2011).

[91] W-C Chang and J-R Yeh, 'Judges as Discursive Agent: The Use of Foreign Precedents by the Constitutional Court of Taiwan' in T Groppi and MC Ponthoreau (eds), *The Use of Foreign Precedents by Constitutional Judges* (Hart Publishing, 2014).

[92] ibid 382.

[93] ibid.

[94] B Cossman, 'Migrating Marriages and Comparative Constitutionalism' in S Choudhry (ed), *The Migration of Constitutional Ideas* (Cambridge University Press, 2006).

[95] DS Law and W-C Chang, 'The Limits of Global Judicial Dialogue' (2011) 86 *Washington Law Review* 523, 558–62.

[96] R Hirschl, *Comparative Matters* (Oxford University Press, 2014) 22.

and regional proximity, because Israel wants 'to be included in the liberal-democratic club of nations'.[97] In this light, judges, like framers, project what they believe to be the correct blueprint of a country in their opinions when interpreting the constitution. This practice takes place in Israel, India and Ireland.[98]

Similarly, judicial engagement in Taiwan may be attributed in part to the competition between Chinese and Taiwanese constitutional identities. By the standards of conventional wisdom on judicial engagement,[99] few countries are closer to the ROC than the PRC in terms of linguistic similarity, geographical proximity and traditional culture. Nevertheless, the Court has never consulted the Supreme People's Court in China. Instead, it seeks out foreign decisions that are made in completely divergent socio-political environments with which Taiwan is unfamiliar. Similar to its Israeli counterpart, the Court's dialogue with Western courts, instead of Chinese courts, 'stems from a deeper ideational commitment to a certain vision of the good society and of the polity's cultural orientation and place in the international family of nations'.[100] Normally, 'the more established a given constitutional court is or the more developed its jurisprudence, the lesser the likelihood it will refer to foreign precedents'.[101] However, this scenario is not the case in Taiwan. The frequency of judicial borrowing seems to escalate over time, and this trend is consistent with the development of Taiwanese constitutional identity.

Furthermore, the tepidness on originalism also reflects the tendency to imbue foreign elements, rather than Chinese materials, into Taiwanese constitutional identity. In Taiwan, originalism has been rarely invoked by the Court, and no constitutional law scholar has ever advocated for a more extensive application. Original meaning seems to be immaterial to the constitutional understanding in most controversial cases in Taiwan. Part of the reasons for this should be attributed to the transformation of constitutional identity. In addition to the issue of whether the dead should govern the living, originalism in Taiwan faces another challenge: with the rise of Taiwan consciousness, the identity of the founding fathers becomes less clear, and their intention becomes less relevant. Most people who currently live on the island-state do not feel connected with the founding fathers of the ROC. The massacre and despotism of the KMT during the authoritarian period further render the founding fathers (most of them were KMT members) less influential, if no more resentful, to Taiwanese people. In a word, the decline in Chinese constitutional identity and the surge of Taiwanese constitutional identity render originalism quite unpopular in Taiwan.

[97] ibid 23, 43–50. See also F Schauer, 'The Politics and Incentives of Legal Transplantation' in JS Nye and JD Donahue (eds), *Governance in a Globalizing World* (Brookings Institution Press, 2000).

[98] Jacobson (n 12) 142–202.

[99] M Bobek, *Comparative Reasoning in European Supreme Courts* (Oxford University Press, 2013) 36–64.

[100] Hirschl (n 96) 57.

[101] ibid 33.

V. Conclusion

After seven rounds of constitutional amendments, one cannot deny that the Taiwanese constitutional identity has grown symbiotically with the Taiwanese national identity, notwithstanding the lack of a clear constitutional moment. Although the pendulum has swung from the Chinese constitutional identity to the Taiwanese constitutional identity, the former does not disappear, but persists firmly. The high threshold of constitutional revision helps preserve the declining Chinese constitutional identity. Moreover, the landslide victory of the KMT in the 2018 nine-in-one elections evinces the resilience of Chinese identity. The co-existence of the two antagonistic constitutional identities not only mirrors the chasm between people with divergent political viewpoints on this island, but also influences the practice of judicial review in many respects.

10

What's in a Founding?

Founding Moments and Pakistan's 'Permanent Constitution' of 1973

MARYAM S KHAN[1]

> [W]hen we devoted ourselves to the task of making the Constitution, we resolved that we shall give a Constitution … which shall have its roots firmly in the people of Pakistan so that no matter what a convulsion you get, no matter what earthquake you get, no matter how many dictators you bring in, you will not be able to dislodge democratic institutions from this country.[2]

For Pakistan, as for India, decolonisation and the accompanying partition of the Subcontinent in 1947 were cataclysmic transformations. For both states, independence was a 'constitutive' or 'founding moment'.[3] But while India was successful in making a constitution in 1950, Pakistan descended into a constitutional impasse. And while India's founding, despite the heavily elite-driven process of constitution-making, has been commemorated as a 'people's constitution' because of its historical premise in the freedom movement against British colonial rule,[4] Pakistan has attracted epithets like a 'vice-regal system',[5] 'constitutional autocracy',[6] 'military-bureaucratic oligarchy'[7] and 'praetorian democracy'[8]

[1] I would like to express my gratitude for the continuous and generous support of my colleagues at the Institute of Development and Economic Alternatives (IDEAS) in Pakistan, especially Osama Siddique, Faisal Bari and Rabea Malik, who engaged in impromptu discussions on this work on several occasions. Thank you also to the South Asia Legal Studies Working Group at the University of Wisconsin Law School for their critical input on an earlier draft.

[2] Abdul Hafeez Pirzada, Chairman of the Constitution Committee, Official Report of the Second Session of the National Assembly of Pakistan (Constitution-Making) Debates (1972) 11(1), 4.

[3] Ted Svensson, *Production of Post-colonial India and Pakistan: Meanings of Partition* (Routledge, 2013) 28–29.

[4] Granville Austin, *The Indian Constitution: Cornerstone of a Nation*, 2nd edn (Oxford University Press, 1999); Arvind Elangovan, 'The Making of the Indian Constitution: A Case for a Non-nationalist Approach' (2014) 12(1) *History Compass* 1, 1.

[5] GW Choudhury, 'Democracy on Trial in Pakistan' (1963) 17(1) *Middle East Journal* 1.

[6] Khalid Bin Sayeed, 'Pakistan's Constitutional Autocracy' (1963–64) 36(4) *Pacific Affairs* 365.

[7] Hamza Alavi, 'The State in Post-colonial Societies: Pakistan and Bangladesh' (1972) 74 *New Left Review* 59.

[8] Hassan Nawaz Gardezi and Jamal Rashid (eds), *Pakistan, The Roots of Dictatorship: The Political Economy of a Praetorian State* (Zed Press, 1983).

because of its abortive experiments with constitutional change. In this discursive milieu, the towering and revered historical figure of Muhammad Ali Jinnah – the founder of Pakistan and a constitutional lawyer himself – personifies a deeply idealised but unfulfilled vision of Pakistani identity that continues to grip the collective imagination. Not unlike the popular appropriation of founding visions elsewhere, the refrain of 'Jinnah's Pakistan'[9] finds traction across the socio-political spectrum, from those espousing an Islamic state[10] to those arguing for a secular and pluralist state.[11]

Amid the din of competing visions of Jinnah's Pakistan, the despair of a lost founding, the nostalgia for Jinnah and his principled constitutional politics, and the hope for a revival of Jinnah's vision in the future, there is little scholarly recognition of the current constitutional framework of the country: namely, the Constitution of 1973. Despite being a watershed historical event, the making of the 1973 Constitution remains chronically understudied almost half a century later. The period of constitution-making between 1968 and 1973 was tumultuous, yet one of constitutional trailblazing. This was a time when a countrywide social movement brought down the first military dictator;[12] when the country held its first democratic elections based on adult universal franchise;[13] when it experienced the shock of civil war and lost more than half its population with the partition of East Pakistan;[14] when elected leaders first took the reins of government;[15] and when a constitution was drafted for the first time by an elected constituent assembly.[16] The lack of attention to the 1973 Constitution is partially a result of the impoverished state of scholarship among lawyers and legal historians in the region. More importantly, it is a result of the cyclical de-legitimation of democratic politics – and, with it, the 1973 Constitution – by the military governments of General Zia (1977–88) and General Musharraf (1999–2008). These and other political upheavals have led many to be deeply critical, even cynical, about the legitimacy, utility and relevance of the Constitution to democratic norm-building.[17]

[9] Martin Lau, 'Islam and the Constitutional Foundations of Pakistan' in Rainer Grote and Tilmann J. Roder (eds), *Constitutionalism in Islamic Countries: Between Upheaval and Continuity* (Oxford University Press, 2012); Safdar Mahmood, 'Jinnah's Vision of Pakistan' (2002) 23(1) *Pakistan Journal of History and Culture* 39.

[10] Hasan Askari Rizvi, 'Jinnah, Islam and the Political System' *Dawn* (25 December 2014), www.dawn.com/news/1153119.

[11] Syed Jaffar Ahmed, 'Jinnah and the Notion of a Nation-State' (2011) 16(1) Pakistan Perspectives 29; Barbara D Metcalf, *Islamic Contestations: Essays on Muslims in India and Pakistan* (Oxford University Press, 2004); Lawrence Ziring, 'Pakistan: The Vision and the Reality' (1977) 4(6) *Asian Affairs* 385.

[12] Shahid Javed Burki, 'Ayub's Fall: A Socio-economic Explanation' (1972) 12(3) *Asian Survey* 201.

[13] Craig Baxter, 'Pakistan Votes – 1970' (1971) 11(3) *Asian Survey* 197.

[14] Richard Sisson and Leo E Rose, *War and Secession: Pakistan, India, and the Creation of Bangladesh* (University of California Press, 1991).

[15] Robert La Porte, Jr, 'Pakistan in 1972: Picking up the Pieces' (1973) 13(2) *Asian Survey* 187.

[16] GW Choudhury, '"New" Pakistan's Constitution, 1973' (1974) 28(1) *Middle East Journal* 10.

[17] Zulfikar Khalid Maluka, *The Myth of Constitutionalism in Pakistan* (Oxford University Press, 1995); AG Noorani, 'Secular Jinnah and the Islamic Undercurrent' (2012) 6(3) *Criterion Quarterly*, www.criterion-quarterly.com/secular-jinnah-the-islamic-undercurrent; Ardeshir Cowasjee, 'Bring Back Jinnah's Pakistan' *Dawn* (1 November 2009), www.dawn.com/news/499938.

Hence, it is with some trepidation that I set myself to what seems like an intellectually daunting task: envisioning the constitutional bargain underlying the 1973 Constitution as a founding moment of constitutionalism in Pakistan. This chapter advances the argument that the creation of the 'permanent' Constitution of 1973 is central to Pakistan's constitutional identity. I make this claim notwithstanding the failure attributed to the 1973 Constitution in forestalling military coups,[18] the repeated 'suspension' of the Constitution and its bill of rights,[19] and the many 'constitutional deviations' introduced into the Constitution by dictators.[20]

The 1973 Constitution is Pakistan's only surviving constitutional settlement that is both democratic in its origins and has the imprimatur of being a 'consensus constitution' in an otherwise divisive political context.[21] Moreover, it is on the pivot of this Constitution that diverse constituencies in support of democracy and constitutional rights have emerged over the past four decades. The Constitution is the symbolic anchor for the survival and self-perpetuation of democratic political parties.[22] It is also the source of a uniquely South Asian constitutional rights jurisprudence, known as 'public interest litigation' (PIL), which has enabled a wide array of constituencies – involving citizen groups and non-governmental organisations, the media, government employees, lawyers, politicians and political parties – to engage with and construct a rights-based discourse through the courts.[23] Furthermore, it is the normative framework from which the judiciary – one of the most politically interventionist in the world – derives its powers of judicial review.[24]

The 1973 Constitution acquires legitimacy as the founding moment from factors that are grounded both in the past and in the present. They include the historic political conditions of the birth of the Constitution; a broad identification with the Constitution at the time of its making; evolving political support for the Constitution over time; mobilisation around the Constitution for political resistance through constitutional means; and a reconstruction of the current political system on the substratum of the original Constitution. Accordingly, I argue that the Constitution must be judged not on the basis of its substantive flaws or historical failures, or on the basis of continuing impediments or challenges to constitutionalism. Instead, it ought to be appraised on the basis of its instrumental value in

[18] Osama Siddique, 'The Jurisprudence of Dissolutions: Presidential Power to Dissolve Assemblies under the Pakistani Constitution and its Discontents' (2006) 23(3) *Arizona Journal of International and Comparative Law* 615, 623.

[19] Imtiaz Omar, *Emergency Powers and the Courts in India and Pakistan* (Kluwer Law International, 2002) 81–82.

[20] Maryam S Khan, 'Genesis and Evolution of Public Interest Litigation in the Supreme Court of Pakistan: Toward a Dynamic Theory of Judicialization' (2014) 28 *Temple International and Comparative Law Journal* 284, 302–03, 316–17.

[21] Paula R Newberg, *Judging the State: Courts and Constitutional Politics in Pakistan* (Cambridge South Asian Studies, 1995) 138–140.

[22] Leo E Rose and D Hugh Evans, 'Pakistan's Enduring Experiment' (1997) 8(1) *Journal of Democracy* 83.

[23] Khan (n 20).

[24] ibid.

enabling and expanding constituencies for constitutional transformation and sustaining opposition to 'extra-constitutional' interventions.[25] In other words, the 1973 Constitution is a central arena for pro-democracy groups and rights activists to assert their constitutional rights and 'to devise instruments of empowerment to strengthen their endeavours'.[26] It is in this consequentialist sense that the 1973 Constitution is a founding moment in Pakistan. This consequentialist understanding does not negate some very valid criticisms of the Constitution and the politics around it; rather, it underlines the need for continuing and strategic engagement with the political process for entrenching constitutional norms.

This conceptualisation deliberately deviates from the idealised eighteenth-century Western European notion of a founding moment as an immediate and radical break with the *ancien régime*.[27] It also departs from normative characterisations of the American founding as higher law-making that takes place outside the regular constitutional process through the intense participation and deliberation of the people.[28] Not only are these traditional formulations of founding moments the subject of mounting critique in their own contexts, using them as yardsticks for constitutional norm-building in present-day post-colonial societies is both misconceived and counter-productive.[29] The alternative notion of a founding moment I propose is 'instrumental' (as opposed to self-enforcing), 'resurgent' (as opposed to entrenched) and 'negotiated' (as opposed to populist). This calls for a reflexive relation between models of constitution-making and political and historical conditions.[30] Indeed, viewed on a wider scale, a constitutional framework that accumulates legitimacy over time through periodic resurgence allows for the articulation of a more typical present-day political model for rethinking founding moments.[31] It is to this end – to engage with a political model on founding moments that has resonance with many contemporary states in political transition – that I use Pakistan's example as broadly illustrative. I remain cognisant that this is only one amongst a plurality of observable processes of constitutional origination.

The chapter is structured as follows. Section I outlines the original 1973 Constitution and its prominent features within a historical framework of inquiry. Section II shifts the focus from the textual to the conceptual. It makes the fundamental argument that the 1973 Constitution is a founding moment

[25] Tayyab Mahmud, 'Praetorianism and Common Law in Post-colonial Settings: Judicial Responses to Constitutional Breakdowns in Pakistan' (1993) 4 *Utah Law Review* 1225.

[26] Rajeev Dhavan, 'The Constitution as the Situs of Struggle: India's Constitution Forty Years on' in LW Beer (ed), *Constitutional Systems in Late Twentieth Century Asia* (University of Washington Press, 1992).

[27] Andrew Arato, 'Forms of Constitution Making and Theories of Democracy' (1995) 17 *Cardozo Law Review* 191, 207.

[28] Bruce Ackerman, *We the People: Transformations* (Belknap Press, 2000).

[29] Arato (n 27) 211.

[30] ibid 219.

[31] Vicki C Jackson, 'What's in a Name? Reflections on Timing, Naming, and Constitution-Making' (2008) 49(4) *William & Mary Law Review* 1249.

in constitutionalism. In making this argument, section II attempts to situate Pakistan's trajectory within a scholarly framework of political and constitutional development, and lays out the contours of a founding model of 'resurgent constitutionalism' in similar contexts. It puts forward two essential elements of a founding moment – namely, the *ex ante* conditions of constitution-making and the *ex post* endurance of a constitution – and reflects on how Pakistan's historical experience is important for thinking about founding moments generally. Section III presents a historical analysis of constitution-making in Pakistan to illustrate the *ex ante* and *ex post* elements of its founding moment.[32] On a more general level, it reinforces the double-barrelled quality of a founding moment as both a watershed historical event and a process of constitutional consolidation. Section IV offers some concluding thoughts on theorising resurgent constitutionalism in transitional contexts.

I. Pakistan's 'Permanent Constitution': Historical Antecedents and Original Framework

This section presents a discussion of the historical antecedents of the 1973 Constitution. It looks at the constitutional frameworks that preceded the Constitution and the major contestations involved in their making. It then locates the original framework of the 1973 Constitution within this historical context.

Prior to the 1973 Constitution, Pakistan was governed by a number of different constitutional frameworks. Interim arrangements aside, the three main constitutions were the Government of India Act of 1935 (hereinafter the '1935 Act'), the last pre-independence constitution of British colonial India;[33] the Constitution of 1956; and the Constitution of 1962. The 1935 Act was adopted with some modifications as the post-independence constitution pending a new indigenous constitution. The 1956 Constitution was the first 'permanent constitution' to be promulgated by a constituent assembly, only to be abrogated in 1958 in a military coup.[34] The 1962 Constitution was introduced after an interregnum of four years by the same military government that abrogated the 1956 Constitution, but suffered a similar fate when it was abrogated in 1969 by a succeeding military regime.[35] Two interim constitutional frameworks followed, eventually to be replaced by the 1973 Constitution.

Thus, Pakistan's constitutional journey, like India's, began with the 1935 Act, a colonial system of 'bureaucratic despotism' designed for centralised control over

[32] I borrow this nomenclature from Jon Elster, 'Arguing and Bargaining in Two Constituent Assemblies' (2000) 2 *University of Pennsylvania Journal of Constitutional Law* 345, 356.
[33] Lau (n 9) 171.
[34] Wayne A Wilcox, 'The Pakistan Coup d'Etat of 1958' (1965) 38 *Pacific Affairs* 142.
[35] KJ Newman, 'The Constitutional Evolution of Pakistan' (1962) 38 *International Affairs* 352.

the native Indian population.[36] Among its main features was the concentration of executive powers in the office of the Governor General and a centralised judicial system, which was an integral component of the coercive apparatus of the colonial state.[37] While India's Constitution of 1950 was also a modulated form of the 1935 Act,[38] various factors at the time of partition led to divergent legacies of the 1935 Act in Pakistan. The 1935 Act amplified the political power of the executive-dominated state bureaucracy over other civilian institutions in Pakistan, including the nascent founding political party, the Muslim League.[39] The historical conditions that led to the rise of the 'over-developed bureaucratic state'[40] included severe resource constraints, a refugee settlement process of gargantuan proportions, the battle over the accession of princely states and other territories, a preoccupation with state-building and national security, and the de-prioritisation of strong representative institutions.[41] It was in these extraordinary conditions that the first Constituent Assembly of Pakistan – elected through provincial legislatures in the year prior to independence and a rump of the Constituent Assembly of India – was expected to draft a new constitution in addition to acting as the central legislature.

Quite apart from the Governor General's powers, the civil and military elite's resistance to democratisation, and the unravelling contestations between the centre and the provinces, there were two other structural constraints that contributed to thwarting early constitution-making efforts. The first of these was the struggle between secularists and Islamic modernists, and a heterogeneous set of Islamist pressure groups with varying demands for an Islamic constitution, leading to a complex process of accommodation. The second was an ethnically defined geographical divide, which was unprecedented in modern state-formation. At the time of partition, Pakistan comprised two 'wings', East and West, separated by more than 1,000 miles of hostile Indian territory. East Bengal or East Pakistan – situated on the eastern tip of the Indian Subcontinent – was its largest province, consisting of well over half the country's total population.[42] Added to their physical isolation was the fact that the Bengalis in the East, despite being the largest indigenous and regionally discrete ethnic group in Pakistan, were discriminated against in the upper levels of the bureaucracy and military, and had virtually

[36] David Washbrook, 'Law, State and Agrarian Society in Colonial India' (1981) 15(13) *Modern Asian Studies* 649.

[37] ibid.

[38] Surya Deva, 'The Indian Constitution in the Twenty-First Century: The Continuing Quest for Empowerment, Good Governance and Sustainability' in Albert HY Chen (ed), *Constitutionalism in Asia in the Early Twenty-First Century* (Cambridge University Press, 2014) 346.

[39] Ayesha Jalal, *The Sole Spokesman: Jinnah, the Muslim League and the Demand for Pakistan* (Cambridge University Press, 1985).

[40] Alavi (n 7).

[41] Ayesha Jalal, *The State of Martial Rule: The Origins of Pakistan's Political Economy of Defence*, 2nd edn (Vanguard Books, 1991).

[42] Rounaq Jahan, *Pakistan: A Failure in National Integration* (Columbia University Press, 1972).

no control over their industry and commerce.[43] The reluctance of the bureaucratic leadership in West Pakistan to strike a fair constitutional agreement with East Pakistan was premised on a fear of the latter's numerical dominance.[44] Hence, for the first decade, Pakistan was embroiled in a constitutional stalemate. It was only in 1955 that the elites from both wings reached a constitutional bargain, albeit in the larger context of a rapidly worsening civil–military imbalance.[45]

The 1956 Constitution emerged from this elite bargain, which was made possible only after the Constituent Assembly was dissolved and reconstituted by the Governor General.[46] Its central feature was a system of East–West representational parity, with seats in a unicameral central legislature apportioned equally between the two wings. In West Pakistan, this necessitated the dissolution of its provincial territories into a single political unit, known as the 'One Unit' – a measure that was steamrolled against the backdrop of opposition from the smaller provinces.[47] As regards the agreement on the role of Islam, the 1956 Constitution declared Pakistan an 'Islamic Republic', making it one of the first post-colonial 'Islamic States' in the world. In addition, the Constitution adopted as its Preamble the 'Objectives Resolution', a constitutional blueprint dating back to 1949 which struck an uneasy compromise between a liberal democratic framework and Islamic principles.[48]

The 1956 Constitution was short-lived. The new military regime of General Ayub Khan that took over power in a coup in 1958 abrogated the Constitution.[49] The main motivation for the coup was the unpalatable prospect of popular elections.[50] After four years of martial law, Ayub Khan introduced the 1962 Constitution, professing that it was more in line with the 'genius of the people'.[51] The 1962 Constitution reverted to an executive-dominated government, but at the same time attempted to construct a more secular vision of Pakistan by omitting the reference to an Islamic state and other Islam-based provisions. However, reactionary responses from *ulema* (Islamic scholars) 'to make the constitution visibly Islamic' led to the re-insertion, only a year later, of most Islamic provisions contained in the 1956 Constitution.[52] In 1969, Ayub Khan was forced to resign following a massive social movement,[53] paving the way for the country's first democratic transition.

[43] Philip Oldenburg '"A Place Insufficiently Imagined": Language, Belief, and the Pakistan Crisis of 1971' (1985) 44 *Journal* of Asian Studies 711, 711–12.

[44] Yunus Samad, *A Nation in Turmoil: Nationalism and Ethnicity in Pakistan, 1937–58* (Sage, 1995) 194.

[45] Jalal (n 41).

[46] ibid 196–215.

[47] ibid.

[48] Leonard Binder, *Religion and Politics in Pakistan* (University of California Press, 1963) 142–54.

[49] Ayesha Jalal, *Democracy and Authoritarianism in South Asia: A Comparative and Historical Perspective* (Cambridge University Press, 1995) 56–59.

[50] Newman (n 35).

[51] GW Choudhury (ed), *Documents and Speeches on the Constitution of Pakistan* (Green Book House, 1967) 560.

[52] Lau (n 9) 194.

[53] Tariq Ali, *Pakistan: Military Rule or People's Power?* (W Morrow, 1970).

The hegemony of the 'military-bureaucratic complex' and the oscillation between civilian and military governments have been central to constitution-making in Pakistan. But much as military regimes have been at the forefront of constitutional engineering since the 1950s, there have been three major fault lines in constitution-making experiments across time, whether imposed by military regimes or produced by democratic governments. These are: the design of the centre and its institutions; the division of power between the centre and provinces; and the demarcation of the role of Islam in the state. I analyse the original 1973 Constitution from the perspective of these focal contestations and the extent to which the new Constitution departed from historical settlements on these issues.

A. The Centre

Like the Indian Constitution, the 1973 Constitution is a lengthy and descriptive document that encompasses both the general outlines and administrative minutiae of government.[54] The 'core ingredients' of the original Constitution included a bill of rights and a 'power map'[55] establishing a democratic government based on a federal parliamentary form of government and an independent judiciary with express judicial review powers.

The parliamentary form of government in the new Constitution consisted of a titular President, a cabinet and an indirectly elected prime minister as the executive.[56] It stood apart in many ways from previous constitutions. The 1956 Constitution was essentially a cosmetic variation on the 1935 Act as it vested executive authority in a president, with discretionary powers to appoint and remove the prime minister.[57] The 1962 Constitution, on the other hand, made no pretences about military authoritarianism – it was described as a 'Presidential Cabinet without a Prime Minister'.[58] The 1973 Constitution overcorrected for the historical president–prime minister imbalance by granting the prime minister special powers over both the president and the parliament.[59]

The bill of rights, known as 'Fundamental Rights', contained the full spectrum of rights ranging from civil and political rights, socio-economic rights relating to property and work, and collective rights like non-discrimination in respect of religion, access to public places and public employment (Articles 9–28). The Fundamental Rights were directly enforceable by the provincial high courts

[54] The original Indian Constitution of 1950, one of the lengthiest constitutional texts in the world, contained 315 articles and eight schedules. In comparison, the original 1973 Constitution comprised 280 articles and four schedules.

[55] Ivo D Duchacek, *Power Maps: Comparative Politics of Constitutions* (ABC-Clio, 1973) 3.

[56] Baxter (n 13).

[57] GW Choudhury, 'The Constitution of Pakistan' (1956) 29(3) *Pacific Affairs* 243.

[58] Newman (n 35).

[59] Baxter (n 13) 1083–84.

and a centralised apex Supreme Court.[60] These 'Constitutional Courts' were endowed with a special 'original jurisdiction' with expansive remedial powers for the enforcement of the Fundamental Rights (Article 184(3)). The Constitution expressly provided that laws that were inconsistent with or made in derogation of the Fundamental Rights were void (Article 8). The combination of judicial power and the Fundamental Rights contained in the 1973 Constitution was unprecedented. The 1935 Act had no bill of rights and only limited judicial review powers. The 1956 Constitution had a similar framework, but was aborted before it could be implemented. The original 1962 Constitution lacked an enforceable bill of rights.

Overall, the design of the cabinet government in the 1973 Constitution departed fundamentally from historical constitutional frameworks in Pakistan. While the inclusion of strong-form judicial review was ostensibly a check on parliamentary authority, the hyper-powers of the prime minister granted him and his cabinet a fair amount of autonomy from the legislature, making his position more akin to the executive in a presidential form of government. Moreover, some of the powers of the National Assembly – the directly elected lower house to which the prime minister was responsible – were made subject to checks by the Senate, an indirectly elected upper house. Thus, the broader structure of the government looked more like a subtype of the separation of powers system with a federal bicameral legislature subject to constitutional review.

B. Centre–Province Relations and Provincial Autonomy

The 1973 Constitution introduced important innovations in federal design. The 1935 Act had proposed a conditional formula for the federalisation of Indian territories that did not materialise under colonial rule. At partition, the pre-independence demarcation of subterritories carried over into the new state of Pakistan. However, the 1956 Constitution eliminated all internal boundaries in the West wing through the 'One Unit' plan because of the East–West stalemate over the federal question. The 1962 Constitution left this One Unit structure and East–West parity intact.[61] Thus, both the 1956 and 1962 Constitutions suppressed regional territories in the West to create a 'bipolar federation'.[62]

The 1973 Constitution embodied a number of historic firsts for centre–region relations. One of these was the disbanding of the One Unit and recognition of the four main regions – Punjab, Sindh, North-West Frontier Province (now Khyber Pakhtunkhwa) and Balochistan – as de jure ethnic identity-based sub-units with their own provincial governments and law-making powers. This was in direct

[60] Khan (n 20) 297–300.
[61] ibid 100.
[62] Maryam S Khan, 'Ethnic Federalism in Pakistan: Federal Design, Construction of Ethno-linguistic Identity and Group Conflict' (2014) 30 *Harvard Journal on Racial and Ethnic Justice* 77, 98–100.

response to historical demands for the constitutional recognition of minority regions and ethnic groups that were otherwise dominated by the disproportionately large and historically powerful province of Punjab.[63] Another innovation was the establishment of the Senate, a federalist body for the equal representation of the provinces at the centre.

In sum, a number of political demands put forth by democratic constituencies since independence finally found expression in the 1973 Constitution. The adoption of a parliamentary system, accommodation of an ethno-regional federal structure with a bicameral central legislature and a re-distribution of power through provincial autonomy all reflected a political reversal on heated questions that had eluded past constitution-makers. That this agreement came after much acrimonious contestation between the majority party and smaller regional parties, or that it did not go far enough in accommodating minority interests, or that its full implementation was hamstrung by the majority party, or that it was suspended by a dictator shortly after its making, does not take away from the singular achievement of making a 'permanent constitution' through a democratic process in a historical context of constitutional impasse and authoritarian government for almost a quarter of a century.

C. Religion and State

The original 1973 Constitution, like most other post-war constitutions, combined elements of history, ideology and culture. It was also distinctive in that it was an 'Islamic Constitution', though it closely resembled its predecessors. Indeed, the Preamble was a verbatim reproduction of the Objectives Resolution and, as such, reflected a continuity in political demands since independence for an Islamic constitution. The incongruities between Islam and liberal notions of constitutionalism thus carried over to the 1973 Constitution. The Constitution contained other Islamic provisions as well. These included a preambular declaration that 'Muslims shall be enabled to order their lives … in accordance with the teachings and requirements of Islam' (Preamble), along with a set of provisions deriving from this declaration; a provision mandating that the head of state be Muslim (Article 41(2)); and a non-justiciable 'repugnancy clause' declaring that 'no law shall be enacted which is repugnant to such [Islamic] Injunctions' (Article 227(1)) and establishing an advisory body for making recommendations to the parliament on whether a proposed law was repugnant (Article 228). The 1956 and 1962 Constitutions contained these provisions in broadly similar terms.[64] The only

[63] ibid 111–13.

[64] Said Amir Arjomand, 'Religion and Constitutionalism in Western History and in Modern Iran and Pakistan' in Said Amir Arjomand (ed), *The Political Dimensions of Religion* (State University of New York Press, 1993) 89–90.

major addition in the 1973 Constitution was a kind of 'establishment clause' that made Islam the 'State religion of Pakistan' (Article 2).[65]

At the same time, the 1973 Constitution was unique in the degree to which Islamic principles were merged with, and in many ways made contingent on, a progressive framework for socio-economic re-structuring. The progressive character of the Constitution was a novelty, particularly its recognition of labour rights, commitment to a broadening of the economic base, latitude in allowing for an expanded role for the state in regulating private wealth and unprecedented focus on securing gender equality. Thus, although the broad 'legitimating principle'[66] of the new political order was Islamic ideology, the latter was ostensibly a progressive vision of Islam centred on 'an egalitarian society' (Preamble). The merger of an Islamic state with progressivist ideals was most evident in the chapter on 'Principles of Policy', which laid out a prescriptive policy schema for guiding executive and legislative functions (Chapter 2). On the one hand, the Principles iterated the state's role in enabling 'the Muslims of Pakistan, individually and collectively, to order their lives in accordance with the fundamental principles and basic concepts of Islam' (Article 31(1)). On the other hand, they read like a socialist charter, directing the state to safeguard the rights and secure greater public participation of vulnerable and marginalised groups (Articles 32–39); to promote social justice through special treatment of 'backward classes and areas', inclusive education reform, inexpensive and expeditious justice delivery, and improved working conditions and benefits for the working classes (Article 37); and to ensure social and economic well-being through the provision of basic necessities of life and equal opportunities, and the reduction of income and wealth disparities (Article 38). The Constitution contained other socialist provisions as well, including reserved parliamentary powers to alter property relations through land reform and to nationalise private industry and business (Article 253). Thus, in many respects, the Constitution was not unlike other post-colonial Asian constitutions in their detailed references to socio-economic structures and promotion of a welfare state.[67]

Against this backdrop, the question arises as to how the 1973 Constitution has stimulated change in the political trajectory of Pakistan. Appreciating the lived utility of a constitution requires more than an understanding of its substantive qualities; it requires a long-range view of constitutional contestation and transformation in practice. Loewenstein's appraisal of constitutions on the basis of their impact is highly relevant in this regard.[68] Loewenstein argues that constitutions may be 'normative' (in which political process conforms to the constitutional

[65] Lau (n 9) 199.

[66] Dieter F Grimm, 'Types of Constitutions' in Michel Rosenfeld and Andras Sajo (eds), *The Oxford Handbook of Comparative Constitutional Law* (Oxford University Press, 2002) 114.

[67] Brian Beddie, 'Issues and Problems in Asian Politics and Government' in RN Spann (ed), *Constitutionalism in Asia* (Asia Publishing House, 1963) 242–43.

[68] Karl Loewenstein, *Political Power and the Governmental Process* (University of Chicago Press, 1957).

framework), 'nominal' (in which power structures are in conflict with constitutional norms and render them ineffective) or 'semantic' (in which the constitutional text describes the existing system of government without imposing binding rules on it).[69] Loewenstein's typology is dynamic as it emphasises the degree to which political reality conforms to the norms of a constitution at a given point in time. It explicitly recognises that the meaning of constitutions is contingent on political environments in which they are embedded and that constitutions are thus evolving political documents. In Loewenstein's terms, the original 1973 Constitution is a case of a nominal constitution. It is not a case of a failed or aborted constitution like the 1956 Constitution or of a semantic constitution like the 1962 Constitution. Conceptualising the 1973 Constitution as a nominal constitution does not gloss over its many flaws, nor does it reduce these flaws to the problem only of under-enforcement. On the contrary, it makes it possible to engage, simultaneously, with the utility of imperfect constitutions as sites of struggle and contestation, and the normative value of constitutionalism.

The following section outlines a theoretical framework for understanding the 1973 Constitution as a model of resurgent constitutionalism in which a 'nominal' constitution may evolve into a 'normative' constitution over time.[70]

II. Founding Moments and Resurgent Constitutionalism: The Case of Pakistan

The 1973 Constitution emerged from Pakistan's first democratic transition. This was a period of global movement towards democratisation,[71] but like many other newcomers to democracy, Pakistan slid back into authoritarian rule in a 'reverse wave' in less than a decade.[72] Having come into effect as a permanent constitution, the 1973 Constitution was 'suspended' multiple times by military dictators and subsequently amended to legitimate their de facto powers. In 1977, the notorious coup-maker General Zia-ul-Haq suspended the Constitution and imposed martial law on the pretext of organising fresh elections.[73] The promise of elections was a political ruse, and the Constitution remained in cold storage for several years. Zia eventually 'revived' the Constitution in 1985, but only after unilaterally re-structuring government and centre–province relations. One of Zia's damaging amendments has acquired a nomenclature of its own and refers to the autarchic

[69] ibid 147–50.

[70] ibid 149.

[71] Samuel P Huntington, *The Third Wave: Democratization in the Late Twentieth Century* (University of Oklahoma Press, 1993).

[72] ibid.

[73] Omar Noman, *The Political Economy of Pakistan 1947–85* (Routledge 1988) 122.

powers of the President to unilaterally dissolve elected governments.[74] Known as 'Article 58(2)(b)', the amendment was intended for subordinating civilian powers to the military executive. It was emulated as a model of presidential government in the early 2000s by another military autocrat, General Pervez Musharraf, who relied on the precedent set by Zia to suspend the Constitution, subvert the judicial process for regime legitimation and subsequently revive the Constitution in a substantially altered form.[75] Ironically, however, the transitional decade between the military regimes of Zia and Musharraf bore the heaviest brunt of Article 58(2)(b). The dissolution of three popularly elected governments in quick succession between 1988 and 1997[76] demonstrated the monumental impediments in rolling back military-imposed changes to the Constitution. In the first three decades of the Constitution's existence – from the time it was enacted to the time it was revived by General Musharraf in 2002 – it was largely in a state of suspension for, cumulatively, a decade (1977–85 and 1999–2002), and in a state of constitutional deviation for another two decades (1973–77 and 1985–99).

Thus, the life cycle of the 1973 Constitution has been 'nonlinear, fitful, ambiguous and protracted'.[77] Kalhan's study of Pakistan's constitutional politics is a step in the right direction for understanding the phenomenon of constitutional evolution in a wider post-colonial context. Kalhan argues that Pakistan is an example of 'gray zone constitutionalism', in which the military engages in a 'recurring, iterative process of *transformative preservation*, by which its own power and that of its affiliated interests have been extended and entrenched into periods of civilian rule'.[78] Far from being a condition peculiar to Pakistan, this 'gray zone' is common to a large number of states undergoing political transition. Political scientists have persuasively demonstrated the non-linearity of the democratisation process since the 1970s, and the complex path dependencies and local contexts that ultimately shape this process. For instance, Carothers notes that many 'transitional countries' have entered a 'political gray zone', in that they are 'neither dictatorial nor clearly headed toward democracy'.[79] Similarly, Diamond refers to the 'democracy rollback', noting a widespread phenomenon in relatively new democracies of a reversal in the initial gains towards democratisation.[80] Diamond's data also show an 'unprecedented growth' since the 1970s in 'hybrid regimes', namely those that are 'neither clearly democratic nor conventionally authoritarian'.[81] Constitution-making in 'gray zones' and 'hybrid regimes' is thus inherently complicated and does not fit neatly into well-defined temporalities.

[74] Siddique (n 18).
[75] ibid.
[76] ibid.
[77] Anil Kalhan, '"Gray Zone" Constitutionalism and the Dilemma of Judicial Independence in Pakistan' (2013) 46(1) *Vanderbilt Journal of Transnational Law* 4.
[78] ibid 10.
[79] Thomas Carothers, 'The End of the Transition Paradigm' (2002) 13(1) *Journal of Democracy* 9.
[80] Larry Jay Diamond, 'Thinking about Hybrid Regimes' (2002) 13(2) *Journal of Democracy* 21.
[81] ibid 25.

There is, of course, a great deal of pessimism about the democratisation potential of grey zones and hybrid regimes. With respect to Pakistan, some argue that the country is unlikely to recover in the foreseeable future from setbacks to the democratic process that occurred in the 2000s.[82] Others assert with bewildering certainty that Pakistan's 'illiberal democracy' is an 'end-state'.[83] Still others pontificate over Pakistan's 'sham constitution' in the conviction that 'naming and shaming' can be 'an effective strategy for achieving positive change in and of itself'.[84] With few exceptions, there is little recognition of the contribution of the 1973 Constitution as an instrument of constitutional struggle towards a democratic order.

However, while there is scepticism about the democratic development of grey zones, there is growing scholarly appreciation of the empirical diversity in methods of constitution-making across political contexts. Conscious cross-fertilisation of these two fields of knowledge would help immensely in terms of understanding constitution-making in grey zones. Some recent works on constitutional change in transitional contexts point in this direction. They refer to the 'achievement of constitutionalism',[85] 'transitional constitutionalism'[86] or 'constitutional tipping points'.[87] Implicit in these concepts is the idea that far from being idealised norm-descriptors, constitutions are instruments of contestation and change towards a normative constitution in transitional contexts.

What does resurgent constitutionalism look like in Pakistan? Jackson's typology of constitution-making, derived from diverse contexts, provides an instructive counterpoint to the case of Pakistan. It encompasses three models of constitutional origination – 'quick clean break', 'incremental' and 'interim'.[88] In some ways, the making of the 1973 Constitution resembles Jackson's 'incremental' constitution, in which a constitution is reconstructed over a long period of time in a post-conflict setting through open-ended and reflexive processes of informal negotiations, legislative actions and judicial interpretation – as in the cases of Poland and Hungary.[89] At the same time, it resembles Jackson's 'interim' constitution, in which a constitution is created through a staggered process with various predetermined mechanisms for different constitution-making activities – South Africa being a

[82] Larry Jay Diamond, 'Is Pakistan the (Reverse) Wave of the Future?' (2000) 11(3) *Journal of Democracy* 91.

[83] Chaitram Singh and Michael Bailey, 'Praetorian Democracy, Illiberal But Enduring: Pakistan as Exemplar' (2013) 35 *South East Review of Asian Studies* 103.

[84] David S Law and Mila Versteeg, 'Sham Constitutions' (2013) 101 *California Law Review* 863, 870.

[85] Albert HY Chen, 'The Achievement of Constitutionalism in Asia: Moving beyond "Constitutions without Constitutionalism"' in Chen (n 38) 1–16.

[86] Jackson (n 31) 1252–59; Jiunn-Rong Yeh and Wen-Chen Chang, 'The Changing Landscape of Modern Constitutionalism: Transitional Perspective' (2009) 4(1) *National Taiwan University Law Review* 145–48; Arthur J Jacobson, 'Transitional Constitutions' in Michel Rosenfeld (ed), *Constitutionalism, Identity, Difference, and Legitimacy: Theoretical Perspectives* (Duke University Press, 1994).

[87] Victor V Ramraj, 'Constitutional Tipping Points: Sustainable Constitutionalism in Theory and Practice' (2010) 1(2) *Transnational Law Theory* 191.

[88] Jackson (n 31) 1260.

[89] ibid 1265–66.

paradigmatic example of this kind of constitution-making process.[90] But neither model fully captures the cyclical nullification and revival of the 1973 Constitution. Unlike Jackson's 'incremental' constitution, the 1973 Constitution was not intended to be provisional. And unlike Jackson's 'interim' constitution, the 1973 Constitution was suspended by a dictator only a few years after promulgation.

Pakistan's resurgent constitutionalism has followed a different path. It is incremental in that it is rooted in a 'permanent constitution' that has been buffeted through successive cycles of suspension–amendment–revival by de facto regimes, surviving at times only in a formal sense, to be salvaged and reclaimed again through a return of electoral democracy. Thus, the same constitutional document has been heavily contested and negotiated along the way. It has experienced multiple iterations of extra-constitutional change, but also compounding periods of democratic reconstruction. This incremental process has allowed for extended public discussion on the Constitution and its meaning over a significant period of time. It has provided a common platform for invoking challenges to and mobilising resistance against competing norms that are antithetical to democratic constitutionalism – including military authoritarianism and constitutional theocracy – and in the process consolidating incremental victories for democracy. Authoritarian forces have also instrumentalised the Constitution, but have refrained from abrogating it for fear of provoking a political backlash.[91] Thus, the Constitution is the cornerstone of Pakistan's political discourse as well as the central site of struggle for constitutionalism, notwithstanding the 'complex and multidimensional currents of constitutional thought and practice in the country'.[92]

Deriving insights from Pakistan's historical experience, I make three theoretic arguments regarding founding moments in grey zones. Foremost, I argue that in order for a founding moment to be consequential to constitutional development, it need not have revolutionary origins or break completely with the old legal order. In a post-colonial milieu where the military is a dominant institution and has all too often invoked doctrines like 'revolutionary legality' and 'necessity' to misappropriate power,[93] insisting on a sweeping and radical break with the past would force proponents of constitutionalism to choose between the extremes of impossibility and self-annihilation.[94] Further, I argue that a founding moment can be reduced neither to the particularities of the originating processes of a new constitution nor the substantive design of a constitution. A founding moment – and indeed constitution-making in general – is endogenous to and contingent upon political conditions. What imbues a constitutional moment with the normativity

[90] ibid 1267–70.

[91] Mohammad Waseem, 'Constitutionalism and Extra-constitutionalism in Pakistan' in Mark Tushnet and Madhav Khosla (eds), *Unstable Constitutionalism: Law and Politics in South Asia* (Cambridge University Press, 2015) 133.

[92] ibid 128.

[93] TKK Iyer, 'Constitutional Law in Pakistan: Kelsen in the Courts' (1973) 21(4) *American Journal of Comparative Law* 759.

[94] Arato (n 27) 218–19.

of a 'founding' is its historical grounding in a broad democratic movement as well as its resurgence or the degree to which it acquires social and political ownership for the transition to constitutionalism over time. Finally, I argue that recognising a founding moment in grey zones is an exercise in retrospective reflection. Whether the moment transpires in a short period of time or through a 'quick clean break', or whether it extends across a substantial period or happens incrementally over successive periods of regression and revival, the process of determining whether it matters as a concrete reality is inherently intertemporal.[95]

The following section deconstructs the abstract notion of a founding moment in the historical context of the 1973 Constitution, and contemplates how the making of the Constitution has mattered for constitutional change in Pakistan – specifically, how it has provided a tangible rallying point for upholding a democratic-constitutional order against 'constitution-wreckers'.[96]

III. 'Permanent Constitution' as a Founding: *Ex Ante* and *Ex Post*

The resurgent model of founding moments has *ex ante* and *ex post* elements: *ex ante* in the sense of historical conditions that enable an unprecedented democratic consensus; and *ex post* in the sense of post-enactment exogenous struggles to entrench constitutional norms.

The *ex ante* conditions in which the 1973 Constitution is grounded relate to a series of events beginning in the late 1960s and culminating in the actual drafting of the Constitution between 1971 and 1973. The late 1960s was a period of major socio-economic flux. The military experienced its first political backlash in the Indo-Pakistan conflict of 1965.[97] By 1968, the deteriorating economic situation resulting from this conflict, combined with rising discontentment over regional disparities and political oppression, put in motion a wave of popular unrest across Pakistan against Ayub Khan's military regime.[98] A number of different social and political movements, including students, workers, and new and revived political parties, catalysed widespread agitation against the regime.[99] This 'anti-Ayub movement' compelled a transfer of power to another military strongman, General Yahya Khan, who immediately imposed martial law and abrogated the 1962 Constitution.[100] Growing political pressure on the military eventually led

[95] Jackson (n 31) 1278.

[96] Elster (n 32) 356.

[97] Rounaq Jahan, 'Ten Years of Ayub Khan and the Problem of National Integration' (1970) 2(3) *Sage* 277.

[98] Burki (n 12).

[99] Talukder Maniruzzaman, '"Crises in Political Development" and the Collapse of the Ayub Regime in Pakistan' (1971) 5(2) *Journal of Developing Areas* 221.

[100] Lawrence Ziring, 'Militarism in Pakistan: The Yahya Khan Interregnum' (1974) 6(1) *Asian Affairs: An American Review* 402.

to the first general election in 1970 based on universal adult franchise. The 1970 election is widely accepted as the most free and fair in Pakistan's history[101] and marked the first formal victory for pro-democracy forces. The electoral winners within each wing won significant majorities: the Awami League in the East and the Pakistan People's Party (PPP) in the West.[102] However, at the same time, this East–West divide was exploited by the military to its political advantage,[103] resulting in a military operation in East Pakistan, the secession of the latter with military and diplomatic aid from India, and finally the retreat of the Pakistan military in 1971.[104] Paradoxically, this phase of deep crisis opened up a critical window of opportunity for constitution-making. Where the country had struggled to create a permanent constitution for almost a quarter of a century because of the East–West imbalance and the political dominance of the military, the removal of these impediments in the aftermath of East Pakistan's secession enabled a constitution to be made within a short span of fifteen months. Regardless of the many flaws in the process, the outcome was an unprecedented constitutional settlement.[105]

In complete contrast to past constitutions, this consensus imparted a high degree of democratic legitimacy to the 1973 Constitution. Yet, the populist *ex ante* context and the consensus producing the Constitution were not sufficient conditions for ensuring the long-term survival of the Constitution. The evolution of social and political support for the Constitution over time is a major determinant in explaining the resurgence of the Constitution.

Ironically, the Constitution suffered its worst setbacks during the early phase of its life, starting with the rapid centralisation of power by the majoritarian PPP government and leading to General Zia's military coup in 1977.[106] In 1979, billions of dollars of military aid poured into Pakistan from the US and Saudi Arabia, setting the country on a path of religious radicalisation to resist the Soviet invasion in Afghanistan.[107] From 1977 to 1984, the Constitution remained suspended and the Constitutional Courts were barred from exercising judicial review powers.[108] The Constitution was revived after extra-constitutional amendments in 1984 to reconsolidate the military's political control prior to elections.[109] However, what is often missed in this oft-regurgitated narrative on Zia's defacement of the 1973 Constitution is the fact that the revival of the Constitution was not merely an act of political gratuitousness or, alternatively, regime legitimation.

[101] GW Choudhury, 'The Last Days of United Pakistan: A Personal Account' (April 1973) 49(2) *International Affairs* 229.
[102] Khan (n 62) 105–06.
[103] Muhammad Rizwan, 'Aftermath of the Elections 1970: From Disparity to Dissection' (2014) 3(4) *Asian Journal of Management Sciences and Education* 127.
[104] Sisson and Rose (n 14).
[105] Khan (n 62) 108–13.
[106] Jalal (n 49) 90–91.
[107] Omar Noman, 'Pakistan and General Zia: Era and Legacy' (1989) 11(1) *Third World Quarterly* 28.
[108] Noman, *The Political Economy of Pakistan* (n 73) 140–50.
[109] Hasan-Askari Rizvi, 'The Civilianization of Military Rule in Pakistan' (1986) 26(10) *Asian Survey* 1067.

On the contrary, the dictator was compelled to change tack because of unrelenting opposition against his regime. One powerful locus of this opposition was the massive, populist left-wing political alliance of major political parties known as the 'Movement for the Restoration of Democracy' (MRD).[110] The central demand of the MRD was the restoration of the 1973 Constitution,[111] and it was instrumental in mounting pressure on Zia to resuscitate the constitutional process and hold elections, and to thereby force open institutional avenues for political contestation.

Zia's death in a mysterious plane crash in 1988 paved the way for another transition to civilian rule. Tenuous as this transition was, it nonetheless brought about two major transformations that catapulted the Constitution to the centre-stage of politics. One was the political rise of the judiciary and the other was a deepening of political party identification with the Constitution. The judiciary's power derived from two main sources in the Constitution: the Fundamental Rights[112] and, ironically, the presidential power to dissolve governments under Article 58(2)(b). The revival of the electoral process created the space for the courts to re-invent and propagate their role as custodians of a new, democratic order through judicial activism.[113] In the process, they evolved jurisprudential tools like PIL to ensure their institutional survival and enlarge their capacity to intervene in political questions. Alongside this, the involvement of the courts in dissolution cases under Article 58(2)(b) empowered them to judge the fate of elected governments.[114] The politics of the 1990s was thus crucial in moulding the role of the courts as mediators between the deep state and civilian political parties – an institutional trend that persists up to the present day.[115] Political parties also emerged as important political forces in the 1990s.[116] They boldly invoked Fundamental Rights in the courts against military encroachment in politics,[117] removed Article 58(2)(b) from the Constitution through a unanimous vote in parliament in 1997[118] and jockeyed for leverage in the courts through strategic judicial appointments and court-packing.[119] That all these contestations were anchored in the 1973 Constitution was a major factor in enhancing the political ownership of the Constitution.

In 1999, General Musharraf overthrew a civilian government in a military coup. Musharraf suspended the 1973 Constitution, purged the courts for regime

[110] Tariq Ali, 'Movement for the Restoration of Democracy in Pakistan' (1984) 11(1) *India International Centre Quarterly* 57.

[111] ibid 59.

[112] Khan (n 20) 297–300.

[113] ibid 304–07.

[114] Siddique (n 18).

[115] Khan (n 20) 307–09.

[116] Haris Gazdar, 'Pakistan's Precious Parties' (2008) 43(6) *Economic and Political Weekly* 8.

[117] Khan (n 20) 304–07.

[118] Anwar H Syed, 'Pakistan in 1997: Nawaz Sharif's Second Chance to Govern' (1998) 38(2) *Asian Survey* 116.

[119] Lorne Neudorf, *The Dynamics of Judicial Independence: A Comparative Study of Courts in Malaysia and Pakistan* (Springer, 2017) 172–74.

legitimation, marginalised political parties, sponsored new parties and alliances, re-inserted Article 58(2)(b) through a fresh set of unilateral constitutional amendments in 2002 and engineered elections on the basis of the revived but heavily amended Constitution.[120] However, unlike in the 1980s, Musharraf had to contend with a burgeoning media, an activist judiciary, and international pressures for rule of law reform and democratisation.[121] The fragile state of the regime became apparent in 2007 when the Supreme Court's constitutional challenges to Musharraf – grounded in the Fundamental Rights jurisprudence[122] – provoked the dictator to move the process for the Chief Justice's removal. This event ignited a large-scale street mobilisation that was spearheaded by lawyers, but was, importantly, supported by a host of other actors, including political parties, the media and civil society organisations, that cohered around the rhetoric of restoration of the Constitution and the rule of law to depose Musharraf. This 'Lawyers' Movement', as it came to be known, culminated in fresh elections, a new democratic government, the re-instatement of the judges and a humiliating exit of the military from politics.[123]

The transition stimulated by the Lawyers' Movement led to a period of constitutional rehabilitation. The most prominent feature of this period was the restoration of the 1973 Constitution to its original form by the landmark Eighteenth Constitutional Amendment.[124] The Eighteenth Amendment was introduced by the first post-Musharraf civilian government and received unanimous parliamentary approval in 2010.[125] It modified or substantially rewrote over one-third of the Constitution with the overarching objective of reversing illegal constitutional amendments since the Zia era, and is arguably the most crucial political consensus in Pakistan since the making of the 1973 Constitution. The provision-enhancing changes in the Amendment include the removal of Article 58(2)(b), the restoration of a semi-parliamentary system with more powers to the Senate, the establishment of an independent and permanent Election Commission for conducting elections, the strengthening of judicial tenure and mechanisms for judicial appointments, and the expansion of judicial review powers through the new Fundamental Rights.[126] Further, the Amendment has made significant strides towards a decentralised federation, devolving some highly important issues to

[120] TA Qureshi, 'State of Emergency: General Pervez Musharraf's Executive Assault on Judicial Independence in Pakistan' (2009–10) 35 *North Carolina Journal of International Law and Comparative Regulation* 485.

[121] Zahid Shahab Ahmed and Maria J Stepan, 'Fighting for the Rule of Law: Civil Resistance and the Lawyers' Movement in Pakistan' (2010) 17(3) *Democratization* 492.

[122] Khan (n 20) 323–27.

[123] Ahmed and Stepan (n 121).

[124] Katharine Adeney, 'A Step towards Inclusive Federalism in Pakistan? The Politics of the 18th Amendment' (2012) 42(4) *Publius* 539.

[125] 'Pakistan's National Assembly Passes Key Constitutional Reforms' *Sunday Telegraph* (8 April 2010), www.telegraph.co.uk/news/worldnews/asia/pakistan/7567994/Pakistans-national-assembly-passes-key-constitutional-reforms.html.

[126] Adeney (n 124).

provincial governments[127] and, to a more limited extent, to local governments as envisaged by the original Constitution.[128]

Developments in the aftermath of the Eighteenth Amendment have edified the normative relevance of the Constitution. These include the completion of an elected government's tenure for the first time in Pakistan's history followed by a peaceful electoral transition in 2013; peaceful transfer of power by two army chiefs since General Musharraf; the completion of tenure of five Chief Justices of the Supreme Court since the retirement of Chief Justice Iftikhar Chaudhry in 2013; the re-distribution of a larger proportion of national revenues to the provinces and the re-allocation of interprovincial shares in favour of historically marginalised regions; and the devolution of power to the provinces and the operationalisation of local governments through elections. Although the Eighteenth Amendment is by no means an uncontested and irreversible reality – especially given the abiding civil–military imbalance – these are nonetheless far-reaching political shifts, accompanied by major institutional overhauling, and signify a deepening of constitutional accommodation.

The following section summarises the main theoretical insights on founding moments based on Pakistan's experience with constitutional evolution.

IV. Rethinking Founding Moments: What Pakistan's Experience Demonstrates

The making of the 1973 Constitution is a case of resurgent constitutionalism. This process of periodic resurgence shares many attributes with diverse examples of constitution-making in grey zones around the world. It neither fully breaks with the past, nor is it immediately entrenched through an open process of public participation. It is characterised by protracted and tenuous non-linear progress, at times degenerating into a reverse wave before accumulating any positive gains for constitutionalism. The paradox that resurgent constitutionalism raises for founding moments in grey zones is not merely that the enabling conditions of constitution-making are also those constraining constitution-making;[129] the real paradox is that contexts that are new to a democratic constitution are also those that invariably need an incubatory period for evolving constitutional norms. Thus, I have argued that 'founding moments' are key periods of democratic constitution-making from which the conditions of constitutionalism emerge temporally in grey zones, largely irrespective of judgements about the original constitution being 'good' or 'sham'. I have further argued, as a necessary corollary to this, that

[127] ibid 9–11.

[128] 'Devolution Talk: Local Government Polls, is Devolution Anathema to Political Parties?' *Herald Forum* (15 May 2015), herald.dawn.com/news/1153045.

[129] Jackson (n 31) 1249.

a founding moment in a transitional context has two elements: *ex ante* historical and political conditions of constitution-making – that give the constitution its initial democratic legitimacy – and *ex post* resurgence and revalidation of the constitution over time.

One of the big contributions of the present case study on Pakistan's founding moment to theories of constitutional origination is the centrality of the *ex post* element of constitution-making. The almost exclusive focus on the *ex ante* element, as well as the particularities of the immediate process of constitution-making in extant theories of founding moments, is not only of limited value to but also deeply ignorant of the political and structural conditions obtaining in contemporary grey zones. The theoretical privileging in constitutional foundings of the *ex ante* notions of a clean break with the past and the immediate entrenchment of constitutions does not coincide with the historical reality of constitution-making in new and transitional democracies. A constitution that is expected to not only define the rules and norms of the political game but also to provide the moorings of democratic transition necessitates an *ex post* struggle for constitutional entrenchment. The ex post pushback against anti-constitutional and anti-democratic forces is the concrete test of a constitution's superlative value as a founding. Thus, I have emphasised the importance – indeed, the necessity – of the *ex post* element to a founding. It is only the *ex post* progress – of what is always a nominal constitution at birth to a normative one over time – that legitimates any constitution through an iterative process of negation, resurgence, contestation, engagement and ownership. Unlike the traditional notion of a collective expression of community during a limited moment of higher law-making, the political model of resurgent constitutionalism facilitates multiple opportunities for collective validation of a founding constitution. It is the *ex post*, then, that gives real meaning to a founding, which, devoid of any real test of survival, only remains an intellectual abstraction.

None of this ought to detract from the continuing fallouts and challenges of resurgent constitutionalism in Pakistan or other transitional democracies. Inherent within resurgent constitutionalism is the deep tension between structural continuity and change, and hence the risk of constitutional reversal. In Pakistan, the staying power of the military as well as supporters of an Islamist constitutional dispensation – the two often buttressing each other – is an obvious challenge. Because of ongoing security problems in the region, the unstable diplomacy between Pakistan and India over the long-standing Kashmir issue, the militarisation of Pakistan's marginalised province of Balochistan, the uncertainties plaguing the border between Pakistan and Afghanistan, the military and drone operations in Pakistan's troubled Tribal Areas in the northwest, and the military's unchanging policy of protecting certain militant and terrorist groups for strategic purposes,[130] the military avows both sufficient cause and institutional power to retain its political ascendance, though perhaps no longer in the guise of military dictatorships

[130] Hasan-Askari Rizvi, 'New Dimensions of Security' *Express Tribune* (20 October 2014), tribune.com.pk/story/777943/new-dimensions-of-security.

and martial laws. The most recent general elections of 2018 are widely believed to have been rigged and engineered by the military on a large scale in favour of its preferred candidate.[131] Thus, a complex civil–military power-sharing arrangement continues to persist, demonstrating that a 'clean break' from authoritarianism is a very long-term political project in transitional countries – one that no constitution can enforce without an equally long-term *ex post* political commitment and institutional evolution.

Despite Pakistan's many current and foreseeable constitutional challenges, resurgent constitutionalism has both empowered and broadened constituencies of constitutionalism over time. Just as the military appears to have firmly reasserted control over the political process, another social movement is surging in the northwestern province of Khyber Pakhtunkhwa and the adjoining Tribal Areas that have been sites of military operations related to the War on Terror for many years. Describing itself as the '*Pashtun Tahafuz* Movement' (translated as '*Pashtun* Protection Movement' or PTM), the Movement calls, among other things, for an end to enforced disappearances, extra-judicial killings and other rights abuses allegedly committed at the hands of Pakistan's military and intelligence services.[132] That the core express demand of the PTM is that people of the region (mostly ethnic Pashtuns) be granted equal protection of the Fundamental Rights and that this demand has found resonance in non-*Pashtun* communities across the country is a powerful testament to the socialisation of the 1973 Constitution.

[131] 'Viewpoint: Pakistan's Dirtiest Election in Years' *BBC News* (23 July 2018), www.bbc.com/news/world-asia-44923565.

[132] M Ilyas Khan, 'Manzoor Pashteen: The Young Tribesman Rattling Pakistan's Army' *BBC News* (23 April 2018), www.bbc.com/news/world-asia-43827660.

11

A Founding Moment in Iraq

A Gender Perspective

NOGA EFRATI*

I. Introduction

Founding moments or landmark events that break ties with an *ancien régime* and lay the foundations for the establishment of modern states are not gender-neutral. Indeed, moments of constitution-making, which are considered ultimate founding moments, have spurred feminist activism and scholarly writing, as women and women's issues have been largely absent. The study of constitutions from a gender perspective has uncovered the different impact these documents had on men and women, has revealed successes as well as failures of women's participation in constitution-making and has documented the process of constitutionalising women's equality around the world.[1] But can a gender perspective actually bring to light founding moments?

Iraq's constitutional past had received little attention in academic literature until the US-led invasion in 2003 and the subsequent efforts at drafting a new constitution for the country. But even then, researchers were inclined to treat Iraq's past constitutional developments in a cursory fashion, as a prologue to more elaborate discussions of the post-2003 drafting process. Many tended to dismiss the importance of constitutional developments occurring between 1925, when the British-backed Constitution was introduced, and 2004, when the American-backed Transitional Administrative Law was promulgated.[2] The interim period

* I wish to thank the Gerda Henkel Foundation for the generous grant that made the research for this chapter possible.

[1] Helen Irving (ed), *Constitutions and Gender* (Edward Elgar, 2017); Ruth Rubio Marin and Helen Irving (eds), *Women as Constitution-Makers: Case Studies from the New Democratic Era* (Cambridge University Press, forthcoming).

[2] See, eg, Andrew Arato, *Constitution Making under Occupation: The Politics of Imposed Revolution in Iraq* (New York, Columbia University Press, 2009); Haider Ala Hamoudi, *Negotiating in Civil Conflict: Constitutional Construction and Imperfect Bargaining in Iraq* (University of Chicago Press, 2013); Jonathan Morrow, 'Deconstituting Mesopotamia: Cutting a Deal on the Regionalization of Iraq' in Laurel E. Miller and Louis Aucoin (eds), *Framing the State in Times of Transition: Case Studies in*

between the 1958 ousting of the Hashemite monarchy and 2003 was depicted for example, as 'forty-five years of tinkering with successive constitutions' that 'had thoroughly undermined any commitment to constitutionalism or the rule of law'.[3] At first glance, then, the period between 1925 and 2004 would not appear to be fertile ground when seeking founding moments. However, in my study of women's history in Iraq, I encountered formative moments that deserve more careful consideration.[4] True, women's history often exhibits its own timeline, periodisation, patterns of continuity and defining moments, but this chapter will argue that a gender perspective undermines the prevailing notion of the period between 1925 and 2004 as a constitutional void. It is my contention that researchers have thus far underappreciated that the struggles of women's rights activists during the Hashemite period (1921–58) were conducted against constraints placed on women by the 1925 Constitution. Following activists' efforts at gaining suffrage and improving women's standing in the realm of personal status will offer particular insight into this. Only when we understand how the 1925 Constitution constructed female citizens of the new Iraqi state can we appreciate the significance of legislation and actions affecting women that were inspired by the constitutional replacement in 1958. Moreover, I will then argue that activists' struggles after 2003 also articulated that the 1958 constitutional replacement was a founding moment in Iraq's history.

II. Historical Setting

The 1925 Iraqi Constitution, which remained essentially unchanged throughout the Hashemite period, was to a large extent a British legacy.[5] British occupation of the three Ottoman provinces – Basra, Baghdad and Mosul – began as a preemptive move in 1914 to protect British interests at the head of the Persian Gulf. These interests had, in large part, been born out of Britain's concern to protect its trade route to India. They grew as trade with the Gulf area developed, but especially with the discovery of oil in commercial quantities in southern Iran in 1908 and with the British Navy's decision to convert its fleet from coal to oil fuel. After the outbreak of the First World War, when it became obvious that the Ottoman

Constitution Making (US Institute of Peace Press, 2010), www.usip.org/sites/default/files/Framing%20the%20State/Chapter21_Framing.pdf; Saad Jawad, 'The Iraqi Constitution: Structural Flaws and Political implications' *LSE Middle East Center Paper Series* 1 (November 2013), eprints.lse.ac.uk/54927/1/SaadJawad_Iraqi_Constitution_LSE_Middle_East_Centre_WP01_Nov2013.pdf. A more detailed discussion is provided by Nathan J Brown, *Constitutions in a Nonconstitutional World: Arab Basic Laws and the Prospects for Accountable Government* (SUNY Press, 2002).

[3] Feisal Amin Al-Istrabadi, 'Reviving Constitutionalism in Iraq: Key Provisions of the Transitional Administrative Law' (2005) 50 *New York Law School Law Review* 270.

[4] See especially Noga Efrati, *Women in Iraq: Past Meets Present* (New York, Columbia University Press, 2012).

[5] For the full text of the 1925 Constitution in English and Arabic, see CA Hooper, *The Constitutional Law of Iraq* (Mackenzie & Mackenzie, 1928); and 'Abd al-Razzaq al-Hasani, *Ta'rikh al-wizarat al-'iraqiyya*, vol 1, 7th edn (Afaq 'Arabiyya, 1988) 339–54.

Empire would join with the Central Powers, Britain sent troops to occupy Faw and Basra. The occupation of Basra in November 1914 began a process that ended with the occupation of Baghdad in March 1917 and of Mosul in November 1918. In 1920, Britain was awarded the mandate over Iraq and accepted responsibility for building an Iraqi state. In 1921, at the Cairo Conference, Britain's plan for Iraq coalesced. It was there, in Phebe Marr's words, that 'the three pillars of the Iraqi state were conceived'.[6] These pillars were a British-backed Arab monarchy, a treaty that would legitimise the British presence in Iraq, and a constitution. Iraq's first constitution had been drafted and re-drafted starting in 1921, but was not promulgated until March 1925. A 'gift from the West', as a British judge in Iraq once termed it,[7] the 1925 Constitution shaped the political and legal landscape in Iraq for years to come. While promising all Iraqis equal status as pertaining to their rights and obligations as well as equality before the law, the Constitution also legalised British strategies aimed at imposing order and enabling their indirect rule of the country. Specifically, the British sought to control Iraq through those individuals they perceived as, or found useful to construct as, Iraq's authentic leaders. Yet, the articles of the Constitution that were designed to tie tribal, religious and secular-oriented leaders to the British-dominated state had harsh and long-lasting implications for Iraqi women, particularly their political and legal enshrinement as second-class citizens.

III. Women and the Political System before 1958

From the inception of the Iraqi state, women's rights activists struggled to gain political rights for women. According to the 1925 Constitution, Iraq was to function as a constitutional monarchy, with a king, cabinet, two legislative chambers and democratic rights for the populace. In practice, for decades, the constitutional system allowed Britain, the British-installed royal family and Sunni former Ottoman officers to effectively control formal politics. The parliamentary system intended to tie urban intellectuals to the new state. But in order to ensure that the power of the Hashemite government would not be undermined, the Constitution and election law facilitated the exclusion of all but an elite few from the seats of power. Considerable obstacles hindered many men from entering Parliament and totally blocked women from participating in formal politics.[8] Indeed, the struggle for women's political rights repeatedly stumbled over the obstacle of the Iraqi Constitution, on which the election laws that prescribed women's disenfranchisement were based. Although the Constitution stated, in Articles 6 and 18, that all Iraqis were equal as pertaining to their rights and obligations, two other

[6] Phebe Marr, *The Modern History of Iraq*, 2nd edn (Westview, 2004) 24.
[7] Hooper (n 5) 15.
[8] See art 30 in ibid 84.

articles in the document restricted this provision to men only. Article 36 required that the Chamber of Deputies be composed on the basis of one deputy for every 20,000 male inhabitants, while Article 42 stipulated that any Iraqi male who had reached the age of 30 and who was not disqualified by certain provisions stated in the Constitution could be elected as a deputy.[9] Based on these articles, election laws restricted the right to vote and to be elected to men.[10]

Throughout the Hashemite period (1921–58), women protested against their exclusion from formal politics. As early as 1924, when the Constituent Assembly was convened to discuss Iraq's Constitution, Paulina Hassun, publisher of the first women's magazine to appear in Iraq, appealed to the Assembly not to ignore women's rights. Participation in democratic life, she wrote, is not the right of men alone.[11] However, it was not until the 1950s that the government allowed women activists to conduct an organised campaign for political rights. Earlier requests to establish organisations for this purpose were rejected by the Ministry of Interior.[12] In the 1950s, organised efforts of middle-class activists for political rights intensified. But only one women's organisation, the Iraqi Women's Union (al-Ittihad al-Nisa'i al-ʿIraqi, established in 1945), many of whose members were wives and relatives of the ruling elite,[13] was authorised to act for women's rights. The left-leaning League for the Defence of Women's Rights (Rabitat al-Difaʿ ʿan Huquq al-Mar'a, founded in 1952) was unauthorised and had to conduct its activities underground.

The union stepped up its efforts in the early 1950s by a variety of means. Members sent missives to successive prime ministers, heads of Parliament and party leaders. They met with senior state figures and initiated special activities and events devoted to women's enfranchisement. In 1953, during the premiership of Muhammad Fadil al-Jamali, for example, the union succeeded in organising a special week in support of women's political rights. The events during that week included lectures, a symposium, radio programmes and a meeting with the Prime Minister, all dedicated to women's suffrage. Union members mobilised

[9] Compare arts 6 and 18 with arts 36 and 42 in ibid 41, 59, 87–88, 93.

[10] See, eg, Iraq Ministry of Justice, *Compilation of Laws and Regulations Issued between 1st January 1924 and 31st December 1925* (Government Press, 1926) 45–51.

[11] *Layla* (Baghdad, 15 March 1924) 242.

[12] 'Women's Clubs Taboo' (May 5 1934) Report on Current Events for the Period April 15 to 30, 1934, Paul Knabenshue to the Secretary of State, US National Archives (Washington) 890G.00 General Conditions/29; Naziha al-Dulaymi, 'Rabitat al-mar'a al-ʿiraqiyya' (1982) 5 *Al-Thaqafa al-Jadida* 104, 107.

[13] Sara Fadil al-Jamali, who founded the Women's Temperance and Social Welfare Society, was the American wife of Muhammad Fadil al-Jamali, who filled high posts at the Ministry of Education in the 1930s and was Foreign Minister in 1946, 1947 and 1952 and Prime Minister between 1953 and 1954; Asiya Tawfiq Wahbi, President of the women's branch of the Child Protection (or Welfare) Society during the 1940s, was married to Tawfiq Wahbi, who was at different times the Minister of Economics, Minister of Education and Minister of Social Affairs; ʿIsmat Sabah al-Saʿid, Vice President of the women's branch of the Red Crescent in the mid-1940s, was Nuri al-Saʿid's daughter-in-law; Zakiyya Pachachi, Chairperson of the Iraqi Women's Union in the 1940s, came from a family that had produced several prime ministers, ministers and others who had attained key roles in Iraq's government.

the press by giving interviews, providing information to the media and making sure that daily newspapers regularly covered union actions.[14] But their demands were often rejected outright as unconstitutional, and even when prime ministers expressed support, the complicated process of amending the Constitution was never begun.[15]

The Hashemite government, as I elaborated elsewhere, utilised the notion of 'gradual modernisation' to constantly postpone activists' demands for suffrage during the 1950s. The notion that reforms were best introduced gradually, taking into consideration the country's 'reality and its possibilities',[16] enabled the government to set goals before reforms could be introduced. Education was set as prerequisite for women's suffrage. But while the government demanded that women, unlike men, exhibit such 'progress' as a prerequisite for gaining rights, it was far from doing its utmost to enable women this kind of progress. Indeed, the government's lack of effort was clearly reflected in the 1957 census, which indicated that under the monarchy, the literacy rate even among the urban, more privileged women did not exceed 10 per cent.[17] However, in the context of this chapter, it is important to note how the Constitution was used to postpone enfranchisement. It was, in fact, the mechanism of introducing amendments to the Constitution itself which served to slow down and even stave off this reform. Indeed, Article 119 of the Constitution required that any amendment of its provisions be approved by a two-thirds majority, both by the Chamber of Deputies and the Senate. After approval, the Chamber of Deputies had to be dissolved and a new Chamber elected. The amendment then had to be resubmitted. Again, after approval by a two-thirds majority of both houses, the amendment had to be submitted to the king for assent and publication.

Amendment to the 1925 Constitution became inevitable in early 1958. The formation of the United Arab Republic prompted Hashemite Iraq to establish the Arab Union with Hashemite Jordan, which required amendments to be made to the Constitution. Now that the complicated process of changing the Constitution had to be set in motion, women activists seized the moment and mobilised with greater vigour to fight for women's political rights. In March 1958, it seemed that their efforts would finally bear fruit. On 26 and 27 March, the Chamber of Deputies and the Senate voted unanimously in favour of an amendment stating

[14] *Sada al-Ahali* (Baghdad, 12 December 1951) 2–3; *al-Zaman* (Baghdad, 20 June 1952) 2; *al-Ahali* (Baghdad, 9 November 1952) 2; *al-Akhbar* (Baghdad, 18 October 1953) 4; *al-Bilad* (Baghdad, 7 March 1956) 5; *al-Zaman* (Baghdad, 26 February 1958) 3.

[15] Ruth Frances Woodsmall and Charlotte Johnson, *Study of the Role of Women, Their Activities and Organizations in Lebanon, Egypt, Iraq, Jordan and Syria, October 1954–August 1955* (International Federation of Business and Professional Women, 1956) 39; *al-Sha'b* (Baghdad, 20 October 1953) 2; *al-Zaman* (Baghdad, 7 March 1956) 4; *al-Bilad* (Baghdad, 12 March 1956) 4; *al-Zaman* (Baghdad, 22 February 1958) 4.

[16] See, eg, *al-Ittihad al-Dusturi* (Baghdad, 22 August 1950) 1.

[17] Al-Jumhuriyya al-'Iraqiyya, Wizarat al-Dakhiliyya, Mudiriyyat al-Nufus al-'Amma, *Al-majmu'a al-ihsa'iyya li-tasjil 'am 1957*, vol 2, part 16 (Government Press, 1964) 24. For more, see Efrati (n 4) 105–10, 137–53.

that 'the Iraqi Constitution may be amended within a year from the enforcement of this law, and this shall include the granting of political rights to educated women'. It added that 'if the [future] two chambers approve this [second] amendment, it shall be forwarded for Royal assent without dissolving the Chamber of Deputies [in contrast to the usual procedure]'.[18]

While the Women's Union, as well as some observers at the time, presented this as a reform,[19] the government, in utilising Article 119, actually deferred women's citizenship rights to some later point in time. For the educated, this future seemed near; for the illiterate masses, it was more distant. The former had to wait a year before gaining their rights, but the latter would have to attain an education or wage a new campaign to amend the Constitution yet again. However, a closer look at the wording of the amendment reveals that even the educated were not given any solid assurances that they would enjoy full rights within a specified period of time. Rather than guaranteeing a future change in the Constitution, the amendment stated only that the Constitution 'may be changed'. It did not clearly state that women would receive both the right to vote and the right to be elected, nor did it specify the level of education required for gaining rights. It ensured a swift passage of any future amendment if a future Parliament approved it. Thus, only a future Parliament could decide whether educated women should receive political rights, the minimum level of education required for political participation and the nature of the rights that women would be granted. In other words, had the ousting of the Hashemite monarchy in July 1958 not occurred, this amendment would have been just another ploy in deferring the granting of political rights to women.

It is important to emphasise that the planned amendment also ensured that, even if it were implemented, only a negligible number of women would enjoy political rights. The census conducted in Iraq in 1957 showed that the number of women aged 20 (the legal voting age) and older who had at least an elementary school education was less than 20,000. At the time, the total number of women aged 20 and older in Iraq was one and a half million. Even a broader definition of 'educated', one that included women who, according to the census data, could 'read and write' or 'read only', would thus have resulted in political rights for only five per cent of all women of voting age.[20]

IV. Women and the Legal System before 1958

Activists' struggle for improving women's standing in the realm of personal status during the Hashemite period reveals another even more problematic aspect

[18] *Al-Zaman* (28 March 1958) 5; Sir M Wright to Foreign Office (26 March 1958) National Archives (London), FO 371/134198/VQ1015/33.

[19] George Grassmuck, 'The Electoral Process in Iraq, 1952–1958' (1960) 14 *Middle East Journal* 397, 400; Matthew Elliot, *'Independent Iraq': The Monarchy and British Influence, 1941–1958* (IB Tauris, 1996) 187; *Al-Sha'b* (26 March 1958) 8.

[20] Al-Jumhuriyya al-'Iraqiyya (n 17).

of the 1925 Constitution. Although the Constitution stated in Article 6 that there would be no differentiation in the rights of Iraqis before the law,[21] it created a highly divisive legal system. The Constitution established that state courts be divided into three classes: religious, civil and special courts. Religious courts were divided into shari'a courts for the Muslims and Spiritual Councils for other religious communities. It affirmed that shari'a courts alone were to handle matters pertaining to the personal status of Muslims in accordance with the shari'a provisions particular to each Islamic sect.[22] While stating that civil courts would have jurisdiction over all Iraqis in all civil and criminal matters, it also allowed for the establishment of special courts for settling criminal and civil cases relating to the tribes in accordance with their customs.[23]

The establishment of special courts for the tribes facilitated the state's adoption of the Tribal Criminal and Civil Disputes Regulation (TCCDR). Introduced during the First World War by the British occupying forces, the TCCDR bolstered tribal leaders and tied them to the British by granting them authority to settle disputes among their tribesmen. After an exhausting world war, as it became necessary to devise a policy that would hasten the evacuation of troops from Iraq and reduce expenditure, the British clung to the TCCDR, which facilitated the cheap, indirect administration of vast territories and the securing of order in the countryside. At the insistence of the mandate authorities, provision for a separate tribal jurisdiction was included in Iraq's Constitution and, in 1924, the Tribal Regulation became a state law. It remained in force throughout the Hashemite period.[24] This regulation divided the citizens of Iraq into two groups with two different legal systems. The urban population was subject to civil and criminal courts. Urban crime fell under the jurisdiction of the Baghdad Penal Code enacted by the British in 1918 and was based primarily on the Ottoman and Egyptian penal codes, which, in turn, had been framed according to the French Penal Code.[25] But the rural population was subject to the TCCDR, which sanctioned and institutionalised customary practices.

Women's activists of the Hashemite period set out to expose the serious implications of the legal system with which they were presented. The Constitution institutionalised state non-intervention in personal status issues, thus offering no recourse to women when faced with unfavourable interpretations of Islamic rules by kin and husbands, as well as in legal procedures pertaining to family relations. In adopting the TCCDR as state law, tribal customs with harsh ramifications for

[21] Hooper (n 5) 41.

[22] ibid 124 and 132–33.

[23] ibid 128 and 145.

[24] *Tribal Criminal and Civil Disputes Regulations* (The Times Press, 1916), L/P&S 10/617, India Office Library (London); 'Tribal Criminal and Civil Disputes Regulation (Revised)' in *Iraq Administration Reports: 1914–1932* vol 8, sources established by Robert L Jarman (Archive Editions, 1992) 144–56; 'The Tribal and Civil Disputes Regulations Amendment Law of 1924' in Iraq Ministry of Justice (n 10) 169–72.

[25] Great Britain, General Officer Commanding-in-Chief, Mesopotamia Expeditionary Force, *The Baghdad Penal Code* (np, 1918).

women in the countryside gained legitimacy. Activists expressed concern about child marriages and polygamy. They criticised the ease with which a man could divorce his wife, and her difficulty in dissolving a marriage and maintaining custody of her children. Indeed, books published at the time with the aim of providing *qadis*, lawyers, and law students with a clear and easy-to-use summary of Shi'i Ja'fari and Sunni Hanafi laws concerning matters of personal status determined that a Shi'i mother had the right to custody of her son only prior to weaning – that is, until the age of two – and of her daughter until the age of seven; according to Sunni Hanafi law, a mother's right to custody continued until her sons were seven and her daughters were nine, at which time the children passed into their father's care.[26]

Intellectuals, such as the poet Nazik al-Mala'ika (1922–2007), decried the ability of fathers to tear children away from their mothers as the harshest, most unreasonable type of deprivation. Activists such as Naziha al-Dulaymi (1923–2007), the leader of the underground League for the Defence of Women's Rights, protested that women, especially those of the 'peasant class', were treated as work tools first by their fathers and later by their husbands. Child marriages, more prevalent in years of drought and grave economic need, saw fathers offering their daughters at a very young age for paltry sums or even without *mahr*[27] so as to be absolved of the burden of supporting them. Like animals, she argued, women were bought and sold in marriage. Polygamy was perceived as a means of expanding the labour force. Divorce was the inevitable lot of the peasant woman who became weak, disabled or unable to work for any other reason or even if her 'owner' simply got tired of her. The threat of divorce compelled women to be obedient and endure hard work, beatings and humiliations; otherwise, they could find themselves homeless, poor and devoid of any rights, even concerning their own children.[28]

Activists also condemned abuses resulting from the state sanctioning of customary practices detrimental to women under the TCCDR. They protested against *shighar*, exchange marriages, when one woman serves as another's *mahr*; confiscation of the *mahr* by guardians; *al-nahwa*, the right of a cousin to forbid the marriage of a female relative; and *fasl* marriage, in which women are given in marriage as part of a dispute settlement. Women handed over in *fasl* marriage were known to be enslaved and maltreated with no right to demand a divorce. Prominent women also protested against the legitimisation of honour murders. In her poem 'Washing off Disgrace', Nazik al-Mala'ika lamented the brutal murder of a young woman in the name of honour. The poem was seen as expressing a new

[26] 'Abd al-Karim Rida al-Hilli, *Al-ahkam al-ja'fariyya fi al-ahwal al-shakhsiyya*, 2nd edn (al-Muthana 1947) 99 and 101; Husain 'Ali al-A'zami, *Ahkam al-zawaj* (Sharikat al-Taba' wa-l-Nashr al-Ahaliyya 1949) 210–13.

[27] According to Islamic law, *mahr* (plural *muhur*) is a sum of money or other property given by the husband to the wife as an obligation of marriage.

[28] Nazik al-Mala'ika, *Al-tajzi'iyya fi al-mujtama' al-'arabi* (Maktab al-Aswar, 1978) 36; Naziha al-Dulaymi, *Al-mar'a al-'iraqiyya* (al-Rabita, [1950?]) 39–40.

generation's aversion to the archaic practices preserved in society.[29] However, her description of the murderer as he sat in a tavern boasting of his deeds and cleaning his dagger also bemoaned the fact that he could get away with it. Her criticism, subtle though it was, clearly conveyed the notion that women lived in fear and submissiveness because there was no law to protect them from their kin.[30] The activists Sabiha al-Shaykh Da'ud (1912–75), a member of the directorate of two of the Iraqi Women's Union's constituent organisations, and Naziha al-Dulaymi concurred that rural women were subjected to 'double servitude' – enslaved like rural men to the landlords and enslaved by their husbands as well. Rural women were overworked, abused and lacked any personal freedom. Like beasts of burden, al-Dulaymi protested, rural women might, without recourse, bear the brunt of their husbands' anger, be beaten or otherwise maltreated. They understood that opposition might have harsh consequences, for they could easily be disposed of through murder. Such an act could easily be covered up under the pretext of 'washing away the shame', which was officially recognised as justification for murder.[31]

Activists were not alone in their critique of the separate legal systems that constructed Iraqis as unequal before the law. However, their criticism brought to light the ramifications of the TCCDR and the state's non-intervention in the realm of personal status on women. The constitutionally backed legal system left all female citizens unprotected from harsh treatment by kin and husbands and from uncompromising rulings by religious clerics. It constructed rural women – the majority of women in Iraq – as tribal possessions and allowed men unbridled power over their lives.

V. Women's Political Rights and Personal Status Issues after 1958

On 14 July 1958, under Brigadier 'Abd al-Karim Qasim and his ally Colonel 'Abd al-Salam 'Arif, a military coup swiftly overthrew the British-installed monarchy. Many inside and outside Iraq, among them numerous scholars, saw the ousting of the Hashemite government and the developments in its aftermath as a revolution.[32] The new Republican government, headed by Prime Minister

[29] Khalid Kishtainy, 'Women in Art and Literature' in Doreen Ingrams, *The Awakened: Women in Iraq* (Third World Center, 1983) 149–50.

[30] Nazik al-Mala'ika, *Diwan Nazik al-Mala'ika*, vol 2 (Dar al-'Awda, 1986) 351–54. For an English translation, see Ingrams (n 29) 150–51.

[31] Al-Dulaymi (n 28) 8–11; Sabiha al-Shaikh Da'ud, *Awwal al-tariq ila al-nahda al-niswiyya fi al-'iraq* (al-Rabita, 1958) 223–29.

[32] See, eg, Hanna Batatu, *The Old Social Classes and the Revolutionary Movements of Iraq* (Princeton University Press, 1978); Marion Farouk-Sluglett and Peter Sluglett, *Iraq since 1958*, 3rd edn (IB Tauris, 2001); Juan Romero, *The Iraqi Revolution of 1958: A Revolutionary Quest for Unity and Security* (University Press of America, 2010).

ʿAbd al-Karim Qasim (1958–63), was quick to annul the 1925 Constitution and to issue a provisional constitution. Most researchers focused on the political aspects of the document and on the new power structure it established. They did not attach much importance to what seemed to be nothing more than generic articles promising Iraq's citizens equality before the law 'in their public rights and obligations' as well as the protection of their rights and liberties (Articles 3 and 9).[33] However, juxtaposing activists' struggles during the Hashemite period with the new legislation and actions pertaining to women's rights these articles inspired reveals a different picture. To begin with, the new republican regime gave a clear signal that it intended to end women's exclusion from formal politics. Article 9 of the Interim Constitution promising all citizens equal 'public rights' was, unlike in the past, generally interpreted as granting all women the right to vote and to run for office.[34] Moreover, in July 1959, Naziha al-Dulaymi, head of the Women's League, was appointed Minister of Municipalities. She not only became the first female cabinet member in Iraq, but also in the entire Arab world.

True, the post-1958 government failed to establish a parliament; thus, any provision that could have been understood as granting women political rights became a dead letter. However, it is noteworthy that since 1958, all succeeding constitutions were understood as granting women political rights. The Interim Constitution of 1964, drafted under President ʿAbd al-Salam ʿArif (1963–66), stated that election is a right of all Iraqis and that their participation in public life is a national duty (Article 39).[35] Based on the 1964 Constitution, Iraq's National Assembly Electoral Law of 1967 passed under President ʿAbd al-Rahman ʿArif (1966–68) recognised women's right to vote (Article 1) and to be nominated as a candidate (Article 20).[36] But again, the promised National Assembly did not come into being. After the Baʿth Party seized power in 1968, its two interim constitutions, published in 1968 and 1970, reaffirmed equal rights and duties for all citizens, and prescribed the establishment of a National Assembly.[37] Similar to ʿAbd al-Karim Qasim, the Baʿth appointed a female minister, Suʿad Khalil Ismaʿil, as Minister of Higher Education (1969–72). In 1980, a National Assembly was established and, for the first time in their history, Iraqi women participated in national elections.[38]

[33] *Al-Waqaʾiʿ al-ʿIraqiyya* (27 July 1958) 2.

[34] *Al-Ahali* (23 August 1959) 3 and 6; *Al-Bilad* (24 December 1959) 3; *Iraq Times* (9 March 1960) 1.

[35] *Weekly Gazette of the Republic of Iraq* (20 May 1964) 5.

[36] *Al-Waqaʾiʿ al-ʿIraqiyya* (9 February 1967) 27 and 32.

[37] Article 19 of the 1970 Constitution is often translated as stating that all citizens of Iraq are equal before the law regardless of gender (*jins*), language, religion or social origin. However, the official translation for the word 'jins' at the time was 'race' rather than 'sex' or 'gender;' *cf Weekly Gazette of The Republic of Iraq* (10 March 1971) 4 with International Labour Organization, 'Iraqi Interim Constitution', ilo.org/dyn/natlex/natlex4.detail?p_lang=en&p_isn=42152 and with Amal Rassam *Women's Rights in the Middle East and North Africa – Iraq*, 14 October 2005, www.refworld.org/docid/47387b6b16.html.

[38] See arts 12 and 14 in *Al-Waqaʾiʿ al-ʿIraqiyya* (17 March 1980) 487; Marr (n 6) 180–81. However, it is noteworthy that the new Electoral Law, promulgated in March that year, required all candidates to obtain permission from an election commission; this meant that only women affiliated with the Baʿth Party could be elected.

In light of activists' pre-1958 struggles, the 1958 Interim Constitution emerged even more clearly as a turning point when we turn to look at the new legal system it set in place. It is noteworthy that on the very same day that the 1958 Interim Constitution was approved, the TCCDR was abolished. This move, the government stated, was 'out of the desire to bring about equality among the citizens' and based on the Constitution's Article 9.[39] With the stroke of a pen, women's formal 'tribalisation' was erased.

In addition, in December 1959, based on the Interim Constitution and with the declared intent 'to ensure women their legal rights and family independence',[40] the government introduced a Personal Status Law. The new law brought family matters under the purview of the state and, in borrowing lenient provisions from the various schools of Islamic law, was attuned to criticism regarding family matters and gender relations raised by activists prior to 1958. The law required a woman's consent to marriage, emphasised her entitlement to the *mahr* and made an effort to tackle the issue of child marriages. It placed severe limitations on polygamy, imposed a number of restrictions on a man's ability to divorce his wife (*talaq*) and allowed women to seek dissolution of marriage through judicial proceedings (*tafriq*) on various grounds. It also stated that a mother had a preferential right to custody of her children. Maternal custody following divorce was granted until the child was aged seven, but the court was empowered to extend this if the welfare of the child so required. Although based on Islamic law and claiming to be derived from its principles – 'from those rules in the shari'a which were generally agreed upon' – the new law contained a daring reform: Islamic laws of inheritance were abandoned, according women an equal share with men. As the TCCDR was eradicated, the law significantly offered the same treatment for both rural and urban women.

The 1959 legislation also created a framework which legitimised women's participation in the legislative process concerning family matters and, as women became part of the administration, they took part in formulating this law. Minister Naziha al-Dulaymi was among the specialists, jurists, *'ulama* and politicians who prepared the new Personal Status Law; the League, which received official recognition in December 1958, had presented a draft law to the Ministry of Interior that had been discussed and approved by its executive committee. Interviews with the then senior members of the League, Mubejel Baban and Bushra Perto, reveal that the most far-reaching reform included in the law, which gave men and women equal shares in inheritance, was the result of their efforts.[41]

Following the 1963 coup, Ba'thists and Arab nationalists' perpetrators promptly amended the Personal Status Law. This short-lived regime introduced

[39] *Al-Waqa'i' al-'Iraqiyya* (3 August 1958) 7.

[40] *Al-Waqa'i' al-'Iraqiyya* (30 December 1959) 1 and 8.

[41] Interview with Mubejel Baban (London, 20 August 1997); interview with Bushra Perto (London, 18 August 1997).

some limited adverse changes regarding polygamy and repealed the articles granting women equality in inheritance, replacing these with rules consonant with the shari'a, but all other provisions favourable to women remained in force.[42] In 1964, after 'Abd al-Salam 'Arif and military allies ejected the Ba'thists from power, their new interim constitution adopted the Ba'thist move concerning inheritance. In an effort to secure that legislation according women an equal share with men would not repeat itself, Article 12 stated that inheritance rights would be determined according to Islamic law.[43] However, all other reforms introduced by the 1959 law remained untouched.

Yet, from the early 1970s reforms in the realm of personal status continued. Limited pluralism allowed women activists again to exert pressure on the regime to address unfavourable loopholes and provisions. Members of the Ba'thist General Federation of Iraqi Women (established in 1969) pushed for far-reaching reforms, hoping for a new law rather than an amendment. Some favoured the secularisation of family law.[44] Members of the Women's League became involved again in formulating a draft family law which was presented to the regime in 1975.[45] By 1978, an extensive amendment to the law was introduced. Based on a selective integration of Sunni and Shi'i laws that were favourable to women, the amendment eliminated an ambiguity in the law regarding the minimum age for marriage and, for the first time, placed severe restrictions on detrimental practices that were still prevalent in the countryside. Punishments were set not only for forcing women into marriage, but also for preventing women from marrying, as had been made possible by such customs as *fasl* marriage and the *nahwa*. The 1978 legislation also took steps to extend the conditions under which women were permitted to seek dissolution of their marriage as well as prolonged maternal custody until the child reached the age of 10.[46] Activists expressed disappointment with the modesty of the reform, but some of their demands were heeded.[47] During the 1980s and 1990s, under Saddam Hussein, many of their achievements were eroded. Still, several amendments favourable to women were introduced as a result of appeals on the part of the Ba'thist General Federation of Iraqi Women. It is important to note that all of Iraq's leaders after 1958, even Saddam Hussein when he was seeking the support

[42] *Al-Waqa'i' al-'Iraqiyya*, 785 (21 March 1963) 1–2; JND Anderson, 'Changes in the Law of Personal Status in Iraq' (1963) 12 *International and Comparative Law Quarterly* 1026.

[43] *Weekly Gazette of the Republic of Iraq* (20 May 1964) 4.

[44] *Al-Mar'a*, 65 (1976) 6–7; Marion Farouk-Sluglett, 'Liberation or Repression? Pan-Arab Nationalism and the Women's Movement in Iraq' in Derek Hopwood, Habib Ishow and Thomas Koszinowski (eds), *Iraq: Power and Society* (Ithaca, 1993) 67; Suad Joseph, 'Elite Strategies for State Building: Women, Family, Religion and State in Iraq and Lebanon' in Deniz Kandiyoti (ed), *Women, Islam, and the State* (Macmillan Press, 1991) 184.

[45] Su'ad Khayri, 'Al-Mar'a al-'iraqiyya tunadil did al-diktaturiyya' (1980) 118 *al-Thaqafa al-Jadida* 120; al-Dulaymi (n 28) 106.

[46] *Al-Waqa'i' al-'Iraqiyya* (20 February 1978) 314–15.

[47] Joseph (n 44) 184; Khayri (n 45) 120–21.

of tribal shaykhs and religious leaders, shied away from cancelling Iraq's 1959 Personal Status Law or officially resurrecting the TCCDR.[48]

VI. A View from Post-Saddam Iraq

The struggle of women's rights activists in Iraq after 2003 also brings to the fore the notion that the 1958 constitutional replacement was a founding moment. The US-led invasion in 2003 was accompanied by promises to turn Iraq into a free and democratic country in which women's rights would be enshrined. All too soon, however, Iraqi women's rights activists began cautioning that developments were pulling Iraqi women back to the past. It was not only the memory of life under Saddam's regime that fanned their fears; they were also haunted by ghosts of a more distant history. Activists often alluded to the British attempt at state building and its harsh long-lasting consequences for women.

The fear that under the American-led coalition, Iraq would revert to past British policies of reliance on tribal leaders and sanctioning customary law was not unfounded. Following the 2003 invasion, British forces, faced with the urgent need to re-establish law and order across the southern part of the country, searched for precedents from their earlier experience in Iraq. Military lawyers, it was reported, were 'dusting down the system of law used during the 38-year British Mandate in Iraq in an urgent effort to reach a workable interim criminal and civil code before a new constitution and legal system is agreed'.[49] What they were in fact contemplating was a resurrection of the TCCDR.[50] By 2005 and even before the Americans' massive use of the tribal 'Awakening' fighters, coalition forces, increasingly desperate to impose order, were recruiting tribal elements to secure borders and protect oil facilities. Under the mounting disorder, tribal courts were convened, sanctioning coercive practices pertaining to women. At the same time, in debates regarding the permanent constitution, some negotiators were pressing for the recognition of tribal justice.[51]

Activists' response to the threat of 'retribalisation' was informed by the struggles of their predecessors during the monarchy period. From the onset of the war in 2003, notwithstanding support for the idea that all groups with a stake in

[48] For more about post 1958 developments in Iraq's Personal Status Law, see Noga Efrati, 'Negotiating Rights in Iraq: Women and the Personal Status Law' (2005) 59 *Middle East Journal* 577–95.

[49] See reports from al-Amara by Donald Macintyre in *The Independent* (24 April 2003) and by Glen Owen in *The Times* (24 April 2003).

[50] Toby Dodge, *Inventing Iraq: The Failure of Nation Building and a History Denied* (Columbia University Press, 2003) 168.

[51] James Glanz, 'Thanks to Guards, Iraq Oil Pipeline is up and Running, on and fff' *New York Times* (3 September 2005), www.nytimes.com/2005/09/03/international/middleeast/03oil.html; Dumeetha Luthra, 'Tribal Justice Takes Hold' *BBC News* (2 February 2004), news.bbc.co.uk/2/hi/middle_east/3449869.stm; Rory Carroll, 'Women Battle for Rights in New Iraq' *The Guardian* (15 August 2005), www.guardian.co.uk/world/2005/aug/15/iraq.gender.

Iraq's future should be included in decision-making, activists expressed concern regarding the incorporation of tribal leaders in positions of power. Turning tribal leaders into a political mainstay, they warned, might result in acquiescence to values and customs detrimental to women.[52] Songul Chapuk, a member of the interim Iraqi Governing Council (IGC) and a women's rights activist, cautioned, for example, that if the tribes were to take over matters of civil society, women would be deprived of their rights and would be dragged back to 'the days of the monarchy and the feudalist regime'.[53] The tribal system, Chapuk noted, does not recognise women's rights; it does not view women as independent entities, but as possessions. Women's rights supporters thus sought to write into the interim and permanent constitutions clauses that would afford legal protection to women against gender-based tribal laws and practices.[54] Their protest apparently led to a modification of the article in the Constitution promising that the state would seek the advancement of Iraqi tribes and uphold their noble human values to also guarantee that 'the state shall prohibit tribal customs that are in contradiction of human rights' (Article 45.2).[55]

In the realm of personal status, activists also found themselves struggling to preserve past gains. In December 2003, the US-appointed IGC passed Resolution 137 abolishing the 1959 Personal Status Law. Clerics of each and every community in Iraq were to take the state's place in administering matters of personal status for members of their respective sects or religious groups. Iraqi activists were quick to react. They warned of the consequences of wresting control over family affairs from the hands of the state. Retired judge Zakiyya Isma'il Haqqi reflected most clearly the reason for women politicians and activists' protests. Since 1959, she said, Iraqi family law has developed and been amended under a series of governments, giving women a 'half-share in society' and an opportunity to develop as individuals. Referring to Resolution 137, she said: 'This new law will send Iraqi families back to the Middle Ages. It will allow men to have four or five or six wives. It will take children away from their mothers. It will allow anyone who calls himself a cleric to open an Islamic court in his house and decide who can marry and divorce and have rights.'[56]

[52] Woodrow Wilson International Center for Scholars, Conflict Prevention Project, Middle East Project and Women Waging Peace, *Winning the Peace Conference Report: Women's Role in Post-conflict Iraq* (Supplemental material, Woodrow Wilson International Center for Scholars, 2003) 8 and 16, www.wilsoncenter.org/sites/default/files/ACF34.pdf; Shereen Gharouf and Elena Gordon, *The Heartland of Iraq Women's Conference Preliminary Report* (Iraq Foundation, 2003) 16, www.peacewomen.org/assets/file/hr_heartlandofiraqwomensconference_womenforafreeiraq_october2003.pdf.

[53] 'Nashitat: Al-Mukallafun bi-Kitabat al-Dustur Mutalabun bi-l-I'timad 'ala al-Qawanin al-Dawliyya' *al-Zaman* (4 August 2005), www.azzaman.com/index.asp?fname=2005\08\08-03\973.htm&storytitle.

[54] *Winning the Peace Conference Report* (n 52) 16.

[55] An English text of the Constitution is available at: http://investpromo.gov.iq/wp-content/uploads/2013/06/iraqi-constitution-En.pdf.

[56] Quoted in Pamela Constable, 'Iraqi Women Decry Move to Cut Rights' *Washington Post Foreign Service* (16 January 2004), www.washingtonpost.com/archive/politics/2004/01/16/iraqi-women-decry-move-to-cut-rights/74decc2e-6724-470e-b521-8df09ec30fd2/?utm_term=.8e847bd0dade.

Fierce resistance, spearheaded by Iraqi women politicians and activists, facilitated the repeal of this resolution two months later. However, this did not prevent further moves to annul the law on the part of both clerics and religious politicians who sat on the committee charged with the drafting of a new permanent constitution. In fact, Article 41 of the 2005 Constitution adopted Resolution 137 to a large extent, stating that 'Iraqis are free in their commitment to their personal status according to their religions, sects, beliefs or choices, and this shall be regulated by law'. While clearly securing the religious option, Article 41 did not refer explicitly to an alternative recourse to secular family law, and the 1959 Personal Status Law was not given as a clear option. While not closing the door completely on the existing Personal Status legislation, it reduced it to an exception rather than the rule. Activists were angry and disappointed. Maysun al-Damluji, a politician and women's rights activist, said that Iraqi women had gained many rights in the past 45 years and it was absurd to give up these achievements. Safiyya Suhayl who worked closely with the George W. Bush administration and was appointed as Iraq's Ambassador to Egypt, protested: 'When we came back from exile, we thought we were going to improve the rights and position of women. But look what happened – we have lost all the gains we made over the last 30 years. It's a big disappointment.'[57] Activists' disappointment stemmed not only from the loss of achievements for which their foremothers had struggled long and hard for decades, but also from the weakening of the very channel that after 1959 made advancements in the realm of personal status possible.

VII. Conclusion

The constitutional replacement of 1958 has received little study as a founding moment in Iraq's history. However, a gender perspective suggests that a more careful look is warranted. Juxtaposing activists' struggles during the Hashemite period against women's political and legal enshrinement as second-class citizens by the 1925 Constitution with the new legislation and actions pertaining to women's rights after 1958 offers a new perspective into this moment in history. While this juncture should not be idealised, as any advancement achieved after 1958 left much to be desired, the annulment of the 1925 Constitution and the introduction of legislation inspired by the 1958 Interim Constitution signalled a new direction. Women were no longer constitutionally barred from formal politics or left outside state jurisdiction and protection. The annulment of the TCCDR ended the formal construction of female citizens as tribal possessions. Suffrage and the introduction

[57] Andrew Buncombe, 'Iraqi Activist Taken up by Bush Recants Her Views' *The Independent* (27 August 2005), www.independent.co.uk/news/world/middle-east/iraqi-activist-taken-up-by-bush-recants-her-views-308604.html.

of the Personal Status Law created a means for women, as activists, lawyers and politicians to advance their rights in relation to the family and society.

The struggle of women's rights' activists in post-Saddam Iraq also affirms the notion that the 1958 constitutional replacement was a founding moment. Activists' sense of déjà vu after 2003 was informed by the generation of activists who had exposed and fought against the harsh implications the 1925 Constitution had on women. Moreover, their struggle was in defence of achievements made possible by the 1958 constitutional replacement that the founding mothers of the Iraqi women's movement had helped bring about.

Conclusion

Rethinking Founding Moments

NISHCHAL BASNYAT

> The death of the contemporary forms of social order ought to gladden rather than trouble the soul. Yet, what is frightening is that the departing world leaves behind it, not an heir, but a pregnant widow. Between the death of the one and the birth of the other, much water will flow by, a long night of chaos and desolation will pass.
>
> Alexander Herzen

> The people made the Constitution, and the people can unmake it. It is the creature of their will, and lives only by their will.
>
> John Marshall

The chapters in this edited volume are a result of a two-year collaborative process that began with a symposium entitled *Founding Moments in Constitutionalism* held at Yale Law School in April 2016. The conference brought together scholars from around the world with the objective of understanding the relationship between 'founding moments' – landmark events that break ties with the *ancien régime* and lay the foundations for the establishment of modern states – and the constitutional order. The symposium produced insightful and unique perspectives on founding moments in constitutionalism, often with fascinating singular examples from around the world, that broadened our understanding of what founding moments are and how they impact our understanding of constitutional regimes.

From Ming-Sung Kuo's opening chapter on the role of narrative, Yair Sagy's insight on Israel's delayed constitutional order to Noga Efrati's exploration of the gendered perspective of founding moments in Iraq, the chapters in this volume shed light on the different casual mechanisms in which founding moments impact – or sometimes fail to impact – constitutionalism and the narratives of various agents (founding fathers, judges, historians and citizens) that are influential in constitutionalising founding moments. While this volume has produced myriad themes worth analysing, these concluding pages will focus on providing an overview of the book. In addition, the following pages will highlight some of the broader issues raised throughout this volume and how they have reconfigured our understanding of founding moments in constitutionalism.

I. Founding Moments: A Reductionist Understanding

To understand the impact of this volume, it is worthwhile to begin by providing a reductionist view of founding moments in constitutionalism. The objective is to use this as a touchstone to help us understand the concept at its most basic level. Thereafter, I will elaborate upon how the chapters in this book add a new dimension to this basic understanding and how each contribution lays the foundation for further inquiries, especially with regard to the notion of causality and narrative legitimacy.

A reductionist view of founding moments in constitutionalism would involve at least four components. First, there is a major 'nation-making' or 'nation-changing' event(s) – violent revolution, war, struggle for independence, the establishment of a modern nation-state or the abolition of deep-rooted institutions like slavery or apartheid.

Second, in the wake of this crisis, a nation creates or re-creates its core identity. A nation distinctly different – both in its normative character and in its underlying institutions – is born. The American Revolution of 1776, the independence of India and Pakistan, and the creation of Israel are examples of such landmark 'nation-making' or 'nation-changing' founding moments.

Third, the founding moment has a guiding 'spirit'. This 'spirit' is formed largely as a reaction to the previous order. They may also be influenced by the political debates that result during the birth or rebirth of a new nation: 'The debates over how to respond to the failure of the old regime, the wrangling over the process and substance of the new constitutional order, and the tabulation of the votes cast in the convention or the referendum on the adoption of the new constitution.'[1] This guiding 'spirit' created by the founding moment – which may even entail words of those considered 'founding fathers' – influences how this new nation views itself normatively. A previously colonised state, for example, may come to hold, as part of its new national identity, anti-colonial or even anti-government tendencies. Likewise, a state once defined by apartheid may be reborn after its founding moment with deeply held egalitarian values.

Fourth, the 'spirit' of the founding moments establishes the constitutional order. This occurs through a process often referred to throughout this volume as constitutionalisation – this may be through the guidance of the preamble, the text of the constitution, the institutions and rights that the constitutional order establishes, or through those who retrospectively interpret the text in light of the character and 'spirit' of the founding moment.

On the one hand, a cursory read of the contributions in this volume may give the impression that the chapters largely conform to this reductionist understanding. Throughout the book, there is discussion of founding moments across

[1] Ming-Sung Kuo, ch 1 in this volume.

history and from different parts of the world; there is analysis of how such founding moments have resulted in different narratives and subsequent constitutional regimes. However, a closer read of the chapters demonstrates that the work contained in this volume not only deviates from this reductionist view in fascinating ways, but in doing so expands both the scope and depth of our understanding of this phenomenon.

The following sections provide a glimpse into how this collection has changed our understanding of founding moments in constitutionalism in relation to three broad themes: (1) narrative legitimacy; (2) temporality; and (3) what founding moments may mean for minority groups and secessionist movements.

II. Narrative Legitimacy: Rethinking Agency in Founding Moments

The reductionist view of founding moments in constitutionalism would assume that the so-called 'spirit' – the new normative character of a nation that follows a founding moment – is agreed upon and largely uniform. However, a key variable largely left uninvestigated by this basic understanding is agency: who should be trusted to dictate or interpret what the 'spirit' is? Who decides what the founding moment means for the country? If it is the 'people', are they the citizens, the founding fathers, or the current or former government? The contributions in this volume delved into the issue of narrative legitimacy and offered a broad range of views. Some found that narrative legitimacy should reside in the citizenry; others offered examples where the courts, legislature, national institutions and even historians held agency. As a result, the chapters in this volume have expanded our notion of agency and narrative legitimacy in founding moments.

The opening chapter by Kuo lays the theoretical foundation for questions of narrative legitimacy. For Kuo, it is desirable that the citizens are in control of the narrative. He argues that contemporary constitutional theories can be divided into the historicist view and the normativist view. In the historicist view, the founding moment is fact only, 'a historical object to be faithfully represented',[2] and, in the normativist view, those historical events and political actions are seen 'as the embodiment of normative principles and values'.[3] Alternatively, Kuo proposes a 'relational' approach to constitutionalising founding moments – one between fact and norm – where the 'founding moment is related to the constitutional order by virtue of narratives that substantiate the constitutional order with meaning'.[4] His argument that the relational view is superior because citizens will be the driving force behind the narrative assumes that democratising this process is desirable.

[2] ibid.
[3] ibid.
[4] ibid.

However, for many people, a constitution should also serve an anti-majoritarian purpose – it is a document that cannot and should not be easily swayed by the whim of the people. Does the relational approach not strengthen the potential for the 'tyranny of the majority' by giving citizens in every era the right to dictate the meaning behind the country's founding moment? Further scholarship stemming from Kuo's contribution could also explore another predicament left largely unanswered by the author: certain citizens will have louder voices in creating that narrative under the relational approach. In other words, how does the relational view of constitutionalism deal with the predictable problem that the socio-economic elite – politicians, the media and the wealthy elite – may have more influence than other citizens in crafting this narrative in each generation?

Simon Gilhooley's chapter provides another dimension in understanding agency and narrative legitimacy in founding moments. While Kuo posits that citizens can narrate and therefore re-interpret the meaning of the founding moment at a later point in time, thereby also democratising the process, Gilhooley suggests that the founding moment itself can be reconceptualised. That is, instead of future generations giving meaning to one singular moment in history, Gilhooley believes that the founding moment can be 'reconfigured … not just in terms of what the founders advocated, but actually in terms of whom exactly the founders were and what it was that they founded'.[5] In doing so, his contribution demonstrates that not only the 'normativist' narrative – to use Kuo's terms – but even the 'historicist' understanding of founding moments can be reconfigured. Gilhooley opens the door to the question of whether there is any objectivity in the historical founding moment. In other words, if we re-create founding moments as we need them, and in a way that suits our desirable narrative at a given time, will these historic events be condemned to be victims of revisionist history?

Swati Jhaveri's chapter adds another dimension to the debate on narrative legitimacy and agency, arguing that the courts in Hong Kong and Singapore may be able to play a role in constitutionalising the founding moment. Jhaveri, however, realises the potential pitfalls of the argument. Throughout the chapter, she acknowledges that 'the judicial branch lacks democratic legitimacy' and is cautious not to propose 'judicially *initiated*' constitutional moments.[6] Her contribution returns us to the dilemma in Kuo's opening chapter regarding the question of narrative agency and legitimacy. Jhaveri's argument assumes that the courts will play a democratising or constitutionalising role by funnelling the will of the people into the process of constitutionalisation through the courts – as the author notes, courts will be 'a proxy for ventilating issues on the part of the citizens'.[7] This leads us, once again, to ask the following: should citizens be trusted with controlling the narrative of the founding moment and thereby influencing the process of constitutionalisation? Additionally, should the courts – as the supposed proxy of

[5] Simon Gilhooley, ch 5 in this volume.
[6] Jhaveri, ch 2 in this volume.
[7] ibid.

the people – be trusted with controlling the narrative? Finally, to a more fundamental assumption, can courts and jurists understand and faithfully carry out the will of the people given that they themselves 'lack democratic legitimacy'?

In this regard, Mikolaj Barczentewicz's chapter offers a different perspective on narrative legitimacy, one that posits a standard for narrative legitimacy for founding moments in constitutionalism. Barczentewicz argues that in order to be a 'legally relevant' constitution-maker, that entity should either: (1) exercise pre-existing legal authority to make the constitution; or (2) have one's intentional act purporting authoritatively to make the constitution as law recognised as the reason for acceptance of the constitution as law.[8] Judging Kuo's relational approach according to Barczentewicz's understanding, the citizenry of the future may not be a legally relevant constitution-maker. Under Barczentewicz's definition, it would be arguable whether the citizenry have the *legal* authority to make the constitution or retrospectively have the legitimacy to purport authority to make the constitution as law. Jhaveri's argument that the courts may play a pivotal role in constitutionalising founding moments may also be problematic according to Barczentewicz's standard. First, the courts in Hong Kong and Singapore did not exercise *pre-existing* legal authority to make the constitution. Even with regard to the second prong – that one's intentional act purporting authoritatively to make the constitution as law recognised as the reason for acceptance of the constitution as law – would be a difficult argument to make, as courts lack not only democratic legitimacy, but also the legal authority of constituent assemblies and similar bodies entrusted with the responsibility of crafting constitutions. Thus, under Barczentewicz's rubric, while the citizenry and courts may be viewed as 'agent[s] behind making a constitution as law', they may not be 'constitution-makers' per se.

Regardless of whether scholars agree with Barczentewicz's standard for narrative legitimacy, he helps us appreciate that a standard is perhaps needed. Not having a standard would risk the founding moment – an historical event – being re-interpreted in subsequent generations to fit their narrative as needed.

The chapters by Sagy, Chien-Chih Lin and Mel A Topf offer other examples of how the narrative of founding moments can be influenced by other actors. Sagy's contribution on Israel demonstrates the role of historians and historiography in forming the narrative about founding moments. Lin, on the other hand, demonstrates how through the amendment process, Taiwan's legislature was able to craft a national identity distinctly different from that of the People's Republic of China (PRC), despite having the same constitutional core. Topf's chapter adds to the debate about narrative legitimacy by injecting the idea that institutions – not just the citizenry, courts or founding fathers – can have agency.

The chapters in this volume have expanded our knowledge of agency and narrative legitimacy in founding moments. While the question of who should

[8] Mikolaj Barczentewicz, ch 4 in this volume.

have the legitimacy to give meaning to the founding moment is anything but resolved, the aforementioned writers have nonetheless laid the foundation for future scholars to continue this debate.

III. Temporality and Tenuousness: Rethinking the Concept of Timing in Founding Moments

In the reductionist view, a founding moment occurs within a particular timeframe, whether a revolution, civil war or abolition of apartheid; it may span months, years or decades, but it has clear temporal demarcations. It has a beginning and an end. The chapters in this volume have challenged this simplistic understanding and by doing so have also opened the door to future scholarship in this area.

In her chapter on Pakistan, Maryam S Khan argues that a founding moment can be incremental. Although Pakistan had one permanent constitution, she argues that through multiple suspension-amendment-revival cycles, the country was able to have an 'extended public discussion on the Constitution and its meaning over a significant period of time'.[9] Khan's chapter raises several questions. First, should subsequent 'rebirths' – the revival of a constitution following a suspension – be considered founding moments at all? If so, would future leaders not have the incentive to suspend and revive the constitution and thereby re-define the meaning of the constitution order – or constitutional identity – by manufacturing another founding moment? Second, her argument assumes that the spirit of a so-called permanent constitution can survive despite multiple suspensions and amendments. How tenuous can the relationship between the original – or permanent – constitution and the ultimate constitutional order be, especially if the constitutional suffers numerous suspensions? Juliano Zaiden Benvindo's chapter on Brazil and Chile raises similar questions regarding so-called incremental founding moments.

Sagy's Chapter on Israel also requires us to delve further into both temporal questions about founding moments and questions regarding its tenuousness. In the Israeli context, there was a clear founding moment – the creation of the State of Israel. However, there was no formal written constitution. Sagy argues that instead of a formal constitution, a 'distinct Israeli constitutional order' came into being about four decades after the foundation of Israel when a 'Constitutional Revolution' occurred after the adoption of two basic laws in 1992 in addition to a short list of basic human rights.[10] This fascinating chapter leads to questions that are slightly different from those arising from Khan's chapter: should claims of legitimacy regarding a declared constitutional order – and the claim that it stems from the founding moment – be entertained if the initial project was abandoned

[9] Maryam S Khan, ch 10 in this volume.
[10] Yair Sagy, ch 6 in this volume.

and was followed four decades later not by a formal written constitution, but by a largely *informal* one?

In addition, Sagy's chapter leads us to consider several other assumptions about founding moments. While many contributions in this volume focus their attention on what constitutes a founding moment, Sagy's chapter forces us to consider what constitutes *constitutionalism*. In other words, in the absence of a formal written constitution, can basic laws or a list of rights be considered a constitutional order? Moreover, should we understand founding moments only as they exist in relation to a constitutional order? That is, is a 'nation-making' event still a founding moment in constitutionalism if it does not lead to a formal written constitution?

Lin's chapter on Taiwan adds an interesting dimension in our understanding of the relationship between founding moments and the constitutional order. Lin separates the notion of a constitutional identity and a national identity, assuming that different national identities can result from a shared constitutional identity. He argues that multiple amendments in Taiwan have moulded a different understanding of national identity, despite sharing its constitutional identity with the PRC. He also argues that the old constitutional identity was retained because of the 'high bar of constitutional revision'. The question of whether the old constitutional identity can be said to remain intact after multiple significant amendments and where we should draw the line is an important one. In other words, can national identity change while constitutional identity remains the same, especially if the former traces its legitimacy from the latter? If subsequent amendments help change the *national* identity of the country, can it do so by retaining the same *constitutional* identity?

Mazo's chapter on the former Soviet republic represents unchartered territory for our understanding of temporality and founding moments. Mazo notes that the founding moment that established the presidential system came not after but before the creation of modern independent states that were once part of the former Soviet Union. His chapter parts with our reductionist view that founding moments are those that break with the *ancien régime*; in fact, he argues that some aspects of a new state – post-founding moments – may even come directly from the *ancien régime*.

The varying examples and arguments in this volume have shed new light in our understanding of temporality and the tenuous relationship between founding moments and constitutional order. In doing so, the authors have opened the door for future scholars to continue the debate on this issue.

IV. Minority Groups and Secessionist Movements

Various chapters in this collection have also shed light on what the phenomenon of founding moments in constitutionalism may mean for minority groups or secessionist movements around the world. The fact that certain segments of society may interpret a founding moment differently from the majority or may feel marginalised by the greater constitutional narrative is a fascinating area for further scholarship. Equally, the ability of a minority group or a secessionist movement to utilise the 'spirit' of the founding moment to specific causes is another potential area for future research.

Lin's chapter on Taiwan adds a fascinating dimension to this volume as it explains how Taiwan has used the 1947 founding moment and constitutional order of the PRC and interpreted it differently in order to create a separate Taiwanese constitutional identity. In doing so, his chapter points us to a potential weakness of founding moments in constitutionalism – it implies that founding moments and constitutions are so malleable that it may be interpreted in different, even contradictory ways. His chapter could also pave the way for future scholars to investigate how secessionist or nationalist movements have used the original constitution of former home state as a springboard for recalibrating a new national identity, instead of developing their own constitution. This chapter may help bring to the fore the important idea of how secessionist movements may adopt the founding moments of the country they separate from as part of their own revolutionary narrative, and ways in which separationist movements have been able to utilise the founding moment narratives of the state they used to be a part of in order to argue that their own independence is a continuation of that narrative.

This phenomena could also be studied at the intra-state level, where minority groups may use the founding moments narrative to legitimise their own struggle against the new state; although the country itself fought against the oppression of foreign colonisers, now 'we' – the minority group – continue that fight, but against the oppression of the majority.

Likewise, Noga Efrati's chapter on the constitutional history of Iraq offers a gendered perspective of founding moments. She shows how one particular segment of society may view certain constitutions – or provisions within constitutions – as founding moments for their particular cause. She notes that most observers in 1958 'did not attach much importance to what seemed to be nothing more than generic articles promising Iraq's citizens equity before the law'.[11] However, from a gendered perspective, the 1958 move to include women in public life was a founding moment for women, although it may have gone unnoticed by others.

Efrati's chapter opens the door to numerous questions regarding founding moments and minority groups. First, is an event a founding moment if only a subsection of society views it as a watershed moment or is it necessary that most of the society – if not all – view it as a founding moment? To use another example, should the reconstruction amendments in the US – which abolished slavery and involuntary servitude – be seen as a founding moment for one subsection of the American population or for everyone in the US?

[11] Noga Efrati, ch 11 in this volume.

V. Future Scholarship and the Ongoing Debate

In addition to expanding our understanding of founding moments in constitutionalism, the chapters in this book have also touched upon other topics that require deeper investigation and could potentially help push the boundaries of scholarship in this flourishing subfield.

First, there needs to be a detailed study of constitutions devoid of founding moments. Although the reductionist view has been that founding moments lead to constitution-building, this volume has demonstrated that this is not always the case. The question of why and how a constitution may come into fruition without a founding moment and how a society may form a cohesive constitutional narrative without a founding moment will be another intriguing area of research. Second, there is also a paucity of research on founding moments that are devoid of grand narratives. Jhaveri's chapter on Singapore and Hong Kong has shed some light on the phenomenon that may be called 'pragmatic constitutionalism', where a constitutional order comes into existence not because of revolutions or war, but rather because of immediate practical need. How does a society create an underlying 'nomos' when the guiding document itself was built more on administrative necessity as opposed to a 'higher' political and social purpose? And are citizens in such societies also driven less by a sense of cohesive national purpose and more by pragmatism?

Another potential subcategory for founding moments in constitutionalism could be on the question of constitutions written by foreign powers and minority groups. In the first case, future scholars can address the relationship between national narrative and the constitution when – as in the case of post-war Japan and Germany – the founding document was written not by the citizens, but by foreign powers. In other words, can the citizenry still derive a national 'nomos' from a document that was not written by them, but rather for them? And are there founding moments – such as defeat in war – that are not conducive to narrative-building constitutionalism? In the case of constitutions written by the ruling minority, questions around how the founding moment is interpreted by the majority and whether the majority can grant any legitimacy to such a document would be a fascinating area of exploration.

When the *Founding Moments in Constitutionalism* symposium was organised in 2016, it was the intention of the organisers that research in this area not be confined to the chapters in this volume. While the chapters in this collection have expanded our knowledge and understanding of founding moments in constitutionalism, this book is also an open invitation to continue the debate on this captivating topic. It is the desire of the editors of this volume that scholars will accept this invitation and that this burgeoning field of legal study will be further expanded.

INDEX

www.ingramcontent.com/pod-product-compliance
Lightning Source LLC
LaVergne TN
LVHW011754200926
848484LV00003B/701
9781509930975